The China reader

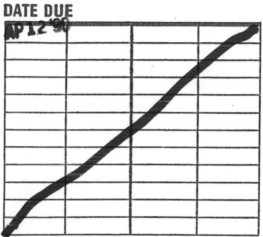

by Franz Schurmann and Orville Schell

THE CHINA READER

★ IMPERIAL CHINA: *The Decline of
the Last Dynasty and the Origins of
Modern China The 18th and 19th Centuries*

★★ REPUBLICAN CHINA: *Nationalism,
War, and the Rise of
Communism 1911–1949*

★★★ COMMUNIST CHINA: *Revolutionary
Reconstruction and International Confrontation
1949–1966*

by Franz Schurmann

IDEOLOGY AND ORGANIZATION IN
COMMUNIST CHINA

Republican China
Nationalism, War, and the Rise of Communism ☯ 1911–1949

2 *The China Reader*

Edited, annotated,
and with introductions
by FRANZ SCHURMANN
and ORVILLE SCHELL

Republican China
Nationalism, War, and the Rise of Communism
 1911–1949

RANDOM HOUSE, New York

The authors wish to thank the following for permission to reprint:
The Cresset Press Ltd. for *The Birth of Communist China* (published in 1952
as *Revolution in China*) by C. P. Fitzgerald.

Harper & Row, Publishers, Inc., for *China Shakes the World* by Jack Belden,
Copyright, 1949, by Jack Belden; *Japan's Dream of World Empire: The
Tanaka Memorial*, edited by Carl Crow, Copyright, 1942, by Carl Crow.

Harvard University Press for *The Communist Conquest of China* by Lionel
Max Chassin, translated by Timothy Osato and Louis Gelas, © Copyright,
1965, by the President and Fellows of Harvard College; *The May Fourth
Movement* by Chow Tse-tsung, © Copyright, 1960, by the President and Fellows
of Harvard College.

International Publishers for *Selected Works* of Mao Tse-tung, Volume I, ©
Copyright, 1954, by International Publishers Company, Inc.

Paragon Book Reprint Corporation for *The Chinese Renaissance* by Hu Shih,
reprint edition © Copyright, 1965, by Paragon Book Reprint Corporation.

Frederick A. Praeger, Inc., for an abridgement of Chapter II, "Old-Style Warlordism," of *China on the Eve of the Communist Takeover* by A. Doak Barnett, Frederick A. Praeger, Inc., Publishers, New York, 1963.

Robert B. Rigg for material from *Red China's Fighting Hordes* (1951).

William Sloane Associates for *The Stilwell Papers* by Joseph W. Stilwell, Copyright, 1948, by Winifred A. Stilwell; *Thunder Out of China* by Theodore White
and Annalee Jacoby, Copyright, 1946, by William Sloane Associates, Inc.

Stanford University Press for *The Tragedy of the Chinese Revolution* by Harold R. Isaacs (second edition, revised), © Copyright, 1951, 1961, by the Board
of Trustees of the Leland Stanford Junior University.

Thames & Hudson, London, for *The Chinese Revolution* by Tibor Mende
(1961).

To the Faculty Peace Committee

F.S.

To my parents

O.S.

"It is of great importance that we try to learn something more about the strange and fascinating Chinese nation, about its past and its present, about the aims of its leaders and the aspirations of its people. Before we can make wise political—and perhaps military—decisions pertaining to China, there are many questions to be asked and, hopefully, answered: What kind of people are the Chinese? To what extent are they motivated by national feeling? To what extent by ideology? Why are the Chinese Communist leaders so hostile to the United States and why do they advocate violent revolution against most of the world's governments? To what extent is their view of the world distorted by isolation and the memory of ancient grievances? And to what extent, and with what effect on their government, do the Chinese people share with us and with all other peoples what Aldous Huxley has called the 'simple human preference for life and peace'? We need to ask these questions because China and America may be heading toward war with each other and it is essential that we do all that can be done to prevent that calamity, starting with a concerted effort to understand the Chinese people and their leaders."

—J. WILLIAM FULBRIGHT

Contents

Introduction

If there is one word to describe China since 1911, it is revolution. Revolution is the sweeping away of an old order—an ancient political system, a traditional culture, an uncreative economy, a ruling class which only exploits, and a system of social organization which no longer satisfies men. China has undergone all these revolutions.

During the nineteenth century, as we saw in Volume I, China slowly gathered momentum for change. Chinese society started to break down for internal reasons. The gentry and officials, complacent in their centuries-old position of dominance, became indifferent to stagnation, poverty, and disaffection in Inland China. When revolts broke out, they suppressed them, attempting to alleviate the situation by temporary and superficial reforms. The arrival of Western imperialism further discredited the dynasty and its ruling classes—they could only acquiesce impotently to the humiliation forced on them. In 1911 the dynasty fell, and thus began the period in Chinese history known as Republican China. China at last had her revolution. For a brief time optimism ran high, but as we know now the demise of the Manchu Dynasty was only the beginning of a long and agonizing period of revolutionary change in China which has not yet ended.

There is little in America's revolutionary heritage which could help us understand the extent and depth of the Chinese Revolution. We drove the foreigner from our soil, and his sympathizers fled to Canada. Our revolution could be compared to the 1911 Revolution in China, but whereas we quickly achieved stable nationhood, China continued on the path of her larger revolution. We never experienced a cultural revolution in which people turned on their heritage. We do not know what a social revolution is, in which people kill their national and local leaders with hatred born of centuries of wrongs. The French underwent such a revolution and recall it to this day.

1911 was only the beginning for China. A new kind of government came into being, but Chinese society remained unchanged. It meant little to the peasant who struggled for subsistence or to the local landlords and officials who continued to rule as before, except that now they owed loyalty to presidents, generals, and warlords. In the new cities foreigners still enjoyed their special privileges, and foreign gunboats still patroled the Yangtze River. Nonetheless, the 1911 Revolution finally set China in motion toward a different future. China's future leaders were then young men passionately convinced that only if she were totally transformed could China resume her rightful position of greatness in the world.

To transform a society so vast as China and so bound to the past was an awesome ambition. China's early revolutionary leaders, like Sun Yat-sen and Chiang Kai-shek, talked about revolution, but it is doubtful that they knew how great a revolution China needed before she could cut herself from the past. Sun Yat-sen gave China revolutionary ideals, but his successor, Chiang Kai-shek, concentrated only on power. As the once-revolutionary Kuomintang turned into cliques of power-hungry politicians and generals, the Communists assumed the revolution's leadership. The Communists' leaders were Western-influenced intellectuals who had been deeply affected by the May Fourth Movement of 1919. The students of Peking, Shanghai, and other cities had demonstrated against their leaders' cowardice in the face of Japanese demands, but more than that, they had gone to the people. Sun Yat-sen had spoken of the power of the people, but the Communists discovered that through revolutionary organization, the people could be made into a political weapon.

We in America believe in the perfectibility of man and society. So do the Communists. But we also believe in progress through gradual reform, that change can be brought about by the earnest efforts of many people working hard, each to improve conditions in his own sector. The leaders of Chinese Communism did not. They saw a people resigned to their plight, to whom the hope of change and improvement was alien. They saw simple reform as too weak a medicine for what ailed Chinese society. When the Russian Revolution broke out, they became convinced that this was the path China must follow.

When the social revolution began in China, it was frightening to foreigners. They were afraid of the Kuomintang when it began its Northern March in 1925, but were relieved when Chiang Kai-shek began his extermination campaign against the Communists in April 1927 (events strikingly similar to those in Indonesia in late 1965). They were afraid of the Communists when they launched their land reform and revolutionary terror in Kiangsi in the late 1920s, but were reassured when it appeared that the Communists were only "agrarian reformers."

The Chinese Revolution has been violent, often indiscriminate and wasteful. As Mao Tse-tung said in 1927 in the hills of Hunan, "a revolution is not a dinner party, or writing an essay. . . ." But let us remember that revolution grew out of China's soil, that a hundred years of rebellion and suppression, of revolution and counter-revolution had so brutalized China that massive violence was inevitable.

We in America are afraid of radical revolution, and our fear prevents us from understanding it when it occurs in other countries. The histories of American and China are very different. Both are proud nations, but America never had to surrender pieces of her territory to foreign rulers. Both are proud peoples, but white Americans have never been labeled an inferior race. Though we have borrowed from abroad, we have always owned the means of our wealth. We have never seen our country fragmented and ruled by absurd warlords who kept themselves in power by looting the population. Aside from our black population, few Americans know what it is to live in a class society in which the great majority of the population is forever condemned to inferior status (though a few may rise). It is difficult for us to understand the frustration and humiliation of a young Chinese intellectual who sees his country abused by foreigners or who is paternally lectured to by foreigners conscious of their own superiority. How can we understand the

hatred of a peasant for landlords, officials, and village teachers
who deprived him of his dignity, since, after all, he was not a
gentleman? Only in the American South do conditions exist
which somewhat resemble those of old China. We would do well
to remember that it was not always poverty or economic deprivation which alone were the causes of revolt in China: the
peasant revolted against indignity—a grievance the gentry found
very difficult to understand.

When revolution is as total as it was in China, only total
organization can build a new society. Few Americans could live
in the present-day People's Republic of China. The Chinese are
friendly to foreigners but do not invite them to join their society;
foreigners would find life disciplined, hard, and not very rewarding to someone who has grown up in a liberal and affluent
democracy. But a liberal and affluent democracy is exactly that
which China was incapable of attaining. People have argued in
the case both of Russia and China that if only the Communists
had not won, liberal, reformist regimes might have been successful. Such arguments are pointless, for Communism did
come to power in both countries, unified them politically, and
launched them on their basic economic development.

China's kind of revolution may be repeated elsewhere in
the world, for many countries have conditions similar to those
of pre-1949 China. It is also possible that aggressive reform
programs may make it possible to avoid the trauma of violent
revolution. But if reform is to work, the reformers must understand and sympathize with the revolutionary drives in the country, and not just regard reform as a counter-revolutionary
device. If reform fails, the kind of polarization of world forces
that Mao Tse-tung and Lin Piao have talked of may come into
being, with the United States fighting on the side of the reactionaries.

Someday the revolution will be completed in China and she
will settle down to a more routinized existence. Such a transition
will be hastened if peace prevails in the world.

I. Revolution and Regeneration: China's Revival in the Early Decades of the Twentieth Century

~§ The 1911 Revolution which created the Republic set China slowly in motion again after a period of passivity and uncertainty. The revolutionary movement had sired a new breed of intellectuals and leaders who had no patience with the traditionalist hair-splitters and their abstract arguments over Chinese spirit and Western substance, and no interest in saving Chinese traditions or Confucianism. Fervent nationalists working for the salvation of their country and its people, and not its archaic culture, China's new youth was a group of iconoclasts who looked forward to the future rather than backward to the past: they were the makers of a new China.

We have called this period revolution and regeneration. China's new leaders were revolutionaries dedicated to the overthrow of the old order and to leading China out of degradation. These young revolutionaries were also searching for a new moral order based on new ideas, for they were convinced that China had to be reborn, that her ancient values and ideas had to be totally replaced by others more able to meet the modern world's challenges.

Sun Yat-sen's Kuomintang overthrew the dynasty and created the Republic, but as we can see from the period of warlordism that followed, the Republic failed to become that workable new order for which the revolutionaries had fought. It had been relatively simple to bring down the tottering Manchu Dynasty, but it proved difficult to replace it with new institutions, ideals, and leadership. The young revolutionaries quickly realized that the 1911 Revolution was only the first step in a long process of rebuilding Chinese society.

Regeneration began shortly after the founding of the Republic. In 1916 Chinese intellectuals called for a "Chinese Renaissance," proclaiming new ideas in a language understandable to the people. The May Fourth Movement of 1919 brought the intellectuals into the streets in popular demonstrations, and so into ever closer contact with the masses. The founding of the Chinese Communist Party in 1921 by intellectuals who had participated in the May Fourth Movement was a further step in the regeneration process. The Kuomintang, by contrast, was then the leading revolutionary party. The subsequent ferment of the 1920s decisively changed the intellectual and political climate of China. Sun Yat-sen had launched the revolution; intellectuals like Hu Shih, Ch'en Tu-hsiu, and Lu Hsün began the process of regeneration. Revolution and regeneration eventually converged in the Chinese Communist Party.

Before new ideologies could take root in China, the vast residue of tradition which persisted despite the 1911 Revolution had to be destroyed. The 1911 Revolution had not changed the bases of the traditional social order: classical education, suppression of women, family system. The new intellectuals called for a total purge of tradition, while simultaneously turning outward in search of substitutes. Some became fascinated by the teachings of John Dewey and Bertrand Russell, some tried to move further along the path sketched by Sun Yat-sen's "Three People's Principles"; the majority, however, turned to Marxism.

The Bolshevik Revolution had a profound impact on many Chinese intellectuals. Russia, vast and backward like China, and with its own "oriental despotism," swept away its old order, skipped over the capitalist stage of development, and became the world's first socialist country. Russia suddenly gave hope to Asia's sick giant that she too could leap from paralysis to strength without going through decades of patient recovery. The new Chinese revolutionaries dreamed of creating a mass movement which could seize power from below, as the Bolsheviks had done in Petrograd, with Marxist ideology and organization.

If many Chinese still had doubts that the Russian Revolution could be repeated in China, Lenin's teachings on bourgeois democratic revolution encouraged them. Lenin admitted that it was unlikely a proletarian revolution could occur in colonial and semi-colonial countries in which, like China, the proletariat was weak, and he maintained that the hold of foreign imperialists must first be broken. He then advanced the argument that since the bourgeoisie was anti-imperialist, the proletariat could unite with them in the first stage of the revolution to destroy foreign domination. The bourgeois democratic revolutions of the colonial countries would converge with the proletarian revolutions of the advanced countries to bring about a worldwide movement to destroy imperialism and capitalism simultaneously.

Chinese intellectuals had finally found a Western ideology which suited China's immediate problems. China's two main enemies were the "feudal" institutions of the past, against which bourgeois and intellectuals alike rebelled, and the imperialist nations, which were slowly seizing control of China's economy; Lenin's theory accounted for a simultaneous revolution against both. Thus when Comintern agents went to China to organize a Communist Party, they found a ready response among intellectuals like Ch'en Tu-hsiu, Li Ta-chao, Mao Tse-tung, and Chang Kuo-t'ao.

Under Comintern guidance the Communist movement gathered momentum during the 1920s. Marxist ideology spread downward into the ranks of the urban proletariat and later into the peasantry. The new Communist Party organized labor unions, peasant associations, student groups. Intellectual activity —the publication of newspapers, journals, and pamphlets—intensified. The Communists, unlike the Kuomintang, turned to the masses as the revolutionary base.

The Communists and Kuomintang, while they cooperated during the 1920s, moved along different paths. The Kuomintang made the seizure of power its one and only goal and, despite verbal adherence to broader ideals, it used all means to achieve power. The Communists, on the other hand, were more interested in mass organization and in the propagation of their new ideology. They, and their Comintern tutors, let the Kuomintang hold the guns—a mistake for which they were to pay dearly in April 1927, after which they never again laid down their arms.

If they failed in the short run, the Communists won in the end. They gave China what the 1911 Revolution had not given it: ideology and organization. Despite repeated setbacks, they continued to build their organized power until the time came to deliver the death blow to their enemy, the Kuomintang.

1. THE OVERTHROW OF THE DYNASTY
AND THE STILLBIRTH OF THE REPUBLIC
☯ A Westernized Doctor, Sun Yat-sen,
Becomes China's First Professional
Revolutionary

IN SPITE of political disagreements, all Chinese agree on one
thing: Sun Yat-sen (1866–1925) was the founding father of
modern China. Sun was China's first real professional revolutionary. Educated as a doctor and well traveled, he was able
to see China from a detached and unprejudiced point of view,
and he concluded that China needed to undergo a total transformation. In his estimation reformers like Liang Ch'i-ch'ao
were indulging in the futile occupation of trying to revive the
dead. There was no question in Sun's mind: the dynasty must be
replaced by a republican government; nothing short of this
would remedy China's problems.

Like many other conquests of China, the Republican
Revolution drew its nourishment from outside of China, and
took its main support from the large number of Chinese students who had gone abroad to study since the turn of the
century. Once out of China, these students were exposed to
a variety of new ideas, and more often than not turned against
the alien Manchu Dynasty. Their experiences abroad made
them extremely vulnerable to revolutionary ideology.

A second source of support for Sun's revolution lay in the
Overseas Chinese communities in Southeast Asia and Hawaii,
who, unlike the culture-bound Chinese at home, were worldly
and much more sympathetic to Western institutions. Fortunately they were also wealthy, thus they could provide Sun
with a vital source of independent funds outside of China
proper.

A third source of support was Japan. In Tokyo there was

a group of influential Japanese who were very sympathetic to Sun's cause. But what is more important, Japan provided China with a close and culturally homogeneous sanctuary in which the Chinese Revolution could incubate. In Japan the movement was born and developed; in Tokyo, Sun established the famous United League (*T'ung-meng hui*), which coordinated revolutionary Chinese student groups all over the world with the underground movement in China. It was through the United League that Sun presented his three-stage program for China: (1) three years of military government following the Revolution, then (2) six years of tutelage under a provisional constitution, finally (3) a constitutional government with a President and a Parliament.

In spite of its success at organizing outside of China, the United League suffered repeated failures within China, and by 1911 Sun admitted to having been involved in ten defeated insurrections. It was not until September of 1911, after a revolt at Wuchang, that the Revolution caught fire and swept the Manchus out of Peking.

When the Revolution itself finally began, Sun was in America. He read in a St. Louis paper of the Manchu collapse, and hurried home to find that the takeover had been virtually bloodless. It was as though the Manchu Dynasty had quietly melted away like a cake of ice in the sun, leaving the Revolution with the simple task of calling people's attention to the fact. The Revolution was as much a process of internal decay as external challenge. Sun's whole credo had been distinctly negative—anti-Manchu—and when the Manchus vanished, the Revolution's main force was destroyed. And as we shall see, it disintegrated into chaos.

The following selection is taken from Sun's memoirs. One is impressed by his tremendous energy and zeal—he was forever traveling, speaking, organizing, and raising money for the Revolution—but he seldom mentioned the Revolution's positive aspects. With what did Sun propose to replace the old and complex system of rule? What dynamic new ideology was he offering as a nucleus of Chinese unity? Did he, in fact, have any realistic plan for China's regeneration?

SUN YAT-SEN *
The Revolution Is the Path to the
Regeneration of China

HOW THE KUOMINTANG ORGANIZED
THE CHINESE REVOLUTION

My appeal for a revolution in China has been successful, and the destructive part of the Revolution, in the shape of the overthrow of the Manchu monarchy, has been achieved; but the constructive part has far from begun. Nevertheless, I do not lose hope in the successful completion of the Chinese Revolution; that is why I have devoted to it all my energies.

In the first year of the Republic, when European writers and scholars were writing thousands of articles about the Chinese Revolution, and approaching its facts more from the point of view of morality than of their meaning, I issued the first chapter of my *Notes on the Chinese Revolution* in which I set forth very briefly and concisely how, twenty years ago, the possibility of a successful revolution in China was a subject of great discussion.

Although I lived at the time in London, I could not name myself as one of the founders of the "Association for the Regeneration of China." This at the time involved the risk of persecution. Today I restore from memory the contents of that chapter of my reminiscences, supplementing them with the facts of the last thirty years, which formerly I had to omit for conspirative reasons which will be understood.

From the moment that the idea of revolutionary struggle awoke within me up to the time of the foundation of the "Revolutionary League" (out of which the Kuomintang developed) I

---

* Sun Yat-sen, *Memoirs of a Chinese Revolutionary* (London: Hutchinson and Co. Ltd., 1918), pp. 184–224 [unable to locate the Chinese version, we have left the Chinese names in their original transliteration].

was a man who practiced revolution, and therefore all my revolutionary activities were not very complicated. I could count on my fingers the names of the persons who at that time recognized my ideas. From the time of the foundation of the "Revolutionary League," the work became much more complicated, and I cannot, of course, recount the names of all the emigrant patriots, still less of all the revolutionary heroes at home. I write my memoirs as materials for a future historian of the Koumintang.

From 1885, *i.e.*, from the time of our defeat in the war with France, I set before myself the object of the overthrow of the Ch'ing Dynasty and the establishment of a Chinese Republic on its ruins. At the very beginning I selected for my propaganda the college at which I was studying, regarding medical science as the kindly aunt who would bring me out onto the high road of politics.

Ten years passed like one day. In the Canton Medical School, I made friends with Chen-Shi-Liang, who had a very large circle of acquaintances amongst widely traveled people who knew China well. When I began talking of revolution, advocating its ideas, he gladly agreed with me, and declared that he would immediately enter a revolutionary party if I would agree to lead it. After staying a year in the school at Canton, I learned that an English Medical School with a wider program than that of the Canton School had been opened at Hong Kong. Thereupon, attracted also by the thought that there I should have a wider field for my revolutionary propaganda, I went to Hong Kong to continue my education. For four years I gave up all my time free from studies to the cause of revolutionary propaganda, traveling backward and forward between Hong Kong and Amoy. At that time I had scarcely any supporters, with the exception of three persons living in Hong Kong: Chen-Shao-Bo, Yu-Shao-Chi, and Yang-Ho-Lin, and one man at Shanghai, Lu-Ko-Tung. The others avoided me, as a rebel, as they would one stricken with plague.

Living together with my three friends Chen, Yu, and Yang, in Hong Kong, we were constantly discussing the revolution. Our thoughts were fixed on the problems of the Chinese Revolution. We studied chiefly the history of revolutions. When it happened that we came together and did not talk of revolution, we did not feel happy. Thus a few years went by, and we received from our friends the nickname of "the four great and inseparable scoundrels." For me this was a period of revolutionary disputes and preparation. . . .

THE FIRST REVOLT

Our committee was in Hong Kong and our branch at Yang-Chen. There worked at that time in the committee Ten-Yin-Nan, Yang-Tsui-Yun, Haun-Yun-Shan, Chen-Shao-Bo, and others, while in the branch at Yang-Chen there were Lu-Ko-Tung, Chen-Shi-Liang, and some instructors from America, and some generals. I often traveled between Canton and Hong Kong. Our tasks by that time were quite well defined. Preparations were in full blast. We had accumulated considerable strength, and we could by a single blow have effected a great deal. But just at this time the authorities discovered the arms we had smuggled in (five hundred revolvers), and one of our worthiest comrades, Lu-Ko-Tung, was executed. This was the first sacrifice made by us on the altar of the Chinese Revolution. At the same time there were arrested and executed Tse-Hsi and Chu-Gui. About seventy people were arrested, among them the Canton Admiral Tsin-Kui-Guan.

The day of September 9, 1895, I consider to be the day of my first revolutionary defeat. Three days after the defeat I was still in Canton, but ten days later I was forced to escape to Hong Kong by byroads, and thence left for Japan with comrades Chen-Shi-Liang and Chen-Shao-Bo, intending to land at Yokohama. I cut off my pigtail and put on European clothes, as the date of my return to China was indeterminate. Then I left for the Philippine islands. Chen-Shi-Liang returned to China to restore matters to the point reached before our defeat, while Chen-Shao-Bo remained in Japan to study the political situation. I was introduced at that time to the Japanese Sugawora, and later we made the acquaintance of Sonei and Miasaki, with whom we established connections. This was the beginning of friendly relations between the Chinese revolutionaries and the Japanese.

Having arrived in the Philippines, I began to gather comrades to strengthen our Association for the Regeneration of China, but even old comrades, owing to our defeat, did not conceal their despair, while some simply forswore our ideas. Owing to the absence of the necessary factors for the development of a revolutionary movement, the latter slowed down somewhat. There was no reason why I should stay long in the Philippines, and I decided to leave for America, in order to establish connections with the organization of Chinese emigrants there. . . .

Amongst the Chinese emigrants in America I found an even more sleepy atmosphere then in the Philippines. I crossed the continent from San Francisco to New York. On my way I stopped at various places for a few days—for ten days at the most—everywhere preaching that to save our mother country from threatening destruction we must overthrow the Ch'ing Dynasty, and that the duty of every Chinese citizen was to help to reconstruct China on a new democratic basis.

Although I spared no effort in this propaganda, the people to whom it was directed remained apathetic and little responsive to the ideas of the Chinese Revolution. . . .

Although my stay in America was of little importance for the further destinies of the Chinese Revolution, it nevertheless aroused fears and misgivings on the part of the Imperial government. Therefore on my arrival in London I almost fell into the clutches of the Imperial Embassy, but I was saved from peril by my teacher Kandeli. It was owing to him that I was saved from the great danger which threatened me.

After escaping from London, I went to Europe to study the methods of its political administration, and also to make the acquaintance of representatives of the opposition parties. In Europe I understood that, although the foremost European countries had achieved power and popular government, they could not accord complete happiness to their peoples. Therefore the leading European revolutionaries strive for a social revolution, and I conceived the idea of the simultaneous settlement, by means of the revolution, of the questions of national economy, national independence, and popular freedom. Hence arose my so-called *"san-min-chu,"* or the idea of democracy based on three principles.

The revolution was my principal aim in life, and therefore

I hastened to conclude my business in Europe, in order not to lose time dear to the Revolution. I left for Japan, considering that there, nearer to China, we could more successfully carry out our revolutionary plans. . . .

There were fully ten thousand Chinese emigrants in Japan, but an atmosphere of inertia prevailed amongst them. They were terribly afraid of the idea of revolution, just like the Chinese emigrants in other countries. Our comrades had worked amongst them for some years, yet it turned out that only a hundred-odd had joined the revolutionary movement, which did not represent one per cent of our emigrants in Japan. While the propaganda of revolutionary ideas amongst the emigrants was so difficult and thankless, it was even more difficult in China. The Chinese were not repelled by the idea of overthrowing the Manchu Dynasty, and willingly entered our party; but their intelligence was very weak, there was little solidarity amongst them, and they had no convictions. They could be used as a passive force, but under no circumstances could they be an active force.

From 1895, *i.e.*, from the moment of our first defeat, until 1900, five years went by, which were a period of great difficulty and suffering for the Chinese revolutionary movement. The revolutionary foundation we had built up in the course of ten years, both in the sense of the work of each of our comrades and in the sense of the positions we had secured, was destroyed. Propaganda abroad had little success. At this time, too, monarchist organizations grew up and became very active on the political arena. Our hopes were almost destroyed, but our comrades did not fall into despair and courageously looked ahead. . . .

Very soon there took place the amalgamation of the Association for the Regeneration of China with organizations which had sprung up in the Kwantung province and other provincial organizations of the Yangtze Valley. . . .

At this time nearly all the provinces began to send students to Japan to receive their education there. Amongst the students who came to Tokyo there turned out to be many people with young and clear heads. They seized on revolutionary ideas at once, and soon entered the revolutionary movement. All the arguments of the students of that day, and all their thoughts turned around revolutionary questions. At a students' New Year's Day meeting Lu-Chen-Yui made a big speech on a revolution to overthrow the Manchu Dynasty. He was expelled from the University at the demand of the Imperial Minister in Tokyo. Other students . . . published popular newspapers to spread revolutionary ideas.

This revolutionary movement amongst the Chinese students found its way into China. At Shanghai the students Chang-Tai-Yang, Wu-Wei-Hoi, Cho-Chang, and others utilized the Christian papers for revolutionary propaganda. Their actions were complained of by representatives of the Imperial authorities, in consequence of which they were arrested and imprisoned on the territory of the foreign concession. One of them, however, managed to escape abroad. Then there followed the only trial of its kind, in which the dynasty brought an action against an individual in the foreign court, and won its case. Cho-Chang was sentenced only to two years' imprisonment.

During this period the popular movement grew stronger and stronger. . . . This period I consider to be the beginning of the epoch of the wide development of the Chinese revolutionary movement. . . .

In the spring of 1905 I arrived in Europe once again, and the majority of the students there were supporters of the Revolution. They had only just arrived in Europe from Japan or China. The revolutionary wave seized on them, and they soon began to go on from arguments about the Revolution to direct revolutionary activities. I then set forth my long-guarded ideas about democracy embodied in three principles and the "Fivefold Constitution," in order to create a revolutionary organization on their basis. Our first meeting took place at Brussels, and thirty people entered our League [*T'ung-meng-hui*]. The second meeting was organized in Berlin, and there twenty-odd persons joined. The third meeting was in Paris, where ten people entered the League; but at the fourth meeting in Tokyo several hundred new members joined. There were in our League representatives of all the provinces of China, with the exception of Kansu, as Kansu had not yet sent any students to Japan. At the time our

League was being set up the word "revolution" was still terri-
fying, and therefore our League was simply called the "United
League," which name it retained for fairly long.

After the creation of the United League, I began to believe
that a new era of the Chinese Revolution was opening before us.
Previously, I had more than once met with great difficulties, I
had been spat upon and ridiculed by all. I more than once
suffered defeats, but I audaciously moved forward, although I
must confess that I did not dream of the accomplishment of the
overthrow of the Manchu Dynasty still in my lifetime. However,
from the autumn of 1905 onward, after the creation of the revolutionary United League, I became convinced that the great
cause of the Chinese Revolution would be accomplished during
my lifetime. It was then that I decided to put forward the watch-
word of a Chinese Republic, and to advocate it before all the
members of our party, in order that when they returned home
each to his own province they should widely support the necessity of revolution to set up a Republic. Scarcely a year had
passed before ten thousand people joined our United League.
Branches were organized in almost all of the provinces, and
from this time forward the revolutionary movement went ahead
with great strides. Its further development exceeded all my
anticipations. . . .

From the very foundation of the United League we published newspapers which spread far and wide the ideas of the
Chinese Revolution, democracy embodied in the three principles
and the Fivefold Constitution. A wave of revolutionary thought
rolled all over China, but it reached its highest point when we
began to publish journals. . . .

Up to the creation of our United League, there were very
few people who helped the revolutionary army in money, and
those only from amongst my personal friends. No one else dared
to help us. After the creation of our United League we began
to be helped from outside. . . .

After my repeated defeats, I could not live freely either in
Japan, Hong Kong, or Annam, or generally in the districts
bordering on China. Thus work within the boundaries of my

native country was almost impossible for me. Therefore, entrusting the leadership to comrades Huang-Kai-Tsiang and Hu-Han-Min, I myself once more set out on a journey round the world, with the special purpose of collecting resources for the Chinese Revolution. . . .

We worked out a plan of action. I went to the Dutch possessions, but was not admitted, and was also refused a passage through the British possessions; so that I had nothing else left but once again to leave for Europe or America. I went to America, where I traveled from corner to corner, agitating amongst the Chinese emigrants and urging them to help us and to subscribe money for the cause of the Revolution. On this occasion there were very many sympathizers amongst the emigrants in America.

At this time took place the Kwantung rising. All the most heroic revolutionaries took part, and although we once again suffered defeat, the glorious deeds of the seventy-two heroes resounded throughout the world. This was our tenth defeat.

Even before the rising, comrades Chen-Yin-Shin, Sun-Tun-Chu, Tan-Shi-Bin, Tsui-Tsiao-Shen, and others, seeing that in the province of Kwantung we were suffering one defeat after another, decided to transfer the center of their attention to Hankow, Wuchang, and Hanyang, *i.e.*, to work amongst the garrisons there, consisting as they did of newly mobilized soldiers. After some agitation had gone on amongst them, their state of mind was so revolutionary that the Governor-General of the Hupeh and Kwantung provinces ordered the most revolutionary units to be transferred to the province of Szechuan. However, after the last Kwantung rising, the number of supporters of the Revolution began to increase daily. The Imperial authorities of the Ch'ing Dynasty were in a state of panic terror, fearing most of all a blow from Wuchang, and therefore the Governor-General of the above-mentioned provinces, Jui-Chen, made an agreement with the Consul of a "certain" state that, when the revolutionaries rise in revolt, he must land his troops and bombard the city.

The atmosphere in Wuchang was electrical. Comrades Sun-Wu, Liu, and others decided to act and raise a rebellion of the troops. However, quite unexpectedly, our committee was discovered, and thirty people were imprisoned; but Hi-Yin-Shan, while in the prison at Wuchang, succeeded in notifying Chen-Yin-Shin and giving him warning, so that he should not too fall into the trap. At this time, there fell into the hands of the Imperial authorities a list of our artillerymen and other soldiers who were taking part in the work of the Revolution. With the object of saving these comrades from inevitable destruction, it was necessary to act immediately with great urgency. Therefore, Sun-Bi-Chen first went into action, followed by Tsao-Tsi-Min and others. At the head of their detachments they attacked the Governor-General's office and began bombarding it.

Governor Jui-Chen, hearing the noise of the cannonade, immediately fled to Hankow. . . .

The first revolutionary outbreak thus took place in the provinces of Hunan and Hupeh, but unity of action was not established between them. Our success at Wuchang was due in great measure to the flight of Jui-Chen, since, if he had not fled, Chang-Hu would not have fled also, and then the troops subordinated to him undoubtedly would not have mutinied. The majority of the mobilized soldiers at Wuchang were on the side of the Revolution; but most of them were transferred earlier to the province of Szechuan. Of the troops who remained in Wuchang there were only the artillerymen and the engineering troops, but they would have sold their lives dearly if their officers had not fled. And so, "Heaven itself helped China."

The object of our Revolution, of course, was not limited to the capture of Wuchang alone. The comrades began to display activity throughout the country. Very rapidly we seized fifteen provinces. Earliest of all Shanghai went over to us, immediately after the fall of Hankow. Chen-Yin-Shin was acting there, and immediately after Shanghai he seized Nanking. Thus the seizure of Wuchang, Hankow, and Hanyang gave us the keys to the whole of Central China, while Chen-Yin-Shin at Shanghai was also growing in strength.

While the rising was taking place at Wuchang, I arrived in Columbia [*sic*]. Ten days before my arrival there, I received a telegram from Huan-Kai-Tsiang from Hong Kong, but as the cipher was in my baggage, I could not read the telegram, and only deciphered it when I arrived in one of the towns of the State of Columbia. The telegram stated that Tsui-Chen had arrived at Hong Kong and reported that money was necessary to assist the rising of the recently mobilized soldiers. Being in Columbia, I had not any money, of course, and could not procure it, and intended to send a telegram postponing the rising. But night fell, and, being tired by my journey, I postponed it till the morning, in order to think over the question again with a clear head. I woke up the next morning at 11 o'clock and, being hungry, went out to a restaurant. On my way I bought a newspaper and, arriving at the restaurant, unfolded it; immediately my eyes were met by a telegram about the capture of Wuchang by the revolutionary troops. I thereupon sent a detailed telegram to Huan-Kai-Tsiang, in which I explained the reason for my silence.

In twenty days I could come to Shanghai and take a personal part in the revolutionary struggle, but for us our diplomatic front was more important even than the military front for the moment. Therefore, I decided to concentrate my efforts on diplomatic affairs, and only after settling this business to return home. . . .

Thus, the international situation was a question of life or death for the Chinese Revolution. The most important of all for us, at the moment, was the attitude of England, for we considered that if England took our side Japan would not delay in following her example. Therefore, I decided to leave for England.

When going through St. Louis, I read a newspaper statement to the effect that a revolution had broken out at Wuchang on the orders of Sun-Yat-Sen, and that in the proposed Republic, Sun-Yat-Sen would be the President. After this I had to hide from the press correspondents, as it turned out that rumor was in advance of fact.

Accompanied by Comrade Chu-Cho-Wen, I continued my long journey to England. On arrival in New York, I received information that the comrades were making an attack on Canton, and I sent a telegram to Governor Chang-Ni-Hsi proposing that he should surrender the city, in order to avoid bloodshed, and ordered the comrades to grant him his life, which was later on carried out.

On my arrival in England, I entered through my English friend into negotiations with the Banking Consortium of the Four Powers, with a view to stopping all loans for the Imperial Manchu House. The position was that the Consortium had already granted one loan of a hundred millions on the security of the Chuan-Hang Railway, and then a further loan of a hundred millions. On one of these loans the money had already been partly paid, but on the other, although the signature was appended, the bonds had not yet been issued. My intention was to secure the stoppage of payment on the loan which had been carried through, and to prevent the issue of bonds for the other loan. I knew that the settlement of this depended on the Foreign Secretary, and therefore I instructed the Director of the Wei-Hai-Wei Arsenal to enter into negotiations with the British government on three questions, on the settlement of which I insisted. The first was the annulment of all loans to the Ch'ing Dynasty. The second was to prevent Japan from helping the dynasty, and the third was to withdraw all orders prohibiting me from entering British territory, so that I could return to China more conveniently.

Having received a favorable settlement of these questions from the British government, I then turned to the Banking Consortium to secure a loan for the revolutionary government. I received the following reply from the manager of the Consortium: "Since the Government has stopped the loans for the dynasty, our Consortium will grant these loans only to a firmly established and officially recognized Government. The Consortium proposes for the present to send a representative with you on your return, and when the official recognition of your Government takes place, it will be possible to open negotiations." This was all I could do during my stay in England. I then returned home through France, and during my passage through Paris met representatives of the French opposition parties. I received expressions of sympathy from all, particularly from Premier Clemenceau. Thirty days after my departure from France I arrived at Shanghai. The Peace Conference of South and North was taking place at this time, but the Constitution of the future Republic was not yet determined.

Even before my arrival at Shanghai, all the foreign and

Chinese newspapers were spreading widely the story that I was returning home with a large sum of money to help the Revolution. When I arrived at Shanghai, both my comrades and the reporters of the foreign and Chinese newspapers expected this, but I replied that I had not brought with me a farthing; but had brought with me a revolutionary spirit, and that, until the aim of the Revolution had been achieved, there could be no question of peace conferences.

Soon after this the deputies from all the provinces of China, assembled in the city of Nanking, elected me Provisional President of China. In 1912 I assumed office, and ordered the proclamation of the Chinese Republic, the alteration of the lunar calendar, and the declaration of that year as the First Year of the Chinese Republic.

Thus thirty years passed as one day, and only after their completion did I achieve my principal aim, the aim of my life—the creation of the Chinese Republic.

₰ The Generals Grab Power

LIKE MOST revolutions, the Chinese Revolution of 1911 gave rise to great euphoria and hope, and Chinese patriots everywhere looked to the Revolution as a panacea for all China's afflictions. The demise of the old dynasty seemed to be the only hurdle between the humiliating past and a promising future, but as in most revolutions, the arduous task of filling the vacuum created by the destruction of the old order proved to be frustrating and bewildering. No sooner had Sun Yat-sen been proclaimed President, when Yüan Shih-k'ai forced his abdication and pompously assumed the position himself. It was not long before the Republican leaders' lofty ideals were forgotten and Yüan was proclaiming himself founder of a new dynasty.

The Revolution's principles and hopes were betrayed almost before the news of the Manchu abdication had reached the distant corners of China, and a feeling of helplessness and disillusionment slowly spread across the country. There was gradual recognition that the transformation of China into a modern democratic nation could not be completed in one night with one simple revolution. Perhaps for the first time China's intellectuals understood the enormity of their task and saw how deeply their country was steeped in its traditions and the past. Before the Revolution the Manchus were a convenient scapegoat for all of China's problems, but their collapse meant that men like Sun Yat-sen had to look beyond the anti-Manchu whipping post and confront a plethora of staggeringly complex problems, most of which, it soon became obvious to anyone who cared to look, China was ill equipped to deal with. From 1911 to 1925 China floundered in one of the most chaotic, confusing, and disunited periods in her history.

In this excellent chapter from *The Birth of Communist China*, C. P. Fitzgerald traces the collapse of the Revolution through the tragicomedy of Yüan Shih-k'ai's "reign" to the disintegration of all central control into warlordism. He points out that the Revolution discredited not only the old monarchical system but also the ideals of republican government, which had been the whole movement's substance. As Fitzgerald said, the Chinese became "completely disillusioned with the false Gods of the West. They turned restlessly to some other solution." It was not long before news of the Bolshevik Revolution reached China, and it did not fall on deaf ears. Here was a new model, and what is more important, a model bearing none of the stigma of Western colonialism. To young Chinese intellectuals trapped in the dark ages of modern Chinese history between warring factions of venal warlords and encroaching foreign powers eager to "cut up the Chinese melon," this new doctrine had a strong appeal.

C. P. FITZGERALD *
The Early Republic: "Min Kuo" Period

Not far from Peking, in the Western hills, there is an ancient temple, where grew a strange and rare plant. This plant flowered at long intervals, and then only at the accession of a new emperor. Then it put forth a single blossom. When the Empire fell the plant flowered again, but this time was covered with a multitude of small flowers. So, at least, the Peking people will tell you. The monks were asked to explain this strange phenomenon. To republican officials, visiting foreigners, and other persons of

* C. P. Fitzgerald, *The Birth of Communist China* (London: Penguin Books, 1964), pp. 43–54.

modern cut, they said that the crowd of little flowers symbolized the rule of the many, the people of China. To the more old-fashioned inquirers the monks would say that perhaps the explanation of the miracle was that in place of one sovereign, the Empire would now suffer the oppression of many small despots.

It was under the dreary and disastrous rule of the warlords that this story became popular in Peking; at the fall of the Empire, even in the ancient capital, there was perhaps a less cynical outlook. The Republic which was established early in 1912 following the abdication of the Manchu Dynasty was, the revolutionaries hoped, to be a democracy modeled closely on those of the United States and France, the two republican countries which were most familiar to the Chinese intellectuals. In the intention of its other chief founder, the former Imperial Commander-in-Chief and first President of the Republic, Yüan Shih-k'ai, it was to be a brief interregnum ending in the foundation of his own Imperial dynasty. The event proved that both were wrong; the Republic was destined to end neither in democracy nor in a new dynasty, but in chaos.

Between the republicans, who were led by men long out of touch with their own country, exiles who had worked for years abroad, and the vast mass of the Chinese people, there was only one idea in common: that the Manchu Dynasty was beyond reform and must go. It had been in full decline for many years, and that decline had involved the decay of China as a power, the invasion of her sovereignty at home, and mounting economic distress in the countryside. Already in 1840 the ancient pattern of dynastic decline had begun to show its well-known symptoms. The failure of the Empire to defend itself against the English in the Opium War revealed its weakness; the Taiping Rebellion was the first great peasant rising caused by oppression and corruption and inspired, like many of its predecessors, by an esoteric creed. It was suppressed only after years of devastation by new armies which the court could but imperfectly control.

Further disastrous foreign wars, the Anglo-French attack which took Peking in 1860, the war with France in 1884 which lost China her suzerainty over Indo-China, and finally the war with Japan in 1895 which lost Korea and Formosa had ruined the prestige of the dynasty. The Empress Dowager, Tz'u Hsi, a familiar type in history, the forceful woman of few scruples who dominates a decadent court, had arrested the fall of the dynasty at the expense of paralyzing every tendency to reform. She had virtually dethroned, and actually imprisoned, the Emperor Kuang Hsü for his part in the sudden wave of reforms which were initiated in 1898 in a last attempt to imitate the Japanese restoration movement and modernize the Empire. The Empress Dowager by the force of her personality and the support of the conservatives had held China stiff and rigid in the old hierarchic pattern; beneath that mask the corpse of the Empire was fast decaying, and when she died in 1908 the swift crumbling of the Imperial power brought all to ruin.

Yüan Shih-k'ai had been the instrument which the Empress Dowager had used to overthrow the reformers and the Emperor Kuang Hsü. He had also been the last Chinese Viceroy in Korea and he was the commander and creator of the modernized army, armed at least with rifles and artillery instead of bows and arrows and spears, which had been formed after the Taiping Rebellion and the war with Japan. He was disliked by the Regent who took power in the name of the child Emperor when Tz'u Hsi and the Emperor Kuang Hsü died, on the same day, in 1908. Yüan was then dismissed from all his posts. Four years later the revolt of the garrison of Wuchang, on the Yangtze, following the acci-dental discovery of a republican conspiracy which involved officers of that garrison, brought the dynasty face to face with a vast insurrection. The Southern provinces, always anti-Manchu, and more affected by foreign contacts, rose without resistance and joined the republican cause. The North, nearer to the throne, less interested in foreign ideas, remained passive. The only hope which remained to the dynasty was the modern army, which Yüan had created. Unless he also commanded it, it would most probably join the rebels. Yüan was recalled, given supreme command, and took the field.

Yüan certainly did not intend to save the dynasty which was in any case beyond rescue. But he was able and intended to defeat the rebels and then, the saviour of the monarchy, to usurp the throne. His chance had come, following the pattern of past history. Such had been the career of more than one of the founders of great dynasties, and of many more transitory re-

gimes. At first all went as Yüan expected. The rebels had
fewer trained troops, mostly southerners, and less artillery. The
Imperial Army gained some successes and easily held the line
of the Yangtze. China could have been divided between Monarchy and Republic, for the Western rebels who had joined the
Republic would have been crushed by Yüan's superior force.
But one factor appeared which upset the calculations of the
Commander-in-Chief. It became apparent before many weeks
were past that the Republicans had the sympathy and support
of the foreign powers, and that support meant much.

The Western powers had no cause to love the Manchu Dynasty. It had resisted them when it dared, yielded when it must,
tricked them when it could, and finally, in 1900, allowed the
peasant rising—called the Boxer Rebellion—to engage in large-
scale massacres of foreign missionaries and attacks upon the
Legation Quarter in Peking itself. It was agreed on all sides that
now that the Chinese were showing themselves anxious to introduce democracy and possibly even Christianity into the old
Empire they should be supported by the "civilized world."

Yüan, who had few modern ideas, could make a shrewd
estimate of a situation. He had driven the Boxers out of Shantung, the province he then governed, and thus deserved the
good will of the West. He saw that the foreigners wished the
Manchus to go, but also wanted peace and order in China to
promote their trade. A strong man would be to their liking. Also,
the conquest of the south in the name of the Manchu Dynasty
was going to be difficult. He cared nothing for the dynasty; the
Empress Dowager, his old mistress, was dead, and the Regent his
enemy.

He therefore betrayed the dynasty, offered peace to the
Republicans, the unity of China, the abdication of the Manchus,
on one condition: that he should be the first President of the
Republic. Negotiations to consummate this betrayal went on,
while the helpless dynasty, unable to enforce loyalty or resist
treason, bargained behind the scenes for life and property. They
were accorded both. The abdication agreement granted the
Emperor his title, the Summer Palace for his residence, a shadow
court to wait upon him, and large revenues. Yüan, after all, did

not want the Imperial dignity to be smirched or reduced, for one day it would be his own.

The Republicans walked into this parlor with astonishing insouciance. Sun Yat-sen, their leader, resigned his provisional Presidency of the Republic. The new capital was to be in Nan-king, but since Yüan delayed the transfer (with the backing of the Diplomatic Corps) and then arranged a mutiny of his troops to provide an excuse for staying in Peking, the unwary Republicans yielded on this point also. By agreeing with Yüan they hoped to gain the peaceful abdication of the Emperor, the reunion of the country, and the end of the civil war. It would not have been so easy to conquer the north, and the real fear of foreign intervention, perhaps by the Japanese on Yüan's side and by the Tsar in Mongolia or Sinkiang, urged them to accept the terms and trust Yüan.

The Republicans mistook the widespread anti-Manchu feeling in the South for republican fervor; they believed that democracy held a virtue proof against all reaction, and that the mere adoption of a constitution based on those of the West would ensure the modernization of China and the recovery of her power. For the most part these men had little or no knowledge of government or of the Chinese political scene; they had imbibed democratic ideas in their student days abroad, they felt bitterly the contempt expressed in foreign countries for antiquated and powerless China, and they believed that by adopting the usages of Europe or America they would also secure the friendship and protection of those powers.

Nothing could have been less true. Of the foreign powers only America was really sympathetic to the Republican cause, and the United States at that time took but a secondary interest in the Far East, confining her active support to words. American religious interests were enthusiastic and hopeful, American business houses followed the views of their British and European colleagues and were dubious and unconvinced. The European powers were all either covertly or actively hostile to the Republic.

Britain, then the ally of Japan, believed that the Japanese model, the reformation of the Empire rather than its overthrow, was the true and proper pattern for Oriental progress.

Any wild flight into democracy could only have unsuitable repercussions in India. Insofar as the new Republic might make China strong and modern it would threaten the established privileges and colonial possessions of the European powers in the Far East. In so far as it might disorganize China and breed civil war or disorder it would prejudice the trading interests of the Western powers in this region. France and Germany, then both colonial powers enriched at the expense of China, felt the same; Russia, an absolute monarchy, could not be expected to welcome a democratic republic in Asia.

Above all Japan was necessarily hostile. Japan had humbled the Empire and seized Korea and Formosa. She had established herself in Manchuria and virtually extinguished the nominal Chinese sovereignty there. She had shared the special privileges of the West in trade and extraterritorial rights, concessions, and tariffs. She was a divine empire, to whom the spectacle of a successful republic in China would be offensive and even dangerous. The rise of China would banish forever her dream of continental empire. The Empire had been surrounded with foes or half-friends all anxious to profit from its demise; the Republic was surrounded with enemies determined to strangle it at birth.

It must also be admitted that the Republic soon confirmed the doubters and discountenanced its few friends. The Parliament, elected in 1912, was a travesty of democracy. Votes were openly sold and openly quoted on the market. The members, when they met, devoted all their time to appropriating large salaries to themselves. Without roots in Chinese history, without tradition and without honesty, the organs of democracy presented a shameful picture of irresponsibility and corruption. Truly "a monkey had dressed up in the robes of Duke Chou."

To the President, Yüan Shih-k'ai, the spectacle was not disagreeable. The more quickly the Republic discredited itself, the sooner would China be ready for his solution, the new dynasty. He knew that he could count on the Western powers, already alarmed at the decline of order and the evident incapacity of the Republicans. He knew, too, that he could count on the main part of the older generation of officials, who would welcome a return to the system they knew and understood. He thought that he could at least count on the passive acquiescence of the peasantry who knew nothing of politics or democracy. Finally he felt sure he could count on his troops.

Preparations were soon put in order. Yüan secured a large loan from the European powers, without the consent of Parliament, and thus flouting the Constitution he made himself independent of it. The few capable Republicans were either exiled or assassinated; organizations were formed to petition for the establishment of a monarchy. They were favorably entertained, renewed, and at last, after due delay, accepted. The dynasty was proclaimed, the President, Emperor-elect, performed, for the last time in history, the ancient rite of ploughing and sacrifice at the Temple of Agriculture and the Altar of Heaven, and the date of his enthronement was announced.

All had gone forward in accordance with the precedents of history: the old dynasty had yielded to the constraint of its own most powerful military commander; he had assumed full power and was now about to ascend the vacant throne, with the customary delays and polite refusals. To Yüan and to many of his contemporaries this seemed natural and right. The Republic was just an ephemeral fantasy of returned students; there was no revolution, only a change of dynasty.

And then things began to go wrong. Japan suddenly, in the middle of the First World War, May 1915, presented to China the famous Twenty-one Demands, which if accepted would have placed China under a virtual Japanese protectorate and extinguished her independence. The Western powers were now at death grips with each other; they had need of Japan. America, who could have acted, was not prepared to intervene on a large scale. Yüan temporized, accepted some of the demands, postponed others, tried to obtain foreign support to reject the most outrageous. His prestige was destroyed, the Chinese people were roused to real alarm and indignation.

Yüan got little help from the divided and hostile European powers, and earned, by exposing the scheme, the cold implacable enmity of Japan. It was in vain that Yüan now pursued his plans. He could still count on the support of his officials and his well-pruned Legislative Assembly, but the army was wavering. On Christmas Day 1915, the commander of the forces in the remote province of Yunnan rose in revolt and denounced the pretender. Other garrisons hesitated, then joined the revolt. In a few weeks it became obvious that any further attempt to establish a monarchy must mean widespread civil war. Yüan gave way, dropped his plans in March 1916, and died, a broken-hearted man, in June.

This sudden collapse of what had apparently been a natural and universally accepted development astonished the world at the time, and still requires explanation. Three things were the main causes of Yüan Shih-k'ai's failure. Firstly his own character, which was treacherous and untrustworthy. He had already thrice betrayed those who had put faith in his loyalty: first the Emperor Kuang Hsü, whom he betrayed to the Empress Dowager; next the Regent, who recalled him to defend the dynasty, and saw him betray it instead; lastly the Republic, which had accepted his terms, made him President, and trusted him to the full. The Chinese at that period were still under the strong imprint of Confucian tradition. Loyalty is the highest of the Confucian virtues, and loyalty was conspicuously absent from Yüan's career. He might have founded a dynasty in other times; it is doubtful whether it would have lasted more than a generation; one of those transitory regimes which arise between the great enduring dynasties of China.

The enmity of the Japanese was the second main cause of the collapse of Yüan. The Japanese provided the money to finance the revolt of the generals, they sheltered his enemies and discouraged his friends. Yüan was unacceptable to Japan because they feared that he would succeed. A restoration of the Empire was to the Japanese the only conceivable way in which China might emerge from her troubles. If she did so, and became a strong modern power, Japan had no prospect of empire on the mainland. Yüan must therefore be cast down, and the chaotic Republic restored so that chaos might deepen until Japan was ready to gain her ends. Had Yüan rejected all the Twenty-one Demands, made himself the leader of a national movement of resistance, and accepted the risk of war with Japan, he might have anticipated history and led China forward to a new order, under a new dynasty. But Yüan was not such a man, and perhaps China was not yet ready for such a struggle. The old order had still many bastions standing, only the throne was gone, and the basis for a national resistance was still lacking.

The third cause of Yüan's failure was the ambition and jealousy of his generals. These men suddenly found, in the confused scene of the Republic, that they, the military, were the real holders of power: the Emperor, the symbol of civil control, was gone. The viceroys and governors of the old Empire had passed away. The new governors, men without prestige or experience, were feeble barriers to military ambition and only too anxious to share with the generals in the spoils of office. Now Yüan wished to restore the Empire, to reimpose the control of a strong and lawful goverment, to humble the army and promote his own relatives to princely rank. It was clear to the generals that as arbiters of the factions of a weak Republic they would count for more than as the obedient generals of a new Empire. Moreover, all could aspire to do what Yüan wished to do. The dynasty was fallen, so any able general could found another. Why leave this to Yüan, who was aging, who had no capable sons to follow him; once Yüan was gone the field would be clear for all comers.

The early progress of Yüan's monarchical movement and its subsequent swift collapse alike prove how little as yet the Revolution had achieved. None of the objectives of 1911 were any nearer to realization. China was weaker than before, more subject to outside pressures and spoliations. The internal situation was deteriorating; no remedy for the peasant discontents had been produced, modernization was only making superficial changes, industry was still tiny and bound up with foreign controls. The Republic had, up to Yüan's death, been merely the old Empire without the Emperor, without prestige and without sanctity. Nor was the Republic able to defend itself. Whatever causes had operated to frustrate Yüan Shih-k'ai, the sentiment for democracy and the activity of the Republican party played no part in them. No one had seriously opposed Yüan except his own generals. Not one of the Republican leaders had any hand in his overthrow.

Consequently, when he fell, the Republic did not recover its former position, but became the sport of the military. For several years after 1916, a succession of ephemeral cabinets occupied the ministries of Peking, assumed the name of the government of China, endeavored to collect loans from the Western powers, and were one and all the creatures of whatever military commander had won the last civil war. In the South, the Republican party, under their leader Sun Yat-sen, established themselves in Canton, repudiated the title of the Peking government to rule, claimed to be the only legitimate government of China, and were equally dependent on the fickle favors of the local military satraps. These generals, like those of the north, were only interested in money. They supported or betrayed the government for money; they warred upon each other to secure richer revenues, they organized the opium trade, sold the official posts, taxed the people for years in advance, squeezed the merchants, and finally, immensely rich, allowed, for a last payment, their troops to be defeated, and retired to the safety and ease of the foreign concessions in Shanghai or the British colony of Hong Kong.

If matters were so conducted in the great cities and in the capital, in the provinces things were often far worse. Under the Empire there had been few troops in the countryside. The landlords lived in their villages, the peasants paid them rent. When times were bad, the landlords remitted rent, to alleviate the distress around them. If they did not they were in danger of being burnt out or slain. The magistrate and the governor were careful not to overtax the people, lest revolt occur. Revolt might mean calling upon the court for troops. The court would also inquire into the disorder and probably execute the over-covetous officials.

There was a natural balance; the poor were oppressed, but not too far; they could react with success, or at least with danger to the oppressor. The troops were armed with sword and spear, so were the peasants. Rifles did not exist, machine guns were unknown. Jack was as good as his master on the battlefield. Or nearly as good; trained troops could of course easily rout a peasant rabble, but trained troops were few.

Now the general balance of the countryside was upset. There was no court to rebuke or decapitate a greedy official; there was, instead, a horde of soldiers, vagabonds in uniform, without discipline or pay, who fattened on the land. They were allowed to pillage, to rob granaries, and slay without punishment. The landlords fled to the cities from these disorders. They left bailiffs behind to collect their rents. The bailiffs found that the only way to live, and to grow rich at the same time, was to go into partnership with the military. If both agreed to collect from some village, good times or bad, all opposition could be overcome. Those who resisted would be shot. The soldier with his rifle and machine gun could lord it over thousands of peasants.

Throughout the period of warlord rule, from 1916 to 1925, conditions steadily deteriorated. Little was heard of the distress of the countryside in the cities or abroad. Missionaries might report what they saw, but few realized how great the change was, nor what storms were brewing. The Chinese Revolution had become an incomprehensible confusion. No principles appeared to be in conflict; no contest between democracy and tryanny was visible, no climax and no conclusion. The Western world, when it gave any attention to this scene, either despaired of China and foresaw Japanese conquest or clung to the belief that a strong man would emerge to restore some kind of order. Japan, well pleased at the rapid decline of China, continued her slow penetration and prepared for swifter and more decisive strokes.

The warlord period was, however, not without lasting importance. It consummated the destruction of two main pillars of the old order. The civil service, still more or less intact when the Empire fell, perished in the Age of Confusion. The older officials withdrew to retirement. The younger either joined the hangers-on of some general for a brief period of spoliation or, leaving politics aside, endeavored to obtain a post at one of the many new universities. In the warlord period the scholar class, at least the best elements of it, withdrew from government into academic life. Government and administration were left to ignorant soldiers and self-seeking careerists.

The flight of the rich from the countryside, the prevalence of banditry hardly differing from the exactions of the military destroyed the balanced economy of the countryside, drove the peasants down further into misery, drained money away to the coast, and left the great irrigation and drainage works uncared for and in decay. Disastrous floods, famine for which no relief, unless from foreign sources, was available, the decline of inland trade, the dislocation of communications, all contributed to the ruin of the older order of society. The military rule had alienated both scholars and peasants; it had defied every moral restraint and outraged every hope of improvement; it was the direct cause of the second phase of the Chinese Revolution.

It was not generally realized in the West, which continued to proffer good advice to China and still made no sustained attempt to comprehend her problems, that in this sad period of disorder democracy and with it all that the West hoped to see flourish in China had been discredited and cast aside. It is true, of course, that democracy had never had any trial at all; had never taken root in this alien soil, and that the pitiful travesty of the early Republic was neither an example of democracy nor a proof of its failure. Yet that is how it appeared to the Chinese people. In the name of Parliament they had seen gross and shameless corruption; in the name of democracy they had seen nothing but weak and bad government, military usurpation, violation of law, every kind of oppression and national decline. By the end of the second decade of the twentieth century the Chinese people were completely disillusioned with the false gods imported from the West. They turned restlessly to some other solution.

There were many who would now have welcomed a restoration of the Empire; many who regretted even Yüan Shih-k'ai. Other attempts to restore the monarchy had been made. In 1917 one of the least progressive generals had occupied Peking and clapped the young Manchu ex-Emperor on the throne. For a week the Empire was restored—in Peking, where the shopkeepers dutifully produced their dragon flags, kept stored away for such an eventuality. The other generals, who had been maneuvering to effect just such a restoration, but had not yet composed their jealousies nor agreed upon the division of the spoils, now combined to oust Chang Hsün and conduct the young Emperor back to retirement. Chaos returned once more.

The one effect of this comedy was to discredit still further the fallen Empire. Whatever others may have planned, or hoped to effect, there was never another movement to restore the

Manchus, or to found another dynasty. The Japanese showed singular lack of understanding of China when they believed that the restoration of P'u Yi to the throne in Manchuria would reconcile the Chinese to the loss of that country.

The Chinese are not romantic, particularly in politics. No lost cause appeals to the Chinese, no fallen house receives sympathy or support. What has fallen is down and can never be raised up. There have been no restorations in China, no Jacobites, no ghosts from the political past. Under the Manchu Dynasty, it is true, the secret societies, such as the Triad, did proclaim their objective to be the restoration of the Ming Dynasty. Dr. Sun Yat-sen, when the Manchus abdicated, solemnly proceeded to the tomb of the founder of the Ming Dynasty at Nanking, and announced to the august shade of Ming Hung Wu the ruin of the enemies of his house. He did not, however, ever suggest that the living representative of the Ming family, the Marquis Chu, who had with his ancestors been a pensioner of the Manchu Dynasty, should be invited to ascend the throne. In Chinese terms expressions of loyalty to the fallen Ming Dynasty were merely an assertion of opposition to the reigning dynasty, and in no way predicated the restoration of the Ming or mortgaged the political future of the opposition movement. The Ming themselves, also succeeding to a foreign dynasty, the Mongols, had declared their aim to be the restoration of the rule of the T'ang and the Sung—but had never sought out any surviving descendants of those dynasties. The mass of the people neither regretted the Empire, nor hoped for its return. They probably expected a new dynasty, they disliked what they saw of the Republic, yet in a vague way they felt that the Empire could no longer meet the need. Something was required which would suit Chinese ways and yet adapt itself to changed conditions. No one really thought that a new dynasty, encumbered by the memories of the past, would prove able to steer China on to a new course. By 1920 it was clear that Western democracy was not the solution, and tacitly it was abandoned even by the revolutionary element. . . .

❧ Provincial Warlords:
Progeny of the Republican Revolution

YÜAN SHIH-K'AI believed that once he had power, he need only proclaim himself Emperor and all of China would bow before the new Mandate of Heaven. What he did not realize was that the "Son of Heaven" raised in the post-1911 Chinese mind unpleasant images of a richly robed figure hidden in some walled-off palace. When this portly, bemedaled general proclaimed his intention of becoming Emperor, the country laughed; less than a year later he was dead. What counted in the China of this time was power, not the trappings of office. After Yüan's death, "President" after "President" came to office in Peking, but more important was what happened in the provinces, where powerful generals allied themselves with civil governors to set up autonomous governments, and some even declared their *de facto* independence from Peking.

For over a decade the map of China was carved and re-carved by a group of warlords, the progeny of Yüan's former armies. Each was his own master, and each depended for power on his private army which in turn depended for its survival on what could be taken from the countryside. They fought constantly, and since wars are expensive and the warlord could not put the squeeze on foreign businesses, the peasant was forced to pay.

Alliances, betrayals, intrigues marked the post-1911 years with almost comic regularity. Modern arms and dashing uniforms emblazoned with impressive medals were the main lessons the warlords learned from the West. In *East Asia, The Modern Transformation,* John K. Fairbank describes this period as a spiritual desert in which "the ancient Confucian ethical sanctions and the ceremonial forms of Imperial rule had lost their potency, while modern beliefs and institutions of popular government, either parties in competition or party dictatorship, had not yet become established." A misapplication of Western technological principles (one warlord, the "Christian general" Feng Yü-hsiang, was said to have had an armed cavalry mounted on bicycles) coupled with the crumbling of her own traditional institutions left China in an interregnum in which power and force alone counted.

Although the following selection by A. Doak Barnett, Professor of Government at Columbia University, describes conditions during the late 1940s, it gives a clear picture of the warlords at their worst and best. Yen Hsi-shan, one of the most powerful interregnum warlords, had so entrenched himself for decades in his native province of Shansi that Chiang was unable to dislodge him. For all intents and purposes, Shansi was a small nation ruled from Taiyuan rather than from Nanking. Yen had a big army, and even built a notable industry in Taiyuan. He aped many Communist practices, hoping thereby to gain the peasants' allegiance, while his loyal secret police cracked down on resistance. But whatever institutional changes he brought about, his main concern was power and its maintenance, and so he taxed and retaxed the peasantry. When the Red armies came, his private empire, like those of so many of the other warlords throughout China, collapsed. In his *From One China to the Other*, Henri Cartier-Bresson's photograph of a fat general, Ma Hung-kuei, staring out into space, is captioned in part:

> General Ma was the big warlord of Northwest China. His secretaries were dressed as hospital nurses. He adored ice-cream and always had bucketfuls handy, and offered it to his guests. Shortly after this photograph was taken, General Ma was abandoned by his troops.

A. DOAK BARNETT *
Old-Style Warlordism

Taiyuan (Shansi)
March 1948

Thirty-seven years ago, when the wave of revolt stirred by the
Nationalist Revolution in central China reached the city of Taiyuan, in Shansi Province, a young colonel named Yen Hsi-shan
made an important decision. On October 29, 1911, he went over
to the Revolution, taking with him all the Imperial troops under
his command. Since that day, the career of Yen Hsi-shan and
the history of Shansi province have been inseparable. Today,
Yen is a living myth in China, and he still rules in Taiyuan,
capital city of Shansi.

Shansi is a distinct geographical entity in the heart of North
China. Although a part of the extensive highlands of China's
North and Northwest—an area distinguished by its thick covering of yellow, wind-deposited, loess soil—Shansi has natural
boundaries that set it apart. Mountains such as the Taihang and
Wutai ranges cover most of the province, except for the Tatung
Plain in the north, the Fen River Valley near Taiyuan, and the
Chiehchow Plain in the south. Plateaus intersperse these ranges,
but they are cut by deep gorges and valleys that lie between
vertical walls of loess, and the plateaus are almost as rugged as
the mountains. To the east, the mountains drop abruptly to the
North China Plain, and the Shansi border follows this terrain
line. The province's western boundary is clearly defined by the
north-south course of the Yellow River, and the river curves and
forms most of the southern boundary as well. The inner loop of
the Great Wall forms the northern limit of the province, and a
special southern branch of the wall separates Shansi from Hopeh.

The mountainous terrain of Shansi tends to isolate the province, and this has resulted in distinct Shansi dialects and customs.

* A. Doak Barnett, *China on the Eve of Communist Takeover* (New York:
Frederick A. Praeger, 1963), pp. 157–180.

Isolation is one of the major factors that has made it possible for a leader such as Yen Hsi-shan to establish a provincial regime that has long maintained a high degree of political independence. There have been extended periods during the past thirty-seven years when the inclusion of Shansi within China has been more nominal than real.

Present-day Shansi cannot be understood without some knowledge of the background of its dominating personality, Marshal Yen Hsi-shan. Born in the Wutai district of northern Shansi, in 1883, Yen completed his basic education in a military institution in Taiyuan, and from there went on to take infantry courses in the Military Cadets' Academy in Tokyo, from 1908 until 1910. While in Japan, he joined the T'ung Meng Hui, forerunner of the Kuomintang, and made his first contacts with Chinese revolutionary leaders. After returning to Taiyuan, he started to build up a model brigade in the province, and then, in 1911, the spark lit by the Nationalist Revolution presented him with the opportunity to start his climb to power. He emerged almost immediately as a key military figure in the province, and was granted recognition by the Nationalist leaders. In March 1912 he was appointed Military Governor of Shansi. In June 1914 he was made a general, with the special title "Tung-Wu." In September 1917 he was appointed acting Civil Governor. By this time, he had achieved undisputed control in Shansi. Over the years, more titles and honors were added. In the autumn of 1918, he was officially designated "Model Governor" of China by the Central Government in Peking. In January 1920 he was awarded the "First Order of Merit." In February 1923 he was made a full general, and in November of the same year, he became a Marshal. These titles and appointments, however, were merely *ex post facto* recognition, by successive national authorities, of Yen's unshakable position in his home province. National regimes rose and fell, and other local leaders came and went during this chaotic period of China's history, but Yen remained in control of Shansi.

Although Yen focused his attention at home, he did not refrain completely from participating in national politics. He was, in fact, extremely shrewd in making opportunistic political alliances with other Chinese leaders to strengthen his own position. From 1912 to 1915, he gave moral support to President Yüan Shih-k'ai, only to desert him when he was losing his power. During the next four years, until 1919, he supported Tuan Ch'i-jui's Anfu Clique. When that clique lost power, Yen played both sides of the fence in the struggle between the anti-Anfu warlord Wu P'ei-fu and General Feng Yü-hsiang. In 1925, Yen formed a new political alliance, this time with the Manchurian warlord Chang Tso-lin, who had defeated Wu P'ei-fu. Then, when the Kuomintang successfully fought its way northward and set up its capital in Nanking in 1927, Yen came to terms with Chiang Kai-shek.

These complicated maneuvers enabled Yen to maintain his power and protect Shansi. As a result, Shansi experienced an unusual degree of peace and stability during a period when much of North China was engulfed by civil wars between numerous warlords. In Shansi, Yen carried out extensive reforms in the early years. He reorganized the provincial administration from the villages up, reformed the school system, built roads, launched campaigns against queue-wearing and foot-binding, and encouraged the development of irrigation and agricultural improvement. Accounts written by visitors to the province during those years indicate that much progress was made, and evidently Yen's popularity among Shansi people was real. Previously, Shansi had been considered an area of unusual backwardness— one explanation undoubtedly being its mountain isolation. According to one story, perhaps apocryphal, Confucius once traveled to a point a few miles west of Taiyuan and then turned back because of disgust at the ignorance of the people. In any case, Yen introduced many reforms into this backward area, particularly emphasizing the development of schools and roads.

During the years following 1927, when the Nanking government was attempting to consolidate its power, Yen Hsi-shan was drawn more closely into its orbit. In the spring of 1928, he was appointed Commander-in-Chief of the Nationalist's Third Army Group in North China; in the summer, he was appointed Garrison Commander of the Peiping-Tientsin Area; in September, he was elected to membership in the Kuomintang Central Executive Committee and the Central Political Council, and in

October, he was made a member of the State Council in Nanking.

Soon thereafter, however, Yen's independence reasserted itself. Although he was appointed Minister of Interior, he did not take up the post. Then, during the following two years, 1929–1930, Yen became the leader of a revolt of Northern generals against Chiang Kai-shek. After a quarrel with Chiang in the summer of 1929, Feng Yü-hsiang, whom Yen had previously fought on two occasions, sought sanctuary in Shansi. Yen soon became involved in the quarrel, and open revolt broke out, with Yen, Feng, Wang Ching-wei, and others cooperating against the Central Government. Over ten provinces "elected" Yen as Commander-in-Chief of the "National Army, Navy, and Air Forces"; from May to September 1930, these Northern forces fought against Chiang. Yen was even "elected" President of China by an "Enlarged Committee of the Kuomintang," which tried to establish a new government. All these machinations were fruitless, however. The Northern forces were soon defeated, and Yen was forced to go into temporary exile in Dairen. But his retreat was short-lived. The very next year, 1931, he returned to Shansi.

During the early 1930s, Yen again concentrated his efforts on the internal development and reform of Shansi, emphasizing this time a policy of "building up industries for the salvation of China." An extensive industrial program was launched in 1932, under a provincial Ten Year Plan.

However, when the Japanese reopened their undeclared war against China, in 1937, Shansi was not exempted from attack. Yen's troops reportedly fought well for a brief period, but then retreated to a mountain position near Chihsien in southwest Shansi, and there set up a headquarters called "Konanpo" ("Hillside of Conquering All Difficulties"), where Yen remained during most of the war. The facts of what happened in much of North China from 1938 to 1945 are difficult to establish, but it is claimed that during the latter stages of the war, active opposition to the Japanese in Shansi was carried on mainly by the Communists, while Yen maintained a delicate buffer position between the forces of the Nationalists, Communists, and the Japanese, attempting to play each against the others. There is no doubt that during this period, some of Yen's troops, in particular the so-called "New Army," left him and joined forces with the Communists' Eighth Route Army. . . .

Within this besieged stronghold, Yen is now carrying out drastic economic and political policies, which are profoundly affecting the lives of the entire population. His motives and objectives are not simple to analyze. He proclaims the policies he has instituted in Shansi to be radical, progressive, and reformist, but these terms can have many meanings. Yen is familiar, in a vague and incomplete way, with the issues involved in the ideological struggle between capitalism and Communism as economic systems. His writings (he is prolific) are full of pseudo-intellectual discussion of these issues, but they actually show a remarkable lack of information and understanding of the issues. His inadequacies have not prevented him, however, from formulating a "new system" of his own. He outlined this system in a long conversation with me. He accepts, he says, the thesis that capitalism should be abolished because of its weaknesses and injustices. Furthermore, Communism is, in his opinion, the best substitute that has been developed to date. The principal trouble with Communism, he says, is that its methods are wrong. Therefore, he has worked out a program that has much in common with what he believes Communism to be, but which supposedly uses better methods. The manner in which Yen's policies are implemented, however, leads one to conclude that the ideological glamour in which he tries to clothe them is simply camouflage. But, in conversation, he places much emphasis on ideology. He will assert, in one breath, that his policies are designed specifically to meet current conditions in Shansi, and then in the next he will suggest, somewhat coyly, that possibly they would be the solution to China's, and even the world's, present problems. He is not a modest man.

In some respects, Yen's policies simply represent an effort to fight the Communists by using their own methods, slogans, and catch-phrases. He has borrowed freely from them, and frankly admits that he has done so. He is shrewd in recognizing and sizing up the popular appeal of a radical reform program such as that of the Chinese Communists, and unlike some Chinese, he does not underestimate its power and appeal. Like the Communists, also, Yen has appeared to be obsessed, since the 1930s, with the aim of mobilizing all resources for increased production, and especially for industrialization.

The two programs that embody the major elements of Yen's economic policies are labeled Soldier-Farmer Unification and the People's Economy. The former is the program for rural areas, and the latter is designed for, and applied to, Yen's one important urban center, Taiyuan.

The Soldier-Farmer Unification Program was begun in 1943, admittedly as a method of increasing the number of men available for active military service. Today, this still seems to be one of its major objectives. The essence of the program, in theory, is as follows: all agricultural land is redistributed. The government neither buys nor expropriates it, however, and landowners keep title to their land, but they lose all right to till it, decide how it will be used, or fix rents. In short, land is indirectly nationalized—by a not very indirect method.

The basis for redistribution of the land is an arbitrary "land unit" that, theoretically, is large enough to support eight persons and would normally require two men to till. The average size of such a unit is said to be about forty *mou* (six to seven acres). Six of these units are combined into one "large land unit," which is assigned to six (not twelve) able-bodied men between the ages of eighteen and forty-seven and physically fit to farm. These men form a mutual aid "small group." One of the six must go on active duty into the army. Another is classified as a reservist on call; since war is in progress, he, too, must now join the regular army. The remaining four, enrolled in the People's Self-Defense Army, are responsible for farming the "large land unit," in a semicollective manner, and must support all families. In this way, one third of all able-bodied men are drafted, and the other two thirds are made militiamen. The men on active duty must serve at least three, and in some cases, four years, after which they are replaced by two others from the group; cultivation of the land unit is thus rotated among the six. Since the large units are of a size that would require twelve men to farm them, and there are only four men assigned to farm, these men must rely on the assistance of their family members and on men above

or below the eighteen to forty-seven age limits, who in theory
are assigned among the land units as they are needed. . . .

The People's Economy program is a more recent innovation. It was put into effect last May, when the economic situation
in Taiyuan became critical. It is as comprehensive a program
for Taiyuan and its suburbs as the Soldier-Farmer Unification
is for rural areas. It includes a system for rationing basic necessities, price control, establishment of cooperatives, regulation of
consumption, limitation of profits and interest, prohibition of
speculation, and control of housing and rents. A separate, special, organizational structure has been established for this program as well. At the base are "consultative conferences" composed of family heads in the basic territorial districts, assisted
by representatives of higher authorities. They are supposed to
meet weekly to discuss proposals sent to them, and to make
suggestions to higher authorities. They also elect a People's Mobilization Committee to provide liaison with higher authorities.
The main responsibility of this body, which has scheduled
monthly meetings, is to help enforce the program. The top body
is the People's Economics Executive Committee. Presided over
by the Mayor of Taiyuan, it has eighteen members: four elected
by administrative districts inside the city wall, two by districts
outside the wall, and two each by various population groups—
merchants, laborers, farmers, factory workers, self-defense
bodies, and women. Under the Executive Committee, there are
a Standing Committee of ten members, a Secretariat, and sub-
committees or bureaus for investigation and control, cooperatives, price control, labor distribution, housing and building
control, people's mobilization, and others. In theory, bureau
heads are elected by a representative municipal body called the
Lü People's Representative Assembly, and they are responsible
for administering the numerous aspects of the program. . . .

Many of the special bodies established by Yen to carry out
his own programs are not officially recognized by Nanking, and
this makes it necessary for Yen to engage in a certain amount of
financial chicanery. He depends for his bank notes, and for considerable financial support, upon the Central Government. Because of this fact, he now allows a branch of the Central Bank

of China to operate in Taiyuan; before the war, he did not. In many parts of China, this bank is looked upon as a stronghold of conservative, even reactionary, supporters of the government. In Taiyuan, however, because it is an important Central Government agency, it is eyed suspiciously and looked upon as being almost subversive. Its officials feel uncomfortable and unwanted, and their functions are extremely limited. Almost all they do, in fact, is to funnel bank notes into Yen's Shansi Provincial Bank, which handles all of the province's monetary affairs. Every month, the Central Bank brings in, by air, a large sum (recently about CNC $400 to $500 billion a month) that is provided as a Central Government subsidy to pay the troops and salaries of officials and employees in provincial government bodies that are recognized by the Central Government. The current basis for computing the monthly total is a salary index of CNC $200,000 for civil officials and employees within the city of Taiyuan itself and CNC $85,000 for everyone else. Yen, however, pays everyone on the basis of the CNC $85,000 figure and uses the money saved to pay the employees of provincial bodies not recognized by the Central Government. The Central Bank of China does not siphon any money out of the province. The amount that the Central Government Direct Tax Bureau in Taiyuan is now able to collect each month in income and commodity taxes is so small that it is hardly worth bothering about. Shansi Province does not send the Central Government a share of its land tax receipts, as specified in the national statutes.

On paper, much of what Yen Hsi-shan is now doing in Shansi sounds fairly progressive, but there is a terrible chasm between theory and practice. Most of the major policies, such as the redistribution of land, have been put into effect, but in ways disastrous to average people. Yen's Shansi is, in practice, a police state, ruled with an iron hand, and a place of near-starvation, fear, and despair. The evidence for this is readily available, even to an outsider visiting the province, if one probes below the surface by talking with people of varied sorts—although talking with private citizens usually has to be done in a conspiratorial manner.

In practice, the Soldier-Farmer Unification program, and the type of taxation that accompanies it, have imposed a terrible

burden on the farmers in Yen's territory. Farmers are reported
to be in almost universal opposition to it. There are many reasons for this. In fact, as contrasted with theory, the assigned land
units are often not capable of providing support for the number
of people who must depend on them. Moreover, taxes tend to be
based on overestimates of the probable production of land and/
or underestimates of the probable food needs of those who depend on the land. As the system works, many persons not in
the eighteen to forty-seven age group are deprived of their means
of existence; often they are farmers still able to work the land,
and in many cases, land is actually taken away from them.
Furthermore, the farmers dislike being shifted, arbitrarily, from
one piece of land to another. Local villagers often do not have
any real voice in how the land is apportioned. And because of
their natural conservativeness, most farmers disapprove, on
principle, of a system that disorganizes their existing life, prevents them from acquiring land they can call their own, and
forces them to move their place of residence every few years.

Despite these objections, the system might be bearable if
the government's taxation policies were not so ruinous. Officially,
it is claimed that land taxation is based on Central Government
regulations. The tax that these regulations, as interpreted and
described by Shansi officials, permit is not light in itself. For
every twelve *mou* of "good land" (adjustments are made for
different qualities of land), the provincial authorities may levy
seven *tou* of grain (one *tou* is about sixteen and a half pounds)
in a direct tax, and seven *tou* as a forced loan (on which interest
payments and repayments are indefinitely deferred). In addition,
the authorities may "purchase" twenty-one *tou,* paying for it
with paper currency. (Payment may be temporarily deferred,
also, and thereby made in depreciated currency.) The "real
taxes" amount to twenty *tou*. This would not be too unreason-
able. However, in practice, the entire system is ignored, and
virtually everything except what is necessary for bare existence
is taxed away. In many cases, even this limit is exceeded. The
farmers have no recourse. If they cannot pay the tax demanded,
they have to sell personal possessions and buy grain to turn over
to the government. If a farmer has a surplus after payment of his
regular taxes, various methods are used to deprive him of it.

One is to make him pay the taxes of some neighboring farmer who cannot pay in full. Another is to force him to "sell" his grain and then to make payment in bolts of cloth, matches, or cigarettes. When this is done, the grain is usually undervalued and the commodities used for payment overvalued. Moreover, the farmers have difficulty converting these commodities into food, or even into money with which to buy food. Sometimes a farmer's grain surplus is simply requisitioned, without all these camouflaging niceties. As a result of these taxation policies, a considerable number of farmers have actually abandoned their land. Tracts of such abandoned land can be seen between Taiyuan and Taiku.

Partly as a result of all these factors, the food situation in the Taiyuan region is now extremely critical for civilians. There is a threat of famine. Even now, many farmers are known to be subsisting on such things as wheat chaff, sorghum husks, and ground-up corn cobs. The food shortage is not entirely the result of the government's taxation policies; last year, there was a severe drought in the province that reduced the output in some areas by 50 per cent. But the government's tax policies are largely responsible for the plight of the farmers. . . .

These grim economic facts give only part of the picture of how people are affected by Yen's regime, however. Government controls and interference affect almost everything the people do, and the prevailing practices of a police state are accompanied by all the usual police-state trappings. Everywhere one sees groups of men, women, and boys being publicly lectured, drilled, and given political indoctrination. Passes are required for almost any activity, and travel is difficult almost to the point of being impossible for most people. For example, to enter the city of Taiyuan, a person not only needs a special pass, but he must also have guarantors willing to attest to his political reliability. Once he enters the city, he must obtain an additional permit to buy foodstuffs. Every household must make detailed reports to the police about all visitors. Political slogans, many of which the people must memorize, have almost displaced commercial advertising on walls and buildings. Political meetings, at which attendance is compulsory, are held frequently. People are sub-

ject to many kinds of forced labor without recompense. Groups
of forced laborers can be seen in many areas building pillboxes,
digging trenches—or working on the new airfield that Yen is
building closer to the city wall than the existing one. Sometimes,
the entire population of a village or city must perform forced
labor. When I visited Taiku, almost the only activity visible in
or near the city, apart from trench-digging by gangs of labor
near the railway station, was the feverish moving of bricks by
everyone—men, women, and children. An order had just been
issued that within a ten-day period, each person in the city had
to carry two hundred bricks from certain brick dumps to specified sites where new pillboxes were to be built. This work was
not to be counted as a part of the twenty days unpaid labor that
everyone is legally required to perform for the government
each year.

Arrests of people suspected of political disloyalty are frequent and arbitrary in Yen's territory. And a much-dreaded
secret-police force reaches into the privacy of virtually every
individual's life. Freedom of speech does not exist; any grum-
bling or criticism leads to suspicion of political disaffection.
Thought control is the aim of the government's extensive propaganda. Teachers in schools are gradually being given special
indoctrination. And Central Government textbooks have been
replaced by provincial texts in which even language lessons are
based on readings about the People's Economy and Soldier-
Farmer Unification programs. Shansi University, theoretically a
national institution, has a bad reputation even within the province. Its academic standards are said to be very low. And when
student political demonstrations sweep the country, Shansi University students are conspicuously quiet.

The most recent innovation in Shansi, however, is the
"Three Self" program, aimed at "self-purification, self-defense,
and self-government." Self-purification is the core of the program. It is handled by Liang Hua-chih, one of the nine provincial commissioners, who has the reputation of being Yen's
strong-arm, secret-police man. Every man, woman, and child
over the age of thirteen within Yen's territory must go through
the process. It consists of three stages and takes three to four
hours every day for a period of thirty days. The first stage is one

of political indoctrination. The second is one of confession, during which each individual must relate everything he or she has done—since the age of thirteen, or since the date when Communist activities in Shansi first began—that might have any conceivable political significance. The final stage is *Tou Cheng* ("Struggle"), in which the people accuse, sentence, and punish those guilty of collaboration with the Communists.

This "Three Self" program is carried out in small groups, by the members of a village or an administrative district, and the basic objective is to root out all Communist sympathizers or collaborators. A person who confesses and repents, however, is supposed to be forgiven. But he or she must go through a special training course. Unrepenting criminals are sentenced by general "agreement of the group." Often the sentence is slow death by beating, with sticks. Liang, and other government officials including Yen himself, blandly explained to me that this is the result of spontaneous enthusiasm on the part of the people; popular justice, even if it is somewhat crude, cannot be interfered with by the government, they say. Actually, it is clearly a fact that the meetings are planned, scheduled, directed, and manipulated by the government. Special authorities handle them. I myself was an uninvited spectator at one of the meetings and saw it managed by men, well identified by red ribbon badges, who explained to me their managerial duties.

This form of "popular justice," including the term *Tou Cheng,* has been borrowed directly from the Communists, as have other aspects of Yen's "reforms." I do not know how it works in Communist territories, but in Yen's region it is primitive and medieval. In fact, it produces a reign of terror. In Shansi today, a person never knows who might accuse him of disloyalty, or on what grounds, or for what motive. Not a few suicides and suicide attempts have resulted simply from the strain of the process, evidence of which I saw in local hospitals. The actual number of people sentenced and executed is probably relatively small, considering the number of people involved, but it is large enough to make a very great impression on the population as a whole. On one particular day this year, for example, more than a hunded persons were beaten to death in the vicinity of Taiku. . . .

Yen relies considerably, however, on an important body of close supporters, most of whom depend completely upon him for their livelihood, position, and whatever power or influence they wield. Theoretically, the broad base of Yen's support is his own political party. This party, organized in the city of Linfen during the retreat from the Japanese in 1938, is called the People's Revolutionary Comrades' Party. Yen's top officials claim it has had as many as eight hundred thousand members, and that two hundred thousand of them are in Yen's territory at present. They also say that the party is connected somehow with the Kuomintang, but the connection certainly appears to be tenuous, even though it is true that members of the Comrades' Party can be, and often are, members of the Kuomintang. The Kuomintang itself, although it has branch party units in Yen's area, has few members; it is really an orphan organization in Shansi, without any real power.

Members of the Shansi bureaucracy and army form a more closely knit and important core of group support for Yen; these men are dependents of Yen's in almost every way. The quality of this group of men is difficult to judge. A man close to government circles claims that the small circle of top officials around Yen probably is fairly free from corruption, because they are under Yen's own vigilant surveillance, but that Yen himself has accumulated, and is still accumulating, substantial personal wealth outside of the province, and that many minor officials and bureaucrats are profiting from corruption on a small scale. It is certainly of some significance that no complete provincial budget or accounting is made public.

The inner circle of Yen's closest supporters is a somewhat mysterious group referred to as the thirteen Kao Kan (which might be loosely translated as "top bosses"). This is an informal group that is said to advise Yen on all important policy matters. Its existence is supposedly secret (although it is a rather open secret). People do not talk about the group; it is not mentioned even by government officials. Its members are known, nevertheless. Some of the thirteen are members of the group by virtue of their government positions, while others hold jobs that sound unimportant but exercise real power behind the scenes. A few of them have had affiliations of various sorts with the Communists in the past, which may be one explanation for Yen's eclecticism in regard to Communist methods. People in Shansi do not venture to name Yen's probable successor, but if he tried to groom an heir, the man would doubtless come from this group. . . .

For the present, however, Yen Hsi-shan still rules in Taiyuan. There is no doubt that the character of this man is extremely complex. In some respects, he appears to be the most notable surviving relic of China's warlord era. In others, he shows surprising modernity, superficially at least. He professes to be a reformer; it is even possible that he has convinced himself that his reforms are progressive, despite the fact that he is certainly not unaware of the tragic results of some of his policies. Personally, he is witty, charming, and delightful. And, although some aspects of his character are confusing, one thing is absolutely clear: he is an extremely shrewd old man. Some people suggest that when the time is ripe he may come to terms with the Communists. This does not seem likely, but Yen's imagination does not seem to have disappeared yet, and he may still have a trick or two up his sleeve.

A man who knows Marshal Yen well, and for many years was closely associated with him, says that his egotism and his lust for personal power have, if anything, increased during the past few years, so it seems unlikely that he will disappear from the Shansi stage if he can possibly hang on. Even if the curtain does fall on his thirty-seven-year-long performance, he will not be soon forgotten, for the imprint and memory of his rule will be indelible for many years to come.

2. INTELLECTUALS TRANSFORM
THE MIND OF CHINA
❧ The Cultural Revolution

COMMUNISTS AND NATIONALISTS alike look upon the May Fourth Movement of 1919 as the high point of China's cultural revolution. Equally important, it marked the beginning of modern nationalist struggle against foreign domination. Chinese intellectuals, for decades, had been unraveling the threads of Chinese tradition, and by 1919 they were ready to proclaim the death of the old culture and the birth of the new. Sun Yat-sen sowed the seeds of nationalism with his assertion of Chinese identity in the face of Manchu rule. When the Manchus fled, nationalism subsided temporarily but soon burst out again—directed this time against the foreign imperialists, mainly Japan.

Cultural revolution and anti-foreign nationalism converged in the May Fourth Movement. Humiliation from abroad, occasioned by the Japanese-provoked injustices at the Versailles Peace Conference, and the ineptness and cowardice of traditionalistic governments in Peking enraged all those frustrated at China's hopeless plight. The students who marched through the Peking streets, and the masses of other people who later struck in sympathy with them throughout China, symbolically brought together the two great currents of China's degradation described in earlier selections: humiliation from without and decline from within.

We have chosen two selections to illustrate the May Fourth Movement's two main currents. The first is a speech delivered by Hu Shih, a key figure in the Movement and former Nationalist Ambassador to the United States. Here he recalls one important aspect of the May Fourth cultural revolution—the literary renaissance, which began in 1916 with the publication of the *avant-garde* journal *New Youth;* but May Fourth made its message the credo of all young Chinese intellectuals

Classical Chinese, the traditional form of written Chinese, was far too difficult and esoteric for the average man to learn. Intellectuals of the May Fourth Movement, like Hu Shih, Ch'en Tu-hsiu (who later became a Marxist), and other members of the New Culture Movement, realized that it was futile to try and build a popular movement and spread new ideas if the common man could not read. Thus they embarked on a campaign to publish magazines, newspapers, and books in the vernacular (*pai-hua*). But as Hu Shih points out, attempts to spread the use of the vernacular were only one phase of the cultural revolution, and he says of his contemporaries, "they want a new language, a new literature, a new outlook on life and society, and a new scholarship." They called for a total rejection of antiquity, for as Hu Shih says, China needed to overthrow "Confucius and Sons." The May Fourth Movement's leaders fought to destroy the old Confucian virtues and replace them with the new ideas of equal rights, individualism, and female suffrage.

In the second selection Chow Tse-tsung, Professor of History at the University of Wisconsin, gives a clear picture of the new nationalism which swept through China in the wake of the Versailles settlement. After reading his description of the May Fourth Incident, it is difficult not to sympathize with the young Chinese students' sense of betrayal as they watched Wilson's Fourteen Points trampled at Versailles. They were furious with the weak and feuding Peking warlords who sold out to the Japanese abroad while suppressing the patriotic student movement at home.

Today we see powerful student movements sweep country after country. In the China of 1919 it was the students who banded together to protest, who went out onto the streets to demonstrate, and who finally went to the people—not easy to do for Chinese intellectuals, who for centuries had prided themselves on their aloofness from the "ordinary people." But they were successful, at least in regard to their immediate goals: the Peking government refused to sign the Versailles Treaty.

The May Fourth Movement was the culmination of years of development. It combined many different interests and issues together under one standard, and for a few weeks the united students marched in protest. But the strands soon separated, and leadership was soon split down a new fault line by the entrance of Marxism onto the Chinese scene.

HU SHIH *

The Chinese Renaissance

The Renaissance was the name given by a group of Peking University students to a new monthly magazine which they published in 1918. They were mature students well trained in the old cultural tradition of the country, and they readily recognized in the new movement then led by some of their professors a striking similarity to the Renaissance in Europe. Three prominent features in the movement reminded them of the European Renaissance. First, it was a conscious movement to promote a new literature in the living language of the people to take the place of the classical literature of old. Second, it was a movement of conscious protest against many of the ideas and institutions in the traditional culture, and of conscious emancipation of the individual man and woman from the bondage of the forces of tradition. It was a movement of reason versus tradition, freedom versus authority, and glorification of life and human values versus their suppression. And lastly, strange enough, this new movement was led by men who knew their cultural heritage and tried to study it with the new methodology of modern historical criticism and research. In that sense it was also a humanist movement. In all these directions the new movement which began in 1917 and which was sometimes called

* Hu Shih, *The Chinese Renaissance* (New York: Paragon Reprint Corp., 1963), pp. 44–62.

the "New Culture Movement," the "New Thought" movement, or "The New Tide" was capturing the imagination and sympathy of the youth of the nation as something which promised and pointed to the new birth of an old people and an old civilization.

Historically, there had been many periods of Chinese Renaissance. The rise of the great poets in the T'ang Dynasty, the simultaneous movement for a new prose literature modeled after the style of the Classical period, and the development of Zen Buddhism as a Chinese reformation of that Indian religion —these represented the First Chinese Renaissance. The great reform movements in the eleventh century, the subsequent development of a powerful secular neo-Confucianist philosophy which gradually overshadowed and finally replaced the medieval religions—all these important developments of the Sung Dynasty may be regarded as the Second Renaissance. The rise of the dramas in the thirteenth century, and the rise of the great novels in a later period, together with their frank glorification of love and the joys of life, may be called the Third Renaissance. And lastly, the revolt in the seventeenth century against the rational philosophy of the Sung and Ming Dynasties, and the development of a new technique in classical scholarship in the last three hundred years with its philological and historical approach and its strict emphasis on the importance of documentary evidence—these, too, may be called the Fourth Renaissance.

Each of these historical movements had its important role to play and contributed to the periodic renewals of vitality in an old civilization. But all these great movements which rightly deserve the term of "renaissances," suffered from one common defect, namely, the absence of a conscious recognition of their historical mission. There was no conscious effort nor articulate interpretation; all of them were natural developments of historical tendencies and were easily overpowered or swept away by the conservative force of tradition against which they had only dimly and unconsciously combated. Without this conscious element, the new movements remained natural processes of evolution, and never achieved the work of revolutions; they brought in new patterns, but never completely dethroned the old, which continued to coexist with them and in time absorbed them. The Zen movement, for instance, practically replaced all the other schools of Buddhism; and yet when Zen became the officially recognized orthodoxy, it lost its revolutionary character and resumed all the features against which its founders had explicitly revolted. The secular philosophy of neo-Confucianism was to replace the medieval religions, but it soon made itself a new religion embodying unwittingly many of the features of medievalism. The new critical scholarship of the last three centuries began as a revolt against, and ended as a refuge for, the fruitless philosophizing and the sterile literary education, both of which continued to dominate and enslave the vast majority of the literati. The new dramas and the new novels came and went, but the government continued to hold the literary examinations on the classics, and the men of letters continued to write their poetry and prose in the classical language.

The Renaissance movement of the last two decades differs from all the early movements in being a fully conscious and studied movement. Its leaders know what they want, and they know what they must destroy in order to achieve what they want. They want a new language, a new literature, a new outlook on life and society, and a new scholarship. They want a new language, not only as an effective instrumentality for popular education, but also as the effective medium for the development of the literature of a new China. They want a literature that shall be written in the living tongue of a living people and shall be capable of expressing the real feelings, thoughts, inspirations, and aspirations of a growing nation. They want to instill into the people a new outlook on life which shall free them from the shackles of tradition and make them feel at home in the new world and its new civilization. They want a new scholarship which shall not only enable us to understand intelligently the cultural heritage of the past, but also prepare us for active participation in the work of research in the modern sciences. This, as I understand it, is the mission of the Chinese Renaissance.

The conscious element in this movement is the result of long contact with the people and civilization of the West. It is only through contact and comparison that the relative value or worthlessness of the various cultural elements can be clearly and critically seen and understood. What is sacred among one people may be ridiculous in another; and what is despised or rejected by one cultural group, may in a different environment become the cornerstone for a great edifice of strange grandeur and beauty. For ten long centuries, by a peculiar perversion of aesthetic appreciation, the bound feet of Chinese women were regarded as beautiful; but it took only a few decades of contact with foreign peoples and ideas to make the Chinese people see the ugliness and inhumanity of this institution. On the other hand, the novels which were read by the millions of Chinese but which were always despised by the Chinese literati, have in recent decades been elevated to the position of respectable literature, chiefly through the influence of the European literature. Contact with strange civilizations brings new standards of value with which the native culture is re-examined and re-evaluated, and conscious reformation and regeneration are the natural outcome of such transvaluation of values. Without the benefit of an intimate contact with the civilization of the West, there could not be the Chinese Renaissance.

In this lecture I propose to tell the story of one phase of this Renaissance as a case study of the peculiar manner of cultural response in which important changes in Chinese life and institutions have been brought about. This phase is sometimes known as the Literary Renaissance or Revolution.

Let me first state the problem for which the literary revolution offers the solution. The problem was first seen by all early reformers as the problem of finding a suitable language which could serve as an effective means of educating the vast millions of children and of illiterate adults. They admitted that the classical language which was difficult to write and to learn, and for thousands of years incapable of being spoken or verbally understood, was not suited for the education of children and the masses. But they never thought of giving up the classical language, in which was written and preserved all the cultural tradition of the race. Moreover, the classical language was the only linguistic medium for written communication between the various regions with different dialects, just as Latin was the universal medium of communication and publication for the whole of medieval Europe. For these reasons the language of the classics must be taught, and was taught, in the schools throughout the country. All the school texts, from the primary grades to the university, were written in this dead language; and teaching in the primary schools consisted chiefly in reading and memorizing the texts which had to be explained, word for word, in the local dialects of the pupils. When European literature began to be translated into Chinese, the translations were all in this classical language; and it was a tremendous task and exceedingly amusing to read the comic figures in the novels of Charles Dickens talking in the dead language of two thousand years ago!

There was much serious talk about devising an alphabet for transcribing Chinese sounds and for publishing useful information for the enlightenment of the masses. The Christian missionaries had devised a number of alphabets for translating the Bible into the local dialects for the benefit of illiterate men and women. Some Chinese scholars also worked out several alphabetical systems for the Mandarin dialect, and publicly preached their adoption for the education of illiterate adults. Other scholars advocated the use of the *pai-hua* [vernacular], that is, the spoken tongue of the people, for publishing periodicals and newspapers in order to inculcate useful information and patriotic ideas in the people who could not read the literary language of the scholars.

But these scholar-reformers all agreed that such expedient measures as the use of the vulgar tongue or the adoption of an alphabet were only necessary for those adults who had had no chance to go to the regular schools. They never for a moment would consider the idea that these expedients should be so universally used as to replace the classical language altogether. The *pai-hua* was the vulgar jargon of the people, good enough only for the cheap novels, but certainly not good enough for the scholars. As to the alphabet, it was only intended for the illiterates. For, they argued, if the pupils in the schools were taught to read and write an alphabetical language, how could they ever hope to acquire a knowledge of the moral and cultural heritage of the past?

All such attempts of reform were bound to fail, because nobody wanted to learn a language which was despised by those who advocated it, which had no more use than the reading of a few cheap magazines and pamphlets that the reformers were kind enough to condescend to publish for the benefit of the ignorant and the lowly. Moreover, it was impossible for these reformers to keep up enough enthusiasm to continue writing and publishing in a language which they themselves considered to be beneath their dignity and intelligence to employ as their own literary medium. So the *pai-hua* magazines were always short-lived and never reached the people; and the alphabetical systems remained the fads of a few reformers. The schools continued to teach the language of the classics which had been dead over two thousand years; the newspapers continued to be written and printed in it; and the scholars and authors continued to produce their books and essays and poems in it. The language problem remained unsolved and insoluble. . . .

Being a pragmatist in philosophy, I proposed to my friends to experiment with the *pai-hua* in writing my own poetry. On July 26, 1916, I announced to all my friends in America that from now on I resolved to write no more poems in the classical language, and to begin my experiments in writing poetry in the so-called vulgar tongue of the people. Before a half-dozen poems were written, I had already found a title for my new volume of poetry: it was to be called *A Book of Experiments.*

In the meantime, I began to study the history of our literature with a new interest and with a new methodology. I tried to study it from the evolutionary standpoint and, to my great surprise and unlimited joy, the historical development of Chinese literature presented to me a continuous though entirely unconscious movement of struggle against the despotic limitations of the classical tradition, a continuous tendency to produce a literature in the living language of the people. I found that the history of Chinese literature consisted of two parallel movements: there was the classical literature of the scholars, the men of letters, the poets of the Imperial courts, and of the elite; but there was in every age an undercurrent of literary development among the common people which produced the folk songs of love and heroism, the songs of the dancer, the epic stories of the street reciter, the drama of the village theater, and, most important of all, the novels. I found that every new form, every innovation in literature, had come never from the imitative classical writers of the upper classes, but always from the unlettered class of the countryside, the village inn, and the market place. I found that it was always these new forms and patterns of the common people that, from time to time, furnished the new blood and fresh vigor to the literature of the literati, and rescued it from the perpetual danger of fossilization. All the great periods of Chinese literature were those when the master minds of the age were attracted by these new literary forms of the people and produced their best works, not only in the new patterns, but in close imitation of the fresh and simple language of the people. And such great epochs died away only when those new forms from the people had again become fixed and fossilized through long periods of slavish imitation by the uncreative literati.

In short, I found the true history of Chinese literature to consist in a series of revolutions, the initiative always coming from the untutored but unfettered people, the influence and inspiration often being felt by the great masters in the upper classes, and the result always bringing about new epochs of literary development. It was the anonymous folk songs of antiquity that formed the bulk of the great *Book of Poetry* and created the first epoch of Chinese literature. It was again the anonymous folk songs of the people that gave the form and the inspiration in the developments of the new poetry in the Three Kingdoms and later in the T'ang Dynasty. It was the songs of the dancing and singing girls that began the new era of *Tz'u* or songs in the Sung Dynasty. It was the people that first produced the plays which led to the great dramas of the Mongol period and the Mings. It was the street reciters of epic stories that gave rise to the great novels some of which have been best sellers for three or four centuries. And all these new epochs have originated in new forms of literature produced by the common people, and in the living language of the people.

So my argument for a new national literature in the spoken language of the people was strengthened and supported by a wealth of undeniable facts of history. To recognize the *pai-hua* as the national medium of Chinese literature was merely to bring into logical and natural culmination a historical tendency which had been many times thwarted, diverted, and suppressed by the heavy weight of the prestige of the classical tradition. . . .

What surprised me most was the weakness and utter poverty of the opposition. I had anticipated a formidable opposition and a long struggle, which, I was confident, would ultimately end in our success in about twenty years. But we met with no strong argument; my historical arguments were never answered by any defender of the cause of the classical literature. The leader of the opposition was Mr. Lin Shu, who, without knowing a word of any European language, had translated 150 or more English and European novels into the language of the classics. But he could not put forth any argument. In one of his articles, he said: "I know the classical language must not be discarded; but I cannot tell why"!! These blind forces of reaction could only resort to the method of persecution by the government. They attacked the private life of my friend and colleague, Mr. Ch'en Tu-hsiu, who was then Dean of the College of Letters in the National University of Peking; and the outside pressure was such that he had to resign from the University in 1919. But such persecutions gave us a great deal of free advertising, and the Peking University began to be looked upon by the youth of the whole nation as the center of a new enlightenment.

Then an unexpected event occurred which suddenly carried the literary movement to a rapid success. The Peace Conference in Paris had just decided to sacrifice China's claims and give to Japan the freedom to dispose of the former German possessions in the province of Shantung. When the news reached China, the students in Peking, under the leadership of the students of the Peking University, held a mass meeting of protest and, in their demonstration parade, broke into the house of a pro-Japanese minister, set fire to the house, and beat the Chinese minister to Tokyo almost to death. The government arrested a number of the students, but public sentiment ran so high that the whole nation seemed on the side of the University students and against the notoriously pro-Japanese government. The merchants in Shanghai and other cities closed their shops as a protest against the peace negotiations and against the government. The Chinese Delegation at the Paris Conference was warned by public bodies not to sign the treaty; and they obeyed. The government was forced by this strong demonstration of national sentiment to release the students and to dismiss from office three well-known pro-Japanese ministers. The struggle began on May 4, and lasted till the final surrender of the government in the first part of June. It has been called the "May Fourth Movement."

In this political struggle, the Peking University suddenly rose to the position of national leadership in the eyes of the students. The literary and intellectual movements led by some of the professors and students of the university, which had for the last few years been slowly felt among the youths of the nation, were now openly acknowledged by them as new and welcome forces for a national emancipation. During the years 1919–1920, there appeared about four hundred small periodicals, almost all of them published by the students in the different localities—some printed from metal types, some in mimeographs, and others on lithographs—and all of them published in the spoken language of the people—the literary medium which the Peking University professors had advocated. All of a sudden, the revolution in literature had spread throughout the country, and the youths of the nation were finding in the new literary medium an effective means of expression. Everybody seemed to be rushing to express himself in this language which he could understand and in which he could make himself understood. In the course of a few years, the literary revolution had succeeded in giving to the people a national language, and had brought about a new age of literary expression.

The political parties soon saw the utility of this new linguistic instrument, and adopted it for their weeklies and monthlies. The publishing houses, which at first hesitated to accept books written in the vulgar language, soon found them to sell far better than those in the classical style, and became enthusiastic over the new movement. Many new small book companies sprang up and published nothing but books and periodicals written in the national language. By 1919 and 1920 the vulgar tongue of the people had assumed the more respectable name of the "National Language of China." And in 1920 the Ministry of Education—in a reactionary government—reluctantly proclaimed an order that, from the fall of the next year, the textbooks for the first two grades in the primary schools were to be written in the national language. In 1922 all the elementary and secondary textbooks were ordered to be rewritten in the national language. . . .

The question has often been asked, Why did it take so long for this living language of such wide currency and with such a rich output in literature to receive due recognition as the most fitting instrumentality for education and for literary composition? Why couldn't it replace the dead classical language long before the present revolution in Chinese literature? Why was the spoken language so long despised by the literary class?

The explanation is simple. The authority of the language of the classics was truly too great to be easily overcome in the days of the Empire. This authority became almost invincible when it was enforced by the power of a long united empire and reinforced by the universal system of state examinations under which the only channel of civil advancement for any man was through the mastery of the classical language and literature. The rise of the national languages in modern Europe was greatly facilitated by the absence of a united empire and of a universal system of classical examination. Yet the two great churches in Rome and in East Europe—the shadowy counterparts of the Roman Empire—with their rigid requirements for advancement in clerical life, have been able to maintain the use of two dead classical languages throughout these many centuries. It is therefore no mere accident that the revolution in Chinese literature came ten years after the abolition of the literary examinations in 1905, and several years after the political revolution of 1911–1912.

Moreover, there was lacking in the historical development of the living literature in China the very important element of conscious and articulate movement without which the authority of the classical tradition could not be challenged. There were a number of writers who were attracted by the irresistible power and beauty of the literature of lowly and untutored peasants and dancing girls and street reciters, and who were tempted to produce their best works in the form and the language of the literature of the people. But they were so ashamed of what they had done that many of the earlier novelists published their works anonymously or under strange *noms de plume*. There was no clear and conscious recognition that the classical language was long dead and must be replaced by the living tongue of the people. Without such articulate challenges the living language and literature of the people never dared to hope that they might some day usurp the high position occupied by the classical literature.

The greatest contribution of the recent literary revolution was to supply this missing factor of conscious attack on the old tradition and of articulate advocacy of the new. The death knell of the classical language was sounded when it was historically established that it had died at least two thousand years ago. And the ascendancy of the language and literature of the people was practically assured when, through contact and comparison with the literature of the West, the value and beauty of the despised novels and dramas were warmly appreciated by the intellectuals of the nation. Once the table of values was turned upside down, once the vulgar language was consciously demonstrated to be the best-qualified candidate for the honor of the national language of China, the success of the revolution was beyond doubt. The time had been ripe for the change. The common sense of the people, the songs and tales of numberless and nameless men and women, have been for centuries unconsciously but steadily preparing for this change. All unconscious processes of evolution are of necessity very slow and wasteful. As soon as these processes are made conscious and articulate, intelligent guidance and experimentation become possible, and the work of many centuries may be telescoped into the brief period of a few years.

CHOW TSE-TSUNG *
From *The May Fourth Movement*

[*Chinese indignation and concern had been building ever since Japan's seizure of German concessions in Shantung in 1914 and her infamous Twenty-one Demands in 1915. Nonetheless, Chinese leaders and intellectuals placed high hopes in a just postwar settlement, believing that the Allied victory would herald the triumph of democracy over despotism, that the secret treaties would be abolished, and that the Japanese-held German concessions in Shantung would be returned to China.*

It was with a sense of profound disillusionment that the Chinese received news of the Paris Peace Conference, and with great bitterness that they learned that Wilson's lofty principles of self-determination and war without victory did not apply to the Far East.]

DISILLUSIONING NEWS FROM PARIS

When the disheartening news that the Paris Peace Conference would give Japan Germany's place in Shantung reached China in the latter part of April, the Chinese public suddenly fell into a state of dejection and indignation. First of all they wanted to know who was responsible for the disaster at Paris. Wilson was reported to have asked the Chinese delegates in the meeting of the Council of Four on April 22: "In September 1918, when the Allied forces apparently were about to win the war and the armistice was at hand, and Japan was not able to threaten China, why did the Chinese government still make the exchange of notes stating 'gladly agree' to Japan's terms concerning the Shantung question?" This aroused the Chinese public's suspicions that their government willingly sold out the sovereignty of the nation

* Chow Tse-tsung, *The May Fourth Movement* (Cambridge, Mass.: Harvard University Press, 1960), pp. 92–120.

instead of doing it under duress. A few days later, upon receiving Liang Ch'i-ch'ao's telegram of April 24 to the Citizens' Diplomatic Association reporting that the Paris Peace Conference would turn over Tsingtao to Japan, Lin Ch'ang-min commented in newspapers on May 2 that, since the conference had reversed its earlier proposal to submit the Shantung question to the disposal of the five Great Powers (Great Britain, the United States, France, Italy, and Japan) with the requirement of consent from the nations concerned, and now accepted Japan's demand of Shantung, China was going to be subdued.

Meanwhile the Chinese delegates, fearful of being held responsible for the failure, reported back to China that "two factors had caused China to lose her case in the Peace Conference: one was that Japan had already secured secret pledges from Great Britain and France in February and March of 1917 that she would receive the German concessions in Shantung after the war; another was that our government had made the 'gladly agree' exchange of notes with Japan in September 1918 in respect to the Shantung question. These two *faits accomplis* made it impossible for those who wished to help us to do so." The contents of this report were published by the Peking daily, *China Press,* on May 1, and disclosed to the public by other newspapers and foreign teachers in Peking on May 3. In this way the Chinese at home learned on the eve of the May Fourth Incident that the Paris Peace Conference was, far from what they had hoped, controlled by power politics and that their own government had "sold out" the interests of their nation to Japan even before the conference opened. The students formally explained their disappointment at the failure of Wilson's idealism and promises:

> Throughout the world, like the voice of a prophet, has gone the word of Woodrow Wilson strengthening the weak and giving courage to the struggling. And the Chinese have listened and they too have heard. . . . They have been told that in the dispensation which is to be made after the war unmilitaristic nations like China would have an opportunity to develop their culture, their industry, their civilization, unhampered. They have been told that secret covenants and forced agreements would not be recognized. They

looked for the dawn of this new era; but no sun rose for China. Even the cradle of the nation was stolen.

The feeling of unrest among the students and their disappointment with the Western countries in the days immediately preceding May 4 was later described by a graduate of Peking University:

> When the news of the Paris Peace Conference finally reached us we were greatly shocked. We at once awoke to the fact that foreign nations were still selfish and militaristic and that they were all great liars. I remember that the night of May 2nd very few of us slept. A group of my friends and I talked almost the whole night. We came to the conclusion that a greater world war would be coming sooner or later, and that this great war would be fought in the East. We had nothing to do with our Government, that we knew very well, and at the same time we could no longer depend upon the principles of any so-called great leader like Woodrow Wilson, for example. Looking at our people and at the pitiful ignorant masses, we couldn't help but feel that we must struggle!

This situation began to look ominous to those in the know. "Even before the demonstration of May 4," Chiang Mon-lin said, "some of the leaders in the new educational movement who had been observing the spirit of unrest among the students predicted that something was going to happen." Paul S. Reinsch, then American Minister to China and a close observer of the movement, described the public feeling of the Chinese, as well as the Americans and British in China before May 4, as follows:

> Probably nowhere else in the world had expectations of America's leadership at Paris been raised so high as in China. The Chinese trusted America, they trusted the frequent declarations of principle uttered by President Wilson, whose words had reached China in its remotest parts. The more intense was their disappointment and disillusionment due to the decisions of the old men that controlled the Paris Conference. It sickened and disheartened me to think how the Chinese people would receive this blow which meant

the blasting of their hopes and the destruction of their confidence in the equity of nations. . . .

The Americans in China, as well as the British and the Chinese, were deeply dejected during these difficult weeks. From the moment America entered the war there had been a triumphant confidence that all this sacrifice and suffering would establish just principles of world action, under which mankind could live more happily and in greater security. That hope was now all but crushed.

This dejection and indignation among the Chinese students was by the beginning of May turning into a threat of a furious demonstration in protest against the "traitors in the government" and the resolutions of the Great Powers at Paris.

THE STUDENTS: THEIR CHARACTER AND ORGANIZATION

It is important to note the character and temper of the Chinese students in general and of those in Peking in particular before describing in detail their reactions to the Versailles crisis. Chinese students, especially since the beginning of the twentieth century, have had a more active political and social consciousness than those of the Western democracies. They were more inclined to participate in public affairs and to attempt reform in politics. This characteristic can be explained by a number of factors.

First of all, China's repeated humiliating defeats by foreign countries which she had previously considered barbarous and inferior, her corrupt and divided governments, prolonged civil wars, and backward and collapsing economy, certainly alarmed the young intellectuals. Taught customarily by their teachers that someday they were bound to be the saviours and hope of the nation, the Chinese students were more sensitive than other groups to any hurt to their national and cultural pride. At the same time, they were aware of the long tradition of influential student political movements and of their own privileged status among the few who possessed the ability to read and write a difficult language. Thus they took for granted their own exceptionally significant position in public affairs and their mission to save China.

Moreover, the Chinese students were psychologically prepared to take part in social and political activities. The abolition of the traditional civil service examination system in 1905 left the youth uncertain regarding their postgraduate professional prospects of which the major goal had been and still was, conventionally, to enter government as officials. The fact that this personal frustration was offset by the opportunity of being powerful as leaders of mass action tended to make Chinese students, as Bertrand Russell observed, reformers or revolutionaries instead of, as was the case with some highly educated youths of the West, cynics. Living as they did in a nation without a genuine legislature or election system, they saw that gradual improvement was obstructed and public opinion suppressed; this situation enraged them and justified their resort to revolt or protest in unorthodox political action. Since the old order appeared so hopeless, the appeal of novelty and modernism to youth was strengthened.

In this connection, we must note the striking contrast in age and education between the new intellectuals and their opposition. The college student leaders at the time were all in their early twenties and many of their schoolmates and almost all the middle school students were teen-agers. In 1919, active students like Fu Ssu-nien, Tuan Hsi-p'eng, Lo Chia-lun, and Chou En-lai were all twenty-three years old, and Hsü Te-heng, who was considered an older student than average and was sent as one of the few student representatives of Peking to Shanghai and Nanking and subsequently played a significant role in spurring student, merchant, and worker strikes in those cities, was twenty-four. Their professors purveying the new thought were in their twenties or thirties. In contrast, most of the old scholars in the opposition had passed sixty and the warlord leaders were middle age or older. Generally speaking, they and the majority of the governmental officials had received an old-fashioned education under the former Imperial regime, which differed greatly from that given to the new intellectuals, a difference far exceeding that between ordinary successive generations. This discrepancy in education and ideology made the views and actions of many government and school authorities unbearable to the young students.

Moreover, several factors facilitated the Chinese students' taking part in mass activities. Unlike their counterparts in the West, they customarily lived together in crowded dormitories and were well regimented in study and recreation activities. Collective and cooperative rather than individualistic attitudes prevailed in Chinese life in general and among the more idealistic young intellectuals in particular. Their concentration in urban centers furthermore alienated them in habit and thinking from their parents, a great number of whom were old gentry or landlords living in the country. The techniques of mass action, such as demonstrations, strikes, and boycotts, which were either introduced by returned students from abroad or learned from Chinese history and Western publications, provided suitable means for the expression of grievances or indignation that could find no other vent. The intellectuals' experiences in frugal study by means of labor and in the work-and-study program in Europe during World War I, as described earlier, had of course helped to draw them closer to the experience of the labor movement which was ascending in the West. On the other hand, there had been in China no strong objection in public opinion to student interference in politics.

While the above analysis might be applied to Chinese students in general during the May Fourth period and since, a few points should be borne in mind with regard to the students in Peking prior to the May Fourth Incident. Peking had long been the political and cultural center of traditional China. Most of the active and ambitious intellectuals, except those with merely economic aspirations, had for centuries gathered in this old capital. The intellectuals came mostly from landlord, bureaucrat, or other well-to-do families. Traditionally, a number of them had maintained close relations with the bureaucracy, and quite a number of the students had been prodigals. Their goals of life had always been, for the most part, to enter officialdom and share power with the old bureaucrats. Not many of them had troubled to pay attention to foreign policy, social problems, or the tide of new thoughts.

The temper of the students, however, underwent a considerable change near the end of World War I, especially after the 1917 reforms of Ts'ai Yüan-p'ei. On the eve of the May Fourth

Incident college students in Peking might be classified, according to their character, into three categories: the remnant of the prodigals who still lived more or less luxurious and corrupt lives, the diligent students who devoted their attention more to study than to current affairs, and the third group who were most affected by the new ideas. This third group probably constituted only 20 per cent of the student body, but it was the most active. These students followed foreign and domestic affairs closely and were deeply interested in social, cultural, and intellectual problems. Compared with their fellow students, they absorbed more Western thought, and read more Western literature— Ibsen, Tolstoy, Maupassant, Kropotkin, and Shaw. A consciousness of mission and a spirit of skepticism prevailed among them. These were the students who led the later student movements.

Actually, the thoughts and activities of the whole student body in Peking at the time were quite complex. All the ideas which had been championed in the West and the East in past centuries crowded together and conflicted with each other in the minds of the students. They had not, of course, studied these vast ideas very deeply. But their enthusiasm for what they believed was unsurpassed. It was like a man just coming into a lighted room out of one long darkened and finding everything curious.

As has been mentioned, after the petition of May 1918 the students organized many small groups, public or secret, liberal or radical, among which the New Tide Society and the Citizens Magazine Society were the most influential. (Secret organizations had come into vogue at this time among citizens, politicians, merchants, and some military men.) Though most of the student organizations were nonpolitical, there were a number interested in political events. For many active students, anarchism became popular in Peking early in 1919. Indeed, Ts'ai Yüan-p'ei himself had been an enthusiastic nihilist, anarchist, and socialist propagandist in the first decade of this century. This was true of many other intellectual leaders as well. After the 1911 Revolution many of them had retained their anarchist convictions more in the sense of humanitarianism, liberalism, and altruism than of terrorism. Under the rule of the ruthless warlords, radical ideas mushroomed inevitably among the youth. Revolutionary or anarchist publications such as the *Liberal Record* (*Tzu-yu lu*), *Collected Essays on Tiger Taming* (*Fu Hu chi*), *Voice of the People* (*Min-sheng, La Voco De La Popolo*), and *Evolution* (*Chin-hua*) were secretly passed about among the students. Kropotkin and Tolstoy became popular, and K'ang Yu-wei's *One World* (*Ta-t'ung shu*) and T'an Ssu-t'ung's *Philosophy of Benevolence* (*Jen hsüeh*), as well as the old nationalistic *Record of the Ten Days at Yangchow* (*Yang-chou shih-jih chi*) about the massacre by the Manchu troops, were still widely read and admired by the youth. These works by K'ang and T'an bore some marks of anarchism and utopian socialism. Among the student groups under this ideological influence, a very radical one was the Work-and-Study Society (*Kung-hsüeh hui*), established by a group of students and alumni from the Peking Higher Normal College, predecessor of the Peking Normal University, on February 9, 1919. The society promoted a kind of doctrine of work-and-study (*kung-hsüeh chu-i*). It rejected Mencius' idea that "mental laborers are governors and manual laborers the governed," and attempted to unite the functions in one person, that is, to have mental laborers do physical work and manual laborers, study. The major purposes of the society were to realize certain anarchist ideals in China, to serve the interest of the laboring classes, and to build a nation based on work-and-study units. It also accepted John Dewey's idea that education is life and school is society. Although its members were very iconoclastic and rebellious, they still committed themselves to the belief that social reform should be carried out bit by bit. In the student activities we are going to describe in the following sections, this group performed behind-the-scenes and sometimes pivotal functions in turning them to a positive and radical direction. Other organizations such as the Common Voice Society (*T'ung-yen she*) and the Cooperative Study Society (*Kung-hsüeh hui*) were more moderate but also influential in student circles.

THE MAY FOURTH DEMONSTRATION

When the news of China's failure in the Paris Conference reached Peking at the end of April 1919, student organizations, including the New Tide Society, the Citizens Magazine Society, the Work-and-Study Society, the Common Voice Society, and the Cooperative Study Society, held a meeting wherein they resolved to hold a mass demonstration on May 7, National Humiliation Day, the fourth anniversary of Japan's ultimatum in the Twenty-one Demands. This resolution was soon approved by the student bodies of all the universities and colleges in Peking, led by Peking University, the Higher Normal College, the Higher Industrial College, and the College of Law and Political Science, together with a plan for participation in the forthcoming demonstration by all the students of those educational institutions. Thus it is clear that the immediate causes of the May Fourth Incident were not only the disaster at Paris but also the continuing indignation aroused by the Twenty-one Demands of 1915. At the same meeting the students also decided to telegraph the following declaration to the press and public organizations throughout the country:

> Our demand for the restoration of Tsingtao is going to fail; and May 7 is near at hand. All of our people must awake to this situation. We hope that you will one and all hold protest meetings on that day to oppose unanimously foreign aggression. Only in this way can our nation survive the crises.
>
> [Signed] 25,000 students of the schools of higher learning (*Chuan-men i-shang hsüeh-hsiao*)

After this meeting, on May 1 and May 3, the news from Paris grew alarming. It was reported that China's demand for a just settlement of the Shantung question was about to be rejected by the Peace Conference and that China's case had been handicapped by the "gladly agree" exchange of notes engineered by the Chinese "traitors." Chang Tsung-hsiang, the Chinese Minister to Japan, hastily returned from Tokyo at this time. After his return, he stayed in Tientsin for several days. Lu Tsung-yü, another outstanding pro-Japanese official in the government, went to Tientsin to talk with him; on April 30 Chang came to Peking without announcing his purpose and lived in Ts'ao Ju-lin's home, though Chang had his own house in the capital. The following day the foreign press reported that Chang would not return to his post. Rumors also circulated that he would succeed Lu Cheng-hsiang as Foreign Minister and chief delegate to the Paris Peace Conference. This news aroused great suspicion on the part of the public, who believed that persons high in the government were plotting against the interests of the country. On May 3, public sentiment in Peking reached fever heat; political and social groups rushed to hold emergency meetings in an effort to save the situation. The Chamber of Commerce of Peking telegraphed to similar organizations in many other cities, asking them to support China's claims in Paris; the Chamber of Commerce of Shanghai resolved to hold a conference on May 6 to discuss methods of handling the matter. The Citizens' Diplomatic Association sent representatives to see the President, Hsü Shih-ch'ang, requesting him to order the Chinese delegation in Paris to refuse to sign the Peace Treaty in the event that the Shantung question was not reasonably solved. It also resolved on May 3 to invite other social and political groups to join a citizens' meeting (*kuo-min ta-hui*) to be held in Peking on May 7. The Corps of Chinese Students in Japan for National Salvation telegraphed the President that "it would be better to face an open rupture than to live in shameful submission."

Under this public pressure, the Peking government took drastic measures to quell the uproar, which made the public still angrier. The students in Peking felt impelled to hold the scheduled mass demonstration earlier than originally planned. The mounting urge for action during the time from May 1 to May 3 was described by one of the students, who took part in the subsequent events, as follows:

> Since May 1st we had been thinking and moving around to seek some way to express our discontent at the corruption of our Government and of the militarists, both Chinese and Foreign. . . . Finally, we came to the con-

clusion that the only immediate thing we could do was to call a great mass parade of the students in Peking.

A group of the most active students, in view of the emergency, posted a notice at Peking University on May 3 at 1:00 P.M., calling for an informal meeting of student representatives from all the universities and colleges of Peking. The informal meeting took place that evening at 7:00 in the assembly hall of the Law School (or "Third School") of the National University of Peking, was attended by more than one thousand students, and presided over by Yi K'e-ni, a nationalistic student at Peking University from Hunan, who was a leader of the Citizens Magazine Society and took a moderate attitude to the old and new culture problems. Most of the participants were from Peking University. Shao P'iao-p'ing of the Society for the Study of Journalism at that university delivered a speech analyzing the Shantung question; it was followed by a number of agitating speeches by other students. Several resolutions were adopted, of which the most significant was passed at 11:00 P.M. It called for a mass meeting of all the students of the universities and colleges in Peking the next day, May 4, instead of May 7, to protest against the government's foreign policy. This meeting of May 3 was described later by a student of the National University of Peking:

> We first discussed the problem of our national crisis and we all agreed that the Shantung problem was caused by corruption and injustice, and that we as students must fight to show the world that "might should never be right"! Four methods of procedure were then discussed. They were as follows: (1) to get the people of the country to fight together; (2) to send telegrams to the Chinese delegates in Paris and ask them not to sign the treaty; (3) to send telegrams to the people of all provinces in the country asking them to parade on May 7th, National Humiliation Day; (4) to meet [with] on May 4 the students of all the schools in Peking at "Tieng-Ang Mien" [T'ien An Men, the Square of Heavenly Peace] and to show our discontent by a great mass parade.

During the meeting, a student of the Law School, Mr. Tshia [Hsieh Shao-min], deliberately cut open his finger and wrote on the wall in blood "Return Our Tsingtao." The students were all quiet.

Obviously the meeting on the evening of May 3 proceeded in a highly emotional atmosphere. This was also recalled by Hsü Te-heng, a student leader who had spoken at the meeting and was one of thirty-two later arrested in the incident, and by Chang Kuo-t'ao, another student at Peking University, who had also spoken at this meeting and later became a Communist leader but left the Party in 1938. It was also said that in the meeting a young student of about sixteen or seventeen years of age shouted in tears that he would commit suicide on the spot if the meeting did not reach a positive resolution for the demonstration.

It must be pointed out, however, that the meeting was carried on in an orderly fashion and that the majority of students and student representatives had no intention that there should be violence in the scheduled demonstration. The meeting was conducted mainly by members of the New Tide Society and the Citizens Magazine Society, most of whom from the beginning disavowed violent action. The demonstration seemed to have been carefully prepared. John Dewey and his wife, who had arrived in China on May 1, 1919, wrote home from Peking on June 20, 1919:

> I find, by the way, that I didn't do the students justice when I compared their first demonstration here to a college boys' roughhouse; the whole thing was planned carefully, it seems, and was even pulled off earlier than would otherwise have been the case, because one of the political parties was going to demonstrate soon, and they were afraid their movement (coming at the same time) would make it look as if they were an agency of the political faction, and they wanted to act independently as students. To think of kids in our country from fourteen on, taking the lead in starting a big cleanup reform politics movement and shaming merchants and professional men into joining them. This is sure some country.

Some of the radical groups, nevertheless, had planned to turn the demonstration into more than mere orderly protest. On the evening of May 3, both before and after the informal meeting of student representatives, many small student groups, secret and public, held meetings at their respective schools to discuss methods and procedures for the forthcoming demonstration. It is reported that some groups in their meetings planned to attack three pro-Japanese officials, Ts'ao Ju-lin, Chang Tsung-hsiang, and Lu Tsung-yü. Ts'ao, Minister of Communications and Managing Director of the Bank of Communications, Chang, Minister to Japan since 1916, and Lu, the Director General of the Currency Reform Bureau, Chairman of the Bank of Communications, and Chinese Director of the Chinese-Japanese Exchange Bank, were regarded as the most pro-Japanese officials in the Peking regime.

Another report has it that some of the students had also planned in advance to burn Ts'ao's house and that secret student societies, mostly anarchist, had intended in the latter part of April to start a demonstration. According to the story, on the eve of May 4 they convened in secret and resolved to punish the three officials severely. At the time an old member of the T'ung-meng-hui gave these students Chang Tsung-hsiang's photograph so that they might identify him. (Photographs of Ts'ao and Lu were often displayed in various studios, so the students could identify them.) They decided to carry small cans of fuel and matches to burn Ts'ao's house, but kept their plans secret from the majority of the students. Because the societies feared that the secret might leak out, they persuaded the students at the informal meeting on May 3 to carry out the demonstration three days earlier than previously scheduled. This account appears to offer a possible explanation of the later violence. But it would be an exaggeration to say that the demonsration itself was directed by those secret societies. It is more likely that they made use of the popular sentiment as an occasion for using violence.

The students' resolution on May 3 to change the date of the demonstration was apparently known to the administrators of the National University of Peking. Before this student meeting Ts'ai Yüan-p'ei had called a faculty meeting to discuss the problem of the student activities. Because of the hostile attitudes of the warlord government toward the university and their own indignation at the government's weak stand on the Sino-Japanese issue, the faculty did not wish to impede the students' activities. On the eve of May 4, Ts'ai called in one of the student leaders, Ti Fu-ting and, reportedly, expressed his sympathy with the students.

On the morning of May 4, a Sunday, at ten o'clock, student representatives met at the Peking College of Law and Political Science, as scheduled by the meeting on the previous evening, to prepare the demonstration. Student representatives from thirteen colleges and universities, including the National University of Peking, attended. An Army Cadets Academy (*Lu-chün hsüeh-hsiao*) also sent student representatives as observers. At this meeting which lasted about an hour and a half, five resolutions were adopted: (1) that telegrams be sent to all organizations concerned at home and abroad urging them to protest the Shantung resolution of the Paris Peace Conference; (2) that efforts be made to awaken the masses of the people all over the country; (3) that a mass meeting of the Peking people be arranged; (4) that a permanent and united organization of all Peking students be established to take charge of student activities and of relations with other organizations; and (5) that the route of the demonstration that afternoon was to be from the T'ien-an Gate, through the Legation Quarter (*Tung chiao-min hang*), and thence to the Hatamen (*Ch'ung-wen-men*) Boulevard business area. At this meeting the student representatives displayed considerable efficiency and harmony in making these important decisions.

By 1:30 in the afternoon over three thousand students had gathered at the T'ien-an Gate . . . to take part in the demonstration. They represented thirteen colleges and universities in Peking. The first to arrive were from the National Higher Normal College of Peking and from Hui-wen University (established by American missionaries). They were followed by students from the National College of Law and Political Science, National Industrial College, National Agricultural College, National Medical College, Academy of Police Officers, Institute of Railroad Administration, Institute of Tax Administration, China University, University of the Republic, and Ch'ao-yang

University. The National University of Peking students arrived last, but played a leading role in the demonstration.

The Peking government had made efforts to prevent the mass meeting. A representative of the Ministry of Education accompanied by several garrison and police officers was sent to Peking University on May 4 about 11:00 A.M. and in the presence of Ts'ai Yüan-p'ei advised the students not to join in, but, after a long argument with the representative, they refused to follow his advice. The only effect of this episode was to delay the students of the university for a time.

When the students had gathered in the big square in front of the T'ien-an Gate, standing in order, group after group by school, a student representative of Peking University introduced the representative of the Ministry of Education to the audience and explained the delayed arrival of the university students. The representative from the ministry "advised the students to go back to their respective schools and to send their representatives to call upon the Government or the Allied Ministers to talk over the matter, instead of parading in such numbers." General Li Ch'ang-t'ai, the commander of the infantry, and Wu Ping-hsiang, the chief of the constabulary, also persuaded them to give up the parade. The students did not accept the proffered advice; they fully realized that their aim was not going to be achieved at once either by petitions or by mass demonstrations anyway. Their immediate purpose was to publicly demonstrate indignation against the warlords and against the national humiliation brought about by power politics.

At the mass meeting and the following demonstration, a printed brief "Manifesto of All the Students of Peking" was distributed describing this purpose:

> Japan's demand for the possession of Tsingtao and other rights in Shantung is now going to be acceded to in the Paris Peace Conference. Her diplomacy has secured a great victory; and ours has led to a great failure. The loss of Shantung means the destruction of the integrity of China's territory. Once the integrity of her territory is destroyed, China will soon be annihilated. Accordingly, we students today are making a demonstration march to the Allied lega-

tions, asking the Allies to support justice. We earnestly hope
that all agricultural, industrial, commercial, and other
groups of the whole nation will rise and hold citizens' meetings to strive to secure our sovereignty in foreign affairs and
to get rid of the traitors at home. This is the last chance for
China in her life and death struggle. Today we swear two
solemn oaths with all our fellow countrymen: (1) China's
territory may be conquered, but it cannot be given away;
(2) the Chinese people may be massacred, but they will not
surrender.

Our country is about to be annihilated. Up, brethren!

This manifesto was written in vivid and clean-cut vernacular
Chinese, which reflected the effect of the literary revolution, and
was considered an excellent expression of the spirit of the young
intellectuals. Besides this, a more formal declaration written in
the literary language was adopted at the meeting. It advocated
"citizens' meetings," "public speeches," and pistols and bombs
for the traitors as last expressions of student reaction. The declaration, which seemed to have been drafted by the militant, nationalistic students before the meeting, was not printed and distributed at the meeting and the demonstration, but it circulated
throughout the country afterwards. It reads:

Alas, citizens! Our dearest, most respected, and most
patriotic brethren! The five Great Powers first promised to
seek our consent for the solution they will reach regarding
the humiliating secret and dangerous treaties forced upon
us by Japan and the long-prayed-for return to us of Tsingtao
and other German privileges in Shantung. But now they
leave these problems to direct negotiation between China
and Japan. This ominous news robs the light from our skies.
When the Paris Peace Conference was convened, was it not
our hope and happy anticipation that right, humanitarianism, and justice would prevail in the world? To return
Tsingtao to us and to abolish the Sino-Japanese secret
treaties and military conventions and other unequal treaties
are right and just; to surrender right to might, to place our
territory at the disposal of the five Great Powers, and to
treat us like the defeated Germany and Austria are not right

and are unjust. Now right and justice have been further
violated; the Great Powers ask China and Japan to negotiate
the Shantung question directly. Japan, tiger-like and wolf-
like, has been able to wrest privileges from China simply
by sending us a sheet of paper, the Twenty-one Demands.
Our further negotiation with her will certainly mean the loss
of Tsingtao and Shantung. Shantung, strategically controlling Chihli and Shansi to the north and Hupei and
Kiangsu to the south, and situated in the middle of the
Peking-Hankow and Tientsin-Nanking Railroads, is actually the throat and heart of the South and North. The loss
of Shantung means the subjugation of China. How can our
brethren, dwelling in this land as owners of these mountains and rivers, while looking on the insult and oppression
and the attempt to enslave us, refrain from crying out for
last-ditch salvation? The French in their struggle for Alsace-
Lorraine cried, "Give us our wish or give us death." The
Italians in their struggle for the Adriatic Straits cried, "Give
us our wish or give us death." The Koreans in their struggle
for independence also cried, "Give us our wish or give us
death." We now approach a crisis in which our country is
threatened with subjugation and her territory is going to be
ceded. If her people still cannot unite in indignation in a
twelfth-hour effort to save her, they are indeed the worthless
race of the twentieth century. They should not be regarded
as human beings. Are there not some of our brethren who
cannot bear the torture of being slaves and beasts of burden
and steadfastly desire to save their country? Then the urgent
things we should do right now are to hold citizens' meetings,
to make public speeches, and to send telegrams to the government in support of our stand. As for those who willingly
and traitorously sell out our country to the enemy, as a
last resort we shall have to rely on pistols and bombs to
deal with them. Our country is in imminent peril—its fate
hangs on a thread! We appeal to you to join our struggle.

At two o'clock, after the meeting, the students marched
from the T'ien-an Gate southward through Chung-hua Gate. At
the head of the procession two janitors carried huge five-colored

national flags. After them was a pair of funeral scrolls on which were written traditional Chinese mourning phrases (*wan-lien*) doctored with sarcasm:

> The names of Ts'ao Ju-lin, Lu Tsung-yü, and Chang Tsung-hsiang will stink a thousand years;
> The students of Peking mourn for them with tears.

Besides distributing leaflets to the spectators on the streets, the students carried white flags made of cloth or paper, bearing slogans written in Chinese, English, and French and caricatures expressing the purposes and sentiments of their demonstration. The slogans may be classified into the following categories:

(*A*) *Externally, struggle for sovereignty, or resist the Great Powers.*

Examples:

Return our Tsingtao.
We may be beheaded, but Tsingtao must not be lost.
Reclaim Tsingtao unto death.
Abolish the Twenty-one Demands.
China has been sentenced to death [by the Paris Conference].
Refuse to sign the Peace Treaty.
Boycott Japanese goods.
Protect our country's soil.
Protect our sovereignty.
China belongs to the Chinese.
Self-determination.
International Justice.
Oppose power politics.

(*B*) *Internally, throw out the traitors.*

Examples:

Down with the traitors.
Ts'ao Ju-lin is a traitor.
Death punishment for the traitors, Ts'ao, Lu, and Chang.
The people should determine the destiny of the traitors.
Don't just be patriotic for five minutes.

The people of Peking were deeply impressed by the demon-strators. Many spectators were so touched that they wept as they stood silently on the streets and carefully listened to the students shout their slogans. Many Western spectators greeted them with ovations and by taking off or waving their hats. The students paraded along the streets in order. Boy Scouts and students from elementary schools joined in and distributed leaflets. Even the police and secret agents, who were sent by the government to patrol, did not find any signs of intended violence on the part of the students.

FROM THE LEGATION QUARTER TO TS'AO JU-LIN'S HOUSE

But the temper of the students changed and became less disci-plined during the latter part of the demonstration. Passing the Chung-hua Gate, the procession turned to the east and reached the western entrance of the Legation Quarter. The students were refused entrance to the extraterritorial district by the Legation Quarter police. After several telephone conversations with lega-tion officials, four student representatives, including Lo Chia-lun and possibly Chang Kuo-t'ao, were appointed to enter the American Legation to see the minister. When they found him absent, the students left for the minister a memorandum. Paul S. Reinsch later recalled:

> A crowd of students appeared before the legation gate on the 5th [4th] of May clamouring to see me. I was absent, that day, on a trip to the temple above Men T'ou-kou and so missed seeing them. Their demonstration, as it turned out afterward, was the first step in the widespread student movement which was to make history. Their patriotic fer-vour had, on that morning [afternoon], been brought to the boiling point by the first inkling of the Paris decision on Shantung. . . .
>
> The Chinese people, discouraged in Peking, had cen-tered their hopes on Paris. When hints of a possible accep-tance of Japan's demands were received in Peking, the first impulse of the students was to see the American minister,

to ask him whether this news was true, and to see what he
had to say. I escaped a severe ordeal.

The student representatives also found the British, French,
and Italian ministers absent, and left letters at their legations.
After a long wait (about two hours) they failed to secure the
permission of the Legation Quarter police to pass through the
quarter. At the same time, Chinese police and troops, surrounding the entrance of the quarter, violently intervened and tried
to force the students back. Under this double disappointment
and pressure, the students, now joined by other citizens, became
irritated and angry. Suddenly, they cried, "On to the Foreign
Ministry!" "On to the house of the traitor!" At this critical
moment, Fu Ssu-nien, as the elected "marshal" of the student
demonstration, urged his fellow students not to go; but he could
not control the situation in the uproar and agitation.

The students then marched northward along Hu-pu Street
and Tung-ch'ang-an Street, to the Tung-tan Arch and Shih-ta-
jen Hu-t'ung (side street). On the road they shouted slogans
and called the traitors by name, including Ts'ao Ju-lin, Lu
Tsung-yü, Chang Tsung-hsiang, as well as the leader of the warlords, Tuan Ch'i-jui, and his chief of staff, Hsü Shu-cheng.
About 4:30 P.M. the procession arrived at Ts'ao's residence
which was at 2 Chao-chia-lou Street, close to the office of the
Foreign Ministry.

Up to this time, things had not yet really gotten out of control. As a British correspondent reported, the students "arrived
at Ts'ao Ju-lin's house in an orderly procession, quite worthy of
the students of an enlightened nation. But the wrath of the demonstrators was roused by the repressive measures taken by the
Police, whereupon they broke out into acts of unbridled violence."

The students found the doors of the house all firmly closed
and the mansion guarded by police and gendarmes. The crowd
demanded that Ts'ao appear in person and explain why he had
made the secret agreements with Japan. To this demand the police and gendarmes turned a deaf ear, and tried to force the
students back. At this the demonstrators flew into a rage, yelling
loudly, "The traitors! The traitors!" Many of them threw stones

and white flags into the windows and over the walls and tried to enter but in vain. When they were about to withdraw and go back to their schools, five intransigents among them climbed up the wall, broke open a window, and jumped into the house. These five students encountered more than a dozen of Ts'ao's armed bodyguard, who, startled by the students, without resistance let them open the front door. Thus the mass of students stormed into the house.

The students supposed that the three pro-Japanese officials were holding a secret conference in the house. But they could not find anyone, except Ts'ao's sick father, son, and young concubine. They let them go away with the bodyguard, but, shouting and hysterical, smashed all the furniture and set the house on fire.

At this instant (about 5 o'clock) some of the students found Chang Tsung-hsiang in a sitting room with Ting Shih-yüan, director of the Aviation Department, Ministry of the Army, concurrently managing-director of Peking-Suiyuan Railroad and Peking-Hankow Railroad, and a well-known Japanese journalist Nakae Ushikichi. Chang was immediately beaten to the ground. When Ting rushed out to call the police, they were reluctant to intervene. Chang lay on the ground pretending to be dead. Seeing the fire, the confused students feared they had overreached themselves and many dispersed to return home or to their schools. Nakae and some of the police took this opportunity to help Chang escape to a dark room in a neighboring salted-egg store. There he was found once again by another group of students who dragged him to the door of the store. When he refused to tell who he was, the students beat him into insensibility with banner staffs and pelted him with eggs; later he was taken to the Japanese T'ung Jen Hospital by the police. Chang's house in Tientsin was reportedly destroyed by students on the same date.

Ts'ao himself had actually been at home in conversation with Chang, Ting, and Nakae at the moment the students attacked the house. He had escaped in disguise with a servant through a window and a narrow alley, and been driven in a motor car to the foreign-owned Wagons Lits Hotel (*Liu-kuo fan-tien*) in the Legation Quarter. Lu Tsung-yü had not been present. The following account of the attack on his house was given in Ts'ao Ju-lin's letter of resignation to the President the next day, May 5:

> I was asked to attend the banquet in the office of the President on the morning of May 4. I went to my home on Chao-chia-lou Street in the east side of the city at 2:30 P.M., and had a talk with Mr. Chang Tsung-hsiang, the minister to Japan. All of a sudden, we heard wild shouts and noises coming from afar, as furious tides rolled toward the entrance of the lane, with the patroling police passively looking on. About ten or more minutes later we saw over one thousand students—some of them jumping over the wall and breaking the door—storm into my house. They smashed everything they saw and beat everybody they met. My paralyzed father who was cared for in the house was also beaten. Then they set fire to my house. Its eastern wing which served as my bedroom was immediately burnt to the ground. All the other things were also completely destroyed. Mr. Chang was caught by the mob when he hastily escaped to a neighboring house. He was violently thrown to the ground, and beaten into insensibility with sticks and stones. His head bore nine deep wounds and bled incessantly. . . .

During these disorders there were some struggles between the police and the students in the courtyard. The attitude of the police, however, was very moderate under the circumstances. Some of them actually "observed an attitude of 'benevolent neutrality.' " But they were forced to interfere after several urgent orders were received from the higher commanders. Consequently, in the fight some students and police were wounded. A student of the National University of Peking named Kuo Ch'in-kuang died three days later in a French hospital in the city. The death was attributed to injury and overstrain in the incident. This became one of the events which heightened indignation among the students in the days that followed.

The fighting lasted until 5:45 P.M., by which time most of the demonstrators had dispersed and only a few dozen remained to see what would happen. Only then did Wu Ping-hsiang and General Li Ch'ang-t'ai arrive accompanied by troops, police, and gendarmes. The police and troops, who had been moderate before, suddenly changed their attitude, probably because of the presence of their commanders. They fired a few shots into the air. Upon the orders of Wu, who had been sent by Premier Ch'ien Neng-hsün (*tzu*: Kan-ch'en, 1869–1924), they made several arrests near the scene and more along the streets. As a result, thirty-two students, including Yi K'e-ni, Ts'ao Yün, Hsü Te-heng, Chiang Shao-yüan, Li Liang-chi, Yang Chen-sheng, Hsiung T'ien-chih (Peking University), and Hsiang Ta-kuang (the Higher Normal College), were imprisoned at police head-quarters. The students arrested were, judging from all the evidence, distributed as follows: twenty from the University of Peking, eight from the Higher Normal College, two from the Higher Industrial College, and one each from China University and Hui-wen University.

The students arrested, although only a few of them were among the leaders or had participated in the violence, went to the police station with a show of heroism. As a student later recalled:

> The students (only ten at first) were taken to the police station in pairs. The soldiers pushed them with the ends of their guns or slapped them if they protested. They were at once put into prison; five being paired off with a group of robbers and thieves. They were not allowed to speak. Three hours later more students arrived at the prison. . . . At 7 P.M. the students were carried to the central police station. On the road these student-prisoners met a few Westerners passing them in an automobile. They greeted the student-prisoners by clapping, and the students returned the salutation. After they reached the station they were put together in a room and not allowed to talk.

After the arrests, martial law was at once proclaimed for the area surrounding the Legation Quarter. Firemen rushed to Ts'ao's house. They came with a fine display of banners and much blowing of horns. A half-inch stream was turned on the buildings which were already burning like tinder. They put out the fire at about eight o'clock. The water flooded adjacent streets carrying with it the gossip that the college boys had burnt the traitor's house. The news immediately spread all over the capital.

The event at once made a profound impression on Chinese
political and social circles. The subject of most comment was the
fact that in the very brief skirmish before Ts'ao's gates there
had been no fierce fighting between the police and the students. "It seems very bitter irony to the local Chinese audience," one of the first reports said, "that the man who has found
the money and the arms for all the Northern armies, who
through his associates could command several hundred thousand
men, should be mobbed in his own house and have no one fire
a shot or strike a blow for him."

From the foregoing description, it seems clear that, thus far,
the demonstration had been purely a public expression of indignation by the students which had resulted in an uncontrolled
disturbance unanticipated by the majority of the demonstrators.
Their prime motive had been devoted patriotism. The significance of the demonstration would have been limited if there had
been no developments following the events of May 4. It might
have been counted merely a defiant gesture on the part of the
students against the warlords and a protest against the unpopular
resolutions of the Shantung question by the Great Powers at
Paris. Or it might have been considered merely a riot by a
youthful mob, or at least by its radical wing, as it has in fact
been interpreted by a few observers who did not understand the
history and development of the movement.

But the students in Peking started immediately after the incident to organize the new intellectuals of the nation in the support of their cause. They also tried to win over the sympathy of
the general public by means of publicity, mass meetings, and
demonstrations. In this process they began to establish closer
contacts with the masses of illiterate people, and to secure strong
and effective support from the new merchants, industrialists,
and urban workers. Hence the students' new ideas were spread
to an unexpected extent throughout the cities of the country,
the antiquated civilization began to crack up, and new socio-
political developments were set afoot. The unique place occupied by the May Fourth Incident in the history of modern
China is due to these consequences rather than to the demonstration alone.

3. THE INTELLECTUALS AND THE PEOPLE: IDEOLOGY AND DISCONTENT UNITE TO MAKE THE CHINESE REVOLUTION

⚘The Chinese Communist Party:
The Impact of the May Fourth Movement
and the Russian Revolution

ONE OF the wellsprings of Chinese Communism was the May Fourth Movement (see pp. 63–86). The student-led demonstrations and the great general strike in Shanghai, organized by students in response to their Peking comrades, convinced many Chinese intellectuals that alliance with the masses was the only road to revolution and regeneration. Students began to go forth from the universities into factories and villages, much as Russian students had done several decades earlier.

The other source of Chinese Communism was the October Revolution in Russia. Before 1917 not even the word "Marxism" was widely known in China. One month after the February Revolution the future Communist leader Li Ta-chao wrote prophetically of Russia and China's common revolutionary destiny. By 1919 small Marxist study groups had formed in many of China's larger cities. Within a decade Marxism had become the dominant mode of thinking in both Communist and non-Communist intellectual circles. Despite the Comintern's high-handed treatment of the Chinese Communist Party (CCP), its ruinous political advice, and worse its misuse of the CCP for internal Soviet purposes, the link then forged between the Soviet and the Chinese Communist Parties has continued, albeit weakened. Even after the debacle of 1927, for which Stalin bore major blame, the Chinese Communist Party remained loyal to the Comintern, and even the unorthodox Mao Tse-tung never at-

tacked the Comintern. In subsequent years, one would again see
Soviet duplicity in China, yet the CCP never completely broke
with Moscow.

The Chinese Communist Party was formed in Shanghai in
July 1921 by a small group of Marxists assisted by Comintern
Representative Gregor Voitinsky. The infant Party was immediately beset by a myriad of problems, not the least of which was
survival. It had no organization, no funds, and precious little
experience. In short, it desperately needed allies. The warlords,
who ruled bits and pieces of China while playing musical chairs
for the theatrical honor of being titular head of the Peking government, were unacceptable candidates for obvious reasons.
Clearly representing a "feudal" class, they were thus anathema
to the young Communists. The alternative was Sun Yat-sen, who
led the struggling Kuomintang faction in Canton. They approached Sun, who was also badly in need of allies, and proposed a two-party alliance with the Kuomintang. At first Sun
rejected their offer, but after repeated assurances from various
Comintern advisors that he need not worry about Communism
since the Soviet system was "unsuitable to Chinese conditions,"
Sun began to think otherwise, though he remained wary. But
promises of Soviet aid and assistance were tempting.

Sun was not the only hesitant member of the proposed alliance. CCP members like Ch'en Tu-hsiu had grave doubts
whether the Kuomintang (officially designated as bourgeois)
was truly a revolutionary group. How could the CCP maintain
its own proletarian identity in an alliance with the bourgeoisie?
How could the CCP carry out the class struggle if forced to
keep company with such strange bourgeois bedfellows? These
were only a few of the distressing contradictions which confronted the young Chinese Marxists and made them reticent to
join the Kuomintang under Sun's terms.

The Comintern, directed by Moscow's iron hand, prevailed,
and Ch'en's protestations were overruled. Moscow claimed that
the Kuomintang was a revolutionary force which would serve
well in the first stage of the socialist revolution to expel the warlords and imperialists. (This stage of the Revolution was called
National Revolution rather than the Proletarian Revolution.)
Purity of dogma yielded to practical compromise. Ch'en's mis-

givings were dismissed as erroneous thinking and negotiations were opened with Sun. In January 1924 the awkward alliance was consummated: "If Ch'en disobeys our Party," said Sun, "he will be ousted." It was an ominous note on which to begin, but Moscow had clearly won the first round.

We have seen that some CCP leaders were reluctant to join the United Front. Why was Sun agreeable?

Virtually abandoned by the Western Powers, Sun was receptive to any and all friendly overtures. Soviet promises to help reorganize the faltering Kuomintang along Leninist lines (it is interesting to note that even today on Taiwan the Kuomintang retains its Leninist form of organization) and to supply it with arms were extremely tempting. Sun could hardly afford to reject the offer. He hoped that the Communists, entering the Kuomintang ranks as individuals, would eventually be absorbed. (This is exactly what Ch'en Tu-hsiu had feared.) But Sun unfortunately failed to appreciate Moscow's real intentions: to use the Kuomintang, as Stalin later said, like a lemon, to squeeze it until dry and then discard it. The Kuomintang was an important power structure into which Moscow hoped the CCP could burrow and thus transform it into Moscow's image. It took little perception to see the contradictions inherent in the United Front and that if it was expedient to do so, neither side would hesitate to pull out. In 1925 Sun died in Peking, depriving the United Front of the one personality around which both sides could muster. His death boded ill for Kuomintang-Communist Party relations.

By 1927 both the Kuomintang and the CCP had achieved their primary objectives. The Kuomintang under Chiang Kai-shek had assembled an impressive military apparatus with Russian help, and the CCP had succeeded in winning a considerable following among labor and peasant organizations; by 1927 each had the means to undermine the other. The question was: Who would strike first?

By the spring of 1927 Chiang had almost completed his Northern Expedition, giving China the first semblance of unity since the fall of the Manchu Dynasty. The Kuomintang position was infinitely stronger than it had been five years before. As the contradictions between the Kuomintang and the CCP became more obvious and irritating, Chiang's patience grew shorter. In 1926, while declaring fealty to the United Front principle, he purged all CCP members from high-ranking positions in the Kuomintang and sent his Russian advisors home. The CCP leadership was deeply worried; they began to feel like sitting ducks decoyed by the Comintern, and they resented allegations that they were doing "coolie service" for the Kuomintang. But Stalin was adamant that the United Front be continued, so Chinese opposition was silenced and once again Comintern discipline prevailed despite the storm clouds.

In April 1927 Chiang struck a blow of unparalleled ferocity at the CCP in Shanghai, and began a systematic extermination of all Communists in the city. The White Terror, as this brutal bloodbath came to be known, quickly spread to other parts of China. One might think that this would have been ample proof to Stalin that the United Front was dead, but directives from Moscow remained unchanged: the United Front must continue! Just because Chiang had shown his feudal imperialist colors, said Stalin, was no reason to reject the whole Kuomintang, and actually, Stalin claimed, Chiang's defection from the ranks of the otherwise revolutionary Kuomintang was a progressive step which helped purify the Kuomintang. This explanation may have sounded reasonable from Moscow, but to many Chinese Communists, to whom Comintern decisions meant the difference between life and death, it had a confusing and hypocritical ring. They wanted to know what was to be gained by perpetuating the United Front. Unfortunately the answer lay deep within the Kremlin walls and had little to do with actual conditions in China.

After Lenin's death in 1924, Stalin and Trotsky became locked in a death struggle for the leadership of the Communist Party of the Soviet Union (CPSU). By the time of the White Terror, Trotsky had launched a relentless attack on Stalin's China Policy, advocating the dissolution of the United Front and the immediate establishment of soviets in China. He accused Stalin of being the "gravedigger of the Chinese Revolution." According to Trotsky, "To enter the Kuomintang meant to bring one's head voluntarily to slaughter." He pointed an accusing finger at Stalin, saying, "The bloody lessons of Shanghai [the White Terror] passed without leaving a trace. The Communists as before are being transformed into cattle herders for the Party of the bourgeois executioners [the Kuomintang]."

China and the CCP unwittingly became the battleground for the Kremlin power struggle. By late 1927 Stalin had succeeded in exiling Trotsky to Kazakhstan, and had emerged the victor. But still the idea of the United Front could not be abandoned, for that would vindicate the Trotsky position, so Stalin ordered the alliance to continue, although by this time most of the CCP had either been exterminated or gone underground.

Stalin's failure was not complete until 1931, when the battered Central Committee was finally forced to flee the cities into the mountains to rendezvous with the young revolutionary leader Mao Tse-tung. The whole orthodox Communist movement had been crushed in one of the bloodiest episodes in Communist history. It is hard to know how men like Chou En-lai, Liu Shao-ch'i, and Chang Kuo-t'ao must have felt as they retreated to the mountains, their party in ruins. They were obviously disheartened and disillusioned, and it is difficult to believe that they were unaware that their ruin had been largely Stalin's fault.

The following selections are taken from Harold Isaacs' classic, *The Tragedy of the Chinese Revolution*. In the opening selection Isaacs traces the revolutionary legacy handed down from the May Fourth Movement, discussing the development of the Kuomintang and the CCP, and the formation of the United Front in 1924, and then describing the consolidation of Kuomintang power and control in South China.

The second selection is an account of the White Terror in Shanghai in 1927. In anticipation of the Kuomintang advance northward against the warlords in the Yangtze Valley, the Communist labor unions and organizations having seized control of Shanghai, held the city and awaited the arrival of Chiang's troops. When Chiang's troops finally did arrive, they remained bivouacked outside the city for an ominously long time. They finally entered the city in the middle of April and launched a savage extermination campaign with the aid of the prolific Shanghai underworld. This was one of the most crucial events in the development of Chinese Communism: henceforth the Chinese Revolution went its own way, although formally allied to Moscow. It ultimately became apparent that the Chinese had developed their own model of revolution, which today rivals that of the Russians. The Russians made their revolution in the cities; the Chinese made it in the villages. Today, with the split, two nations are competing not only for leadership in the Communist movement but for two different models of revolution.

HAROLD ISAACS *
The New Awakening

China's economic spurt during the First World War opened all the sluices of change. Along a thousand channels new ideas, new thoughts, new aspirations found their way into the country and crashed against the dead weight of the past like mighty waves against a grounded hulk. Among the intellectuals the mood of despair and discouragement engendered by the failure of the 1911 Revolution gave way to the beginnings of a vigorous cultural renaissance which rapidly drew a whole new generation into its orbit. New leaders, new forces came to the fore. Out of the thinned ranks of the revolutionary intellectuals of 1911 emerged the figure of Ch'en Tu-hsiu, scion of an Anhwei Mandarin family, who began posing the tasks of revolt more boldly, more clearly, more courageously than anyone who had preceded him. To his side rallied the men who with him were going to make over the life of a whole generation and who in later years would enter and lead opposing armies on the battlefields of social conflict.

The task of the new generation, proclaimed Ch'en Tu-hsiu, was "to fight Confucianism, the old tradition of virtue and rituals, the old ethics and the old politics . . . the old learning and the old literature." In their place he would put the fresh materials of modern democratic political thought and natural science.

* Harold Isaacs, *The Tragedy of the Chinese Revolution* (Stanford: Stanford University Press, 1962), pp. 53–64, 175–185.

We must break down the old prejudices, the old way of believing in things as they are, before we can begin to hope for social progress [wrote Ch'en in 1915 in his magazine, *New Youth*]. We must discard our old ways. We must merge the ideas of the great thinkers of history, old and new, with our own experience, build up new ideas in politics, morality, and economic life. We must build the spirit of the new age to fit it to new environmental conditions and a new society. Our ideal society is honest, progressive, positive, free, equalitarian, creative, beautiful, good, peaceful, cooperative, toilsome, but happy for the many. We look for the world that is false, conservative, negative, restricted, inequitable, hidebound, ugly, evil, war-torn, cruel, indolent, miserable for the many and felicitous for the few, to crumble until it disappears from sight. . . .

I hope those of you who are young will be self-conscious and that you will struggle. By self-consciousness I mean that you are to be conscious of the power and responsibility of your youth and that you are to respect it. Why do I think you should struggle? Because it is necessary for you to use all the intelligence you have to get rid of those who are decaying, who have lost their youth. Regard them as enemies and beasts; do not be influenced by them, do not associate with them.

Oh, young men of China! Will you be able to understand me? Five out of every ten whom I see are young in age, but old in spirit. . . . When this happens to a body, the body is dying. When it happens to a society, the society is perishing. Such a sickness cannot be cured by sighing in words; it can only be cured by those who are young, and in addition to being young, are courageous. . . . We must have youth if we are to survive, we must have youth if we are to get rid of corruption. Here lies the hope for our society.

This memorable call was really the opening manifesto of the era of the second Chinese Revolution. Ch'en Tu-hsiu was a professor at the time at Peking National University, where new ideas and new impulses were stirring and where a new spirit was germinating. Ch'en's magazine was eagerly snatched up by students in every school and college in the country. When it was published, wrote one student, "it came to us like a clap of thunder which awakened us in the midst of a restless dream. . . . Orders for more copies were sent posthaste to Peking. I do not know how many times this first issue was reprinted, but I am sure that more than 200,000 copies were sold." It nourished the impulsive iconoclasm of the young people. It gave direction to the mood of unease and unsettlement that pervaded all classes in the population. It was a call to action that awakened immediate response. An outlet was not long in offering itself.

Japan had taken advantage of the wartime circumstances in 1915 to impose upon China its Twenty-one Demands, which would have reduced China to a virtual Japanese colony. Japanese troops had also occupied the province of Shantung. Woodrow Wilson's promises of self-determination and social justice for all peoples had bred the hope that in the general postwar settlement, China would be relieved of Japanese and Western overlordship. When, at Versailles, these illusions were cynically spiked by horse-trading politicians, the student youth in China rose in fury against the treachery of the Japanophile Peking government. On May 4, 1919, huge student demonstrations took place in the old capital. The homes of pro-Japanese ministers were attacked and wrecked. The movement spread across the country. In it a new note sounded when workers in factories struck in support of the student demands of a new regime.

At the end of 1916 there were already nearly a million industrial workers in China and their number nearly doubled by 1922. An army of nearly two hundred thousand Chinese laborers had been sent to Europe during the war. Many of them learned to read and write and, even more significantly, came in contact with European workers and the higher European standard of living. They returned with new ideas about man's struggle to better his estate. Nationalist sentiment had taken strong hold among them. Many on their way back from Europe had refused to step ashore at Japanese ports during the furor over Shantung. When strikes in factories began to deepen the roar of the May Fourth Movement, the returned laborer was already regarded as "the stormy petrel of the Chinese labor world." These

workers played a key role in the creation of new labor organizations, in which they formed a solid and energetic nucleus. Just
as old family firms and partnerships were beginning to give way
to modern corporations, the guilds were beginning to break up
and to divide into labor unions and chambers of commerce.
Chinese workers, new to their machines and new to the ideas and
techniques of labor organization, were thrust at once into the
political turmoil that rose around them. Their strikes in Shanghai
and other cities in 1919 more than anything else forced the
release of student demonstrators arrested in Peking and hastened
the resignation of the offending government officials.

The tide of May 4 engulfed the entire country. It ushered
in the second Chinese Revolution. It seemed to touch off waiting
impulses of astonishing vigor. Traditional ideas and modes of
conduct were crumbling and the echo of their fall sounded from
one end of the country to the other. Young men and women in
towns and villages began to break with the old authority of the
family and the village elders. A fissure opened between the generations that was never again closed. The old ways of doing and
thinking still governed much of Chinese life but they were now
being mortally assailed. In the colleges and universities there
was a great churning. The disillusionment with the West after
the Versailles Conference turned popular attention among the
students to the Russian Revolution. This new current brought
with it to China belated tributaries of all the main streams of
European social thought, democracy, anarchism, syndicalism,
and Marxism, opening up new horizons and stimulating a veritable revolution in thought, morals, and literature, and rapidly
deepening the channels of political change and social conflict. All
classes of society entered the political arena. Old political organizations took on fresh life. New organizations came into being.

When these fresh political currents began to flow in 1919,
the Kuomintang, heir to the party of the 1911 Revolution, had
fallen into sterile impotence. Its "right" elements, conservative
bourgeois intellectuals, had become helpless dependents of the
warlords. Sun Yat-sen, leader of the more radical wing of the
intelligentsia, was pursuing his schemes for revolution by military
conspiracy, by attempting to use the lesser against the greater
militarists. He had evolved his own political philosophy, summed

up in his "Three People's Principles." These were not distinguished by their clarity or boldness, or even by any consistent radicalism. His principle of Nationalism, which concerned the liberation of China from foreign control, was heavily diluted by Sun's own naïve illusions. As first President of the Republic, Sun had promised the Powers that their perquisites and privileges, extracted by force from the overthrown dynasty, would remain intact and that payments due them on their loans would be assumed by the Republic. After the war of 1914–1918, he counted on the benevolent cooperation of the Powers. He submitted to the various foreign offices a plan for "sincere" collaboration among the different nations in the development of China's resources. He envisaged an idyll in which the foreign holders of privilege would join with the Chinese in a "socialistic scheme" from which all would benefit. "It is my hope," he wrote, "that as a result of this, the present spheres of influence can be abolished, international and commercial war done away with, internecine capitalistic competion can be got rid of, and last but not least, the class struggle between capital and labor can be avoided." Sun's "nationalism" also included the prospect of Chinese domination over minority nationalities within the former Empire. He looked for the "assimilation" of the Manchus, Mongols, Mohammedans, and Tibetans, in a Greater China ruled by the Han. The idea of the self-determination of nations, like that of a vigorous struggle against imperialism, entered his thinking somewhat later.

Sun's second principle, democracy, provided mainly for a period of "political tutelage" during which enlightened leaders would gradually guide the dark and miserable masses toward self-government. Conceived by Sun as a kind of benevolent paternalism, this doctrine became in the hands of his heirs and successors a justification for the most despotic kind of tyranny. There was, in fact, little in common between Sun Yat-sen's concept of democracy and the idea of the direct conquest of political rights and liberties by the people.

The third principle of the People's Livelihood expressed Sun's thinking on future Chinese economic organization and the all-pervading question of the land and the peasantry. He advocated "restriction of capital" and "equalization of rights in the land," two formulas broadly and variously interpreted by Sun himself and by his disciples in subsequent years. By "restriction of capital" Sun hoped to save China from the blights of capitalism, although it was never clearly shown how this was to be done. By "equalization of rights in the land," Sun meant a plan to correct inequalities in such a way that "those who have had property in the past will not suffer by it." His plan was to have land values fixed by agreement with the landlords and for all future increment in these values to revert to the State. By the power of purchase, the State would then proceed to create better conditions for the landless or land-hungry peasant population. Sun Yat-sen never ventured for years, however, to propagate even these plans for fear of alienating his military allies and many of his own followers. Sun totally rejected the idea of a class struggle, and the participation of the masses in political life was quite outside his ken. His hope was to bring about the peaceful and benevolent transformation of Chinese society after first securing power for himself and his followers by purely military means. This was the aim of his long series of invariably fruitless military adventures and alliances.

The renewal of political activity in the country in 1919, however, energized Sun Yat-sen's declining party. Sun himself began appearing before student gatherings, and when General Ch'en Chiung-ming permitted him the next year to establish a government in Canton, he made contact there with the newly organized trade unions. The labor movement had already begun to make headway. Railroad workers had established a union at Ch'anghsintien, near Peking, and students went there nightly to teach the union members. Unions had also begun to spring up along the seaboard and in Canton and Hong Kong in the South. Marxist journals appeared in the schools and universities. Marxist study groups formed in 1918 and 1919 expanded into socialist societies and from these it was but a step, in 1920, to the foundation of the Chinese Communist Party. Its founders included some of the leading figures of the May Fourth Movement, chief among them Ch'en Tu-hsiu. The Party's first naional conference took place in Shanghai in July 1921. Most of the delegates were young intellectuals. It was a mixed group destined to break into many parts. Some, drawn by adolescent sentiment or quickly stifled anarchist leanings, soon dropped away into obscurity or found their way to opposing political camps. Among the founders, for example, was Tai Chi-t'ao, who in a short time became the leading ideologist and spokesman for the Right Wing of the Kuomintang. Others who began their careers as Communists included Ch'en Kung-po, Shao Li-tzŭ, and Chou Fu-hai, all later luminaries in the Kuomintang regime. Ch'en Kung-po ended up as a puppet of the Japanese. Others, like the famous Li Ta-chao, librarian of Peking National University, were destined to lose their lives in the coming battles. Also among the founders was Li's young assistant, a Hunanese named Mao Tse-tung.

The new Communist Party soon had to face the problem of its relation to other burgeoning political groups. At its second national conference, in 1922, it was decided to propose a two-party alliance to the Kuomintang. When this plan was laid before Sun Yat-sen, he rejected it. He said he might permit Communists to join the Kuomintang but would countenance no two-party alliance. Shortly afterward, Maring, the first delegate of the Comintern in China who had already been in contact with Sun in the South, met with the Communist Central Committee at West Lake, Hangchow. He proposed that the Communists simply enter the Kuomintang and use its loose organizational structure as a means for developing their own propaganda and contacts among the masses. Maring based his proposal in the first place on his own prewar experience in Java. There he had been associated with left-wing Social Democrats who joined the Saraket Islam, a mixed political-religious movement opposing Dutch colonial rule. Within the Saraket Islam this group had begun to organize workers' groups and during the war had succeeded in developing a substantial left-wing political movement in the colony. Maring also was convinced that in Sun Yat-sen's group in Canton there was the nucleus of the kind of national revolutionary movement to which Lenin had referred at the Second Congress of the Comintern. He cited Sun's connections with the growing labor movement in the south.

According to Maring, the majority of the Chinese Communist Central Committee accepted his views. Those who opposed his plan did so on the grounds that they doubted the weight of the Kuomintang as a political force and did not believe it would or could develop into a mass movement. Ch'en Tu-hsiu, listed by Maring as among those who agreed readily to enter the Kuomintang, has written an account of the Hangchow conference which differs on this point. He says that all the Central Committee members opposed Maring, claiming that even at that time the Chinese Communist leaders believed such a step "would confuse class organizations and curb our independent policy." This was written, however, after the event. In 1922, Ch'en had written: "Cooperation with the revolutionary bourgeoisie is the necessary road for the Chinese proletariat" and it was obviously in this spirit that he approached the Kuomintang issue when it arose. It seems fairer to assume that the opposition to Maring was based on the belief that the Kuomintang was defunct and not worth considering, a view which he remembers was most strongly expressed by Chang Kuo-t'ao, another of the founding leaders of the Communist organization. In the end the proposal was adopted, although there was considerable doubt whether the Kuomintang, and especially Sun himself, would welcome it.

The Communists entered the Kuomintang as individuals in hopes of winning over to their influence the Southern workers who had already affiliated with the Kuomintang. At the same time they pressed Sun Yat-sen to reorganize his party on the basis of a new program capable of attracting popular support. Sun remained cool to these proposals. Only when he was forced once more to flee for his life, following a revolt by General Ch'en Chiung-ming in Canton in June 1922, did he grow more receptive to the arguments of Maring, supported by Liao Chung-k'ai, the most radical of Sun's immediate entourage. Sun was still unattracted by the role of a mass movement as a political weapon, but he had begun to be attracted by the prospects of direct and concrete aid from Russia.

Several factors combined to start Sun thinking about a Russian alliance. His plan for the international development of China had been rebuffed by all the foreign governments who received it. The Powers had set about regulating their relations in the Far East at the Washington Conference of 1921–1922. But while that conference produced the Nine Power Treaty guaranteeing the territorial integrity of China, the main issue settled there had more to do with Anglo-American relations with Japan than with the needs of China. That conference, to borrow Wang Ching-wei's summary, "freed China from the Japanese policy of independent violent encroachment" only to leave it victim "to the cooperative slow encroachment" of all the Powers. Sun and his followers began to lose some of their faith in Western good intentions. Simultaneously, they began to see in Russia not only a source of material aid but a lever for extracting concessions from the Western Powers.

The Moscow government had already indicated its readiness to put Chinese-Russian relations on a radically new basis. On July 4, 1918, Chicherin, then Commissar for Foreign Affairs, declared that Bolshevik Russia had unilaterally renounced all Czarist "unequal" treaties with China and its agreements with Japan and other countries relating to China. This policy was again set forth in a manifesto issued on July 25, 1919, over the signature of Leo Karakhan, Deputy Commissar for Foreign Affairs. This manifesto said that the Soviet government annulled and repudiated "all the secret treaties concluded with Japan, China, and the former Allies; treaties by which the Czar's government, together with its allies, through force and corruption, enslaved the peoples of the Orient, and especially the Chinese nation, in order to profit the Russian capitalists, the Russian landlords, and the Russian generals." Again, on September 27, 1920, in a formal note to China, the Soviet government reiterated its denunciation of all previous treaties, renounced all Czarist annexations of Chinese territory, and returned to China "free of charge and forever all that was ravenously taken from her by the Czar's government and by the Russian bourgeoisie." Early Soviet missions to Peking, under M. I. Yurin and A. K. Paikes, tried from 1920 to 1922 to negotiate a new treaty on this basis but were blocked, mainly by Western and Japanese pressure on the Peking government.

These first contacts between Bolshevik Russia and China illustrate how, even at this early date, contradictions arose between Russian national purposes and Communist international revolutionary purposes. The declarations from Moscow in 1919 and 1920 had breathed a note of change new in the annals of international diplomacy. The offer of this new revolutionary government to deal with China on a basis of equality nettled the Western Powers and won a delighted and sympathetic hearing for Russia among all classes of Chinese. But there were some significant equivocations, relating to the Chinese Eastern Railway in particular, which strongly suggested second thinking by at least some Russians in policy-making positions at the time.

But even more striking is the fact that the first Soviet agents to reach China, sent by the Chita government and by the Irkutsk Bureau of the Comintern, came looking not for new revolutionary currents to swim in but for a deal with any likely looking band of militarists and politicians who might serve Russian diplomatic interests. The government at Peking was then in the hands of the notoriously pro-Japanese Anfu Clique and the Russians scanned the field for promising opponents. The puny Nationalist movement led by Sun Yat-sen in the South did not impress them as a point of support for Soviet interests. They were more attracted by the military strength of the warlord Wu P'ei-fu, who was interested in overthrowing and replacing the Anfu regime in power. When Wu did seize the government in Peking in 1920 and set up a puppet civilian cabinet of his own, the Far Eastern expert V. Vilensky wrote in *Izvestia*: "Wu P'ei-fu has hung out his flag over the events which are taking place in China and it is clear that under this flag the new Chinese cabinet must take an orientation in favor of Soviet Russia." But Wu's orientation was toward the British; the Rising Sun had merely been replaced by the Union Jack at the back door of the Peking government. That was why, in the final analysis, the 1921 negotiations were without result.

When Maring came to China in the spring of 1921 and established connections with Sun Yat-sen, whom he first visited in Kwangsi, he decided that the main stream of Chinese nationalism flowed through Sun's Kuomintang. This belief was strengthened when in Canton and Hong Kong in January 1922 a major seamen's strike took place and Maring found that the Kuomintang already had substantial links to the young Chinese labor movement. Maring's proposal to the Chinese Communists to enter the Kuomintang marked a reversal of the so-called "Irkutsk line" of the Comintern. When Sun Yat-sen, expelled from Canton by the militarist Ch'en Chiung-ming, arrived in Shanghai in August 1922, Maring met him again and urged him to substitute a campaign of mass propaganda and organization for any attempt to recapture Canton by purely military means. This time he found his views more welcome. Sun, dismayed by the outcome of the Washington Conference, had begun to think in terms of seeking Soviet assistance. This was the report that Maring took back with him to Moscow the next month. On the basis of his findings, the Comintern abandoned the "Irkutsk line" of trying to establish links with Northern militarists and turned its attention instead to Sun Yet-sen. Maring's views were published in the Communist press and became the starting point of an entirely new orientation of Soviet policy. The Soviet government sent Adolph Joffe, one of its top diplomats, to establish formal contact with Sun Yat-sen.

Joffe met Sun in Shanghai. On January 26, 1923, they issued a joint statement in which Joffe agreed that "conditions do not exist here for the successful establishment of Communism or Socialism," that "the chief and immediate aim of China is the achievement of national union and national independence." Joffe assured Sun that, in seeking these aims, the nationalist movement "could depend on the aid of Russia." This diplomatic formula inaugurated the formal entente with Sun. The Russians at the same time pressed their treaty negotiations in Peking and the next year Leo Karakhan, as Soviet envoy, triumphantly concluded the Sino-Soviet Treaty of May 1924. By that time, however, the whole emphasis had shifted to the South. Arms, money, and advisers were beginning to move in to implement the deal with Sun and the Kuomintang.

From the outset, it was automatically assumed that the Chinese Communists would henceforth devote themselves solely to the job of helping to make the Kuomintang a worthy ally. All the elaborate formulations and explanations came later. In the beginning it was a "practical" and obvious outcome of the new turn in Soviet policy. The Russians had entered into an arrangement with the Kuomintang. It became the duty of the Chinese Communists to facilitate and fructify that arrangement. When Michael Borodin took his post as adviser to Sun Yat-sen in the fall of 1923, he came not as a delegate of the Communist International to the Chinese Communist Party, but as adviser to the Kuomintang delegated by the Politbureau of the Communist Party of the Soviet Union. This distinction was far from purely formal. It reflected the underlying political realities. Borodin's job was to reorganize and pump new life into the Kuomintang. All efforts, especially those of the Chinese Communists, had to be concentrated now to that end. The Executive Committee of the Comintern had ruled, on January 12, 1923: "Insofar as the working class . . . is not yet sufficiently differentiated as an absolutely independent force, the E.C.C.I. considers that it is necessary to coordinate the activities of the Kuomintang and of the young Communist Party of China." The Party was "not to merge" with the Kuomintang nor "furl its own banner" but, on the other hand, the "central task" became coordination with the Kuomintang and recognition that it could not be an "absolutely independent force." Some of the members of the Chinese Party may have found these formulas a little tricky but the third conference of the Chinese Communist Party in June 1923 silenced all internal opposition to the Kuomintang entry and raised the slogan: "All work to the Kuomintang!" The conference manifesto declared that "the Kuomintang should be the central force of the national revolution and should stand in the leading position."

Borodin set out to convince Sun Yat-sen that what the Kuomintang needed was a disciplined party organization with a powerful mass movement behind it. Sun had managed to reestablish himself in Canton and in November was again threatened there by Ch'en Chiung-ming's army. Borodin, with the help of the Chinese Communists, managed to demonstrate that the militarist forces could be easily repelled by a show of popular strength. The ease with which this was done finally convinced the Kuomintang leader. With his support, Borodin drafted a new program for the Kuomintang. It was based upon cooperation between the Kuomintang and Soviet Russia as well as the Chinese Communist Party, the idea of a militant anti-imperialist struggle mounted on a mass basis, and a platform of liberal reforms for the workers and peasants. Borodin took over Sun's formulas, "restriction of capital" and "equalization of rights in the land." He translated them into planks for a 25-per-cent reduction in land rents and a promise of a labor code. This new program was adopted and the reorganization of the Kuomintang approved at the First National Congress of the Party, which met in Canton in January 1924, on the day that Lenin died.

The Kuomintang was transformed into a rough copy of the Russian Bolshevik Party. Bolshevik methods of agitation and propaganda were introduced. To create the basis of an army imbued with Kuomintang ideas and to put an end to the previous dependence on old-style militarists, the Russians in May 1924 founded the Whampoa Military Academy. This academy was supplied and operated with Russian funds, staffed by Russian military advisers. Before long, shiploads of Russian arms were coming into Canton harbor to supply the armies which rallied to the new banner as soon as the Kuomintang began to display the new strength with which all these activities endowed it. The Chinese Communist Party, chief organizer of the new movement, confined itself religiously to building the Kuomintang and propagating its program. Its members were the most indefatigable Party workers, but they never appeared as Communists nor presented any program of their own. The Communist Party became in fact and in essence, in its work and in the manner in which it educated its own members, the left-wing appendage of the Kuomintang. In the initial stages, however, the ultimate significance of this fact was overshadowed by the spectacular growth of the mass movement. For neither the tactics of the Communists nor the requirements of the Kuomintang brought the mass movement into being. Its sources were imbedded, like ore in rock, in the conditions of Chinese life.

The Shanghai Coup of April 12, 1927

At four o'clock on the morning of April 12 a bugle blast sounded from Chiang Kai-shek's headquarters at the Foreign Ministry Bureau on Route Ghisi. A Chinese gunboat at anchor off Nantao sounded a blast on its siren. "Simultaneously," reported the *China Press,* "the machine guns broke loose in a steady roll." The attack was launched at the fixed hour in Chapei, Nantao, the Western District, in Woosung, Pootung, and Jessfield. It came as no surprise to anyone except the workers, for as the local British newspaper revealed: "All the authorities concerned, Chinese and foreign, after midnight were made secretly cognizant of the events which were to take place in the morning."

Members of Shanghai's underworld gangs "had feverishly worked through the night organizing secret parties to appear at dawn as though from nowhere." They wore white armbands bearing the Chinese character *kung* (labor). The *North China Daily News* called them "armed Kuomintang laborers." The Shanghai Municipal Police Report referred to "merchants' volunteers." The *China Press* contented itself with "Nationalist troops." More bluntly, George Sokolsky reported: "Arrangements were made with the Green and Red Societies, so that one morning they, as 'white' laborers, fell upon and shot down the Communists." They did not appear from "nowhere," but at the given signal, as the *Shen Pao* and other newspapers frankly stated, they "rushed out of the concessions" and in the adjoining Chinese areas made contact with picked detachments of Pai Ch'ung-hsi's troops. Together or separately, according to detailed, prearranged plans, they attacked the headquarters of working-class organizations scattered throughout the city. In most cases, as at the Foochow Guild in Nantao and the police station in Pootung, the objectives were won after sharp but brief battles. Their quarters once occupied, the pickets and their supporters were given short, brutal shrift. Their arms were seized and "even their clothes and shoes ripped from them." Every man who resisted was shot down where he stood. The remainder were lashed together and marched out to be executed either in the streets or at Lunghua.

In a few places the attackers tried guile. A band of some sixty gangsters began firing on the Huchow Guild in Chapei at about 4:30 A.M. This building housed the headquarters of the General Labor Union and was defended by several scores of pickets. The surprised guards shouted out to ask the attackers what union they belonged to; "To the Northern Expeditionary Army," was the reply, and the attack continued and the pickets returned the fire. Twenty minutes later, a company of soldiers, headed by an officer named Hsin Ting-yu, appeared on the street. Hsin shouted orders to cease firing. "Do not fire at us!" he cried out to the pickets. "We've come to help you disarm these men." The shooting stopped. He proposed from the street that both sides hand over their arms. Ostentatiously he proceeded to disarm some of the gangsters and, under the suspicious eyes of the pickets, even bound some of them in ropes. At that, the gates were opened. Hsin and his men were invited in. The Communist who tells this story, a participant in the scene, adds that tea and cigarettes were brought out for the guests. The officer told Ku Chen-chung, commander of the pickets, that he had been appointed to conduct "armed mediation" under the new martial law regulations. He asked Ku to accompany him to headquarters. The picket leader complied and with six of his men left the premises with Hsin. A few steps down the street Hsin turned to Ku: "We've disarmed those guerrillas. We've got to disarm your squads too," he said. Ku stopped short. "You can't," he said. "Those men are gangsters. Our pickets are revolutionary workers. Why disarm us?" Hsin did not answer. Instead his men closed in on the group. Ku and the six men were disarmed and brought back to the General Labor Union headquarters. A few minutes later a force of some three hundred gangsters who had been waiting nearby rushed into the building and while the soldiers stood by, they savagely attacked the astounded pickets. In the melee, Ku and his vice-commander, a young man named Chou En-lai, escaped. The Huchow Guild had meanwhile fallen. Similar methods achieved similar results at most of the other workers' centers in the city.

By mid-morning the last workers' stronghold was the big building of the Commercial Press, where some four hundred pickets continued to hold out against overwhelmingly superior forces. When the gangsters attacked and the soldiers came on the scene with their demand for a cessation of hostilities, the defenders inside the building answered with a renewed fusillade. The soldiers thereupon simply joined in the attack and all further attempts at deception were discarded. Siege was laid to the building from all sides. Paoshan Road dinned with gunfire for several hours. The defenders fought on until most of them were dead and the rest without ammunition. It was nearly noon before the attackers gingerly stepped inside the bullet-riddled building.

"What action the soldiers took beyond disarming the Communists is naturally not known. It is not going to be advertised by the Chinese authorities," complacently reported the *North China Daily News*. Early foreign reports minimized the casualties of that first day, but the British-controlled Shanghai Municipal Police later came nearer the actual toll when it reported that nearly four hundred workers were killed in the day's operations. Other reports put the death toll at close to seven hundred. Among the missing was Wang Shao-hua, chairman of the General Labor Union. It was not discovered until some time later that he had been kidnaped by gangsters the previous afternoon and carried off to military headquarters at Lunghua, where he was executed. At four o'clock, the military authorities announced they had the situation "in hand."

Ch'en Ch'ün, secretary and aide to the gang leader Chang Hsiao-lin and newly apointed Political Director of Pai Ch'ung-hsi's army, announced plans for the immediate "reorganization" of the General Labor Union along the lines already made familiar in Kiangsi and Chekiang in March. "The policy of the government is to have labor working in harmony with the revolutionary army and the government," he said. "But when labor becomes a disturbing element, when it arrogates to itself tasks which are detrimental to the movement and disturbing to law and order, labor must be disciplined." His newly created "Workers Trade Alliance" at once took over the occupied union quarters and introduced itself as follows:

> The Shanghai General Labor Union was manipulated by a few Communist scoundrels. They bullied and deceived the workers and made them sacrifice themselves. Workers who have lost their jobs owing to strikers are daily increasing in number. The General Labor Union wanted to starve and ruin the workers to create opportunities for committing crimes against society and the state. The aim of the Workers' Trade Alliance is to realize the Three People's Principles of the Kuomintang, to secure for the workers their most concrete interests, to aid in China's reconstruction so as to win freedom and equality in the family of nations. . . . Now the pickets of the G.L.U. have all been disarmed. They can no longer oppress our workers. Now our workers

are completely free. It is hoped that the workers will send delegations to get in touch with us and wait patiently for a settlement.

The General Labor Union and other Communist organizations were still in existence. They were still addressing appeals and petitions to Chiang Kai-shek. The Shanghai *tangpu,* the local Kuomintang branch, long since driven from its headquarters, issued an exhortation: "Our working masses must not shrink from reorganizing their ranks. . . . The military authorities should also more properly protect the workers' organizations and return their arms to them." The defunct Provisional Government still existed in name and it addressed a letter to General Pai: "The workers' pickets made heavy sacrifices to aid the Northern Expeditionary Army and to expel the Chihli-Shantung bandit troops. . . . After the capture of Shanghai, they cooperated with the army and the police to maintain order and they have rendered no little service to the city. Therefore even Commander-in-chief Chiang highly approved of them and presented them with a banner inscribed 'Common Action.' . . ." The letter concluded with a respectful request for the return of the arms taken from the pickets. That night Communist speakers addressed crowds in the streets of Chapei. They complained that the workers "had consistently assisted the Nationalist government for years and had only recently captured Shanghai for them. . . . They had always maintained discipline . . . and had not only observed the law but assisted in upholding it." Resolutions were adopted at these street meetings urging "that the authorities be again requested to give back the arms taken."

It was at this moment, with the battle lost and the moment for action irretrievably buried in the blunders of the past, that the General Labor Union called, on April 13, for a general strike of protest. "We shall fight to the death . . . with the national revolution as our banner. It is glorious to die in such a way." The workers had obediently followed the Communists to the slaughter but were now asked "to be prepared to sacrifice all, to renew the war against the forces of the right wing." They might well have asked: what war against the right wing? They had been told all would be well, that they should retreat, bury their arms, and avert "open" struggle. Now the open struggle had been carried to them by the enemy and they were helplessly caught unprepared. Nevertheless, the strike call of the General Labor Union produced striking evidence of the strength and discipline of these workers. Some one hundred thousand of them quit work. The waterfront was tied up. The tramway workers went out. Most of the textile workers in the Western District and about half the workers in the Yangtzepoo mills answered the call.

At noon on April 13 a great crowd of workers gathered in a mass meeting on Chinyuen Road in Chapei. Resolutions were passed demanding the return of the seized arms, punishment of the union-wreckers, and protection for the General Labor Union. A petition was drafted and a parade formed to march to Second Division headquarters to present it to General Chou Feng-ch'i. Women and children were in the parade. None of the men had arms. They swung into Paoshan Road under a pouring rain. As they came abreast of San Te Terrace, a short distance from the military headquarters, machine gunners waiting for them there opened fire without warning. Lead spouted into the thick crowd from both sides of the street. Men, women, and children dropped screaming into the mud. The crowd broke up into mad flight. The soldiers kept firing into the backs of the fleeing demonstrators. From adjacent alleyways the attackers fell upon the crowd, swinging bayonets, rifle butts, and broadswords. They pursued the fleeing marchers right into the houses in Yi Ping Terrace, Paotung and Tientungan Roads—streets thickly clustered with working-class tenements. Men and women were dragged out. "Those who resisted were either killed on the spot or wounded. . . . Many of the wounded were left to die where they dropped. It was an hour before the street was cleared," reported one eyewitness. Another a little later saw bodies being carted off in vans. He counted eight truckloads filled with corpses. More than three hundred were killed and a much larger number wounded. Many of the wounded were "carried away and buried with the dead."

Foreign forces cooperated directly in the reign of terror now instituted throughout the city. The contribution of the French authorities was especially notable, since the head of the

French Concession detective force was pockmarked Huang Ching-yung himself, leading member of the triumvirate ruling the underworld gangs of the city. In the International Settlement, foreign municipal police and detachments of the British and Japanese defense forces carried out a series of raids beginning on the night of April 11, several of them in Chinese territory adjacent to the so-called extraconcessional North Szechuan Road. These measures were taken "with permission from the Nationalist military authorities at Lunghua." On the night of April 14 British armored cars joined squads of Japanese marines in minor raids in the extraconcessional area during which machine guns were several times brought into play. Everywhere house-to-house searches were carried out and wholesale arrests made. Prisoners were handed over in batches to the military headquarters at Lunghua. There they faced military courts set up under martial law regulations issued by General Chiang Kai-shek. Run by officers expressly empowered to "use their own discretion" in the event of any "emergency," these courts became the chief instrument for a system of official terrorism which in the following months claimed the lives of thousands.

This reign of terror, directed above all at the workers and the Communists, likewise for a time crossed the bounds of property which it was instituted to keep inviolate. The Chinese bankers and merchants had found it necessary to call in Chiang Kai-shek and the gangsters against the workers. Now they were forced to submit themselves to the predatory raids of their own rescuers. Like the French bourgeoisie, which in 1852 "brought the slum proletariat into power, the loafers and tatterdermalions headed by the chief of the Society of December the Tenth," the Chinese bourgeoisie in 1927 elevated over itself the scum and riffraff of the cities headed by the chiefs of the Green Gang and the man who was sometimes called the Ningpo Napoleon, Chiang Kai-shek. Like its French prototype, the Chinese bourgeoisie had now to pay heavily for professional services. It had, again in the peculiarly applicable words of Karl Marx, "glorified the sword; now it is to be ruled by the sword. . . . It subjected public meetings to police supervision; now its own drawing rooms are under police supervision. . . . It had transported the workers without trial; now the bourgeois are transported without trial

. . . [and their] money bags are rifled. . . . The words of the bourgeoisie to the revolution were unceasingly those of St. Arsenius to the Christians: *Fuge, tace, quiesce!* The words of Bonaparte to the bourgeoisie are the same." Like Louis Napoleon, Chiang Kai-shek ordered the moneyed men of Shanghai to flee, be silent, and submit. More explicitly, he added: "Pay!"

The bankers, industrialists, compradores, and merchants had rallied to Chiang's banner on condition that he would free them of the Communists, of the rebellious workers, of strikes and insurrections. With a ruthlessness that should have satisfied the most exacting and worried capitalist, he acquitted himself of this task. He carried out, in the words of a British account, "such a cleanup of Communists as no northern general would have dared to do even in his own territory." But here came the hitch. This same account continued: "The anti-Communist campaign should have ended there and the people [*sic*] would have been happy. But every form of persecution was resorted to on the pretext of hunting Communists. Men were kidnapped and forced to make heavy contributions to military funds. . . . No reason or justice was evident . . . no courts of law were utilized. . . . Men possessing millions were held as Communists. . . . No one is safe, even at this moment, from the inquisition which has been established."

"The plight of the Chinese merchant in and about Shanghai is pitiable," reported the correspondent of *The New York Times* on May 4. "At the mercy of General Chiang Kai-shek's dictatorship, the merchants do not know what the next day will bring, confiscations, compulsory loans, exile, or possible execution. . . . The military authorities have ordered the reorganization of the Chinese Chamber of Commerce and other institutions with new directors, presumably satisfactory to Chiang Kai-shek and Pai Ch'ung-hsi, as they ordered the reorganization of the labor unions. . . . Outlawry against the better class of Chinese is rampant." When the raising of the $30,000,000 loan for the new Nanking government lagged, the merchants received "military advice to subscribe, with intimations that arrests may follow failure to do so. . . ." Even Yung Chung-chin, well-known leading industrialist, was not exempt. Chiang asked him for a half million dollars. When Yung tried to bargain, Chiang had him arrested forthwith. Yung reportedly bought himself out of prison with $250,000. Others had to pay more.

It has been aptly said that Fascist or military dictators are like ferocious bodyguards who sit at the table of frightened employers and help themselves almost at will to the feast that is spread there. Chiang Kai-shek, like other militarists before him, appeared to be a brigand garbed in the authority of state power, but he remained, nevertheless, a hireling. His price was high but it was small compared to what he saved his employers by smashing the mass movement. The bankers and merchants rallied quickly enough to the government that Chiang now set up at Nanking. Within a few days after the Shanghai coup, similar blows were struck at Ningpo, Foochow, Amoy, Swatow, and Canton. In all these cities the turnover took place in circumstances that almost exactly reproduced those at Shanghai.

A delegation of Russian trade unionists en route to Hankow arrived in Canton on April 14. They came in time to be witnesses of the raids on the trade unions, mass arrests, and executions carried out at the orders of General Li Chi-shen, following the lead of Chiang Kai-shek. Li, too, only a short time before, had been one of those listed in Stalin's directory of "revolutionary generals." Trade unionists fleeing from Canton brought to Hankow the belated message: "We regret to say that the cradle of the national revolution has become a stronghold of reaction."

In Hankow the Left Kuomintang and the Communists were, up to the last hours and beyond, still engaged in the business of propitiating Chiang Kai-shek. Wang Ching-wei had arrived there to tell his colleagues about the agreement with Chiang to hold a joint plenary session of the Kuomintang Central Executive Committee for the "peaceful" settlement of all disputes. News now came to Wuhan that Chiang was about to convene his own separate plenary session in Nanking. On April 13, the day after the Shanghai coup, the delegation of the Communist International in Hankow, now led by the Indian Communist, M. N. Roy, sent Chiang Kai-shek the following telegram:

> The delegation of the Third International is now in China and has always been eager to visit you; but it could

not be done because we have been visiting separately distant parts of the country. . . . Now comes news that you
have decided to convene several members of the Central
Committee and the Central Control Committee at Nanking.
This act obviously violates your agreement with Wang
Ching-wei that all questions of conflict inside the party
would be placed before a plenary session of the Central
Committee, which should be called at Wuhan and in which
you would participate. Your convening a meeting of a few
members of the Central Committee at this critical moment
will naturally be interpreted by the enemies of the revolution as a rupture in the ranks of the Kuomintang. At this
moment when international imperialism unites in an insolent
attack upon the Chinese nationalist revolution, the unity
of the revolutionary forces is a supreme necessity. . . . In
view of the dangerous situation, we advise you to abandon
the projected Nanking conference which will practically
split the party. And the grave responsibility for breaking
the nationalist front at this critical moment will rest on you.
We advise you to stand on the agreement to place all con-
tentions on inner party questions before a plenary session
of the Central Committee. If you take this advice, we shall
be glad to visit Nanking in order to discuss with you personally all outstanding questions. The Third International
will lend all its services to help the formation of a united
nationalist front of all revolutionary forces.

Signed, for the delegation of the Third International,
M. N. Roy, April 13, 1927.

This remarkable communication was dispatched more than
twenty-four hours after the beginning of Chiang's coup in
Shanghai. This would seem to exclude the possibility that the
news of what was happening in Shanghai had not yet reached
Hankow. In any case, the Comintern representatives there were
fully aware of the events in Kiangsi, the progressive attacks on
the unions and other organizations from city to city along the
Yangtze and, just before the Shanghai outbreak, in Hangchow.
The telegram of April 13 makes it plain that the Comintern
agents, Roy, Earl Browder, Jacques Doriot, and Tom Mann,

together with Borodin and the other master strategists, were ready to overlook these developments if Chiang would, even now, only accept their "advice." From Peking some days later, the well-informed Walter Duranty, who knew his Kremlin, wired to *The New York Times* his conviction that "the Moscow leaders will do their utmost to restore Kuomintang unity, even at the sacrifice of the more extreme Communists." The plea of the Hankow Comintern agents, dispatched to the executioner even while the heads were rolling in Shanghai's streets, showed how far the Comintern was ready to go in sacrificing the interests of the Chinese Revolution to the Kremlin's conviction that the only ally it could have in China was the Chinese ruling class. It showed how hopelessly the Kremlin had misunderstood and miscalculated the play of forces in China.

In Moscow first there was silence. Information passed around the Soviet capital and in the headquarters of the Comintern only in the form of rumors. News of the Shanghai events came like the blow of some utterly shattering catastrophe. It was, on the face of it, incredible. A full day passed before any statement was made. There is a total blank in the available record as to what went on in the Kremlin in those hours. Finally a brief announcement was made. "After persistently denying reports of serious discord between Chiang Kai-shek and the extremists of the Kuomintang," foreign correspondents were at last able to wire, "the Soviet authorities at Moscow this evening announced it was unfortunately true and deplored the fact that fighting occurred at Shanghai between detachments of the Nationalist Army and 'armed labor fraternities' and that the Nationalist Army is busy disarming labor fraternities in other southern towns." In the Comintern, the surprise was complete and the consternation unbounded. Articles written by Comintern "experts" right up to the day of the coup d'état firmly denying any and all possibility of a coup were still being published in the central organ of the International for days after the coup occurred. The April 16 issue of *La Correspondance Internationale,* for example, featured an article by Ernst Thaelmann, the future leader of the German Communist party who was destined to figure six years later in the capitulation to Hitler. He wrote: "The bourgeois Right wing in the Kuomintang and its leadership had been defeated" back in 1926. Chiang, he said, "must submit." He closed deriding the "illusions" of the imperialists about the chances of Chiang's defection. On April 20 the same publication contained an article by one Victor Stern of Prague which announced that "the hopes of a split . . . and a compromise of the Right wing with the militarists . . . are lies and have no chance of succeeding." The same day, bearing the same date, a special issue was released under the heading THE TREASON OF CHIANG KAI-SHEK!

Chiang's coup, bad enough in itself for the Kremlin's cause, was particularly embarrassing because it so crushingly confirmed the warnings and predictions of Trotsky and the Opposition in the Russian Communist Party. This was in many ways, from Stalin's point of view, Chiang Kai-shek's most unforgivable crime. Events might prove Trotsky right, but the struggle against Trotskyism had to go on. It had been felt all the way to Shanghai where, in Malraux's words, the Chinese Communist leaders, "knowing that the Trotskyist theses were attacking the union with the Kuomintang were terrified by any attitude which might, rightly or wrongly, seem to be linked to that of the Russian Opposition." Accordingly, in the name of unity with the Kuomintang, they had led the workers to the slaughter. Even now it was impossible for Moscow to admit that events had overtaken a thousand lies and specious arguments. A spokesman for the Comintern unblinkingly declared: "The treason of Chiang Kai-shek was not unexpected." Stalin himself, on April 21, announced that events had "fully and entirely proved the correctness" of the Comintern "line."

But papal bulls of infallibility could not displace the facts. In Shanghai the workers had died on the cross of Kuomintang "unity." Under it, the militarists and the bankers now gambled and bargained for the spoils.

Urban Revolution Begins: The Communists Organize the Workers of China

THE CHINESE labor movement was born and reached a zenith of agitation and activity during the 1920s. Labor congresses, demonstrations, and strikes abounded in almost all major cities. Bloodshed and violence were not uncommon, but major concessions were won and the ranks of the newly formed unions swelled with members. Working conditions were shockingly poor; wages were low and hours long. Since there was an almost infinite supply of cheap labor, factory owners could set any terms they wished. During World War I hundreds of thousands of peasants, driven off the land, flocked into China's cities to find work in the burgeoning Chinese industry. The Chinese Communist Party, founded in 1921, was quick to take up their cause. Men like Liu Shao-ch'i, Li Li-san, and Chang Kuo-t'ao, who were recent converts to Marxism, did not fail to appreciate the situation's significance, and their tireless efforts to organize a labor movement soon overshadowed all of the Kuomintang's efforts. Even at this early stage, a keen eye might have discerned the crucial difference between the power bases of the CCP and the Kuomintang. The CCP's efforts were directed toward building a grass-roots power base among the working class, while the Kuomintang was busy negotiating with warlords and winning support from the influential and wealthy urban elite.

The labor movement was not integrated into the revolution as a whole until the formation of the united front between the Kuomintang and the CCP in 1924 (see pp. 87–115). But even then the Kuomintang was singularly unsuccessful in penetrating the Communist-dominated labor unions. Organization on the mass level remained firmly in the CCP's grip despite the fact that in theory the CCP and the Kuomintang were "co-operating" to expel from China the twin evils of "warlordism" and "imperialism."

The following selection is taken from an official Chinese Communist history written by Ho Kan-chih. Like all Communist histories, it suffers from obvious overstatements and oversimplifications—all good is attributed to the Party, while all bad is attributed to the capitalists and imperialists—but the selection serves as an example of the Chinese Communist approach to history, and it clearly shows the value the CCP placed on the labor movement during the 1920s. Until the White Terror in 1927 and the Communists' gradual retreat from the cities to the countryside, organization of the proletariat was the CCP's *raison d'être*. Their efforts at organizing and the ensuing strikes were crucial in galvanizing China's growing industrial proletariat into a conscious and active movement of considerable significance.

HO KAN-CHIH *

Rise of the Chinese Working-Class Movement. The Working-Class Movement in Hunan. The Big Political Strike of the Peking-Hankow Railway Workers

After its foundation in July 1921 the Party concentrated its efforts on leading the working-class movement. The Chinese Trade Union Secretariat was established soon after the Party's First National Congress to guide the workers' struggles. Its chief tasks were to publish newspapers and periodicals and to set up clubs and night schools for the workers and to lead them in their day-to-day struggles. Thanks to the correct leadership of the Party and the revolutionary enthusiasm of the Chinese working class, the first big wave of strikes of the workers occurred from January 1922 to February 1923. It started with the Hong Kong seamen's strike in January 1922 and reached

* Ho Kan-chih, *A History of the Modern Chinese Revolution* (Peking: Foreign Languages Press, 1959), pp. 51–57.

its climax in February 1923 with the Peking-Hankow Railway workers' big political strike, lasting, in all, thirteen months and including over a hundred big and small strikes, with more than three hundred thousand workers taking part. Most of these strikes were crowned with complete success. Encouraged by these victories, workers rushed to join the Communist-led trade unions. With the working-class movement and the workers' organizations rapidly expanding, the important role played by the working class in China's political and economic life became all the more evident.

On January 12, 1922, Chinese seamen of the foreign shipping firms in Hong Kong came out on strike.

The Chinese seamen had been suffering manifold oppression. They earned pitifully low wages that were insufficient even for self-support, and were fleeced by the foremen, who, working hand in glove with the capitalists, enjoyed the exclusive privilege of contracting for and recommending workers. Wage scales were extremely unfair, a Chinese seaman being paid only a fifth of the wage of a foreign seaman. On top of all this was political inequality. Under the influence of the surging revolutionary tide of the postwar world, the Chinese seamen quickly became class-conscious. The strike was for an increase in wages and the right of the trade unions to recommend workers. More than thirty thousand seamen and transport workers came out on strike, with the Chinese Seamen's Union taking the lead. After the outbreak of the seamen's strike, the transport workers were the first to come out in sympathy; then a general strike of all the workers of Hong Kong was called. The strike also received support from workers all over the country. In order to break the strike, the Hong Kong government tried every conceivable means, such as force, bribery, mediation, sowing dissension and recruiting scab labor, but all these intrigues were shattered by the strikers. The chief tactics employed by the seamen was to blockade Hong Kong, which, being an isolated island, could not produce enough to meet the needs of its inhabitants. All foodstuffs and part of its daily needs had to be imported from Kwangtung. Now, with communications between Hong Kong and Kwangtung cut by the strike, there was an acute shortage of grain and other food supplies in Hong Kong and prices soared: rice by over 60 per cent and meat by 20 to 30 per cent.

The vigorous struggle of the Hong Kong workers forced the British imperialists to make concessions. On March 6 the Hong Kong authorities announced the cancellation of the order to close down the seamen's union. The arrested workers were released and a 15-to-30-per-cent increase in wages obtained. On March 8 the big strike came to a victorious end. This marked the Chinese people's first victory in a century of anti-imperialist struggle, and it was won on their own strength. It also revealed the Chinese working class as the most resolute vanguard of the Chinese people in their fight against imperialism.

The victory of the Hong Kong seamen's strike greatly encouraged the workers' struggle in the country as a whole. In answer to the rising tide of strikes and to strengthen the leadership in the working-class movement, the Chinese Communist Party called for the convening of a national labor congress. Under the sponsorship of the Chinese Trade Union Secretariat, the First National Labor Congress was held in Canton on May 1, 1922. It was attended by 162 delegates representing 12 cities, over 100 trade unions and 270,000 trade-union members. Among those present were representatives of the Communist Party, the Kuomintang, and the Anarchist Party, as well as people with no party affiliation. The following problems were discussed at the congress: participation by the workers in the democratic revolution; establishment of the All-China Federation of Trade Unions to eliminate the guild outlook prevalent in local trade unions; and the organization of socialist education among the workers. It adopted the slogans put forward by the Communist Party: "Down with Imperialism!" and "Down with the Warlords"; adopted resolutions on the eight-hour day and the principle of mutual aid in strikes; and recognized the Chinese Trade Union Secretariat as the national liaison center pending the establishment of the All-China Federation of Trade Unions. This last resolution and the whole course of the congress indicated that all the participants unanimously recognized the Communist Party as the leader of the Chinese working-class movement. At

the same time, the congress marked the beginning of nationwide unity of the Chinese working class and thus gave a mighty
impetus to the current strike movement.

The fact that their strikes were everywhere suppressed by
the warlords and the imperialists brought home to the workers
the importance of political freedom. Accordingly they started a
movement for labor legislation under the leadership of the
Party. An "Outline of Labor Law," which aimed at protecting
the rights and freedom of the workers, was drafted by the Trade
Union Secretariat and submitted to the Parliament in Peking for
ratification. It consisted of nineteen clauses, which included
among others freedom of assembly and association for workers;
the right of workers to stage general strikes and the right of collective bargaining; recognition of the eight-hour day; protection
of woman and child labor; establishment of a minimum wage
scale; and recognition of the workers' right to establish international connections. This outline was published in newspapers
throughout the country and widely circulated among the workers.
The workers throughout the country actively responded to the
call of the Trade Union Secretariat to take part in the movement
for labor legislation. Of course it would be the height of naïveté
to expect a parliament under the control of warlords to give the
workers human rights and freedom or to adopt a labor law that
was in their interests. Nevertheless, these nineteen clauses
strongly impressed the workers and became their program of
struggle in the strikes. The movement taught the working class
that no political freedom could be won without persistent
struggle.

The nationwide strikes continued to forge ahead. Hunan
was at that time one of the provinces where the working-class
movement made the greatest headway. After the Party's First
Congress in 1921, Comrade Mao Tse-tung had returned to Hunan to lead the Party's work there. After the First National Labor
Congress in May 1922, the Trade Union Secretariat moved
from Shanghai to Peking, and set up branches in the major
cities of the country. Comrade Mao Tse-tung was elected Chairman of the Hunan branch. He worked hard for the working-
class movement, leading the strikes of Changsha, the Anyuan
Colliery, and the Shuikoushan Lead Mine. Mao Tse-tung, Liu

Shao-ch'i, and others were in close contact with the masses of the workers, kept themselves well informed about their problems and always stood at the very forefront of their struggles.

The year 1922 and the early part of 1923 witnessed a vigorous development of the working-class movement in Hunan and the country as a whole. Heroic strikes for wage increase and political rights spread over the whole province. The one that had the greatest influence over the working-class movement in Hunan and the rest of the country was the great Anyuan strike.

The Anyuan Colliery in Pinghsiang County, Kiangsi Province, had at that time a daily output of over two thousand tons of coal. It supplied the Tayeh Iron Mine and the Hanyang Iron Works (both in Hupeh province) with the fuel they needed. In all, there were about twenty thousand men employed in the mines and on the Chuchow-Pinghsiang Railway.

The Anyuan Colliery was an enterprise owned by bureaucrat-capitalists under the control of Japanese imperialism. The successive directors were all corrupt bureaucrats, real power concerning the mining projects being in the hands of foreign supervisors. The entire enterprise was run on the feudal gangmaster system. The workers groaned under the treble oppression of imperialism, bureaucrat-capitalism, and feudalism. Therefore the Anyuan Colliery contained immense revolutionary possibilities.

After 1921, the Party at first ran spare-time schools for the workers at the mine to carry on Marxist education; then it organized a trade union, which was formally founded on May 1, 1922. Meanwhile, a branch of the Socialist Youth League was formed among the workers, the best members of which were later absorbed into the Party.

The big strike of the Anyuan coal miners, which had repercussions throughout the country, broke out on September 10, 1922. The authorities of the mine and the railway had delayed payment to the workers for several months and attempted to dissolve their union. Further, the workers were encouraged by the victory of the strike in the Hanyang Iron Works. They demanded the safeguarding of their political rights, improvement in their working conditions, and an increase in wages.

Pickets were organized after the outbreak of the strike to keep order in the mining district. When the warlords of Kiangsi Province sent troops to suppress the strike, the workers under the guidance of the Party went to agitate among the soldiers, and succeeded in winning their sympathy to such an extent that the soldiers refused to open fire on them. The authorities tried through sham "negotiations" to arrest Comrade Liu Shao-ch'i, who was leading the strike, but thousands of strikers surrounded the meeting place and foiled the warlords' plan.

Owing to the solidarity of the workers and their vigorous struggle, the authorities were forced to accept the workers' demands on the fifth day of the strike and thus the strike was victoriously concluded.

After the victory of the strike the trade union was organized along new lines. The basic unit of organization was a ten-man group. Each group had a representative, every ten groups an intermediate representative, and each pit or workshop a chief representative. Every pit and workshop had its board of representatives or intermediate representatives; and above them all was the supreme conference of the chief representatives. Thus the workers were better and more strictly organized. Their political rights were extended and their living conditions markedly improved. The workers also expanded their schools and opened consumers' cooperatives. The Anyuan trade union was at that time one of the strongest in the country. It alone stood firm when nearly all the unions in the other big enterprises were destroyed during the low ebb of the working-class movement which followed the massacre of the Peking-Hankow Railway workers on February 7, 1923. In the course of the Northern Expedition in 1926, the Anyuan workers gave strong support to the Expeditionary Army. They also took part in the armed struggle during the Autumn Harvest Uprising in 1927. From 1928 onwards, Anyuan was the liaison center of the Chingkang Mountains revolutionary base.

For two years the Hunan workers won all their struggles. Their success was owing to two factors: the nationwide expansion of the strike movement, and, what was more important, the leadership of the Chinese Communist Party.

Rural Revolution Breaks Out Again: The Communist Organize the Peasants of Inland China

IN THE ideal Confucian social order, the peasant ranked just below the scholar and ahead of the artisan and the merchant. Since the Chinese Revolution was mainly the work of intellectuals and peasants, Confucianism may be credited with having identified Chinese society's two key revolutionary classes. The peasant revolution began in the latter part of the eighteenth century when worsening economic conditions led to the great Buddhist White Lotus uprisings. The Taipings were mainly peasant revolutionaries. Throughout the nineteenth century there were smaller peasant revolts in various parts of China, but by the turn of the century, open peasant rebellion appeared to have waned. The Manchu Dynasty was overthrown by discontented military men in league with revolutionary students. During the early 1920s neither the Kuomintang nor the Communist Party had many peasant adherents. The Comintern looked to the proletariat for the class base of the Chinese Revolution, and its Chinese followers dutifully acquiesced.

Shortly after the May Fourth Movement, some radicals began to look beyond the cities to the land for revolutionary possibilities. Influenced by Russian writings on peasant movements, many Chinese students went to the villages to start a "peasant enlightenment movement." In 1921 the Chinese Communist leader P'eng P'ai founded a peasant association in Kwangtung province. The movement spread rapidly, and by January 1924, 75,000 peasants were organized in associations in Kwangtung; by 1926 the figure had risen to 665,000 in Kwangtung alone. Honan had 270,000 peasants in associations, and Hunan, Mao Tse-tung's province, had 138,000 including many from

Mao's native county of Hsiang-t'an. Mao was elected Chairman of the All-China Association of Peasant Associations. In November 1927 China's first soviet government was proclaimed in the Hai-feng and Lu-feng districts of Kwangtung, where P'eng P'ai had first established himself.

The astounding rapidity with which the movement spread meant that the dormant volcano of peasant revolution had once again erupted, not to quiet down again until the Communists had been swept to victory. In one of his earliest Party writings, "Report on an Investigation into the Peasant Movement in Hunan," of March 1927, from which the following selection is taken, Mao foresaw the immense power of the revolutionary peasantry:

> For the present upsurge of the peasant movement is a colossal event. In a very short time, in China's Central, Southern, and Northern provinces, several hundred million peasants will rise like a mighty storm, like a hurricane, a force so swift and violent that no power, however great, will be able to hold it back.

This movement's cries echoed those of the Taiping Rebellion and scores of other peasant revolts: Down with officials, landlords, and gentry! If Mao had thought little of the peasantry's revolutionary potential while still a young student in Hunan, as an expert on the peasant question for the Chinese Communist Party he remembered his country's history of peasant revolts. Here was revolutionary power that could be tapped.

Mao's chance came in 1927, when Chiang Kai-shek's White Terror had all but destroyed the Communist Party's city organizations. Yet until 1927 Mao may not have been absolutely sure that the great tempest would arise, since the peasant associations had been largely peaceful. But in September 1927 the Autumn Harvest Insurrection broke out in Hunan, which, though a failure, confirmed Mao's estimations of the peasantry's revolutionary potential. As Mao along with Chu Teh organized the Red Army, he raised the banner of revolution in Hunan and Kiangsi. The peasants responded, thus furnishing the Chinese soviets with their power base. The intellectual had come to the peasants as a revolutionary leader and they followed him.

MAO TSE-TUNG *
From *The Peasant Movement in Hunan*

March 1927

THE IMPORTANCE OF THE PEASANT PROBLEM

During my recent visit to Hunan I made a first-hand investigation of conditions in the five counties of Hsiangtan, Hsianghsiang,
Hengshan, Liling, and Changsha. In the thirty-two days from
January 4 to February 5, I called together fact-finding conferences in villages and county towns which were attended by experienced peasants and by comrades working in the peasant
movement, and I listened attentively to their reports and collected a great deal of material. Many of the hows and whys of
the peasant movement were the exact opposite of what the
gentry in Hankow and Changsha are saying. I saw and heard
of many strange things of which I had hitherto been unaware.
I believe the same is true of many other places, too. All talk
directed against the peasant movement must be speedily set
right. All the wrong measures taken by the revolutionary authorities concerning the peasant movement must be speedily
changed. Only thus can the future of the revolution be benefited.
For the present upsurge of the peasant movement is a colossal
event. In a very short time, in China's Central, Southern, and
Northern provinces, several hundred million peasants will rise
like a mighty storm, like a hurricane, a force so swift and violent
that no power, however great, will be able to hold it back. They
will smash all the trammels that bind them and rush forward
along the road to liberation. They will sweep all the imperialists,
warlords, corrupt officials, local tyrants, and evil gentry into
their graves. Every revolutionary party and every revolutionary

---

* Mao Tse-tung, "Report on an Investigation of the Peasant Movement in
Hunan," *Selected Works* (Peking: Foreign Languages Press, 1965), Volume I,
pp. 23–30.

comrade will be put to the test, to be accepted or rejected as they decide. There are three alternatives. To march at their head and lead them? To trail behind them, gesticulating and criticizing? Or to stand in their way and oppose them? Every Chinese is free to choose, but events will force you to make the choice quickly.

GET ORGANIZED!

The development of the peasant movement in Hunan may be divided roughly into two periods with respect to the counties in the province's central and southern parts where the movement has already made much headway. The first, from January to September of last year, was one of organization. In this period, January to June was a time of underground activity, and July to September, when the revolutionary army was driving out Chao Heng-ti, one of open activity. During this period, the membership of the peasant associations did not exceed 300,000 to 400,000, the masses directly under their leadership numbered little more than a million, there was as yet hardly any struggle in the rural areas, and consequently there was very little criticism of the associations in other circles. Since its members served as guides, scouts, and carriers of the Northern Expeditionary Army, even some of the officers had a good word to say for the peasant associations. The second period, from last October to January of this year, was one of revolutionary action. The membership of the associations jumped to two million and the masses directly under their leadership increased to ten million. Since the peasants generally enter only one name for the whole family on joining a peasant association, a membership of two million means a mass following of about ten million. Almost half the peasants in Hunan are now organized. In counties like Hsiangtan, Hsianghsiang, Liuyang, Changsha, Liling, Ninghsiang, Pingkiang, Hsiangyin, Hengshan, Hengvang, Leiyang, Chenhsien, and Anhua, nearly all the peasants have combined in the peasant associations or have come under their leadership. It was on the strength of their extensive organization that the peasants went into action and within four months brought about a great revolution in the countryside, a revolution without parallel in history.

DOWN WITH THE LOCAL TYRANTS AND EVIL GENTRY! ALL POWER TO THE PEASANT ASSOCIATIONS!

The main targets of attack by the peasants are the local tyrants, the evil gentry and the lawless landlords, but in passing they also hit out against patriarchal ideas and institutions, against the corrupt officials in the cities and against bad practices and customs in the rural areas. In force and momentum the attack is tempestuous; those who bow before it survive and those who resist perish. As a result, the privileges which the feudal landlords enjoyed for thousands of years are being shattered to pieces. Every bit of the dignity and prestige built up by the landlords is being swept into the dust. With the collapse of the power of the landlords, the peasant associations have now become the sole organs of authority and the popular slogan "All power to the peasant associations" has become a reality. Even trifles such as a quarrel between husband and wife are brought to the peasant association. Nothing can be settled unless someone from the peasant association is present. The association actually dictates all rural affairs, and, quite literally, "whatever it says, goes." Those who are outside the associations can only speak well of them and cannot say anything against them. The local tyrants, evil gentry, and lawless landlords have been deprived of all right to speak, and none of them dares even mutter dissent. In the face of the peasant associations' power and pressure, the top local tyrants and evil gentry have fled to Shanghai, those of the second rank to Hankow, those of the third to Changsha, and those of the fourth to the county towns, while the fifth rank and the still lesser fry surrender to the peasant associations in the villages.

"Here's ten yuan. Please let me join the peasant association," one of the smaller of the evil gentry will say.

"Ugh! Who wants your filthy money?" the peasants reply.

Many middle and small landlords and rich peasants and
even some middle peasants, who were all formerly opposed to
the peasant associations, are now vainly seeking admission.
Visiting various places, I often came across such people who
pleaded with me, "Mr. Committeeman from the provincial capital, please be my sponsor!"

In the Ch'ing Dynasty, the household census compiled by
the local authorities consisted of a regular register and "the
other" register, the former for honest people and the latter for
burglars, bandits, and similar undesirables. In some places the
peasants now use this method to scare those who formerly
opposed the associations. They say, "Put their names down in
the other register!"

Afraid of being entered in the other register, such people
try various devices to gain admission into the peasant associations, on which their minds are so set that they do not feel
safe until their names are entered. But more often than not they
are turned down flat, and so they are always on tenterhooks;
with the doors of the association barred to them, they are like
tramps without a home or, in rural parlance, "mere trash." In
short, what was looked down upon four months ago as a "gang
of peasants" has now become a most honorable institution.
Those who formerly prostrated themselves before the power of
the gentry now bow before the power of the peasants. No matter what their identity, all admit that the world since last October is a different one.

"IT'S TERRIBLE!" OR "IT'S FINE!"

The peasants' revolt disturbed the gentry's sweet dreams. When
the news from the countryside reached the cities, it caused immediate uproar among the gentry. Soon after my arrival in
Changsha, I met all sorts of people and picked up a good deal
of gossip. From the middle social strata upwards to the Kuomintang right-wingers, there was not a single person who did
not sum up the whole business in the phrase, "It's terrible!"
Under the impact of the views of the "It's terrible!" school then

flooding the city, even quite revolutionary-minded people became downhearted as they pictured the events in the countryside in their mind's eye; and they were unable to deny the word "terrible." Even quite progressive people said, "Though terrible, it is inevitable in a revolution." In short, nobody could altogether deny the word "terrible." But as already mentioned, the fact is that the great peasant masses have risen to fulfil their historic mission and that the forces of rural democracy have risen to overthrow the forces of rural feudalism. The patriarchal-feudal class of local tyrants, evil gentry and lawless landlords has formed the basis of autocratic government for thousands of years and is the cornerstone of imperialism, warlordism, and corrupt officialdom. To overthrow these feudal forces is the real objective of the national revolution. In a few months the peasants have accomplished what Dr. Sun Yat-sen wanted, but failed, to accomplish in the forty years he devoted to the national revolution. This is a marvelous feat never before achieved, not just in forty, but in thousands of years. It's fine. It is not "terrible" at all. It is anything but "terrible." "It's terrible!" is obviously a theory for combating the rise of the peasants in the interests of the landlords; it is obviously a theory of the landlord class for preserving the old order of feudalism and obstructing the establishment of the new order of democracy, it is obviously a counter-revolutionary theory. No revolutionary comrade should echo this nonsense. If your revolutionary viewpoint is firmly established and if you have been to the villages and looked around, you will undoubtedly feel thrilled as never before. Countless thousands of the enslaved—the peasants—are striking down the enemies who battened on their flesh. What the peasants are doing is absolutely right; what they are doing is fine! "It's fine!" is the theory of the peasants and of all other revolutionaries. Every revolutionary comrade should know that the national revolution requires a great change in the countryside. The Revolution of 1911 did not bring about this change, hence its failure. This change is now taking place, and it is an important factor for the completion of the revolution. Every revolutionary comrade must support it, or he will be taking the stand of counter-revolution.

THE QUESTION OF "GOING TOO FAR"

Then there is another section of people who say, "Yes, peasant
associations are necessary, but they are going rather too far."
This is the opinion of the middle-of-the-roaders. But what is
the actual situation? True, the peasants are in a sense "unruly"
in the countryside. Supreme in authority, the peasant association
allows the landlord no say and sweeps away his prestige. This
amounts to striking the landlord down to the dust and keeping
him there. The peasants threaten, "We will put you in the other
register!" They fine the local tyrants and evil gentry, they
demand contributions from them, and they smash their sedan
chairs. People swarm into the houses of local tyrants and evil
gentry who are against the peasant association, slaughter their
pigs, and consume their grain. They even loll for a minute or
two on the ivory-inlaid beds belonging to the young ladies in
the households of the local tyrants and evil gentry. At the
slightest provocation they make arrests, crown the arrested with
tall paper hats, and parade them through the villages, saying,
"You dirty landlords, now you know who we are!" Doing
whatever they like and turning everything upside down, they
have created a kind of terror in the countryside. This is what
some people call "going too far," or "exceeding the proper
limits in righting a wrong," or "really too much." Such talk
may seem plausible, but in fact it is wrong. First, the local tyrants, evil gentry and lawless landlords have themselves driven
the peasants to this. For ages they have used their power to
tyrannize over the peasants and trample them underfoot; that
is why the peasants have reacted so strongly. The most violent
revolts and the most serious disorders have invariably occurred
in places where the local tyrants, evil gentry, and lawless landlords perpetrated the worst outrages. The peasants are clear-
sighted. Who is bad and who is not, who is the worst and who
is not quite so vicious, who deserves severe punishment and
who deserves to be let off lightly—the peasants keep clear accounts, and very seldom has the punishment exceeded the
crime. Secondly, a revolution is not a dinner party, or writing

an essay, or painting a picture, or doing embroidery; it cannot
be so refined, so leisurely and gentle, so temperate, kind, courteous, restrained, and magnanimous. A revolution is an insurrection, an act of violence by which one class overthrows another. A rural revolution is a revolution by which the peasantry
overthrows the power of the feudal landlord class. Without
using the greatest force, the peasants cannot possibly overthrow the deep-rooted authority of the landlords which has
lasted for thousands of years. The rural areas need a mighty
revolutionary upsurge, for it alone can rouse the people in their
millions to become a powerful force. All the actions mentioned
here which have been labeled as "going too far" flow from the
power of the peasants, which has been called forth by the
mighty revolutionary upsurge in the countryside. It was highly
necessary for such things to be done in the second period of the
peasant movement, the period of revolutionary action. In this
period it was necessary to establish the absolute authority of
the peasants. It was necessary to forbid malicious criticism of
the peasant associations. It was necessary to overthrow the
whole authority of the gentry, to strike them to the ground and
keep them there. There is revolutionary significance in all the
actions which were labeled as "going too far" in this period.
To put it bluntly, it is necessary to create terror for a while in
every rural area; otherwise it would be impossible to suppress
the activities of the counter-revolutionaries in the countryside
or overthrow the authority of the gentry. Proper limits have to
be exceeded in order to right a wrong, or else the wrong cannot be righted. Those who talk about the peasants "going too
far" seem at first sight to be different from those who say "It's
terrible!" as mentioned earlier, but in essence they proceed from
the same standpoint and likewise voice a landlord theory that
upholds the interests of the privileged classes. Since this theory
impedes the rise of the peasant movement and so disrupts the
revolution, we must firmly oppose it.

THE "MOVEMENT OF THE RIFFRAFF"

The right wing of the Kuomintang says, "The peasant movement is a movement of the riffraff, of the lazy peasants." This
view is current in Changsha. When I was in the countryside,
I heard the gentry say, "It is all right to set up peasant associations, but the people now running them are no good. They
ought to be replaced!" This opinion comes to the same thing
as what the right-wingers are saying; according to both it is all
right to have a peasant movement (the movement is already
in being and no one dare say otherwise), but they say that
the people running it are no good and they particularly hate
those in charge of the associations at the lower levels, calling
them "riffraff." In short, all those whom the gentry had despised,
those whom they had trodden into the dirt, people with no
place in society, people with no right to speak, have now audaciously lifted up their heads. They have not only lifted up
their heads but taken power into their hands. They are now
running the township peasant associations (at the lowest level),
which they have turned into something fierce and formidable.
They have raised their rough, work-soiled hands and laid them
on the gentry. They tether the evil gentry with ropes, crown
them with tall paper hats and parade them through the villages.
(In Hsiangtan and Hsianghsiang they call this "parading
through the township" and in Liling "parading through the
fields.") Not a day passes but they drum some harsh, pitiless
words of denunciation into these gentry's ears. They are issuing
orders and are running everything. Those who used to rank
lowest now rank above everybody else; and so this is called
"turning things upside down."

4. A POLITICAL KUOMINTANG TAKES POWER; A MILITARY KUOMINTANG LOSES IT

✿ The Success and Failure of a Revolution Without Regeneration

CHINESE HISTORY, like all history, abounds with *if*s. It is frequently claimed that *if* China had not been assaulted by the Japanese and the Communists, the Kuomintang would have been able to carry out a sweeping reform program and would have won the everlasting love of the Chinese people.

Unfortunately for the Kuomintang, Japan did attack China and the Communists remained a small but threatening force in the country. It is undeniable that this double menace sapped much of the Kuomintang's strength and helped throw the country into serious confusion. But the Kuomintang's inability to handle this situation during the 1930s had internal as well as external causes, and the causes of its downfall were within its own ranks as well as without. The war and the extermination campaigns during the 1930s tended to magnify all the inadequacies and shortcomings of Chiang's regime, so that in the end the Kuomintang was defeated not so much by the Japanese or the Communists as by itself.

It was only natural that Chiang Kai-shek, as a military man, saw solutions to China's problems in military rather than social and political terms. He saw the unification of China as a military task, and never stopped to ask what would hold China together after his armies had done their job. After the death of Sun Yat-sen (himself no impressive ideologue) the Kuomintang became an ideological vacuum; in spite of several abortive efforts, Chiang never succeeded in endowing it with a dynamic and persuasive ideology. He ruled China with his armies, not with ideas: as we see in the following selection, his means for halting the spread of Communism in Kiangsi was to launch five massive and costly extermination campaigns. By brute force and technological superiority he drove Mao out of Kiangsi, but he never got to the real root of the problem—peasant discontent.

In a country like China, where the vast majority of the population came from the peasant class, an aggressive land reform policy was the *sine qua non* of popular support. The Kuomintang, heavily dependent on the support of the landowning class, was understandably reluctant to institute any large-scale land-reform program; thus while many handsomely bound plans existed in government files, they were never carried out. The officials upon whose initiative land reform depended were the very men to whom land reform was anathema. It was not surprising that grandiose land-reform schemes were usually pigeon-holed long before reaching the local level—a problem similar to the dispute over reform before the turn of the century. The same axiom holds true for both situations: officials who have a vested interest in the status quo make very poor reformers.

In the last analysis, Chiang's decline began because he was unable to maintain mass support under pressure. His regime was comprised of a tight clique of personal friends, ex-warlords, Shanghai bankers, Whampoa military colleagues, and a small handful of able and dedicated men; but as a whole the Nanking government was not reform-oriented. Priority was consistently given to consolidating political control (exterminating the Communists) while internal reforms (which Sun Yat-sen had referred to in the Three Principles of the People as "people's welfare") went unattended.

During the 1930s, as the war situation worsened, the Kuomintang's failure to deal with China's internal problems became the source of widespread disaffection. Criticism was repressed. All China's ills were blamed on the Japanese and the Communists. As the war dragged on, the Kuomintang became more and more authoritarian. A process of alienation slowly set in, isolating Chiang's harassed government from the people it claimed to be defending.

The following selection is taken from Theodore White and Annalee Jacoby's famous *Thunder Out of China*. The author traces Chiang Kai-shek's rise to power and what he calls the "miscarriage" of the Chinese Revolution. While mincing no words in his criticism of Chiang, he does admit that by 1935 the Kuomintang enjoyed considerable popularity. China was unified, the Communists were on the run, and for a while it seemed as though China was on the threshold of a new age. But this period was short-lived. The real challenges to Chiang's regime lay ahead in the dark years of the late 1930s and 1940s, by which time pressure from within and without had eroded the thin layer of popularity the Kuomintang had once enjoyed. In an almost reflex reaction the Kuomintang moved to defend itself by increasingly repressive measures. This was the beginning of the end.

THEODORE H. WHITE AND ANNALEE JACOBY *
The Rise of the Kuomintang

Out of the misery of the countryside, out of the growing strains and pressures in the villages, an urgency has been generating within China that can be stilled only by change—by peace if possible, by violence if there is no other way. Such revolutionary pressure is not new in Chinese history. Time and again the weight of the old system has grown too heavy for the peasant to bear. At such moments he has punctuated the history of his land with blood, swept it with desperate fury, thrown out the reigning dynasty, and established a new order. Each of the many dynasties of China was born of upheaval; each started with a vigorous administration on top, a reorganization and redistribution of land and feudal obligations on the bottom. And with each new dynasty in turn the process of widening differentiation went on afresh until it was again intolerable, and revolution brewed out of the suffering and discontent burst forth anew.

The crisis today is different from the crisis of years gone by. For one reason, an ordinary historical upheaval would yield

* Theodore White and Annalee Jacoby, *Thunder Out of China* (New York: William Sloane Associates: 1946), pp. 33–47.

only a system of weak peasant equality, and what history demands now is something that will lift Chinese society to the level of the modern world. For another, the normal cycle of revolution and reorganization has been too long frustrated. A hundred years ago an overdue revolution against the moribund Manchu Dynasty swept from Southern China almost to Peking itself; this Taiping Rebellion was a furious movement, yeasty with the first overtones of Christian ideas, and it was whipped finally only by foreign military intervention. Then, as now, it was felt that an orderly, stable China was essential to world peace and that such peace could be assured only by crushing the revolt of the Chinese peasantry. The suppression of the Taiping Rebellion put the cap on fundamental change in China for some sixty years, and the pressure generated by this delay grew more intense with each decade. Eventually, when the lid was lifted, China came apart in a series of explosions; like a string of firecrackers, each sputtering uprising generated another in a chain reaction of growing violence. Out of this chaos two distinct groups emerged, which had clear but diverging ideas about what to do to end the chaos.

The collapse of the Manchu Empire in 1911 stripped China of her outward appearance of changelessness and stability. Within less than five years the first political lesson of government had been learned anew—that the state rests on force. That was the age of the warlords, and China broke up into a patchwork of blood and unhappiness. Each warlord had his own army, each army its district. The great warlords governed entire provinces; their generals governed parts of provinces; their captains governed counties, cities, towns. Three hundred men could keep a county in subjection, levy taxes on it, rape its women, carry off its sons, batten on its crops. All those who were accustomed to govern were gone, and the soldiers who took over found with astonishment that they were government. Their will was law; paper they printed was money. Among themselves they fought as the whim took them; coalitions formed and re-formed; ambition, treachery, and foul play became the code of Chinese politics. And each evil deed was sanctified by its perpetrator, who proclaimed it done for the unity of China. The only enduring legacy left by the warlords was their belief in force; the only conviction that Chiang Kai-shek and the Communists have shared for twenty years is the conviction that armed strength is the only guarantee of security.

The warlords were purely destructive; in earlier ages such a period of anarchy might have lasted for generations before re-integration set in, but this was the twentieth century. All up and down the China coast and far up the rivers concessions had been wrung by foreign powers from the decadent Manchu government. On China's main rivers were steamers of foreign owner-ship, which were protected by gunboats flying foreign flags. Rail-ways owned and managed by foreigners sucked profit out of China to foreign investors. China's tariffs were set and collected by foreigners; so was the most profitable of internal revenues, the salt tax. The foreigners who lived in China had enormous contempt for both the Manchus and the later warlords, but they could not exist in island communities in the vastness of China; for their own purposes they had to create or convert to their use a body of Chinese who could act as a bridge between themselves and the nation they wished to plunder. Western businessmen created Chinese businessmen in their likeness. New Chinese banks were developed; old ones learned to substitute double-entry bookkeeping for beaded counting-boards. The factories, steamships, mines, and railways that foreigners controlled needed a host of skilled Chinese to operate them; their success caused Chinese businessmen to start similar projects, which needed the same kind of management and engineers. A new kind of Chinese began to appear, a naturalized citizen of the modern world; a middle class was developing in a feudal country.

No less forceful than the impact of Western armies and Western business was the impact of Western ideas. The new uni-versities that were set up in China to teach the new sciences and skills created scholars and students of a new sort, who thought less of the Book of Odes and the millennial classics than they did of Adam Smith, Karl Marx, and Henry George. The adepts of the new learning smarted even more than the businessmen under the contempt, the brutality, and the indignity the imperial powers heaped on China; they gave brilliant intellectual leadership to the discontent within the land. The ferment seemed like a great undisciplined anarchy, more froth and foam than substance. But it arose from one basic problem—that statelessness of China. The problem had one basic solution—internal unity and strength in China.

The political instrument of the new merchant and educated class was the party known as the Kuomintang. The architect of the early Kuomintang, its very soul, was a sad-eyed dreamer called Sun Yat-sen. It is customary now in intellectual circles to sneer at the naïveté with which he attacked world problems, but Sun Yat-sen was the first man to formulate a program of action for all the complex problems of the Chinese people. It was as if some Western thinker had attempted to devise one neat solution for the problems of feudalism, the Renaissance and Reformation, the Industrial Revolution, and the social unrest of today. Sun Yat-sen was a Cantonese who had been educated in Hawaii; he participated in almost every unsuccessful revolt against the Manchu Dynasty in the last decade of its existence, and he had lived the life of a hunted exile in Japan, America, and Europe. Almost every warlord who verbally espoused unity adorned his ambition with quotations from Sun Yat-sen; almost all ended by betraying him. The wretchedness of China, the burning eloquence of Sun Yat-sen's cause within him, the examples of Western civilization in the countries of his exile, were all finally synthesized in his book *San Min Chu I,* or *Three Principles of the People.*

The *San Min Chu I* is not a perfect book, but its sanctity in present-day China, among both Communists and Kuomintang, makes it by all odds the major political theory in the land. The book was a long time in maturing; it did not appear in print till shortly before Sun's death and then only as the transcript of a series of lectures he had given just before setting his party off on the greatest adventure in its history. The ideas of Sun Yat-sen, however, were current long before they were put into type. Sun's theory started by examining China. Why was she so humiliated in the family of nations? Why were her people so miserable? His answer was simple—China was weak, uneducated, and divided. To solve the problem, he advanced three principles.

The first was the Principle of Nationalism. China must win

back her sovereignty and unity. The foreigners must be forced out of their concessions; they must be made to disgorge the spoils they had seized from the Manchus. China must have all the powers and dignities that any foreign nation had; she must be disciplined and the war lords purged. The second was the Principle of People's Democracy. China must be a nation in which the government serves the people and is responsible to them. The people must be taught how to read and write and eventually to vote. A system must be erected whereby their authority runs upward from the village to command the highest authority in the nation. The third was the Principle of People's Livelihood. The basic industries of China must be socialized; the government alone should assume responsibility for vast industrialization and reconstruction. Concurrently with the erection of the superstructure of a modern economic system, the foundation had to be strengthened. The peasant's lot was to be alleviated; those who tilled the soil should own it.

The doctrine of Sun Yat-sen won instant acceptance throughout the country. Few accepted it in its entirety, but it was a broad program, and there was something in it to touch the emotional mainspring of almost every thinking Chinese. The new middle class took it to its bosom; even the proud rural gentry could go along on the general thesis that the warlords' strife and the foreigners must go. The years of exile and failure had been years of education for Sun Yat-sen. He began as a dreamer and an intellectual; but he learned, as all China did during the decade following the Manchu collapse, that dreams and theories alone were insufficient for the reorganization of the land. Thousands, perhaps millions, were willing to admit that his theories were right, even to join his party. But the party needed force— an armed tool to work its will. By the early 1920s history had conspired to give Sun the strength he needed. First, the Russians had succeeded in establishing their own revolution against feudalism and were interested in revolution everywhere; they were willing to send to China not only political mentors to aid Sun Yat-sen, but battle-seasoned soldiers who could fashion an army for him. Secondly, the decade-long violence within China had by now produced young soldiers and officers who were interested in more than loot and plunder; they were interested in their country as an end in itself, and they sought political leadership for their military skills.

In 1923, Sun Yat-sen was permitted by the local warlord to set up a nominal government in Canton. He had made such agreements before with other warlords when they had sought inspiring façades for practical despotism; each time he had been betrayed and cast out when he tried to exercise more than nominal authority. This time it was to be different. Within a year this new government of Sun Yat-sen was the seat of an incandescent revolutionary movement. Sun set up in Canton a center that was both military and political. Two Russian agents were his most conspicuous advisers—Michael Borodin as political mentor and a general known as Galen for the new army. Communists were brought into the movement and made members of the Kuomintang. The political center was the training school for a host of flaming advocates of revolution, agents who were to circulate through all China in the next few years to preach the new doctrines. The real strength, however, was in a school on the banks of the muddy Whampoa River, where an academy for the training of revolutionary officers was set up. This was to produce men who, knowing how to wield force, would wield it not for the sake of force alone but in the name of a new China. To head this academy Sun Yat-sen chose a slim and cold-eyed Chekiang youth named Chiang Kai-shek.

No adequate biography of Chiang Kai-shek will appear in our times. Many of those who could best tell of his career are dead; the others are either his bonded servants, who see him as a saint, or his desperate enemies, who seek only his destruction. It has been too dangerous too long in China to record the facts of Chiang's career, so that now all that is known, apart from a few idolatrous official biographies, consists of morsels of gossip.

In Canton, Chiang was already the young hero of the Revolution. The Russian advisers of Sun Yat-sen had been so taken with him that they had sent him to Moscow in 1923 for a six months' course in indoctrination. When he returned to head the Whampoa academy, he rose rapidly from comparative obscurity to dominance. The death of Sun Yat-sen in 1925 gave him almost unchallenged authority.

By the spring of 1926 the revolutionary armies of the Kuomintang were ready to set forth on the famous Northern March from Canton to the Yangtze Valley to reclaim China from the warlords. Chiang Kai-shek was the commander-in-chief. It was a motley host, armed with discarded weapons of every conceivable foreign manufacture. It was staffed with Russian advisers; some of its key armies were commanded by repentant warlords who had seen the light. Before it went the political agents, Communist and Kuomintang, organizing peasants and factory workers and preparing the people of the countryside for the dawn of a new day. The army swept north on the very crest of a wave of revolutionary enthusiasm and seized Hankow, whose workers had already been organized and begun to strike in late summer. From Hankow the armies turned east down the Yangtze Valley, swept through Nanking and on to Shanghai.

The advance of the revolutionary armies sounded like the hammers of doom to the foreign concession of Shanghai. From the interior came stories of riots, bloodshed, and butchery, of strikes that closed down all foreign shipping and factories, of Chinese soldiers killing white men and raping white women. The tide reached Shanghai in the spring of 1927. From within the city Communist agents organized the workers for a revolt, and on March 21, in a tremendous general strike, the entire city outside of the International Settlement closed down. The armed unions went on to make their strike one of the greatest of modern insurrections. They seized police stations, government buildings, and factories so rapidly that by the time Chiang's Kuomintang armies arrived at the suburbs, the workers were in complete control of the native city and turned it over to the revolutionary government.

Three weeks after the climactic victory the alliance of Communists and Kuomintang came to an end. What happened during those three weeks is a matter of mystery. Overnight the racketeering gangs of the waterfront and the underworld materialized in Chiang's support. Trembling foreign businessmen were quickly apprised that Chiang was indeed a "sensible" leader, and foreign

arms and assistance were supplied him. The revolutionary forces
were weak and vacillating; units of Chiang's own armies made
overtures to the Communists, for they sensed an impending
crisis. And then suddenly, without a word of warning, Chiang's
deputies, assisted by cohorts from the underworld and blessed
by foreign opinion, turned on the workers, disarmed them, executed their leaders, and forced the Communists underground
by a purge that was to continue for years (see pp. 104–117).

The Kuomintang itself was astounded by this breach of faith
and split into two separate groups, one under Chiang Kai-shek,
the other under the left wing at Hankow. By 1928, however, the
Kuomintang had knitted together again in a solid anti-Communist front and had achieved stability. The Party was now
completely respectable in the eyes of the foreign world and was
recognized as the only legitimate government of China. It proceeded to transfer the seat of its power from Canton to the
Yangtze Valley. In the cities it controlled, the wheels of industry
began to turn. But in the countryside Sun Yat-sen's program of
peasant reform died stillborn; the old system, aggravated by continuing civil war and commercial speculation, still loomed over
the peasantry. The revolution had miscarried.

What had happened? To understand the tragedy of the
great uprising it is necessary to return to Canton and establish
the personality of the historic antagonist of Chiang Kai-shek—
the Communist Party of China. Like the Kuomintang, the Chinese Communist Party was born of intellectual ferment. It appeared much later on the scene of Chinese history and took its
analysis and solution of China's problems from the example of
the Russian Revolution. The Communists agreed completely
with Sun Yat-sen and the Kuomintang that the foreigners must
be thrown out, the warlords annihilated; but they went a step
further. They asked: For whose benefit should China be reorganized? They answered: For the Chinese peasant himself.

To accomplish this it was necesary not only to achieve all
the aims of the Kuomintang, but to go further, to smash in
every village the shackles of feudalism that chained the peasant
to the Middle Ages. In the cities the new industrial workers of
the factories and mills were to be the constituents of the new

era. The savage exploitation of labor by the coastal entrepreneurs would have to be ended before industry could be a blessing rather than a new curse to China. The Communists brought to their early alliance with the Kuomintang all the discipline and zealotry that are characteristic of their movement everywhere. In its early days the Chinese Communist Party was organically linked with Moscow. The Russian delegation attached to Sun Yat-sen controlled the Party completely and, under the strictest injunction from Moscow, committed it to unreserved subordination to the Kuomintang. Communist agents spearheaded the great organizing drives that led the triumphal Northern March of the revolutionary armies. They converted the areas of combat into quicksands for their warlord enemies; peasant and labor unions developed almost overnight as the masses rose to the first leadership they had ever known as their own.

Chiang saw in the Communists a leadership as coldblooded and ruthless as his own. To his passionate nationalism their connection with Russia was wicked. His brief visit to Russia had given him an insight into the working of a dictatorial state along with a lasting dislike for the Russians. He saw the Communists as Russian agents, possessed of some magic formula that would tear the countryside apart in social upheaval—and he hated them. For the first three years of his alliance with the Communists he bided his time. He needed both Russian arms and peasant support; he could not afford a break. His march to the Yangtze Valley, however, brought him into contact for the first time with the highest rungs of the new Chinese industrial and commercial aristocracy. These men, no less than the foreigners, were terrified of strikes and labor unions; slogans of agrarian reform threatened to upset the entire system of rural commerce and landholding. Chiang suddenly found in the Shanghai business world a new base of support, a base powerful enough to maintain his party and his armies; with these men and their money behind him, he was no longer dependent on Russian aid or agrarian revolution. When he makes up his mind, Chiang acts swiftly. Before the Communist leaders had any inkling of what was happening, their movement had been beheaded, and within a year of the Shanghai coup Communism was illegal from end to end of China.

Chiang Kai-shek was the chief architect of the new China that emerged. Occasionally, in fits of sulkiness, he would withdraw from the government for a few months to prove that only he could hold its diverse elements together; he always returned with greater prestige and strength than before. The new Kuomintang government was a dictatorship. It glossed itself with the phrases of Sun Yat-sen and claimed that it was the "trustee" of the people, who were in a state of "political tutelage." Its secret police were ubiquitous, while its censorship closed down like a vacuum pack over the Chinese press and Chinese universities. It held elections nowhere, for its conception of strengthening China was to strengthen itself, and it governed by fiat. This government rested on a four-legged stool—an army, a bureaucracy, the urban businessman, the rural gentry.

The army was the darling of Chiang Kai-shek. Chiang imported a corps of Prussian advisers to forge it into a powerful striking weapon. Its soldiers learned to goose-step, to use German rifles and artillery. Within the army was a praetorian guard consisting of the original group of Whampoa cadets. The young students of the military academy had been decimated in the early revolutionary battles, but those who survived were loyal to the Kuomintang before all else and faithful to Chiang as the symbol of the new China. As succeeding classes of students entered, the cadets rose in rank from captain to major to colonel. By the time the war against Japan broke out, an estimated forty of the Whampoa cadets were divisional commanders. About Chiang clustered a number of senior military men who shared his own background of warlord education; they were men who belonged to no coherent group. They commanded the campaigns Chiang wished to fight, but never did they have any such affection or loyalty as he gave to the youths he trained himself. Chiang's army was the strongest ever seen in China. From 1929 to 1937 there was not a year he was not engaged in civil war. The base of his strength was the lower Yangtze Valley, while all about him lay the provinces controlled by warlords. These individually and then in coalition challenged his rule, and one by one he would either buy them off or destroy them. He gradually brought central China as far as the gorges of the Yangtze under his control, until all China south of the Yellow River had acknowledged him as its overlord by the time the Japanese struck.

Almost as large a figure as the army in the process of unification was the new bureaucracy Chiang was creating at Nanking. China had never before had even the most primitive form of modern government. The new regime had a real Ministry of Finance, a real Ministry of Railways, a real Ministry of Industry. It had agricultural research stations and health bureaus, and although these bureaus scarcely met Western standards, they were the best China had ever seen. A Central Bank was created, which brought the first stable currency China had had in a generation. New roads were pushed through, stimulating commerce and industry. New textbooks were written, new sciences cultivated. The scholars, students, and engineers who served in these administrations were neither devoutly faithful to Chiang nor happy about the Kuomintang dictatorship, but for all of them it provided the first opportunity to serve their country. They were men of ability and generally of integrity—and here, for the first time, were careers open to their talents.

The other two mainstays were the classes that formed the social basis of the government. The first, a relatively progressive element, was the businessmen on the coast and in the great cities. They had profited by the Revolution. They had loosened foreign control of their customs; they dealt now with Western businessmen as with equals. The new government with its stable finance, its rational structure of taxation, gave them for the first time opportunities that Western businessmen had enjoyed for decades. The government preserved law and order within the Yangtze Valley and constructed new railways. A wave of prosperity lifted Chinese commercial and industrial activity to new levels; exports and imports soared; production multiplied.

In the countryside the Kuomintang rested on the landed gentry. The Kuomintang indeed wrote into its law books some of the most progressive legislation ever conceived to alleviate peasant misery—but the legislation was never applied; it was window dressing. The government reached back into antiquity and revived a system for the countryside that seemed simple. Each county was subdivided into units; each of these, called *pao,* consisted of a hundred families and was further subdivided into *chia* comprising ten families. Each *pao* and *chia* was to choose headmen who would be the transmission belt of all the new reforms the Kuomintang sought to establish. On paper the system looked fine. But actually the *pao* and the *chia* chieftains were the same landlords and gentry who had always ruled the village. Looking up at his government from below, the peasant could see no change. His taxes ran on as before; his rent and interest rates were just as high as ever; his court of appeal consisted of the same men who had always denied his demands. The revolution had brought him nothing. The Kuomintang, the party of the Nationalist Revolution, was now securely established in every village, with roots in local party cells of the wellborn and well-to-do.

The driving spirit of the government was Chiang Kai-shek himself. He could safely leave the tasks of Party organization, administration, and reconstruction to his subordinates; with a minimum of guidance the pent-up talents of educated Chinese could direct the technical tasks of modernizing China. He devoted his own energies and interest to two great problems, the Communists and the Japanese.

The alliance of Chiang Kai-shek and the Communists against the warlords and imperialists had broken over the basic question of the peasant and his land. The Communists had tried—but too late—to bring the uprising to its appointed climax with redistribution of the land and reorganization of the whole system of feudal relationships in the village. In the turbulence that had accompanied the Northern March the peasants had time and again taken the law into their own hands and made their own judgments. You could hardly ask men to overthrow foreign imperialism and corrupt warlords and at the same time condone injustice and oppression in the village, where it struck nearest home. The Kuomintang wanted to limit the revolution to the accomplishment of a few specific aims such as the end of imperialism and warlordism; it promised to take care of rent, credit, and all other peasant problems after it had the government established. But the peasants did not want to wait.

When Chiang forced the Communists underground, he cut

them off from the workers of the city, but he could not break their contact with the agitated peasantry. South of the Yangtze the Communists found the memory of the Revolution still green in the hearts of the villagers, and their troops proceeded to establish a miniature soviet republic. Chiang waged unceasing war against this soviet republic in Southern China. With his government buttressed by loans from America, his troops, German-armed and trained, tightened their blockade ring about Communist areas each succeeding year. The very war against the Communists drew warlords into alliance with Chiang for mutual protection. The struggle against the Communists was savage and relentless. Within the areas that Chiang controlled, his police butchered Communist leaders; families of known Communist leaders were wiped out; students were watched and spied on, and possession of Communist literature was made a crime punishable by death. In Communist areas it was the village landlord who fared worst, and the hatred of the poor for the rich was given full rein.

By 1934 the pressure on the Communists had grown too great, and bursting out of Chiang's blockade line, they performed that spectacular feat known as the Long March. Men and women, with bag, baggage, and archives, the Communists marched from Southern China to re-establish themselves in the Northwest. The winding route of the main column of thirty thousand was over six thousand miles long. The Long March was a savage ordeal that stands out in Chinese Communist history as an emotional mountain peak. The sufferings endured and the iron determination with which they were mastered are beyond description. The countryside through which the march passed is still dotted with stone blockhouses built by the government to hem in the Communists. The ferocity of the fighting ravaged the peasants in hundreds on hundreds of villages; in many districts in Southern and Central China the name of Communist is still hated for the destruction this march wreaked on the countryside. In certain other districts the Communists succeeded in creating a political loyalty among the poorer peasants that lingered for years. The Communists finally established themselves at the end of 1935 in the Northwest, in the areas just north of Yenan in Shensi, which later became their chief base.

The Communists' arrival in Yenan coincided with a turning point both in their own history and in the Party line. By now they had become an independent organization; their ties with Moscow were nominal. The Soviet Union had re-established friendly relations with Chiang Kai-shek and left the Communist Party to fend for itself. From their new base the Communists raised a new call: Chinese unity against the Japanese! The response throughout China was instant, for the most profound emotion was touched. Japan had seized Manchuria in 1931, had pressed on down past the Great Wall, was pouring opium into Northern China, was flagrantly abusing every international standard of decency. China was being humiliated by the Japanese Army in a way never experienced before; nothing, it seemed, would satisfy Japan except control over the whole vast country.

As for Chiang, he hated the Japanese with the stubborn fury that is his greatest strength and his greatest fault. His armies, he felt, were unable to stop the Japanese Army; China's industry could not match the modernized power of Japan's industry; China was disunited. He wanted to wipe out the Communists first, establish unity, and then face Japan. The new Communist slogan forced him into an intolerable position. Its logic was irrefutable: Why should Chinese kill each other when a foreign enemy was seeking to kill all Chinese? The Kuomintang explained in whispers that it was only biding its time against the Japanese—that when it was ready it would turn and defend China. At the same time students were arrested and jailed for anti-Japanese parades and demonstrations. Chinese journalists and intellectuals stood aghast at what they saw. The threat of international annihilation from without became graver with every passing day; within, the government spent its resources not on resistance to Japan but on a Communist witch hunt.

Gradually the call for unity began to penetrate the army. In the North, where the civil war against the Communists was still being pushed, the campaign began to flag and finally came to a dead stop. Chiang, flying to Sian to revive it, flew directly into a conspiracy and was kidnapped—not by Communists but by warlords who refused to fight against Communists any more when they might be fighting against the Japanese. During his two weeks' internment Chiang met the Communists personally for the first time since 1927. No one has ever recorded in full what actually happened during Chiang's kidnapping and at his meeting with the Communists, but the results were electric; the civil war came to an abrupt end. Chiang recognized the right of the Communists to govern their own areas in the North within the loose framework of the Central Government. Their armies were to be incorporated into the national armies. The Communists were to give up their program of revolution in the countryside. The government was to institute immediate democratic reforms, and Sun Yat-sen's program as set forth in *Three Principles of the People* was to be the code of the land.

This news came to the Japanese like an alarm in the night. Ever since China's Nationalist Revolution, Japan had been haunted by two prospects; one was the unity of China; the other, Communism in China. Japan knew that a united, resurgent China would ultimately be the leader of all Asia. Japan feared Communism, too. Her own empire was based on thin, rocky islands poor in every material resource except manpower. Her armed might rested on the unthinking obedience of civilians and soldiers; any system that challenged them to thought was a menace to Japan. Thus, no matter which side won in China, Chiang Kai-shek or Communism, Japan would lose. And to keep China permanently weak, disunited, and subordinate, Japan's continental armies had been constantly pressing down from the North, dabbling in warlord politics, poisoning China with thousands of agents. The new accord between Chiang and the Communists meant that now there was the possibility not only of a united China but of a united China in which Communism was tolerated and condoned. There was no time to be lost.

On the night of July 7, 1937, at the Marco Polo Bridge outside of Peking, Japanese garrison troops were engaged in field maneuvers. Someone fired a shot; the Japanese claimed they had been assaulted—the war had begun.

❧ Moral Precepts
of a General and His Wife

ONE OF the most important effects of Chinese Communism in the 1920s and 1930s was to reveal the Kuomintang as an ideological desert. Other than Sun's Three Principles of the People, the Kuomintang had little to offer in competition with Marxism. Chiang governed China with armies, not ideas. No doubt it was in realization of this poverty of ideas that he and his wife launched the New Life Movement in 1935, which proved from the beginning to be an artificial attempt to provide China with an ideological basis for unity.

The New Life Movement tried to exhume Confucianism and apply it to China's modern problems. The underlying assumption was that the old Confucian virtues which had "made the nation great in remote times" could once again be pressed into service. Through moral exhortation, Chiang hoped to uplift a nation which had only recently rejected its Confucian heritage.

In short, although the Kuomintang was at the apogee of its power during the mid 1930s, the New Life Movement proved to be superfluous. While Mao was telling his followers in the mountains to struggle onward to the dawn of a new world, Chiang was telling his people to turn back to the past and docilely wait for "a fuller enjoyment of life."

Aside from Sun Yat-sen's vague Three Principles of the People (which the Communists superseded with a hard-hitting revolutionary program), Kuomintang ideology thus appeared to consist of bits and pieces of Confucianism and Christianity. Beneath the shallowness of the ideas, however, there was a rationale. The Kuomintang derived its social support from the

landed gentry and the urban middle classes. The former remained Confucian, untouched by the intellectual revolution of
the May Fourth Movement, while the latter showed some predilection for Protestant Christianity. (One of Madame Chiang's
stipulations for marrying Chiang Kai-shek was that he convert
to Christianity.)

Given the revolutionary currents sweeping through Inland
and Coastal China at the time, one may wonder what effect this
ideological amalgam of Confucianism and Christianity had on
the Chinese people as a whole, for whom the gentry were a hated
antiquated class and the urban middle classes a small Western-
ized minority.

The first selection is the Foreword by Madame Chiang
Kai-shek written for a book outlining the New Life Movement
for Kiangsi province, which had just been retaken from the
Communists. The second selection is a short speech broadcast
by Generalissimo Chiang Kai-shek on Easter Eve 1938 to the
Chinese people.

MAYLING SOONG CHIANG *
From *New Life for Kiangsi*

FOREWORD

The demoralization and ruin which characterized the country
recovered from the Communist-bandit hordes inspired Generalissimo Chiang Kai-shek to inaugurate what has become known
as the New Life Movement. During the campaign which freed
the regions in Kiangsi province from the Communists, it was
borne in upon the Generalissimo that more military measures
were required effectively to eradicate the influence of Communists and their propaganda. He realized that definitely realistic

* Mayling Soong Chiang (Madame Chiang Kai-shek), Foreword, in C. W. H.
Young, *New Life for Kiangsi* (Shanghai, 1935), pp. iii–v.

things must be done to give the people something tangible to cling to, to elevate them to an understanding of their duties to their villages as well as their families, and also to the nation as citizens.

Thus took form the idea that a national consciousness and spirit of mutual cooperation must be created through the practical application of measures of social and economic reconstruction in the devastated areas, based upon those four important principal virtues of old China, *"Li," "I," "Lien,"* and *"Chih,"* which made the nation great in remote times.

The idea crystallized into what is now known as the New Life Movement. The Chinese of today seem to have forgotten the old source of China's greatness in their urge to acquire material gain, but, obviously, if the national spirit is to be revived, there must be recourse to stable foundations. In the four principles of ancient times, we have those foundations— *"Li"* means courtesy; *"I"* service toward our fellow men and toward ourselves; *"Lien"* honesty and respect for the rights of others; and *"Chih"* high-mindedness and honor.

A right conception of *"Li"* would bring recognition not of outward pomp but the sterling native qualities of our fellow men. If we practiced *"I,"* we would feel the obligation not to hold wealth and enjoy it wastefully while our fellow countrymen may be on the verge of starvation or suffering from sickness or other evils. With *"Lien,"* if the officials recognized the rights of the people under them, they would not try to benefit themselves at the expense of the people just because the latter were too powerless to fight for their own rights. The standard of official honesty would become so high that corruption could not exist. If *"Chih"* were carried out, no one would become shameless or stoop to anything mean or underhanded.

To the end that these four principles might be applied to actual existing conditions in order to help the moral character of the nation attain its highest standard, the New Life Movement was launched at Nanchang, the capital of Kiangsi province, a year ago. It was then intended as a purely local measure to begin with, but no sooner was it understood than it swept the whole country.

The first step taken was to have the four principles applied to the universal and indispensable facts of life, food, shelter, clothing and conduct, and it was this that caused the movement to grip the imagination of the people. . . .

Scarcely two years have elapsed since the Generalissimo went to Kiangsi to take personal command in the anti-Communist campaign in that province and only recently the New Life Movement celebrated its first anniversary. At this present writing, the Communists are cleared from Kiangsi and the New Life Movement has opened the way to a fuller enjoyment of life for the people of that province.

In ten other provinces in which the Generalissimo and I traversed last autumn, striking evidence of the growing influence of the New Life Movement upon the people and the officials was shown alike in the remote and far-flung Northwestern provinces and the Central and Maritime provinces. Practical application of the principles of the movement were noticeable everywhere, coupled with eagerness for even more effective and fundamental measures to better the lot of the people. For example, in most of the regions visited, the officials established cooperative contacts with the foreign missionary organizations, out of which sprang definite measures for the treatment of opium addicts, the abolition of foot-binding, the cure of trachoma, etcetera.

A few days ago, the Generalissimo came to Szechuan to clear this province of the Communist-bandits. The situation here, today, to the average person, would seem well-nigh hopeless, for Szechuan, apart from the fact that it has suffered from Communist outrages, has for years been bled by equally unscrupulous militarists. But with the example of good government and the creation of a new psychology for the people as exemplified by the concrete results of the application of the principles embodied in the New Life Movement, in Kiangsi, the future seems not unhopeful, especially as the Szechuan people are craving for reform and relief, and when we take into consideration the fact that Szechuan is unsurpassed in fertility of soil, richness of mineral resources, and almost unlimited man power. All that has been lacking so far is a pure motivation to consider first and foremost the good of the people, and that, as in other provinces, is being provided by the New Life Movement. . . .

Chungking,
Szechuan, March 16, 1935.

CHIANG KAI-SHEK *
My Religious Faith

A RADIO BROACAST, ORIGINALLY ENTITLED
"WHY I BELIEVE IN JESUS," DELIVERED TO
CHINESE CHRISTIANS THROUGHOUT THE LAND
ON EASTER EVE, APRIL 16, 1938

One who wishes to succeed in his work, especially one engaged in a revolutionary task, must be free from superstition and yet he must be a man of faith. Especially today, when the evil passions of men are running riot, do we need a firm faith in the ultimate triumph of right. Our country is now being torn asunder; our fellow countrymen are suffering untold agonies; our men are being massacred, and our women are being ravished. The very existence of our nation is threatened. How can we avert such a terrible calamity and resist the brutal enemy upon our soil except by faith? Therefore, while we must eradicate all super-stitions, we must at the same time cultivate a strong and positive faith. For example, if we believe with all our hearts that the *San Min Chu I* (Three Principles of the People) are essentially true and just principles, then we shall have the power to put them into effect, and our enemies will never be able to conquer us, no matter how fierce and cruel they may become. Fearless-ness and confidence have their roots in an unshakable faith.

Tomorrow is Easter Sunday. This evening I have been asked by the National Federation of Chinese Christians to speak

* *President Chiang Kai-shek's Selected Speeches and Messages* (Taipei: China Cultural Service), pp. 20–24.

to my fellow-Christians throughout the country. I propose to
follow my talk of last year with a further testimony on the
subject, "Why I Believe in Jesus."

To my mind the first reason why we should believe in Jesus
is that He was the leader of a national revolution. At the time of
Jesus' birth the Jewish people were steadily weakening under
the heavy oppression of Rome. If we study the history of this
period we find that the Jews were treated like slaves and animals
at the hands of their enemies. The Romans had power of life
and death over them. The Jews had not only failed to resist
the aggressors, but they had even lost the will to resist. Then a
people's revolutionist was born in the person of Jesus, who
courageously took upon Himself the heavy task of regenerating
the nation. With sacrificial determination He set out to save
His people, the world, and all mankind. He took His disciples on
many itineraries, and by means of His preaching and healing,
His Heaven-given wisdom and matchless eloquence, and His
three ideals of truth, righteousness, and abundant life, He
aroused the nation, led the masses, and prepared the way for a
people's revolution.

The second reason why we should believe in Jesus is that
He was the leader of a social revolution. The causes of a nation's
weakness are many. One of the most serious is the inability of
the people to improve their living and economy and to put them
on a rational foundation. Therefore, one engaged in a people's
revolution must begin by ridding society of its darkness and
corruption, and then with fresh spirit create a new, expanding,
abundant life for all the people, thus setting the nation free. Jesus
fully realized that in order to revive His nation and regenerate
His people He must launch a social revolution. He sought by the
inspiration of His leadership and personality to awaken the
perishing masses so that they would give up the ways of darkness, become new citizens, and build the foundations of a new
society.

In the third place, Jesus was the leader of a religious
revolution. Jesus saw that unless there was a radical reform to
sweep away the superstitions and corruption in the organized
religion of His day, the real spirit of religion could not shine
forth. Hence He often denounced those who prayed on the

streetcorners, and strongly opposed the use of religion to exploit the people. All of His acts were designed to lead the Jewish religion from darkness to light, from decay to health, from chaos to order, from corruption to purity, and to lead society from the blackness of night into the brightness of day. How important and yet how difficult was this task of reforming religion and of cleansing the religious society! Yet Jesus went ahead with utter disregard of personal suffering, in order that He might rescue religion and society from the evils that beset them and awaken the people from their spiritual lethargy. I call Jesus a great religious revolutionist.

I have often sought to study the secret of Jesus' revolutionary passion. It seems to me that it is found in His spirit of love. With His wonderful love Jesus sought to destroy the evil in the hearts of men, to do away with social injustices, and to enable everyone to enjoy his natural rights as a human being and receive the blessings of liberty, equality, and happiness. He believed that all men are brothers and that they should love one another and help one another in need. He believed in peace and justice between nations. Throughout His life He opposed violence and upheld righteousness. He was full of mercy and continually helped the weak. His great love and spirit of revolutionary self-sacrifice were demonstrated in all His words and deeds. His purpose to save the world and humanity was firm and His faith was immovable. He gave Himself in utter love and sacrifice for others. He was absolutely fearless, and He struggled to the end. When He was nailed to the Cross and made to suffer unspeakable pain, He faced the ordeal with calm and fortitude. His loyalty to His cause and to His sense of duty, and His magnanimity to friends and associates were virtues as precious as they are difficult to attain. See Jesus lifted on the cross; He still looks to Heaven and pleads with God to forgive His enemies for their ignorance. What marvelous Love! Jesus' revolutionary spirit came from His great love for humanity.

If we compare the situation in China during the past few centuries when our national life degenerated under Manchu domination, we find that it was very similar to that occurring among the Jews under the rule of Rome. Our late leader, Dr. Sun Yat-sen, with his universal sympathy for all oppressed and his profound understanding of Jesus' revolutionary spirit of love and sacrifice, carried on his revolutionary work for forty years and brought about at last the liberation of the Chinese people. In 1911 he overthrew the autocratic Manchu Dynasty and established the Republic of China, thereby completing his mission of national revolution.

As I look at the future of our Revolution I am convinced that we cannot truly regenerate our nation unless we have the spirit—the revolutionary spirit—of struggle and sacrifice such as we find in Jesus. I once said, "We will not abandon peace until all hope of peaceful settlement is gone; but when we reach the limit we will consider no sacrifice too costly." This, I believe, reflected Jesus' spirit. During the past few years, in addition to my regular duties, I have promoted several social movements. The best-known movement, and the one which has achieved some measure of success, is the New Life Movement. And yet I feel that this movement is apt to emphasize outward forms to the neglect of the inner substance, and to put more stress upon material than spiritual values. Where is the trouble? The answer is that many people are thinking only of new modes of living and not of a new quality of life. So I wish to give you this thought tonight: If we want to promote new ways of living, we must have not only a new spirit but also the quality of life that is inspired by the love and sacrificial purpose of Jesus.

In conclusion, Jesus' spirit is positive, sacrificial, sure, true, progressive, inspiring, and always revolutionary. We observe Easter this year at a time of grave national peril. Easter testifies to the immortality of Jesus' spirit. We who share the Christian faith should treasure the Easter message of rebirth and resurrection. We should follow Jesus' way of sacrifice. We should take His life as our example, His spirit as our spirit, His life as our life. Let us march together toward the Cross, for the regeneration of our nation and for the realization of everlasting peace on earth.

5. ANGER, IRONY, AND DISCOURAGE-MENT IN CHINA'S GREATEST MODERN WRITER

LU HSÜN (1881–1936) is perhaps the most gifted writer modern China has produced. Born in a small town on the Yangtze River into a traditional Chinese family, Lu Hsün grew to be one of the most sensitive and articulate voices of the Chinese literary revolution.

Like so many other young Chinese students in 1902, Lu Hsün went to Tokyo to study medicine. During the Russo-Japanese War in 1905, he saw a film showing a Chinese youth, having been accused of spying for the Russians, being bound for execution by Japanese soldiers while a crowd of apathetic helpless Chinese stood by watching. Lu Hsün tells us it was this incident that convinced him that what was needed to save China was not medicine but an entire transformation of national outlook. Lu Hsün abandoned medicine and took up writing.

Until his death in 1936, Lu Hsün wrote fitfully. Sometimes overcome by discouragement and a sense of hopelessness he would stop writing, only to begin again after a short time. As the years passed, he lost much of the optimism he had had during the May Fourth Movement. His writing began to be permeated with a deep sense of despair over China's inability to resurrect herself—a lament that was to became a leitmotif in his writing. Seeing the Chinese people's traditional subservience and apathy as the root of his country's backwardness, he exhorted his countrymen time and time again to stand up, move out from under the pall of Chinese tradition, and step forward with confidence and self-respect. He wrote endlessly, criticizing the small-minded provincialism which still bound China to the past. Lu Hsün portrayed the world of greedy officials and pompous gentry as barbaric and fit only for madmen. It was with great bitterness that he watched the Kuomintang clamp down on intellectual freedom after the purge in 1927. At the same time he deplored the left wing's voluntary dogmatic censorship. "Good literary works," he said, "are never composed in accordance with others' orders."

Discouraged with his own generation, he turned hopefully to China's youth, looking to the new generation in hope that they might at last destroy the shackles binding China to her backwardness. He ends one piece with the final plea, "Save the children!" He concludes one of the following selections by lamenting, "Vast territory, abundant resources, and a great population—with such excellent materials are we able only to go around in circles?"

It was Lu Hsün's inability to disassociate himself from the tragedy of twentieth-century China that, more than anything else, made him a great writer. Sometimes he was satirical, sometimes cynical, but always he was sincere and disturbed. China, like the famous Ah Q, humiliated and saddened Lu Hsün. But try as he would, he could never bring himself to make the final retreat (and he frequently tried) into his own private world and forget China's tragedy. In many ways Lu Hsün himself was a tragic figure caught up in an impossible undertaking. Repelled by the authoritarian Kuomintang, he was driven farther and farther to the left, finally joining the League of Left Wing Writers. But this was a period before Communism in China had shown its own authoritarianism. One senses that Lu Hsün—too ardent a defender of human liberty—would have had difficulty resigning himself to Communism as it later developed, for all ideologies repelled him. He chose the lonely path between the two hostile camps around which China was slowly polarizing. Perhaps it was fortunate that he died when he did, thus sparing himself the anguish of later years.

The following short selections are taken from a translation of the *Selected Works of Lu Hsün,* published in Communist China.

LU HSÜN *
From *Selected Works*

THE GREAT WALL

Our wonderful Great Wall!

This engineering feat has left its mark on the map, and is probably known to everyone with any education the whole world over.

Actually, all it has ever done is work many conscripts to death—it never kept out the Huns. Now it is merely an ancient relic, but its final ruin will not take place for a while, and it may even be preserved.

I am always conscious of being surrounded by a Great Wall. The stonework consists of old bricks reinforced at a later date by new bricks. These have combined to make a wall that hems us in.

When shall we stop reinforcing the Great Wall with new bricks?

A curse on this wonderful Great Wall!

SUDDEN NOTIONS

I used to believe the statements that the twenty-four dynastic histories were simply "records of mutual slaughter" or "family histories of rulers." Later, when I read them for myself, I realized this was a fallacy.

All these histories portray the soul of China and indicate what the country's future will be, but the truth is buried so deep in flowery phrases and nonsense it is very hard to grasp it; just as, when the moon shines through thick foliage onto moss, only

* *Selected Works of Lu Hsün* (Peking: Foreign Languages Press, 1960), V, 43, 107–109, 151; III, 281–282, 287–288, 311–312; IV, 201–202, 260–261.

checkered shadows can be seen. If we read unofficial records and anecdotes, though, we can understand more easily, for here at least the writers did not have to put on the airs of official historians.

The Chin and Han Dynasties are too far from us and too different to be worth discussing. Few records were written in the Yuan Dynasty. But most of the annals of the Tang, Sung, and Ming Dynasties have come down to us. And if we compare the events recorded during the Five Dynasties period or the Southern Sung Dynasty and the end of the Ming Dynasty with modern conditions, it is amazing how alike they are. It seems as if China alone is untouched by the passage of time. The Chinese Republic today is still the China of those earlier ages.

If we compare our era with the end of the Ming Dynasty, our China is not so corrupt, disrupted, cruel or despotic—we have not yet reached the limit.

But neither did the corruption and disruption of the last years of the Ming Dynasty reach the limit, for Li Tzu-cheng and Chang Hsien-chung rebelled. And neither did their cruelty and despotism reach the limit, for the Manchu troops entered China.

Can it be that "national character" is so difficult to change? If so, we can more or less guess what our fate will be. As is so often said, "It will be the same old story."

Some people are really clever: they never argue with the ancients, or query ancient rules. Whatever the ancients have done, we modern men can do. And to defend the ancients is to defend ourselves. Besides, as the "glorious descendants of a divine race," how dare we not follow in our forebears' footsteps?

Luckily no one can say for certain that the national character will never change. And though this uncertainty means that we face the threat of annihilation—something we have never experienced—we can also hope for a national revival, which is equally unprecedented. This may be of some comfort to reformers.

But even this slight comfort may be cancelled by the pens of those who boast of the ancient culture, drowned by the words of those who slander the modern culture, or wiped out by the deeds of those who pose as exponents of the modern culture. For "it will be the same old story."

Actually, all these men belong to one type: they are all clever people, who know that even if China collapses they will not suffer, for they can always adapt themselves to circumstances. If anybody doubts this let him read the essays in praise of the Manchus' military prowess written in the Ch'ing Dynasty by Chinese, and filled with such terms as "our great forces" and "our army." Who could imagine that this was the army that had conquered us? One would be led to suppose that the Chinese had marched to wipe out some corrupt barbarians.

But since such men always come out on top, presumably they will never die out. In China, they are the best fitted to survive; and, so long as they survive, China will never cease having repetitions of her former fate.

"Vast territory, abundant resources, and a great population" —with such excellent material, are we able only to go round and round in circles?

THE SECRET OF BEING A JOKER

Kierkegaard is a Dane with a gloomy outlook on life, whose works always breathe indignation. But he says some amusing things too, as in the passage below:

> A theatre catches fire. The clown steps to the front of the stage to announce it to the audience, who think it a joke and applaud. Then the clown announces again that there is a fire, but they roar with laughter and clap more loudly than ever. No doubt the world will end amid the general applause of these laughter-loving people who take everything as a joke.

What amuses me, however, is not this passage alone, but the way it reminds me of these jokers' cunning. When there is work to be done, they help out. When their masters are bent on crime, they become accomplices. But they help in such a way that in case of bloodshed no bloodstain is found on them, nor any smell of blood.

For instance, if something is serious and everyone is taking it seriously, the joker appears as a clown and makes the thing

look funny, or exaggerates some irrelevant aspects of it to dis-
tract attention. This is known as "playing the fool." If murder
has been done, he describes the scene of the crime and the hard
work of the detectives. If a woman has been killed, so much the
better: he can refer to her as "the lovely corpse" or introduce
her diary. If it is an assassination, he tells the life story of the
victim, relates his love affairs and the anecdotes about him. . . .
Passions are bound to cool down eventually, but cold water—
or to be more refined, "green tea"—will speed up the cooling-off
process. Then this fellow playing the fool becomes a man of
letters.

If a serious alarm is raised before men have grown completely apathetic, of course that is bad for the murderer. But then
the joker can play the fool again, cracking jokes and making faces
on one side, so that the man who has raised the alarm looks
like a clown himself to everyone, and his warnings sound laugh-
able. The joker shrinks and shivers to show how rich and
mighty the other is. He bows and sighs to show the other's
pride. Then the man who raised the alarm is considered a hypo-
crite. Luckily most of these jokers are men: otherwise they
could accuse the one who gives the warning of attempted se-
duction, make public a great many indecent details, and finally
pretend to kill themselves for shame. When there are jokers all
around, the most serious talk loses its force, and amid the suspicion and laughter an end is made of everything unfavorable
to the murderer. This time the joker appears as a moralist.

When there are no incidents of this kind, jokers collect tittle-
tattle for the newspaper supplements every week or ten days
with which to stuff readers' heads. After reading this for six
months or a year, your mind is stocked with stories of how a
certain great man plays mahjong or a certain film star sneezes.
This is naturally quite amusing. But an end will also be made of
the world amid the laughter of these laughter-loving people.

RANDOM THOUGHTS—MURDERERS OF THE PRESENT

Cultured gentlemen say, "The vernacular is vulgar and low,
beneath the contempt of the discerning."

All that illiterates in China can do is speak, so of course they are "vulgar and low." Men like myself, "because they are unlettered, are for the vernacular in order to hide their own ignorance." We are vulgar and low as well—that goes without saying. The sad thing is that those cultured gentlemen cannot be like that waiter in the *Flowers in the Mirror* who remained cultured all the time, using the classical language to describe two pots of wine or a plate of sweetmeats. They can show their lofty, ancient character only in their classical essays, but still talk in the vulgar, low vernacular. All the sounds uttered by China's four hundred millions are "beneath contempt." This is truly lamentable.

Not content to be mortals, they want to be immortal. Living on earth, they want to go up to heaven. Modern men, breathing modern air, they want to ram moribund Confucian morality and a dead language down people's throats—what an insult to the present! These are "murderers of the present." And by murdering the present, they are murdering the future too.

But the future belongs to our descendants.

ON BATS

Men generally dislike creatures that come out at night, probably because they do not sleep as human beings do, and it is to be feared they may observe secrets while men slumber soundly or stir in the darkness.

But though the bat also flies by night, it has a good reputation in China. Not because it preys on mosquitoes and is a friend of man, but more on account of its name which has the same sound as the Chinese word for "good fortune." It is thanks entirely to this that its not too distinguished features appear in paintings. Another reason is that the Chinese have always wanted to fly and imagined other creatures as flying too. Taoist priests want to take wing to heaven, emperors to soar up as immortals, lovers to become birds which flit in pairs, and sufferers to fly from their misery. The thought of "winged tigers" makes men shiver with fear, but when money flies their way they fairly beam. As the flying machines invented by Mo Tzu are lost, we have to raise funds to buy airplanes from abroad now. This is not strange in the least for we laid too much stress in the past on spiritual culture—compelled to by circumstances, for the best of reasons. But though we cannot actually fly, we can do so in imagination; so when we see creatures like rats with wings, we are not surprised. And famous writers even use them as themes for poems, and compose such fine lines as: "At dusk I reach the temple where bats are flying."

The Westerners are not so high-minded or big-hearted. They do not like bats. If we look for the reason, I think Aesop is probably to blame. In his fables we read that when the birds and beasts held their meetings, the bat went to the beasts and was turned away because he had wings; then he went to the birds and was turned away again, because he had four legs. In fact, because he had no proper stand at all, everyone dislikes him as a fence sitter.

In China recently we have picked up some old foreign allusions too, and sometimes make fun of the bat ourselves. But though such fables are pleasant, coming from Aesop, who lived in a time when zoölogy was in its infancy, it is different today when even a child in primary school knows quite well what species whales or bats belong to. If a man still takes these old Greek fables seriously, it simply shows that his knowledge is on a par with that of the ladies and gentlemen who took part in those meetings in Aesop's time.

Professor Liang Shih-chiu, who thinks galoshes are a cross between straw sandals and leather shoes, has a similar mental level. Had he lived in ancient Greece, he might have been second only to Aesop; but today, unfortunately, he is born too late.

ANOTHER FOLK TALE

One morning, twenty-one days later, a cross-examination was held in the police station. In a small dark room sat two officials, one on the right, the other on the left. The one on the right had on a Chinese jacket, the one on the left a Western suit. This latter was the optimist who denied that in this world man eats man. He was here to take down the deposition. Policemen, shouting and swearing, dragged in an eighteen-year-old student. His face pale, his clothes dirty, he stood there before them. The Chinese Jacket, having asked his name, age, and birthplace, demanded: "Are you a member of the woodcut club?"

"Yes."

"Who heads it?"

"The chairman is Ch———. The vice-chairman H———."

"Where are they now?"

"I don't know—they were both expelled."

"Why did you try to stir up trouble in your school?"

"What! . . ." The boy exclaimed in suprise.

"H'm!" The Chinese Jacket showed him a woodcut. "Did you do this?"

"Yes."

"Who is it?"

"A writer."

"What's his name?"

"Lunacharsky."

"Is he a writer? What country does he belong to?"

"I don't know." To save himself, the boy lied.

"You don't know? Don't try to deceive me. Isn't he Russian? Isn't he obviously a Red Army officer? I've seen his photograph in a history of the Russian Revolution. Can you deny that?"

"It's not true!" At this heavy blow, the boy cried out in despair.

"This is only to be expected. As a proletarian artist, you would naturally make the portrait of a Red Army officer."

"No. . . . I tell you I never. . . ."

"Don't argue. Don't be so stubborn. We know quite well that life is hard for you in the police station. You must make a clean breast of things so that we can send you to court for sentencing—conditions are much better in jail."

The boy said nothing. He knew that speech or silence were equally useless.

"Speak up!" The Chinese Jacket sniggered. "Are you C.P. or C.Y. [Communist Party, or Communist Youth League]?"

"Neither! I don't know what you mean!"

"So you can make a portrait of a Red Army officer but don't

understand C.P. and C.Y.? So young yet so cunning. Out!" As he waved one hand in dismissal, a policeman with the skill of long practice dragged the boy away.

I must apologize if this doesn't read like a folk tale any more. But if I don't call it a folk tale, what can I call it? The strange thing is that I can tell you when this happened. It was in 1932.

"TRUST TO HEAVEN FOR FOOD"

"Trust to Heaven for food" is a good old Chinese maxim. In the middle of the Ch'ing Dynasty, a picture entitled "Trust to Heaven" was engraved on a stone tablet. And in the early days of our republic Mr. Lu Jun-hsiang, who had come first in the palace examination, drew a picture of a big character "Heaven" with an old man leaning against it, eating from a rice bowl. Reprints were made of this, and those who believe in Heaven or love the bizarre may still possess copies.

And all of us are putting this theory into practice, the only difference from the picture being that we have no rice bowls. At all events, half this theory is being carried out.

Last month we heard the clamor: "Drought is inevitable this year." Now the rainy season has started and there has been steady rain for more than ten days, as indeed there is every year; but although there have been no great storms, there are floods on all sides. The few trees we planted on the tree-planting festival are not enough to win back the favor of Heaven. Gone are the good old days of Yao and Shun when "every five days a strong wind blew, every ten days it rained." So we trust to Heaven but have nothing to eat, which probably never occurred to the believers. After all, the popular primer *Yu-hsüeh-chiung-lin* is right when it says: "Things light and pure float upwards to become heaven." If heaven is light, pure and floating, how can we lean on it?

Some words that were true in ancient times seem now to have become lies. I fancy it was a Westerner who said that the poor of this world possess nothing but sunshine, air, and water. Yet this does not apply to those who live in Shanghai: those who toil with hand and brain are shut up all day where they have neither sunshine nor fresh air, while those who cannot afford to have tap water laid on cannot drink pure water either. The papers often say: "Recently the weather has been abnormal and epidemics have broken out." This is not because the weather has been abnormal. Heaven has no voice and must suffer calumny in silence.

But if we go on trusting to "Heaven" we shall not survive as "Men." Dwellers in the desert fight more fiercely over a pool of water than our young men over a sweetheart: they fight to the death, not content with merely writing a poem of lament. Didn't that Westerner Dr. Aurel Stein unearth many antiques from the sands of Tunhuang? That was once a flourishing city, but as a result of trusting to Heaven it was swallowed up by sand. Of course, trusting to Heaven is a good way to manufacture relics for the future. But for purposes of living it is not too good.

This leads up to the subject of conquering Nature, but this problem is too remote to be touched on as yet.

SAND

Of late our literati have kept lamenting that the Chinese are a dish of loose sand and quite hopeless, shifting the blame for our troubles to the people as a whole. In fact this is unfair to most Chinese. Though the common people do not study and may not have a clear judgment, they are quite capable of banding together over something which they know affects their interests. The old methods were public penances, insurrection and revolt; while today they still use petitions and similar tactics. If they are like sand, it is because their rulers have made them so. In classical parlance, they are "well-governed."

Is there no sand, then, in China? There certainly is. Not the common people but their rulers, great and small.

We often hear the expression "official promotion and a fortune." In fact the two are not synonymous. Men want official promotion in order to make a fortune; the first is the way to the second. So though high officials rely on the central government, they are not loyal to it. Though small officials rely on the local yamen, they do not love or defend it. The superior may issue an order for honest dealing, but the petty bureaucrats will pay no attention, counteracting this command with false reports. They are all self-centered, self-seeking grains of sand, out to better themselves while they can; and each particle is an emperor, who lords it over others whenever he can. "Tsar" has been translated into Chinese as *"sha-huang"* or "sand-emperor," and that is the most appropriate title for this lot. Where do their fortunes come from? They squeeze them out of the common people. If the common people were to band together, their fortunes would be hard to make; so obviously they must do all they can to change the country into loose sand. Since the people are ruled by these sand-emperors, the whole of China is now "a dish of loose sand."

But beyond the sandy desert are men who band together and walk in as if to "an uninhabited land."

This means a big change for the desert. For such times, the ancients had two extremely apt comparisons: the chiefs become apes and cranes, the common people insects and sand. The rulers take off into the blue like white cranes, or climb up trees like monkeys. "When the tree falls the monkeys scatter." But as there are other trees, they will not come to grief. The people are left below as ants and dirt, though, to be trampled underfoot or killed. If they cannot oppose the sand-emperors, how can they stand up to the sand-emperors' conqueror?

At such a time, however, there is always someone to flourish a quill or wag a reproving tongue. Then the common people are catechized severely:

"What are you going to do now?"

"What are you going to do in future?"

They suddenly remember the people and, keeping silent on all other matters, demand that the people save the situation. This is like asking a man bound hand and foot to catch a robber.

But this is precisely the final act of the sand-emperor's good government, the last gasp of apes and cranes, the end of self-adulation and self-betterment, the inevitable consummation.

II. War: Revolt and Invasion: *1930s and 1940s*

૯⑤ If Chiang Kai-shek thought that the April 1927 purge of the Communists would finally inaugurate an era of peace for China, he was mistaken. From 1927 until 1949 war was an inescapable part of Chinese life. Armies, foreign and Chinese, controlled the fate of China. We have called this section revolt and invasion: during this period China was faced with constant invasion from without, and with an intensifying revolt within. Our selections will examine the dual streams of revolt and invasion.

From 1927 to 1936 Chiang pressed his anti-Communist-bandit extermination campaigns forward with relentless determination, mobilizing hundreds of thousands of troops in a series of massive and costly attempts to destroy the Red Army in the Kiangsi-Hunan regions. Chiang was convinced that until the last Communist had been exterminated, his power would not be secure.

Invasion began in 1931 with the Japanese occupation of Manchuria and the ensuing series of encroachments which finally led to the long and disastrous Sino-Japanese War. It was not until fifteen years later that the Japanese occupation army surrendered and left Chinese soil, but their departure did not resolve China's internal conflict. No sooner had they laid down their arms when the smoldering rivalry between the Communists and the Nationalists erupted with renewed fury, plunging the war-weary Chinese people into five more years of destruction and deprivation.

Chiang Kai-shek's break with the Communists in 1927 had a decisive influence on the future of the entire Communist movement in China. Driven from the cities, the center of the movement shifted to the newly established soviet areas of the inland hills. But the shift was more than geographic: an almost complete change in leadership went hand in hand with a sharp change in Communist revolutionary practice. Old urban revolutionaries like Ch'en Tu-hsiu and Li Li-san, were replaced by advocates of peasant revolution, like Mao Tse-tung and Chu Teh. As we now know, the rise of Mao Tse-tung and his ideas radically changed the face of Chinese Communism.

The Kiangsi Period, as the years from 1927 until the Long March in 1934 came to be known, were years of hardship and struggle for the Communists. Landlocked and constantly under siege from without, the Communists had no choice but to turn to the peasant for support. Mao described the peasant movement as a "colossal event which will rise like a tornado or a tempest, a force so extraordinarily swift and violent that no power, however great, will be able to suppress it"—and it was from the ranks of the common peasant that Mao built the first Red Army. In spite of the mistakes, excesses, and near-fatal failures, Mao laid the groundwork for his future success.

The Kiangsi Period ended with the Long March in 1934. The Communists were almost totally exterminated, and the pursuing Kuomintang troops thought that final victory was within their grasp. But the very fact that Mao and his followers survived turned the Long March into a Communist victory. The bravery and perseverance exhibited on the march became a Chinese legend of heroism and invincibility.

The survivors of the Long March settled at last in Shensi province deep in Northwestern China. These years are known as the Yenan Period, named after the new Communist capital where the Communists developed modern Chinese Communism's organizational and ideological foundations. This period of careful attention to the organization of party, army, and villages contrasted sharply with the previous Kiangsi Period, with its violent peasant jacqueries, disorganized Party, and old-fashioned rebel armies. The Communists took root in their isolated stronghold and built a new movement from the bottom up, block by block. Ideological unity and Party solidarity were their objectives.

The Communists emerged from Yenan with a new unity and sense of direction. By 1945 they controlled 250,000 square miles of territory, had a Party membership of some 1,200,000, and an army roughly of 1,000,000 regular and guerrilla troops. Though still greatly inferior to the Kuomintang armies in num-

bers and weaponry, the Communists were a formidable force
on the eve of the Chinese Civil War.

The second theme of this section is the Japanese invasion.
After 1931, when the Japanese moved into Manchuria and set
up the puppet Manchukuo government, it became increasingly
obvious that Japan was making a bid for complete domination
of China; in subsequent years she was to move persistently
southward until most of Northern China was under her control.
The Japanese invasion left Chiang Kai-shek in an awkward
position. He was reluctant to get involved with Japan before
resolving the Communist problem and unifying the country
behind the Kuomintang, but Chiang's strategy, unfortunately,
tended to disunite rather than unite China. He alienated a large
and important group of potential supporters by his dogged insistence that Chinese fight Chinese at a time when the nation
was in peril of being overrun by Japan.

After the Sian Incident in 1937 the Kuomintang finally
took up the standard against the Japanese, but by this time it
had lost much of the initiative in galvanizing anti-Japanese resentment into a Kuomintang-led resistance movement. Chiang's
troops were handed defeat after defeat in the late 1930s until
finally they were driven up the Yangtze to a temporary capital
at Chungking. As the war continued, Chiang became increasingly
reluctant to commit troops to battle. Hampered by a lack
of equipment, incomplete control over the troops under his command, and a penchant for saving his powder for use against the
Communists, Chiang was a less than aggressive combatant.
American entry into the war after Pearl Harbor only increased
his reluctance to fight. Many Nationalist commanders seemed to
have concluded that since the United States would probably win
the war in the end, there was little point in committing their men
to combat, an attitude which proved to be the source of much
friction and ill will between the Americans and the Chinese, as
we shall see in the following selections.

There is no doubt that Japanese aggression dealt China a
devastating blow. But had Chiang parried the blow with greater
acumen and daring, he could have ridden it to higher ground
rather than allow it to become his undoing.

In 1945 the Japanese surrendered. For the first time in almost a decade China was free from foreign invaders, but there was little cause for rejoicing, for as soon as the Japanese laid down their arms, the old rivalry between the Nationalists and the Communists flared up. For a while during the war, some cooperation between the two sides had been achieved. But with the defeat of their common enemy, the United Front collapsed. As a race to reoccupy Japanese-held areas ensued, the thin veneer of wartime cooperation dissolved into hostile competition. The Nationalists, aided by an American air- and sealift, rushed troops to the important Northern Chinese and Manchurian urban centers. The Communists, on foot, moved into the countryside surrounding the cities. Only after they were sure of their support in the countryside did they move on the cities and deliver the final blow to the isolated Nationalists. While Chiang's troops sat in their urban prisons and waited, Mao's troops swept across the land, organizing villages, denouncing the Nationalists, and unleashing one of the most brutal but effective anti-landlord campaigns in history. The Red Army remained highly mobile, maintained excellent morale, and won strong popular support. Chiang's army, weakened by overextension, was generally immobile, in poor spirits, and almost completely divorced from the people.

The United States government was committed to Chiang's Nationalist regime, of course. After the Japanese surrender the United States government continued to pour aid into China, but as the Civil War raged on, it became increasingly obvious to Washington that much of this aid was being used for personal gain or wasted, or was ending up in Communist hands. The United States was placed in an unenviable position, allied as it was to a shabby regime which was being handed one defeat after another. Conservative critics thundered for more aid and demanded that China be "saved." The question confronting the Administration was: Could China be saved, short of dispatching massive American troop reinforcements? After sending numerous fact-finding missions to China, the State Department concluded that, given the level of corruption, incompetence, and lack of popular support for the Nationalists, it was not within America's power to prevent the "loss" of China.

The Communist takeover of China set off a monumental debate in the United States. The government was accused of having "sold out" to the Communists, but defenders of the government's position maintained that the United States had done everything possible to help Chiang win the Civil War. Was it within the power of the United States to prevent the "loss of China" after World War II?

We hope that the following selections, representing both sides of the arguments, will help the reader resolve this debate in his own mind.

1. THE JAPANESE BEGIN TO MARCH
🌀 The Grand Plan for Conquest

WE MUST mention at the outset that the authenticity of the following selection, the Tanaka Memorial, is questionable, but whether or not it is an authentic document actually written by Baron Tanaka and presented to the Japanese Emperor in July 1927 is irrelevant. The Chinese claim to have obtained a copy shortly after it was supposed to have been written, and they disseminated it widely throughout China as proof of Japanese aggressive intention. The Chinese believed it to be authentic. As such, it had a profound influence on Chinese and world opinion. The Japanese could disclaim it as a forgery, but they could not disclaim their history of encroachment on China, nor could they deny that the substance of the Tanaka Memorial had been set forth time and time again by Baron Tanaka and other members of the militarist faction.

Japanese interest in a foothold on the China mainland antedates the turn of the century. Ever since the Sino-Japanese War [see Volume I] in 1895, after which China was forced to cede Korea, Formosa, the Pescadores, and the Liaotung Peninsula, Japan had designs on China. In 1904–1905 Japan again went to war, this time with Russia, over a conflict of interest in Korea and Manchuria. During World War I the Japanese took another step to establish themselves in China. Conveniently entering the war on the Allied side, they moved into the German concessions on Shantung. In 1915 Japan presented China with the Twenty-one Demands, calling upon her in effect to abdicate her own sovereignty. Unfortunately, China was too weak to resist the endless incursions from her Asiatic neighbors, and the Western Powers, pledged to defend the Open Door in China, were too deeply embroiled in their own problems to lend any assistance. China stood alone.

By 1927 Chiang Kai-shek's Northern March was well under way. Since China appeared to be on the verge of unification, this was perhaps the last moment, concluded Baron Tanaka and the militarist faction, for Japan to move on a still divided China. In 1928 young Japanese officers, fearing growing Chinese influence in Manchuria, blew up the train of the pro-Kuomintang warlord Chang Tso-lin. In 1931, without the authorization of the Japanese Civil Government, they trumped up the famous "Mukden Incident" and occupied Manchuria, and the next year they launched a bold attack on Shanghai. It became painfully clear that the Tanaka Memorial demands were being fulfilled although the main invasion did not come until 1937, when the Japanese finally moved into Peking and began their march south.

There are several points about the Tanaka Memorial to bear in mind. The Japanese people did not regard Japan's invasion of China as militarism for its own sake. Using a rationale similar to the Nazis' in Europe, there were many men in Japan who believed that their country's future depended on expansion. They contended that their small island nation would perish without the natural resources and markets offered by Manchuria and Mainland China. Expansion (*Lebensraum*) was a matter of life and death to the Japanese nation.

The Japanese were also deeply disturbed over the continued Communist threat in China. The militarist faction, which was gradually gaining the upper hand, was notoriously anti-Bolshevik. Chiang's inability to stamp out the stubborn Communists and the anti-Japanese agitation of left-leaning Chinese in the cities conjured up the image of a China that might one day go Red and ally itself with Russia against Japan.

These reasons are intended not to excuse the Japanese, but merely to show that, from where they stood, occupation of the Chinese mainland seemed to be essential. They did not see the occupation of Asia as the mere sport of a few archetypal Fascist villains. Reasonably or unreasonably, Japan believed her future to be bound inextricably to China, and she hoped that by controlling China, she could control her own destiny.

PREMIER TANAKA *

The Tanaka Memorial

MEMORIAL PRESENTED TO THE EMPEROR OF
JAPAN ON JULY, 25, 1927, OUTLINING
THE POSITIVE POLICY IN MANCHURIA

Since the European War, Japan's political as well as economic
interests have been in an unsettled condition. This is due to the
fact that we have failed to take advantage of our special
privileges in Manchuria and Mongolia and fully to realize our
acquired rights. But upon my appointment as premier, I was
instructed to guard our interests in this region and watch for
opportunities for further expansion. Such injunctions one cannot
take lightly. Ever since I advocated a positive policy toward
Manchuria and Mongolia as a common citizen, I have longed
for its realization. So in order that we may lay plans for the
colonization of the Far East and the development of our new
continental empire, a special conference was held from June 27th
to July 7th lasting in all eleven days. It was attended by all the
civil and military officers connected with Manchuria and Mongolia, whose discussions result in the following resolutions. These
we respectfully submit to Your Majesty for consideration.

GENERAL CONSIDERATIONS

The term Manchuria and Mongolia includes the provinces Feng-
tien, Kirin, Heilungkiang and Outer and Inner Mongolia. It
extends an area of seventy-four thousand square miles, having a
population of twenty-eight million people. The territory is more

* Carl Crow, *Japan's Dream of World Empire: The Tanaka Memorial* (New
York: Harper and Brothers, 1942), pp. 22–33.

than three times as large as our own empire not counting Korea and Formosa, but it is inhabited by only one third as many people. The attractiveness of the land does not arise from the scarcity of population alone; its wealth of forestry, minerals, and agricultural products is also unrivaled elsewhere in the world. In order to exploit these resources for the perpetuation of our national glory, we created especially the South Manchuria Railway Company.

The total investment involved in our undertakings in railways, shipping, mining, forestry, steel manufacture, agriculture, and in cattle raising, as schemes pretending to be mutually beneficial to China and Japan, amount to no less than 440,000,000 yen. It is veritably the largest single investment and the strongest organization of our country. Although nominally the enterprise is under the joint ownership of the government and the people, in reality the government has complete power and authority. Insofar as the South Manchuria Railway is empowered to undertake diplomatic, police, and ordinary administrative functions so that it may carry out our imperialistic policies, the company forms a peculiar organization which has exactly the same powers as the Governor-General of Korea. This fact alone is sufficient to indicate the immense interests we have in Manchuria and Mongolia. Consequently the policies toward this country of successive administrations since Meiji are all based on his injunctions, elaborating and continuously completing the development of the new continental empire in order to further the advance of our national glory and prosperity for countless generations to come.

Unfortunately, since the European War there have been constant changes in diplomatic as well as domestic affairs. The authorities of the Three Eastern Provinces are also awakened and gradually work toward reconstruction and industrial development, following our example. Their progress is astonishing. It has affected the spread of our influence in a most serious way, and has put us to so many disadvantages that the dealings with Manchuria and Mongolia of successive governments have resulted in failure. Furthermore, the restrictions of the Nine Power Treaty signed at the Washington Conference have reduced our special rights and privileges in Manchuria and Mongolia to such an extent that there is no freedom left for us. The very existence of our country is endangered.

Unless these obstacles are removed, our national existence will be insecure and our national strength will not develop. Moreover, the resources of wealth are congregated in North Manchuria. If we do not have the right of way here, it is obvious that we shall not be able to tap the riches of this country. Even the resources of South Manchuria which we won by the Russo-Japanese War will also be greatly restricted by the Nine Power Treaty. The result is that while our people cannot migrate into Manchuria as they please, the Chinese are flowing in as a flood. Hordes of them move into the Three Eastern Provinces every year, numbering in the neighborhood of several millions. They have jeopardized our acquired rights in Manchuria and Mongolia to such an extent that our annual surplus population of eight hundred thousand have no place to seek refuge. In view of this we have to admit our failure in trying to effect a balance between our population and food supply. If we do not devise plans to check the influx of Chinese immigrants immediately, in five years' time the number of Chinese will exceed six million. Then we shall be confronted with greater difficulties in Manchuria and Mongolia.

It will be recalled that when the Nine Power Treaty was signed which restricted our movements in Manchuria and Mongolia, public opinion was greatly aroused. The late Emperor Taisho called a conference of Yamagata and other high officers of the army and navy to find a way to counteract this new engagement. I was sent to Europe and America to ascertain secretly the attitude of the important statesmen toward it. They were all agreed that the Nine Power Treaty was initiated by the United States. The other powers which signed it were willing to see our influence increase in Manchuria and Mongolia in order that we may protect the interests of international trade and investments. This attitude I found out personally from the political leaders of England, France, and Italy. The sincerity of these expressions could be depended upon.

Unfortunately just as we were ready to carry out our policy and declare void the Nine Power Treaty with the approval of those whom I met on my trip, the Seiyukai Cabinet suddenly fell and our policy failed of fruition. It was indeed a great pity. After I had secretly exchanged views with the Powers regarding the development of Manchuria and Mongolia, I returned by way of Shanghai. At the wharf there a Chinese attempted to take my life. An American woman was hurt, but I escaped by the divine protection of my Emperors of the past. It seems that it was by divine will that I should assist Your Majesty to open a new era in the Far East and to develop the new continental Empire.

The Three Eastern Provinces are politically the imperfect spot in the Far East. For the sake of self-protection as well as the protection of others, Japan cannot remove the difficulties in Eastern Asia unless she adopts a policy of "Blood and Iron." But in carrying out this policy we have to face the United States which has been turned against us by China's policy of fighting poison with poison. In the future if we want to control China, we must first crush the United States just as in the past we had to fight in the Russo-Japanese War. But in order to conquer China we must first conquer Manchuria and Mongolia. In order to conquer the world, we must first conquer China. If we succeed in conquering China the rest of the Asiatic countries and the South Sea countries will fear us and surrender to us. Then the world will realize that Eastern Asia is ours and will not dare to violate our rights. This is the plan left to us by Emperor Meiji, the success of which is essential to our national existence.

The Nine Power Treaty is entirely an expression of the spirit of commercial rivalry. It was the intention of England and America to crush our influence in China with their power of wealth. The proposed reduction of armaments is nothing but a means to limit our military strength, making it impossible for us to conquer the vast territory of China. On the other hand, China's sources of wealth will be entirely at their disposal. It is merely a scheme by which England and America may defeat our plans. And yet the Minseito made the Nine Power Treaty the important thing and emphasized our *trade* rather than our *rights* in China.

This is a mistaken policy—a policy of national suicide. England can afford to talk about trade relations only because she has India and Australia to supply her with foodstuffs and other materials. So can America because South America and Canada are there to supply her needs. Their spare energy could be entirely devoted to developing trade in China to enrich themselves. But in Japan her food supply and raw materials decrease in proportion to her population. If we merely hope to develop trade, we shall eventually be defeated by England and America, who possess unsurpassable capitalistic power. In the end, we shall get nothing. A more dangerous factor is the fact that the people of China might someday wake up. Even during these years of internal strife, they can still toil patiently, and try to imitate and displace our goods so as to impair the development of our trade. When we remember that the Chinese are our principal customers, we must beware lest one day when China becomes unified and her industries become prosperous, Americans and Europeans will compete with us; our trade in China will be wrecked. Minseito's proposal to uphold the Nine Power Treaty and to adopt the policy of trade toward Manchuria is nothing less than a suicide policy.

After studying the present conditions and possibilities of our country, our best policy lies in the direction of taking positive steps to secure rights and privileges in Manchuria and Mongolia. These will enable us to develop our trade. This will not only forestall China's own industrial development, but also prevent the penetration of European Powers. This is the best policy possible!

The way to gain actual rights in Manchuria and Mongolia is to use this region as a base and under the pretense of trade and commerce penetrate the rest of China. Armed by the rights already secured we shall seize the resources all over the country. Having China's entire resources at our disposal we shall proceed to conquer India, the Archipelago, Asia Minor, Central Asia, and even Europe. But to get control of Manchuria and Mongolia is the first step if the Yamato race wishes to distinguish themselves on Continental Asia.

Final success belongs to the country having food supply; industrial prosperity belongs to the country having raw materials; the full growth of national strength belongs to the country having extensive territory. If we pursue a positive policy to enlarge our rights in Manchuria and China, all these prerequisites of a powerful nation will constitute no problem. Furthermore our surplus population of seven hundred thousand each year will also be taken care of.

If we want to inaugurate a new policy and secure the permanent prosperity of our empire, a positive policy toward Manchuria and Mongolia is the only way.

🏵 The First Attacks
in a Long War

THE JAPANESE set about dismembering China with a methodical persistence during the 1930s. After moving in Manchuria, the Japanese struck a lightning blow at Shanghai, and when asked to explain the attack, Admiral Shiosawa said, "The Imperial Navy, feeling extreme anxiety about the situation in Chapei [a section of Shanghai], where Japanese nationals reside in great numbers, has decided to send troops to this section for the enforcement of law and order in the area." This was the usual statement presaging the arrival of foreign gunboats off the treaty ports, except in this case the Japanese did have reason to fear for the safety of their nationals, for when news of the Japanese takeover in Manchuria reached Shanghai, anti-Japanese feeling swelled to new intensity.

The Japanese had not intended to become bogged down in a long, costly siege of Shanghai, but had hoped, rather, to take the city in a few days with a minimum of effort and publicity, but the Chinese resistance proved to be much stiffer than the Japanese had anticipated: the Chinese soldiers fought bravely and ably, dragging on the incident for several months until finally the Shanghai Armistice Agreement was signed. The Japanese agreed to retreat, and the Chinese agreed not to station troops in Shanghai and to curb some of the violent anti-Japanese sentiment rising throughout China.

The attack on Shanghai was only the beginning of a long and costly struggle destined to last for almost fifteen more years. The devastation wreaked on Shanghai was only a suggestion of the scorched-earth policy with which the Japanese later laid waste a large part of China.

The following selections are accounts of the Japanese at-

tack on Shanghai from two English-language newspapers in
China. Although they describe only one incident in a brutal
war, they are symbolic of the entire war. The Japanese in China,
like the Germans later in Europe, waged total war against civilians as well as soldiers. They believed that the terror of Japanese
bombs could crush the Chinese will to resist. They were wrong
in Shanghai as they would be wrong time and time again in later
years; they would eventually bomb Chungking day after day,
but were to reap only more hatred and stiffer resistance from the
Chinese.

K. N. LEI *
Japanese Occupy Shanghai; Woosung Forts Shelled

Following quickly on top of a proclamation by Rear Admiral
K. Shiosawa, Commander of the First Japanese Fleet in Chinese
waters, that he was determined on military action in Chapei,
despite the acceptance of the Japanese demands by General Wu
Teh-chen, the Mayor of Greater Shanghai, and the Japanese
Consul-General's assurance that the acceptance was considered
satisfactory "for the time being," Japanese marines at 11:10 last
night entered Chapei where, at the time of going to press, brisk
fighting was in progress.

The entry into Chapei came after the voluntary withdrawal
of most of the Chinese forces, apparently after a warning of action had been given to them by the commander of the Japanese
naval landing party. The first parties to enter Chinese territory
met with some resistance, and shots were exchanged. Later the
Japanese found large sections of the city deserted, shops empty,
and streets dead. Carried in motor trucks, the Japanese pursued
their occupation lighting their way with flares which cast a lurid
glow over the scene.

* K. N. Lei, *Information and Opinion Concerning the Japanese Invasion of
Manchuria and Shanghai from Sources Other than Chinese* (Shanghai: Shanghai Bar Association, 1932), pp. 140–141, 210–213, 266–270.

Sterner resistance was met as the invaders approached the Jukong Road area, the sounds of heavy machine-gun fire, punctuated by occasional burst of shell fire, indicating that larger bodies of troops were in conflict. Japanese hurried reinforcements to the scene in motor trucks, their men in the streets being harassed by snipers from the rooftops. From what could be gathered from the sounds—no one being allowed to approach near to the scene of the fighting—the resistance put up was of a spasmodic nature, and the Japanese seemed to be having things almost their own way.

BOMBARDMENT OF WOOSUNG

At 10:30 o'clock twelve Japanese warships commenced a bombardment of the Woosung forts. After ten minutes' firing, in which forty shells were fired by the Japanese warships, a lull in the fighting seemed to indicate that the forts had been silenced. The Japanese then prepared to land marines, but a recrudescence of shell fire at 12:25 A.M. carried the news that the Chinese resistance had not been completely crushed, as had at first been thought. No definite news of the result of the engagement could be got through to Shanghai last night, communications being in the utmost confusion. It was understood, however, that the superior Japanese armaments had taken their toll, and that the capture of the forts was simply a matter of time.

Admiral Shiosawa's proclamation, which came as a thunderbolt after the storm had apparently begun dying away, was immediately followed by another in which Admiral Shiosawa forbade "all meetings deemed as constituting a hindrance in the current situation"—a measure which, it was pointed out last night, will act as a curb not only upon unruly Chinese elements but also upon the fire-eating section of the Japanese community, to whom the decision announced earlier in the day by the Consul-General that the Chinese acceptance of his demands was satisfactory had come as a great disappointment.

Admiral Shiosawa, in his proclamation, gives as reasons for his contemplated action the urgent need for the protection of Japanese life and property within the Chinese areas. After emphasizing the anxiety felt by the Japanese Navy in this regard, Admiral Shiosawa concludes by expressing the hope that the Chinese authorities will "speedily withdraw the Chinese troops now stationed in Chapei and remove all hostile defenses in the area."

CHINESE WITHDRAWAL URGED

An English version of Admiral Shiosawa's proclamation follows:

General restlessness prevails in and outside the International Settlement in Shanghai and there are signs that the situation is being further aggravated. In view of this state of affairs, the Shanghai Municipal Council has proclaimed a State of Emergency in the Settlement and the military and naval forces of various countries have respectively taken their positions for the defense of the Settlement.

The Imperial Navy, feeling extreme anxiety about the situation in Chapei, where Japanese nationals reside in great numbers, have decided to send out troops to this section for the enforcement of law and order in the area.

In these circumstances, I earnestly hope that the Chinese authorities will speedily withdraw the Chinese troops now stationed in Chapei and remove all hostile defenses in the area.

It was explained in Japanese naval circles that the present action had been necessitated in order to give effective protection to Japanese nationals who reside in Chapei and other places adjacent to the North Szechuen Road, where the Japanese fear disorder and lawlessness due to the absence of effective control by the Chinese authorities and also because of the presence of a large number of undisciplined troops. . . .

Local Chinese Troops Show
Great Bravery

(*The China Weekly Review,* Shanghai, February 13, 1932)

Whatever the eventual outcome of the present war between China and Japan—it is war, nothing less, even though for political reasons neither side wishes to make a formal declaration —the battles around Shanghai will form a glorious page in Chinese history. The action of the Japanese Admiral in bombing an undefended town immediately after and despite the acceptance of humiliating terms imposed by him upon the Chinese is an act of perfidy not without parallel, but fortunately not very common. What the Japanese Admiral hoped to do was to walk through the Chinese in a few hours, occupy all the strategic points, grab Hongkew and hold it against all comers, and gloat over his action from the vantage point of a *fait accompli.* However, things didn't work out that way at all. A Japanese friend of ours who was a resident of Hongkew previous to the Japanese attack on the night of January 28 tells us that he was talking with some of the high Japanese naval authorities that very evening and happened to ask them whether it was better to move away from Hongkew or to remain. The Japanese naval people replied, "The Admiral tells us it will be all over in three hours. You just stay where you are." But this Japanese resident, together with nearly all the female residents of the district and a great many of the men, have had no confidence in the kind of protection that the Japanese naval authorities have been giving them and have long since removed from the district. Day after day the steamers from Shanghai to Japan have been crowded with Japanese refugees anxious to get away from this part of the world. A strange commentary indeed, on the oft-repeated statement of the Japanese authorities, particularly the naval authorities, that their object in acting as they did was to protect the Japanese residents of Shanghai!

In the end of course, unless by international action or as

a result of some other at present unforeseen cause, the fighting around Shanghai is suspended, the Japanese will probably be successful in their operations in the Shanghai district. But it has not been and will not be a walkover by any means. The Chinese troops in this district have shown not only bravery, but also military skill way beyond anything that foreign observers had expected of them. While they have for the most part been on the defensive, the Chinese have actually now and then assumed the offensive. The Chinese in recent years have had the advice of veteran German military advisers and their use of machine guns has been most skillful. Even the old mud forts at Woosung, which were equipped with nothing but obsolete heavy guns, which were easily demolished by the Japanese heavy-gun fire, are being held by the Chinese against terrific onslaughts by the Japanese, by the expert use of machine guns. Along the entire water front the Chinese have dug themselves in and built machine-gun nests and from these there was poured out a rain of lead that made the attack by the Japanese most difficult. The Japanese warships day after day continued to shell the forts, but the great majority of the shot only threw up lot of mud. It was at rare intervals that a shot hit one of the machine guns. The Japanese object of "scaring" the machine gunners away by heavy-gun fire didn't work at all. The Chinese took their chances and kept on peppering the approaching Japanese with deadly effect.

It is a most remarkable fact that the little rice-eating Chinese from the South have proved much better fighters than the heavy wheat-eating men of the North. But it is simply one more example of the adage, "Practice makes perfect." The Chinese troops in this part of China have had years of experience in fighting bandits—real ones, not the kind that the Japanese have told the world so much about in Manchuria—and, let it also be said, considerable experience in fighting the troops of rival factions. In many ways the Japanese are doing the Chinese a good turn—they are teaching the Chinese to unite, and they are doing it admirably at present.

There is no telling how long this war will last. It may be over within a few weeks through the Japanese being able to induce some one Chinese faction to turn traitor to the others. Or it may last for months or years. The Japanese may be able to

take all the main positions, but that is quite a different matter
from occupying the whole of China. If the Chinese stick
together, and there is no reason why they should not if they claim
to be a nation entitled to a seat in the family of nations, they can
eventually wear out the Japanese. Even now already the Japanese
populace is becoming restive at the cost of the expedition in
China. The boycott was bad enough, but now when the Japanese
military forces have been repulsed, temporarily at least, and
millions of yen are required to be raised for an expedition the net
result of which is problematical, the Japanese people are not so
enthusiastic in their hearts, nor very much disposed to make still
more sacrifices. When it comes to patient and continued resistance the Chinese are superior in fiber to the Japanese. . . .

In the Wake of Japanese Conquest

(*The China Weekly Review,* Shanghai, March 12, 1932)

Overhead the sky is clear and a blue of purity like early spring.
For a short distance, after I leave behind the torn fabric of
Chapei, there is a ribbon of farmlands and in some of them
peasants till the soil. There is no sound of the big guns that on
my last visit thundered near here. I find it difficult to believe
that over these fields have swept two armies engaged in the
business of slaughter: one a gray-clad army proud of a valorous
defense, in retreat but not vanquished; the other in olive drab,
marching into an alien land, following in the wake of a host of
deadly and destructive machines in which lies the secret of its
might.

In the distance clouds of dense smoke obscure the horizon.
Drawing closer I see on the road broken motor trucks, an
armored car split in half, a Red Cross van struck by an aerial
bomb. With a shudder I visualize the fate of those who rode
in these cars as passengers for death. Taziang appears ahead, or
what is left of it. After a bend in the road, where buses are
smashed and overturned, I enter the village and the smell of

burnt timbers mingles with that other acrid smell of roasting human flesh.

There is the sound of burning bamboo with sharp reports like rifle shots. Japanese civilians are methodically setting fire to those few outlying houses which managed to escape destruction by shells and bombs. In the road appears a huge crater and my driver swerves suddenly into a brief detour to avoid it. Scattered bits of clothing, some of them bloodstained, are noticed. A gang of coolies, mingled with farmers and villagers are at work at odd jobs for their new masters, and over them stand Japanese sentries with naked bayonets held horizontally. Those who lag get a prod in the loins which enlivens them like sluggish trained mice poked at through a cage.

Everywhere there is a desolate prospect. Vicious fires eat into what yet remains undamaged. Piles of debris are heaped ten, twenty feet high on the side of a brook which unperturbably ambles under a quaint arched bridge, miraculously unhurt. But it is a stream dark with bits of charred wood, broken household articles, pieces of garments. Here and there a swollen corpse floats slowly, or nestles against the bank as if reluctant to abandon the soil where it was rooted.

Under the spilt tile and brick, beneath the massed timbers thrust at gaunt angles, lie hundreds of buried men, women, and small girls and boys. Now and then I see legs or arms protruding from the gory mess—or worse, lying detached, or the prey of wolfish dogs. Living Chinese still move among this wreckage. They climb laboriously round the giant gaping holes left by 250-pound high-explosive bombs hurled by Japanese. These are forlorn people who no longer smile and they are on an earnest mission of search. No, not many of them are looters, as the Japanese tell you. The irony of it is patent: there is nothing left to loot. They are villagers looking for something to identify lost members of their family; or perhaps trying to find the spot where their home once stood.

Now I begin to understand the meaning of those naval communiqués. "Our naval planes," said Admiral Shimada, "succeeded in accomplishing their purpose with good effect in Taziang and other villages of the enemy." The "good effects" are nauseating and the anguish of these innocent people adequately describes the Admiral's purpose. . . .

THE ORDEAL OF DEATH

The invitation of the scene is for you to try to reconstruct, in mental image, a picture of the torture undergone by the brigade that held on here. Daily bombed from the air, strafed by machine guns fired from low-flying planes, shelled from destroyers scarcely a stone's throw distant, and raked by the enemy's batteries of heavy modern guns, these men stayed and few of them were left unbutchered. The ordeal here was many times worse than death. They lived for days in constant anticipation of being blown to atoms; they watched their comrades' arms and legs and heads severed or mangled. They suffered all the terror of death a hundred times before a fragment of shell finally cut them to pieces. I think it took great spirit and rare intrepidity for men to face such an assault, fighting with ineffective trench mortars, a few machine guns and rifles which were useless against the vastly superior heavy armament of the invading plunderers. . . .

I have seen enough. In my mind runs a panorama sharp with images of horror and carnage—at Woosung, at Kiangwan, at Chapei, Hongkew, Taziang, and other places. I think of the agony and loss and death of those thousands of simple and guiltless folk, massacred without cause, without warning, and by militarists who assure the world that they are not at war. The thought stirs in you a sense of profound contempt for the Japanese race, though you know that the Japanese people have had little to do with it. But that is the significance of the militarists' backward plunge into an abyss of barbarism: it has degraded the whole nation in the eyes of men. It has sabotaged international good will, respect, and confidence built up so carefully through years of effort. It means Japan's claim to civilized status has been put in forfeit. For a long time to come men of other races will look upon Japan as it regards the jungle tribesman—with frank distrust, suspicion, and piteous contempt. That is the immediate price of the Japanese military aberration at Shanghai.

2. THE REVOLUTION GOES INLAND
❧ The Kiangsi Soviet: A Communist and a Nationalist View

AFTER CHIANG KAI-SHEK'S White Terror of April 1927, the Chinese Communists went inland and turned to peasant revolution. The Central Committee remained in Shanghai for a few more years, but its weakness was demonstrated when the Sixth Party Congress of 1928 had to be held in Moscow. Labor unions, built up so laboriously by the Communists before 1927, were smashed or infiltrated by Kuomintang agents. By 1930 Communist activity in the coastal cities had been driven underground and almost completely halted.

When Mao Tse-tung linked up with Chu Teh in Hunan to form the Red Army, a peasant movement already existed. Except for Kwangtung, Hunan had more peasant associations than any other province. The violence of the Autumn Harvest Uprising of 1927 convinced Mao that the peasant was ready to fight as well as be organized. As the Red Army moved into the hills, more and more peasants joined its ranks. The real weapon, however, was not military but political. The proclamation of radical land reform aroused the age-old grievances of the peasantry against landlords, gentry, and officials. The peasants killed the landlords and seized their lands, and the peasant associations were transformed into "soviets" (*su-wei-ai* in Chinese) of soldiers, peasants, and workers which assumed administrative control over the Red areas.

Though Moscow was suspicious of this peasant Bolshevism and was not well-informed about what Mao Tse-tung was doing, Stalin nonetheless finally did bestow a lukewarm blessing on it. By 1930 the only remaining Chinese Communist movement was in the Kiangsi-Hunan region. In 1931 the Chinese Soviet Republic was proclaimed, with Mao Tse-tung as its Chairman. What was this new style of Communism? What went on in the struggling soviet areas? What were the problems they confronted? In the answers to these questions lie clues to an understanding of the genesis of the Chinese Communist movement.

The Kiangsi Period—a period of violence, mistakes, extreme hardship—is not looked back on with fondness by the Communists today. Chiang Kai-shek's successive extermination campaigns made constantly uncertain the very existence of the soviet areas. The Communists resisted with spears, old fowling pieces, and whatever weapons they could capture from Chiang and his German advisers, and out of this ceaseless struggle against the Kuomintang, Mao began to develop his now-renowed theory of guerrilla warfare: attack where and when the enemy is weak, retreat and conserve your strength when he is strong. The importance of the Red Army cannot be overemphasized during this period, for it was the heart and soul of the Communist movement, without which it would have perished in a few months. In the following selection Mao says that "the struggle in the border areas is exclusively military, both Party and masses have to be placed on a war footing. . . ." He continues, "How to deal with the enemy and how to fight have become the central problems in our daily life."

Mao had long since realized (see pp. 123–132) that while the army was essential, the success of the movement as a whole depended upon the Party's ability to arouse the common peasant into action. And no issue was closer to the peasant's heart than land reform. The inequities of land distribution in China were well known. Each town usually had its one or two big landlords from whom most of the surrounding peasants were forced to rent their land at exorbitant rates. Mao states, "The agrarian policy adopted in the border areas is complete confiscation and thorough distribution," but he does admit to excesses, especially against the middle peasants who technically were a "revolutionary class." There is no doubt that this policy ushered in one of the bloodiest anti-landlord purges ever witnessed in China. But despite the uncontrolled nature of the land program, the Communists were successful in winning peasant support—the source of their strength and their trump card against the Kuomintang, which was all too closely identified with the landholders.

The Kiangsi Soviet period was one of flux. Chinese Communism had been thrown back on itself after the failure of Stalin's attempt to lead the Revolution from Moscow. During the late 1920s and early 1930s the Kuomintang was at the peak of its success and was squeezing the vise ever tighter around Mao and his followers (whom they referred to simply as *Kung-fei,* or Communist-bandits). In 1928 Mao wrote, "we have an acute sense of loneliness and are every moment longing for an end of such a lonely life." These were gloomy times and Communist fortunes were at a low ebb. Political and ideological guidelines were still vague, the army was little more than a ragged force completely dependent on captured weapons, leadership problems were unsettled. Nonetheless, the Kiangsi Soviet was an important beginning in Mao's rise to power. China's future leaders learned much from their mistakes. When the Communists were finally driven out of Kiangsi on the epic Long March in 1934, they were almost beaten, but they took with them the legacy of having been the peasants' saviour, a legacy that served them well in the hard years to come.

The first selection is taken from a report written by Mao in 1928 in which he describes the Party's plight in the mountains and the problems they faced. In each section one is impressed by the frankness with which Mao admits to problems and errors. The Party's future depended on the rectification of mistakes: they could not be swept under the rug and ignored.

The second selection is taken from a book published by the Nationalist Government shortly after the Communists were driven out of Kiangsi in 1934. The author describes the soviet areas as a "veritable nightmare" in which "an indescribable reign of terror prevailed"—allegations containing much truth. The Communists showed little restraint in their treatment of landlords. The land reform program began as a *carte blanche* for mass slaughter of "reactionaries." A thirst for vengeance, which had been growing for centuries against the landlords, poured forth in a wave of violence.

The problem was that the Kuomintang failed to understand the class struggle which was the essence of the Communist movement. And thus, like the author, they tended to miss the real threat posed by their Communist enemies. While admitting that the "Reds were credited with a few good points," and that "the populace at first welcomed the Reds and looked upon them as saviours," the author goes on to excoriate the Communists. The Kuomintang refused to acknowledge the Communists as anything more than a few wily "bandits," and they sought to destroy them by traditional anti-bandit methods—force of arms. What Chiang failed to appreciate (and it comes out clearly in the second selection) was the nature of the enemy he was up against: an idea which proved to be far more seductive to the Chinese peasant than his own New Life Movement.

To this day the Nationalists refer to the Communist regime on the mainland as "bandits." And to this day they have failed to develop a viable counter-ideology.

MAO TSE-TUNG *

The Struggle in the Chingkang Mountains

The phenomenon that within a country one or several small areas under Red political power came into existence amid the encirclement of White political power is one which, of all the countries in the world today, occurs only in China. Upon analysis we find that one of the reasons for its occurrence lies in the incessant splits and wars within China's comprador class and landed gentry. So long as splits and wars continue within these classes, the workers' and peasants' armed independent regime can also continue to exist and develop. In addition to this, the existence and development of such an armed independent regime require the following conditions: (1) a sound mass basis, (2) a first-rate Party organization, (3) a Red Army of adequate strength, (4) a terrain favorable to military operations, and (5) economic strength sufficient for self-support.

The independent regime in a given area must adopt a

* Mao Tse-tung, *Selected Works* (New York: International Publishers, 1954), Vol. I, pp. 71–104.

different strategy against the ruling class forces which encircle it according to whether their political power is enjoying temporary stability or is splitting up.

When splits take place within the ruling classes . . . we may adopt a strategy of comparatively venturesome advance and expand the independent regime over a comparatively large area by fighting. Yet all the same we must take care to lay a solid foundation in the central districts so that we shall have something to rely upon and nothing to fear when the White Terror comes. When the political power of the ruling classes is relatively stable, as in the southern provinces after April this year, our strategy must be one of gradual advance. We must then take the utmost care neither to divide up our forces for venturesome advance in the military field, nor to scatter our personnel and neglect to lay a solid foundation in the central districts in the field of local work (including the distribution of land, the establishment of political power, the expansion of the Party, and the organization of local armed forces).

The failure in various small Red areas has been due either to a lack of favorable objective conditions or to subjective tactical mistakes. The tactics have been mistaken precisely because of the failure to distinguish clearly between the two different periods, the period when the political power of the ruling classes is temporarily stable and the period when it is splitting up. In the period when the political power of the ruling classes was temporarily stable, some comrades, as if oblivious of the fact that the enemy could muster for an attack not only the house-to-house militia, but also regular troops, advocated dividing our own forces for a venturesome advance, and even proposed to leave the defense of an extensive area to the Red guards singlehanded. In local work they utterly neglected to lay a solid foundation in the central districts, but aimed exclusively at unlimited expansion, regardless of whether we were strong enough to achieve this. And anyone who advocated gradual expansion in military work and, in civilian work, concentration of forces to build up a solid foundation in the central districts, thus placing ourselves in an invincible position, was called a "conservative." Precisely such erroneous views were the fundamental cause of the fiasco in August this year in the Hunan-Kiangsi border area and of the simultaneous defeat of the Fourth Army of the Red Army in southern Hunan. . . .

THE CURRENT SITUATION IN THE AREA
UNDER THE INDEPENDENT REGIME

Since April this year the Red areas have gradually expanded. After the battle of Lungyuankow (on the borders of Yungsin and Ningkang) on June 23, in which we defeated the enemy forces from Kiangsi for the fourth time, the border area reached its peak of development. . . . In the Red areas the greater part of the land had been redistributed, and the redistribution of the remainder was in progress. District and township governments were established everywhere. . . . In the villages the workers' and peasants' insurrection corps were extensively organized, and there were Red guards in the districts and counties. In July the enemy forces from Kiangsi launched an attack and in August the enemy forces from both Hunan and Kiangsi jointly attacked the Chingkang mountains; all the county towns and the entire flat country of the counties in the border area were occupied by the enemy. The peace preservation corps and the house-to-house militia, both tools of the enemy, ran amuck, and White Terror reigned throughout the towns and the countryside. Most of the Party organizations and organs of political power collapsed. The rich peasants and opportunists within the Party became turncoats one after another. After the battle in the Chingkang mountains on August 30, the enemy forces from Hunan retreated to Ling, but those from Kiangsi still held all the county towns and most of the villages. However, it has always been beyond the power of the enemy to capture the mountain areas. . . . In July and August one regiment of the Red Army, in coordination with the Red guards of the counties, fought scores of big and small battles with a loss of only thirty rifles, but finally withdrew to the mountains.

As our men were marching back to the Chingkang mountains . . . the enemy forces in southern Kiangsi, the Independent Seventh Division under Liu Shih-yi, pursued us as far as

Suichwan. On September 13 we defeated Liu Shih-yi, captured several hundred rifles and took Suichwan. On September 26 our men returned to the Chingkang mountains. On October 1 we engaged in Ningkang Chou Hun-yuan's brigade under Hsiung Shih-hui, winning the battle and recovering the entire county. . . . The enemy is attempting to destroy our base area by military attacks and economic blockade and we are making preparations to defeat his attacks.

THE MILITARY PROBLEM

Since the struggle in the border area is exclusively military, both the Party and the masses have to be placed on a war footing. How to deal with the enemy and how to fight have become the central problems in our daily life. An independent regime must be an armed one. Wherever there are no armed forces, or the armed forces are inadequate, or the tactics for dealing with the enemy are wrong, the enemy will immediately come into occupation. As the struggle is getting fiercer every day, our problems have also become extremely complicated and serious. . . .

As to the composition of the Red Army, one part consists of workers and peasants and the other of lumpenproletarians. It is of course inadvisable to have too large a proportion of lumpenproletarians. But as fighting is going on every day and casualties mounting, it is already no easy matter to get for replacements the lumpenproletarians, who are good fighters. In these circumstances the only thing to do is to intensify political training.

The majority of the Red Army soldiers came from mercenary armies; but once in the Red Army, they change their character. First of all the Red Army has abolished the mercenary system, making the soldiers feel that they are not fighting for somebody else but for themselves and for the people. The Red Army has not to this day instituted a system of regular pay, but issues only rice, an allowance for oil, salt, firewood, and vegetables, and a little pocket money. Land has been allotted to all Red Army officers and men who are natives of the border area, but it is rather hard to allot land to those from distant areas.

After receiving some political education, the Red Army soldiers have all become class-conscious and acquired a general knowledge about redistributing land, establishing political power, arming the workers and peasants, etc.; and they all know that they are fighting for themselves and for the working class and the peasantry. Hence they can endure the bitter struggle without complaint. Each company, battalion, or regiment has its soldiers' council which represents the interests of the soldiers and carries out political and mass work.

Experience has proved that the system of Party representatives must not be abolished. As the Party branch is organized on the company basis, the Party representative at the company level is particularly important. He has to supervise the soldiers' committee in carrying out political training, to direct the work of the mass movement, and to act at the same time as the secretary of the Party branch. Facts have proved that the better the company Party representative is, the better is the company, while the company commander can hardly play such an effective political role. As the casualties among the lower cadres are heavy, soldiers captured from the enemy a short time ago have often been made platoon or company commanders and some of those captured only last February or March are now battalion commanders. Superficially it might seem that, since our army is called the Red Army, it could do without Party representatives; actually the reverse is the case. The Twenty-eighth Regiment in southern Hunan once abolished this system only to restore it later. To re-name Party representatives "directors" would be to confuse them with the directors of the Kuomintang, who are detested by the captured soldiers. Moreover, changes in title do not affect the nature of a system. Hence we have decided against the change. To make up for the heavy casualties in Party representatives we hope that, besides starting training classes ourselves, the Party center and the two provincial Party Committees will send us at least thirty comrades eligible as Party representatives.

The average soldier needs six months' or a year's training before he can fight, but our soldiers, though recruited only yesterday, have to fight today with practically no training to speak of. Exceedingly poor in military technique, they fight by courage alone. As a long period for rest and training is impossible, we shall see whether we can find ways to avoid certain battles in order to gain time for training. For the training of lower officers we have formed a training corps of 150 men and intend to make it a permanent institution. We hope that the Party center and the two provincial committees will send us more officers from the rank of platoon and company commanders upwards.

The Hunan Provincial Committee has asked us to attend to the material life of the soldiers and to make it at least a little better than that of the average worker or peasant. At present the very reverse is the case, for, besides rice, each man gets only five cents a day for cooking oil, salt, firewood, and vegetables, and it is hard even to keep this up. The monthly cost of these items alone amounts to more than ten thousand silver dollars, which are obtained exclusively through expropriating the local bullies. We have now obtained cotton for the winter clothing of the whole army of five thousand men but are still short of cloth. Cold as the weather is, many of our men are still wearing two suits of clothes of single thickness. Fortunately we are inured to hardships. Furthermore all alike share the same hardships: everbody from the army commander down to the cook lives on a daily fare worth five cents, apart from grain. In the matter of pocket money, if two dimes are allotted, it is two dimes for everybody; if four dimes are allotted, it is four dimes for everybody. Thus the soldiers harbor no resentment against anyone.

After each engagement there are a number of wounded soldiers. And a great many officers and men have fallen ill from malnutrition, exposure to cold and other causes. The hospital up in the mountains gives both Chinese and Western treatments, but is short of doctors as well as medicine. At present there are over eight hundred patients in the hospital. The Hunan Provincial Committee promised to procure medicine for us but so far we have not received any. We still have to ask the Party center and the two provincial committees to send us some iodine and a few doctors with Western training.

Apart from the role played by the Party, the reason why the Red Army can sustain itself without collapse in spite of such a poor standard of material life and such incessant engagements, is its practice of democracy. The officers do not beat the men;

officers and men receive equal treatment; soldiers enjoy freedom of assembly and speech; cumbersome formalities and ceremonies are done away with; and the account books are open to the inspection of all. The soldiers handle the mess arrangements and out of the daily five cents for oil, salt, firewood, and vegetables, can even save a little sum for pocket money (called "mess savings") of approximately sixty or seventy cents for each person every day. All these measures are very satisfactory to the soldiers. The newly captured soldiers in particular feel that our army and the Kuomintang's army are worlds apart. They feel that, though in material life they are worse off in the Red Army than in the White Army, spiritually they are liberated. The fact that the same soldier who was not brave in the enemy army yesterday becomes very brave in the Red Army today shows precisely the impact of democracy. The Red Army is like a furnace in which all captured soldiers are melted down and transformed the moment they come over. In China not only the people need democracy but the army needs it too. The democratic system in an army is an important weapon for destroying the feudal mercenary army.

The Party organizations are now divided into four levels: the company branch, the battalion committee, the regimental committee, and the army committee. In a company there is the branch, and in a squad the group. An important reason why the Red Army has been able to undertake such severe struggle without falling apart is that the *Party branch is organized on the company basis*. Two years ago our organizations in the Kuomintang army did not have any hold on the soldiers, and even among Yeh T'ing's troops there was only one Party branch in a regiment; this is why they could not stand up to any crucial test. In the Red Army today the ratio of Party members to non-Party men is approximately one to three, *i.e.*, on the average there is one Party member among every four men. Recently we have decided to recruit more Party members among the combat soldiers, so as to attain a fifty-fifty ratio between Party members and non-Party men. At present the company branches are short of good secretaries and we ask the Party center to send us for this purpose a large number of the activists from among those who can no longer stay where they are. The working personnel from southern Hunan are almost all doing Party work in the army. In August some of them left us during the flight in southern Hunan, and therefore we have no personnel to spare now.

The local armed forces are the Red guards and the workers' and peasants' insurrection corps. The insurrection corps is armed with spears and fowling-pieces and organized on a township basis with a contingent in every township, the strength of which is proportional to the township population. Its job is to suppress counter-revolution, to protect the township government, and, when the enemy comes, to assist the Red Army and the Red guards in war. The insurrection corps was started in Yungsin as an underground force; it has come out in the open since we captured the entire county. The organization has now been expanded in other counties of the border area and the name remains unchanged. The arms of the Red guards are mainly five-round rifles but also include some nine-round and single-round ones. There are 140 rifles in Ningkang, 220 in Yungsin, 43 in Lienhwa, 50 in Chaling, 90 in Ling, 130 in Suichwan and 10 in Wanan, making a total of 683. While most of the rifles were supplied by the Red Army, a small number were captured from the enemy by the Red guards themselves. Fighting regularly against the peace preservation corps and the house-to-house militia of the landed gentry, most of the Red guards in the counties are daily increasing their fighting capacity. . . .

THE AGRARIAN PROBLEM

The agrarian situation in the border area: Roughly speaking, more than 60 per cent of the land used to belong to the landlords and less than 40 per cent to the peasants. . . .

The problem of the intermediate class: The agrarian situation being such, the confiscation and redistribution of all the land can win the support of the majority of the population. But people in the rural areas are generally divided into three classes: the class of big and middle landlords, the intermediate class of small landlords and rich peasants, and the class of middle and poor peasants. The interests of the rich peasants are often interwoven with those of the small landlords. The land of the rich peasants makes up but a small percentage of the total acreage, yet with the land of the small landlords counted in, the amount is considerable. Perhaps this is more or less the case throughout the country. The agrarian policy adopted in the border area is complete confiscation and thorough redistribution; thus in the Red area the landed gentry and the intermediate class are both under attack. Such being the policy, in actual execution we nevertheless meet with considerable obstruction from the intermediate class. In the early period of the Revolution the intermediate class apparently capitulated to the poor peasantry, but in reality they took advantage of the former social position of the poor peasants as well as of their clannishness, in order to threaten them and delay land redistribution. When no further delay was possible they withheld information about the actual acreage of their land, or kept the good land for themselves and left the poor land to other people. In this period the poor peasants, having long been ill-treated and feeling uncertain about the victory of the revolution, often accepted the proposals of the intermediate class and dared not take positive action. Positive action is taken in the villages against the intermediate class only at a time of real revolutionary upsurge, when, for instance, political power has been seized in one or several counties, the reactionary army has been defeated a number of times, and the prowess of the Red Army has been repeatedly demonstrated. The most serious instances of delaying land redistribution and withholding information about land acreage were found, for example, in the southern section of Yungsin, where the intermediate class was the largest. We actually went ahead with redistribution only after the Red Army had won a great victory at Lungyuankow on June 23 and the district government had dealt with several people for delaying land redistribution. But the feudal patriarchal organizations are widespread in every county, and in most cases one clan inhabits a whole village or several villages; thus it will be quite a long time before the process of class differentiation is completed and the clan sentiment overcome in the villages.

The volte-face of the intermediate class under White Terror: The intermediate class, having suffered blows during the revolutionary upsurge, immediately goes over to the other side when the White Terror comes. It was precisely the small landlords and rich peasants in Yungsin and Ningkang who incited the reactionary troops to set fire to large numbers of houses of revolutionary peasants there. Acting on the directions of the reactionaries, they burnt down houses and arrested people, and quite boldly too. When the Red Army returned to the area of Ningkang, Sincheng, Kucheng and Lungshih, thousands of the peasants there, deceived by the reactionary propaganda that the Communists would kill them, fled with the reactionaries to Yungsin. It was only as a result of our propaganda—"Do not kill peasants who have become turncoats" and "Peasants who have become turncoats are welcome home to reap their crops" —that some of the peasants eventually came back.

When the Revolution in the country as a whole is at a low ebb, the most difficult problem in areas under the independent regime is our lack of a firm hold on the intermediate class. The intermediate class turns traitor to the Revolution mainly because it has received too heavy a blow. But when the country as a whole is in a revolutionary upsurge, the poor peasantry gains courage because it has something to rely upon while the intermediate class dares not get out of hand because it also has something to fear. When the war between Li Tsung-jen and T'ang Sheng-chih spread to Hunan, the small landlords in Chaling tried to placate the peasants; some of them sent pork to the peasants as a New Year gift (by then the Red Army had retreated from Chaling and gone to Suichwan). But after that war was over, no one heard of such things any more. At present, when the tide of counter-revolution is rising high in the country as a whole, the intermediate class in the White areas, having been subjected to heavy attack, has attached itself almost entirely to the landed gentry, and the poor peasantry has become an isolated force. This is indeed a very serious problem.

The pressure of daily life as a cause of the volte-face of the intermediate class: Opposed to each other, the Red areas and the White areas have become two enemy countries. Owing to both the enemy's tight blockade and our improper treatment of the petty bourgeoisie, trade between the two areas has almost en-

tirely ceased; since daily necessaries like salt, cloth, and medicine
are scarce and costly and agricultural products like timber, tea,
and cooking oil cannot be marketed in the White areas, the
peasants' source of income is cut off and all the people are
affected. The poor peasantry is, comparatively speaking, able to
bear such hardships, but the intermediate class will capitulate
to the landed gentry the moment it finds them past bearing. If
splits and wars among the landed gentry and the warlords in
China do not continue, and if the revolutionary situation throughout the country does not develop, then the Red independent
regime in small areas will come under great economic pressure
and its prolonged existence will become doubtful. For such
economic pressure is not only intolerable to the intermediate
class, but will someday prove so even to the workers, poor
peasants, and Red Army soldiers. In the counties of Yungsin
and Ningkang there was at one time no salt for cooking and
supplies of cloth and medicine were entirely cut off, not to mention other things. Salt is now obtainable there but the price is very
high. Cloth and medicine are still totally lacking. Timber, tea,
and cooking oil, all abundantly produced in Ningkang, western
Yungsin and northern Suichwan (all under our independent regime at present) cannot yet be transported to the White areas.

The criterion in land redistribution: The township is taken
as the basis of land redistribution. In regions where there are
more hills and less farm land, e.g., the Siaokiang district in
Yungsin, three or four townships were sometimes taken as one
unit, but such cases were extremely rare. All the country people,
male or female, old or young, received equal shares. In accordance with the Party center's plan, a change is now made whereby
ability to work is taken as the criterion: a person with ability to
work is allotted twice as much as one without.

The problem of making concessions to the owner-peasants:
This has not yet been discussed in detail. The rich owner-peasants have themselves requested that productive power be taken
as the criterion, i.e., those who have more labor power and capital (such as farm implements) should be allotted more land. The
rich peasants feel that neither equal redistribution nor redistribution according to ability to work is to their advantage.
They have indicated that they are willing to put in more labor

power which, coupled with the power of their capital, would enable them to raise bigger crops. They will be unsatisfied if, with their special efforts and extra capital neglected (*i.e.,* left idle), they are only allotted the same amount of land as the people in general. Here the redistribution is still being carried out according to the Party center's plan. But this problem deserves further discussion, and another report will be submitted when a conclusion is reached.

The land tax: In Ningkang it is being collected at the rate of 20 per cent of the crop, exceeding by 5 per cent the rate specified by the Party center; as the collection is already under way, the rate should not be altered just now but will be reduced next year. Besides, the sections of Suichwan, Ling, and Yungsin under our independent regime are all hilly areas, and the peasants are so poverty-stricken that taxation is inadvisable. For the maintenance of the government and the Red guards we rely on expropriating the local tyrants in the White areas. As to provisions for the Red Army, rice can be obtained temporarily through collecting the land tax in Ningkang, while cash is also obtained entirely through expropriating the local tyrants. During our guerrilla operations in Suichwan in October we collected more than ten thousand dollars, which will last for a while, and we shall see what can be done when the sum is spent. . . .

THE PROBLEM OF THE CHARACTER OF THE REVOLUTION

We fully agree with the Communist International's resolutions concerning China. At present China certainly remains in the stage of the bourgeois-democratic revolution. A program for a thorough democratic revolution in China includes, externally, the overthrow of imperialism so as to achieve complete national liberation, and, internally, the cleanup of the influence of the comprador class in the cities, the completion of the agrarian revolution, the elimination of feudal relations in the villages, and the overthrow of the government of the warlords. We must go through such a democratic revolution before we can lay a real foundation for passing on to socialism. Having fought in various places in the past year, we are keenly aware that the revolutionary upsurge in the country as a whole is subsiding. While Red political power has been established in a few small areas, the people of the country as a whole still do not possess basic democratic rights; the workers and the peasants and even the bourgeois democrats have no rights of speech and assembly, and joining the Communist Party constitutes the greatest crime. Wherever the Red Army goes, it finds the masses cold and reserved; only after propaganda and agitation do they slowly rouse themselves. We have to fight the enemy forces hard whoever they are, and scarcely any mutiny or uprising has taken place within the enemy forces. The same is true even of the Sixth Army, which recruited the greatest number of "rebels" after the Incident of May 21. We have an acute sense of loneliness and are every moment longing for the end of such a lonely life. To turn the revolution into a seething, surging tide all over the country, it is necessary to launch a political and economic struggle for democracy involving also the urban petty bourgeoisie. . . .

Up to the present no split has occurred within the regime of the landed gentry, and the enemy's forces for "annihilation" that are deployed round the border area still number more than ten regiments. But if we can continue to find some way out in the matter of cash (food and clothing are not much of a problem now), then, basing ourselves on the foundation in the border area, we shall be able to cope with the enemy force at its present strength, or even at a greater strength. As far as the border area is concerned, once the Red Army moves away a devastation like that of August would befall it. Though not all of our Red guards would be wiped out, the whole basis of the Party and of the masses would be heavily damaged, and although the independent regime in some of the mountain areas might hold out, all of us in the plains would have to go underground as we did in August and September. If the Red Army does not move away, then with our present base we can gradually expand to all the surrounding areas and our prospects are very bright. And for the Red Army to expand, it must engage the enemy in a long struggle in the area round the Chingkang mountains, *i.e.,* the four counties of Ningkang, Yungsin, Ling, and Suichwan, where we have a mass base, taking advantage of the clash of interests between the

enemy forces of Hunan and Kiangsi and of the enemy's need to
man the defenses on all sides and consequently his inability to
concentrate his forces. We must use correct tactics and fight no
battle unless we can win victory and capture the enemy's arms
and men, so as to expand the Red Army gradually. With the
mass base well laid in the border area in the period from April
to July, the Red Army's major detachment could undoubtedly
have expanded itself in August, if it had not made an expedition
to southern Hunan. Although a mistake was made, the Red
Army has returned to the border area where the terrain is favorable and the people friendly, and the prospects are still not bad.
In a place like the border area the Red Army must be fully
determined for the struggle and have the stamina for fighting,
for only thus can it increase its arms and train good men.

For a whole year the Red flag has been kept flying in the
border area; though it has incurred the hatred of the landed
gentry of Hunan, Hupeh, and Kiangsi provinces and even of
the whole country, it has gradually aroused the hopes of the
masses of workers, peasants, and soldiers in the nearby provinces.
Regarding the "bandit-annihilation" campaign against the border area as a major task and issuing statements like "a million
dollars were consumed in a year's campaign to annihilate the
bandits" (Lu Ti-p'ing), and the Communists "number twenty
thousand armed with five thousand rifles" (Wang Chun), the
warlords have gradually directed the attention of their soldiers
and disheartened lower-rank officers to us and thereby supplied
another source for the expansion of the Red Army, because
more and more of such officers and men will come over to us.
Furthermore, the fact that the Red flag has never been struck in
the border area shows not only the strength of the Communist
Party but the bankruptcy of the ruling classes; this is of great
significance in national politics. That is why we have always
held that it is entirely necessary and correct to build up and
expand the Red political power in the middle section of the
Losiao mountain range.

C. W. H. YOUNG *
Life Under the Chinese Soviet Regime

Life under the Chinese soviet regime in Kiangsi province, where the Reds had established Juichin, "capital of the Union of Soviet Socialist Republics of China" until their armies were defeated and scattered by the loyal armies of the Nationalist government under General Chiang Kai-shek, and also in Fukien, was described to me during a visit which I recently made to the recovered areas. I had heard so much of the idealistic side of Communism that I decided to learn as much as I possibly could of the practical side.

The tales told by the scores whom I interviewed were most interesting but somewhat conflicting. Some sung praises for the Communists and their doctrines but these were very few and far between, the majority being at one in condemning Bolshevism. I will attempt in the next few chapters to give a general narrative, as far as I have been able to piece the various stories together. In doing so, attention must be drawn to the fact that, although the Communists have been defeated in Kiangsi, the details presented will tend to give an insight of life under the Chinese Soviet regime, no matter where it may be established.

It was the general consensus of opinion that life under the Reds was not as rosy as Communist propagandists, in Shanghai at least, would make people believe. The Soviet made numerous and all sorts of promises to bring benefits to the people which were not carried out. True, there was equality for a time but the benefits accorded the people were not lasting.

A VERITABLE NIGHTMARE

An indescribable reign of terror prevailed and the populace was forced to undergo unnecessary hardships and sufferings and to

* C. W. H. Young, *New Life for Kiangsi* (Shanghai, 1935), pp. 73–78.

live a life of bondage, a veritable nightmare, instead of receiving equality and benefits and good treatment such as they had been led to believe they would receive.

The manner in which the Communists have devastated the homes of the people in Kiangsi is reminiscent of Chapei after the Sino-Japanese hostilities of 1932 (see pp. 186–194). The official yamen and the houses of the wealthy have been sacked and burned to the ground. Ancestral halls and temples have been desecrated beyond description, leaving only the bare walls.

The humble dwellings of the poor peasants have been left standing in many places but not a piece of woodwork remains within. Heaps of ashes have taken the places of others. All is mute evidence of the "benefits" which Communism is supposed to bring to the people of China. And now hundreds, aye thousands, are living in what purports to be houses, buildings with two or three walls and only temporary covers.

In spite of everything that may be said against them, the Reds were credited with a few good points. They were stated to be considerably better than the former militarists and their henchmen but agreement was general among the many whom I interviewed that the new regime, headed by the Generalissimo and Madame Chiang Kai-shek, has given the people benefits and justice such as they had never expected to receive in this lifetime. They have given the people a New Life and a New Deal, far better than anything the Communists could offer, and they have, furthermore, given them the best and most popular government they have ever lived under.

EVEN NAILS CARRIED OFF

The Generalissimo and his wife believe that nothing is too good for the Chinese people, so they are giving them the best they can offer in a Christianlike manner, for both of them are ardent Christians (see pp. 150–157).

The people with whom I spoke during my recent visit actually lived through the Red occupation and the reign of terror which accompanied it and their tales, for the most part, were heart-rending. Indescribable shambles of filth remain in the places of the stately and palatial homes of the wealthy, as well as the shacks of the farmer. Doorknobs, and even nails, have been carried off. Doors and floors have been torn away to be used as firewood.

Husbands and sons have been seized, carried off, and held until ransom has been paid. Others have been impressed into the Communist army for military or compulsory labor service. Those who have been so fortunate as to escape have been hunted remorselessly and, when caught, treated with ruthless cruelty. Even children have by no means been exempt from the wrath and violence of the Reds and the death penalty is said to have been imposed in many cases by the riffraff of the Red army on the tots who have been unfortunate enough to be born to the families of the wealthy.

Still others have been slain and their families called upon to pay ransom even after they have been tortured and done to death in a manner beyond description. Then, after ransom has been paid, the mutilated corpses of the unfortunate victims have been handed over to their families!

PEOPLE AFRAID TO SPEAK

Many people were afraid to speak or to say anything to the writer, preferring to suffer silently rather than take the risk of being quoted, for fear that the Reds would eventually return and vent their wrath upon them for giving away "state secrets." The people as a whole have lived in great fear of the OGPU system, hence they refuse to speak lest they should be speaking to some secret service agent of the Communists and for fear that their words may, at some future date, be used as evidence against them.

Generally speaking, however, it would appear that the populace at first welcomed the Reds and looked upon them as saviours; for had they not suffered under the merciless grip of the militarists in the past? Had not their crops and their livestock been seized, together even with their homes, to satisfy exorbitant tax demands which had to be met for decades in advance? Had they not been forced to give up the planting of legitimate crops and to grow poppy instead? Had the Reds not promised them equality in everything? Had they not been promised benefits under the Soviet system such as they had never enjoyed before and such as they had never expected they would enjoy?

Now, however, they were disillusioned and refused to heed the words of the Reds any longer, because, as they bitterly complained, the Communists had failed to keep their word and, instead of giving them the promised benefits, proved to be a hundred times worse than the former militarists.

As they told their stories of the grueling experiences they had undergone, tears rolled down the cheeks of the narrators while others who stood by listening remained silent, staring mutely and vacantly before them. They had been through brigand scares and numerous other upheavals scores of times before but never had they experienced the like of this horror. As they spoke, I could well envisage the sufferings they had undergone and realize why they had become disillusioned.

RED PROPAGANDISTS ACTIVE

As might be expected, there is considerable haranguing and soapbox speeches aplenty in Communist territory while nearly every wall carries a painted inscription bearing out the merits of Communism. While most of the slogans that have been painted on the walls of homes, ancestral halls, temples, and other buildings in the areas which, until recently, had been controlled by the Reds, have been whitewashed and covered with new inscriptions and slogans more favorable to the National government, many still remain. For instance, when I visited the place, I noticed a few, such as the following:

Energetically till the state lands of the soviet!
Communism brings equality and benefits to the people!
The soviet has come to save the people and deliver them from their oppressors!

There were, of course, others, such as:

Down with the Nanking government!
Down with the enemies of the people!
Overthrow the capitalists!
Down with Chiang Kai-shek!
Peasants! Rise! Overthrow those who have oppressed you
and who have benefited at your expense!

The entire Communist movement is carried on through
class-hatred tactics. All vestiges of the old civilization are being
wiped out, according to the soviet system, in a horrible and
ruthless fashion. The only classes recognized are the farmers,
the workers, and the soldiers. All other classes are to be completely annihilated, not merely eliminated. There is no room for
the wealthy or the scholar, much less the official.

After they have been rounded up, the wealthy classes are
classified. Rich landowners, wealthy farmers, moneylenders, ex-
ploiters of the people, oppressors of the masses, officials of the
old regime, members of the Kuomintang, and cultured people—
all these are the potential enemies of the soviet and are considered to be counter-revolutionaries if they dare to speak a word
against the soviet regime, and they are dealt with as such, should,
unhappily, they fall into the hands of these people.

"ENEMIES" OF SOVIET CLASSIFIED

The name of each victim is taken. Each case is investigated.
After a thorough investigation has been made, the farmers and
workers are asked what property the victims own, what official
positions they have held, whether they are "good or bad,"
whether they have exploited or oppressed the people, etc., and
the soviet decision is made on the basis of extracting as much
money as possible from the hapless persons who fall into their
clutches.

Communism, under the extreme or radical Bolsheviks, is a
system of open looting and murder, as well as one of propaganda and espionage. Those passed upon as being corrupt are
immediately put to death: others are held for varying sums,

ranging from $200,000 down to as low as $50, according to their worldly possessions. One unfortunate fellow recently paid $8,500 for the release of his uncle but, upon the latter's release, it was found that he had been so badly treated that he died within five miles of his home town!

A most amazing instance of the brutality of the Reds occurred only recently when some five hundred people were caught one evening during a surprise raid on the town where they lived. One of the Red soldiers was told to kill ten persons. Somewhat reluctantly, it must be said, this man was forced to carry out the order. This done, another ten persons were brought forward and their lives were given to another slaughterer. Thus it continued until these five hundred unfortunate human beings had their throats slit like pigs with sharp knives.

The violence of the Reds is by no means exaggerated. In many districts in which they wielded power, they degenerated until the soviet became nothing more than an organization for the gathering of loot.

Very few families, rich or poor, in the territories recovered from the Communists have not suffered in loss of life or property under the soviet regime. Two years ago, the people preferred the Reds and worked for them in a most enthusiastic manner but, when they discovered that they had been deceived and after they had learned of the New Life Movement inaugurated by General Chiang Kai-shek, with its program of social reforms, which compels officers and officials everywhere to take an interest in the welfare of the people, the citizens of the recovered areas turned round, pledged fealty to the National government, and announced their preparedness to accept the government program, a promise which they are honestly and conscientiously observing.

3. STRUGGLE FOR SURVIVAL:
Rebuilding the Communist Movement

THE LONG MARCH from Kiangsi through the Western Chinese wastelands to the new base area in Shensi is the most impressive event in the history of the Chinese Communists. The Long March is for them what the October Revolution is for the Russians. Epic tales have grown up around it, and those on it have become Communist China's heroes. Edgar Snow wrote of it:

> Adventure, exploration, discovery, human courage and cowardice, ecstasy and triumph, suffering, sacrifice, and loyalty, and then through it all, like a flame, this undimmed ardor and undying hope and amazing revolutionary optimism of those thousands of youths who would not admit defeat either by man or nature or God or death—all this and more are embodied in the history of an Odyssey unequaled in modern times.

The Long March was a rebaptism for the Chinese Communists, and credit for it is due Chiang Kai-shek. The Communist record in the soviet areas had not been entirely good: land reform was violent, brutality was not uncommon, government, Party, and organization in general were inefficient, and the army was still a far cry from the great Red Army of later years. Chiang, however, was obsessed by the idea of exterminating every last Communist. Mobilizing a million men and as much equipment as he could, he launched his fifth and greatest bandit extermination (*Chiao-fei*) campaign, with the methodical talents of German General Falkenhausen to advise him. But try as he would, the ever diminishing line of Communist marchers eluded him. By the fall of 1935, the main units of the

Red Army, joined by other units from other provinces, established themselves in Shensi.

Tibor Mende, Professor of Political Science at the University of Paris, notes in the first selection three results of the Long March. First, the Communists became heroes throughout the country, despite all attempts of the Kuomintang-controlled press to suppress news of their exploits. Second, the Communist Party achieved a new internal cohesion. And third, contact with peasants and tribesmen in so many different parts of China gave them a new insight into the minds of the people. Mende concludes: "thus, with their moral stature grown but physically and numerically weakened, the Communists began to organize their new base."

The achievement of internal cohesion cost the Communists dearly at a time when they were already suffering the brunt of Chiang's fiercest attacks. In the winter of 1934–1935 the Party held its famous Tsunyi Conference, in which Mao was attacked from the "left" and the "right." His old comrade Chang Kuo-t'ao split with him on the choice of the new base area, and may have attempted to dispute his leadership of the whole movement. The attacks from the "right," which became evident only in the subsequent period, centered around Wang Ming, chief of the Chinese Communist Party delegation in Moscow, whose advocacy of a more conciliatory policy toward the Kuomintang was in line with Moscow's general approach. But Mao weathered the attacks, retained the loyalty of most of the Party's leading figures, and emerged decisively as the leader of the Chinese Revolution.

Kuomintang pressure against the Communists ceased after the Sian Incident (December 1936), in which Chiang Kai-shek had been arrested by rebellious anti-Japanese armies led by Chang Hsüeh-liang, son of the former Manchurian warlord. Chiang was finally forced to agree to a united front with the Communists. Thus began the Yenan Period of Chinese Communism.

During the first few years in their new base area the Communists set about rebuilding Party and army. In the many Party schools that grew up they debated their Kiangsi Period failures and mistakes, and began to sketch out new principles of organization and policy. The United Front agreement with the Kuomintang ruled out radical land reform as a revolutionary instrument, so the Communists turned their attention to building up stable organization within the villages. Instead of outright confiscation of land, rents were reduced and taxes lightened, while landlords were allowed to retain most of their property. These reformist tactics yielded high returns in peasant support for the Communists.

During the early 1940s the Communists launched a large-scale cooperative movement in Red area villages based initially on traditional forms of labor cooperation and tool sharing. Edgar Snow, in the second selection, describes the movement in its early stages.

As a result of these careful efforts, the Communists managed to build a strong organizational base in the villages. Even after occupation by Japanese or Kuomintang forces, Communist village organization remained intact. The Party, of course, became largely peasant in membership, but in contrast to the Kiangsi Period, great efforts were expended to raise the quality of members: they were taught rudimentary literacy, and continuing thought reform increased their loyalty and effectiveness to the movement.

In contrast to the Kuomintang, which manifested a persistent disinclination to commit its forces in the battle against the Japanese (one of General Stilwell's perennial complaints) (see pp. 269–277), the Communists used combat opportunity to improve morale, discipline, and organization. Though they fought few large-scale battles with the Japanese, the thousands of guerrilla actions they engaged in gave their cadres much leadership experience.

Small guerrilla pockets, in addition to the eleven major guerrilla base areas, appeared over the entire map of Japanese-occupied China. In its simplest form, the guerrilla band was a village unit which fought on some days and on others returned to the village to work—the Communists called this the unity of work and battle. Gradually the Communists developed means of linking the small units together into larger formations and eventually transforming them into regular armies. Yet the guerrillas' roots were in the villages, and when times were difficult, they always returned there.

Part of the first great debate in America on the Chinese Communists was the question of whether they were agrarian reformers or radical revolutionaries. There is no doubt that during the Yenan Period they were the former. But, with the intensification of the Civil War in the summer of 1946, they returned to the more violent tactics of radical land reform pursued during the Kiangsi Period, though in a more systematic and disciplined manner. Even before the Civil War ended, however, the Chinese Communist leaders tried hard to bring the violence under control. Kiangsi had taught them that violent revolutionary approaches may have short-term advantages, but impede the long-term process of organization. Yenan provided the lesson of how to penetrate the village and build solid organizational foundations from within.

TIBOR MENDE *
The Long March to Yenan

In 1931 when the Chinese Soviet Republic was proclaimed with Mao Tse-tung as its President, its authority extended over a fairly large area and over a population of about twenty-five million. Its regular army, composed of nearly sixty thousand men in 1931, grew to nearly three hundred thousand by 1934.

The first Kuomintang offensive launched against the Kiangsi soviets in November 1930 ended in failure before the end of the year. A second one, in the spring of 1931, was not more successful. In July of the same year Chiang Kai-shek personally conducted another campaign at the head of an army of three hundred thousand men. His efforts being temporarily diverted by Japan's activities in the North, this offensive, too, failed. When

* Tibor Mende, *The Chinese Revolution* (Worcester: Thames and Hudson, 1961), pp. 109–112.

it was recommenced in the summer of 1932, it managed to liqui-
date some small Communist bases in Hupeh province, but the
fourth offensive directed against the principal Kiangsi base failed.

It was the fifth campaign, begun in October 1933 with
two hundred airplanes and with more than half a million men,
that was to be decisive. Numerical superiority and the sheer
weight of modern equipment were beginning to tell. Moreover,
success was due primarily to the tactics adopted by General
Falkenhausen, head of the German military mission at that time
advising the Kuomintang. He instituted an inexorable blockade
of the Communist-held areas relying on a network of blockhouses able to frustrate well-tried guerrilla tactics. This, at last,
proved to be effective and by June 1934 Chiang could claim
that only three small regions remained infested by Communists
and that even those would soon be cleared out.

The Communists realized that the ring was closing around
them. Their hope that from Kiangsi they could spread out all
over China, lay shattered. To avoid annihilation, and after much
deliberation, they decided to abandon Kiangsi, to try to break
through the tight blockade, and so to carry with them the Soviet
Republic to a new and more secure base.

Their choice fell on the Northern province of Shensi. There,
in the great bend of the Yellow River, they knew of the existence of another Communist group. But to get there by the
direct route, about twelve hundred miles long, would have been
impossible. It led across regions where the Kuomintang was in
full control. Instead, it was decided to try a roundabout way
which would lead through areas where, owing to distance and
the difficulty of the terrain, the Kuomintang's control was partial
only.

Once the Communists were dislodged from Kiangsi, however, the Kuomintang was triumphant. As in 1927, so in 1934
again, its press and radio announced the final annihilation of
the Communists and the end of the danger they represented for
the Nationalist regime.

What really had happened was rather different.

The evacuation of the Kiangsi region began in October
1934. At the cost of some hard fighting the bulk of the Red
Army managed to break through the concentric lines of be-

sieging troops. They had to move southwest before they could head westward in the direction of the Tibetan borderlands. Thrown back toward the South, they changed direction and crossed the upper Yangtze. Continuing their northward advance, they again had to fight hard battles in order to cross the Tatu River. Beyond it, following the Szechwan border over difficult mountainous country, the trek led through the northwestern Moslem areas and from there over some of the most desolate regions of Kansu province. Finally, about a year after their departure from Kiangsi, the tattered remnants of the Communist armies reached the remote northern part of Shensi. There, at last, they could join up with the guerrilla forces in control of the region.

This prodigious feat of endurance became known as the Long March. It involved an organized trek of some eight thousand miles within a year. It led across eleven provinces, over remote regions inhabited by suspicious peoples, through murderous marshy lands overgrown by grass, and in face of continuous danger from local and governmental forces. It is claimed that the three Communist armies who participated in the march crossed eighteen mountain chains and twenty-four large rivers, broke through the armies of ten warlords, defeated dozens of Kuomintang regiments, and took temporarily sixty-two cities.

The basic aim, to save the Revolution, was thus achieved. But the price was heavy. Of the 130,000 men who had left Kiangsi and Hunan, fewer than 30,000 arrived in north Shensi. Some deserted on the way, intimidated by hardship. Many more perished in battle or succumbed to fatigue, frost, or to the other rigors of a hostile nature. Of several hundred women, no more than thirty survived. Among those who perished was Mao Tse-tung's wife. But those who reached Shensi constituted a hard core of tempered steel, a reliable and disciplined force with which to build the new Soviet Republic.

Three factors connected with the Long March were to help that task.

The first concerned Communist prestige. The Kuomintang continued to claim that the Communists had succumbed and ceased to represent any threat. Its press was tightly controlled and public opinion was preoccupied with Japan's moves so that few people were aware of the historic events in the remote interior of the country. Yet the epic story of the Long March was fast growing into a legend. Its incidents became the themes of songs and stories. Slowly what really had happened became known and the heroes of such a performance could hardly be described any longer as the unprincipled bandits of the Kuomintang's propaganda. On the contrary, a new prestige, springing from the admiration due to national heroes, was beginning to surround the Communists' enterprise.

The second factor was the new, total cohesion of the Communist Party. Next to the Kiangsi Soviet there had existed other Communist-controlled areas and not all of them had been unconditional in their acceptance of Mao's leadership. As the various groups had joined up with the Long March, a number of political meetings had been held on the way which gradually helped to eliminate existing differences. By the time the Communsts reached their destination, the miltary and political leaders had won unanimous support and Mao Tse-tung's "line" and leadership of the Party emerged uncontested.

The third factor was the human experience the Long March had provided. Like an involuntary and monumental study tour, it splendidly completed the Communists' already unrivaled knowledge of the Chinese peasant's psychology. It brought them into contact with new regions and different peoples. Disseminating their ideas among them on their way, they also learned a great deal about the problems and the attitudes of masses they were destined to govern later on. As a significant by-product of the experience, for the first time, the Long March brought the Communists into direct contact with the "national minorities" of the Southwest and of the Western regions and rendered both sides conscious of their ideas and aims.

Thus, with their moral stature grown but physically and numerically weakened, the Communists began to organize their new base.

After a pause, partly spent in negotiations with the local revolutionaries, an attempt was made to bring more territory under the Communists' control. In December 1936 the small town of Yenan was taken and for several years to come it served as the capital of the new Soviet Republic.

The area chosen was less easily accessible to the Kuomin-

tang forces than had been Kiangsi. Also, as in Chingkanshan, this
was once again a border area falling into several provincial juris-
dictions and thus rendering the action of the local, provincial
authorities less effective. Yet the problems to be faced were
enormous. The region was poor and sparsely populated. Food
was scarce. So were recruits for the fighting forces or the arms
they needed.

So it was in an atmosphere of general austerity, and practically ignored by the outside world, that once again the Communists began to build up their base into a veritable social lab-
oratory.

EDGAR SNOW *
Soviet Society

Whatever it may have been in the South, Chinese Communism
as I found it in the Northwest might more accurately be called
rural equalitarianism than anything Marx would have found ac-
ceptable as a model child of his own. This was manifestly true
economically, and although in the social, political, and cultural
life of the organized soviets there was a crude Marxist guidance,
limitations of material conditions were everywhere obvious.

It has already been emphasized that there is no machine
industry of any importance in the Northwest. The region is far
less influenced by industrialism than the Eastern parts of China;
it is farming and grazing country primarily, the culture of which
has been for centuries in stagnation, though many of the economic abuses prevalent no doubt reflect the changing economy
in the semi-industrialized cities. Yet the Red Army itself was an
outstanding product of the impact of "industrialization" on
China, and the shock of the ideas it brought into the fossilized
culture here was in a true sense revolutionary.

Objective conditions, however, denied the Reds the possi-

* Edgar Snow, *Red Star Over China* (New York: Random House, 1938),
pp. 232–243.

bility of organizing much more than the political framework for the beginnings of a modern economy, of which naturally they could think only in terms of a future which might give them power in the great cities, where they could take over the industrial bases from the foreign concessions and thus lay the foundations for a true socialist society. Meanwhile, in the rural areas, their activity centered chiefly on the solution of the immediate problems of the peasants—land and taxes. This may sound like the reactionary program of the old Narodniks of Russia, but the great difference lies in the fact that Chinese Communists never regarded land distribution as anything more than a phase in the building of a mass base, a stage enabling them to develop the revolutionary struggle toward the conquest of power and the ultimate realization of thoroughgoing socialist changes. In *Fundamental Laws of the Chinese Soviet Republic* the First All-China Soviet Congress in 1931 set forth in detail the "maximum program" of the Communist Party of China—and reference to it shows clearly that the ultimate aim of Chinese Communists is a true and complete socialist state of the Marxist-Leninist conception. Meanwhile, however, it has to be remembered that the social, political, and economic organization of the Red districts has all along been only a very provisional affair. Even in Kiangsi it was little more than that. Because the Soviets had to fight for an existence from their beginning, their main task was always to build a military and political base for the extension of the revolution on a wider and deeper scale, rather than to "try out Communism in China," which is what some people thought the Reds were attempting in their little blockaded areas.

The immediate basis of support for the Reds in the Northwest was obviously not so much the idea of "from each according to his ability, to each according to his need" as it was something like the promise of Dr. Sun Yat-sen: "Land to those who till it." Among economic reforms which the Reds could claim to their credit these four evidently counted most to the peasantry: redistribution of land, abolition of usury, abolition of tax extortion, and elimination of privileged groups.

While theoretically the soviets were a "workers' and peasants' " government, in actual practice the whole constituency was overwhelmingly peasant in character and occupation, and the regime had to shape itself accordingly. An attempt was made to balance peasant influence, and offset it, by classifying the rural population into these categories: great landlords, middle and small landlords, rich peasants, middle peasants, poor peasants, tenant peasants, rural workers, handicraft workers, lumpenproletariat, and a division called *tzu-yu chih-yeh chieh,* or professional workers—which included teachers, doctors, and technicians, the "rural intelligentsia." These divisions were political as well as economc, and in the election of the soviets the tenant peasants, rural workers, handicraft workers, and so on, were given a very much greater representation than the other categories—the aim apparently being to create some kind of democratic dictatorship of the "rural proletariat." However, it was hard to see that there was any important basic class division operative in these categories, landlords excepted, as they were all directly attached to agrarian economy.

Within these limitations the Soviets seemed to work very well in areas where the regime was stabilized. The structure of representative government was built up from the village soviet, as the smallest unit: above it were the district soviet, the county soviet, and the provincial and central soviets. Each village elected its delegates to the higher soviets clear up to the delegates elected for the Soviet Congress. Suffrage was universal over the age of sixteen, but it was not equal, for reasons mentioned above.

Various committees were established under each of the district soviets. An all-powerful committee, usually elected in a mass meeting shortly after the occupation of a district by the Red Army, and preceded by an intensified propaganda campaign, was the revolutionary committee. It called for elections or re-elections, and closely cooperated with the Communist Party. Under the district soviet, and appointed by it, were committees for education, cooperatives, military training, political training, land, public health, partisan training, revolutionary defense, enlargement of the Red Army, agrarian mutual aid, Red Army land tilling, and others. Such committees were found in every branch organ of the soviets, right up to the Central Government, where policies were coordinated and state decisions made.

Organization did not stop with the government itself. The

Communist Party had an extensive membership among farmers and workers, in the towns and in the villages. In addition there were the Young Communists, and under them two organizations which embraced in their membership most of the youths. These were called the *Shao-nien Hsien-feng Tui* and the *Erh-t'ung T'uan*—the Young Vanguards and the Children's Brigades. The Communist Party organized the women also into Young Communist Leagues, anti-Japanese societies, nursing schools, weaving schools, and tilling brigades. Adult farmers were organized into the *P'in-min Hui,* or Poor People's Society, and into anti-Japanese societies. Even the Elder Brother Society, an ancient secret organization, was brought into soviet life and given open and legal work to do. The *Nung-min Tui,* or Peasant Guards, and the *Yu Chi Tui,* or Partisan (Roving) Brigades, were also part of the intensely organized rural political and social structure.

The work of all these organizations and their various committees was coordinated by the Central Soviet Government, the Communist Party, and the Red Army. Here I shall not enter into statistical detail, or tiresome tables and charts, to explain the organic connections of these groups, but it can be said in general that they were all skillfully interwoven, and each directly under the guidance of some Communist, though decisions of organization, membership, and work seemed to be carried out in a democratic way by the peasants themselves. The aim of soviet organization obviously was to make every man, woman, or child a member of something, with definite work assigned to him to perform.

Rather typical of the intensity of soviet efforts were the methods used to increase production and utilize great areas of wasteland. I have copies of many orders, quite astonishing in their scope and common-sense practicality, issued by the land commission to its various branches to guide them in organizing and propagandizing the peasants in the tasks of cultivation. To illustrate: in one of these orders that I picked up in a branch land office, instructions were given concerning spring cultivation, the commission urging its workers to "make widespread propaganda to induce the masses to participate voluntarily, without involving any form of compulsory command." Detailed advice was offered on how to achieve the four main demands of this planting period, which the previous winter had been recognized by the Soviets to be: more extensive utilization of wasteland and expansion of Red Army land; increased crop yields; greater diversity of crops, with special emphasis on new varieties of melons and vegetables; and expansion of cotton acreage.

Among the devices recommended by this order to expand labor power, and especially to bring women directly into agricultural production (particularly in districts where the male population had declined as a result of enlistments in the Red Army), the following amusing and ingenious instruction suggests the efficiency with which the Reds went about utilizing their available materials:

> To mobilize women, boys, and old men to participate in spring planting and cultivation, each according to his ability to carry on either a principal or an auxiliary task in the labor processes of production. For example, "large feet" (natural feet) and young women should be mobilized to organize production-teaching corps, with tasks varying from land clearance up to the main tasks of agricultural production itself. Small feet (bound feet), young boys, and old men must be mobilized to help in weed-pulling, collecting dung, and for other auxiliary tasks.

But how did the peasants feel about this? The Chinese peasant is supposed to hate organization, discipline, and any social activity beyond his own family. Well, the Reds simply laugh at you when you tell them that. They say that no Chinese peasant dislikes organization or social activity if he is working for himself and not the *min-t'uan*—the landlord or the tax collector. And I must admit that most of the peasants to whom I talked seemed to support Soviets and the Red Army. Many of them were very free in their criticisms and complaints, but, when asked whether they preferred it to the old days, the answer was nearly always an emphatic yes. I noticed also that most of them talked about the Soviets as *womenti chengfu*—"our government" —and this struck me as something new in rural China.

One thing which suggested that the Reds have their base in the mass of the population was that in all the older soviet districts the policing and guarding was done almost entirely by the peasant organizations alone. There were few actual Red Army garrisons in the soviet districts, all the fighting strength of the army being kept at the front. Local defense was shared by the village revolutionary defense corps, peasant guards, and partisans. This fact may explain some of the popularity of the Red Army with the peasantry, for it was rarely planted down on them as an instrument of oppression and exploitation, like other armies, but was generally at the front, fighting for its food there, and engaged in meeting enemy attacks. On the other hand, the intensive organization of the peasantry created a rear-guard and base which freed the Red Army to operate with the extreme mobility for which it has been noted.

But really to understand the peasant support for the Communist movement it is necessary to keep in mind its economic basis. I have already described the burden borne by the peasantry in the Northwest under the former regime. Now, wherever the Reds went there is no doubt they radically changed the situation for the tenant farmer, the poor farmer, the middle farmer, and all the "have-not" elements. *All* forms of taxation were abolished in the new districts for the first year, to give the farmers a breathing space, and in the old districts only a progressive single tax on land was collected, and a small single tax (from 5 to 10 per cent) on business. Secondly, they gave land to the land-hungry peasants, and began the reclamation of great areas of "wasteland"—mostly the land of absentee or fleeing landlords. Thirdly, they took land and livestock from the wealthy classes and redistributed among the poor.

Redistribution of land was a fundamental of Red policy. How was it carried out? Later on, for reasons of national political maneuver, there was to be a drastic retreat in the soviet land policy, but when I traveled in the Northwest the land laws in force (promulgated by the Northwest Soviet Government in December 1935) provided for the confiscation of all landlords' land and the confiscation of all land of rich peasants that was not cultivated by the owners themselves. However, both the landlord and the rich peasant were allowed as much land as they could till with their own labor. In districts where there was no land scarcity—and there were many such districts in the Northwest—the lands of resident landlords and rich peasants were in practice not confiscated at all, but the wasteland and land of absentee owners was distributed, and sometimes there was a redivision of best quality land, poor peasants being given better soil, and landlords being allotted the same amount of poorer land.

What was a landlord? According to the Communists' definition (greatly simplified), any farmer who collected the greater part of his income from land rented out to others, and not from his own labor, was a landlord. By this definition the usurers and *t'u-hao* (*t'u-hao,* which actually means "local rascals," is the Reds' term for landowners) were put in about the same category as landlords, and similarly treated. Usury rates, according to Dr. Stampar, formerly ranged as high as 60 per cent in the Northwest, or very much higher in times of stress. Although land is very cheap in many parts of Kansu, Shensi, and Ninghsia, it is practically impossible for a farm worker or tenant with no capital to accumulate enough to buy sufficient land for his family. I met farmers in the Red districts who formerly had never been able to own any land, although rates in some places were as low as two or three dollars an acre.

Classes other than those mentioned above were not subject to confiscatory action, so a big percentage of the farmers stood to benefit immediately by the redistribution. The poorest farmers, tenants, and farm laborers were all provided with land enough for a livelihood. There did not seem to be an attempt to "equalize" landownership. The primary purpose of the soviet land laws, as explained to me by Wang Kuan-lan (the twenty-nine-year-old Russian-returned student who was land commissioner for the three Red provinces of the Northwest), was to provide for every person sufficient land to guarantee him and his family a decent livelihood—which was claimed to be the most urgent demand of the peasantry.

The land problem—confiscation and redistribution—was greatly simplified in the Northwest by the fact that big estates were formely owned by officials, tax collectors, and absentee landlords. With the confiscation of these, in many cases the immediate demands of the poor peasantry were satisfied, without much interference with either the resident small landlords or the rich peasants. Thus the Reds not only created the economic base for support in the poor and landless peasantry by giving them farms, but in some cases won the gratitude of middle peasants by abolishing tax exploitation, and in a few instances enlisted the aid of small landlords on the same basis or on the patriotic appeals of the anti-Japanese movement. There were several prominent Shensi Communists from landlord families.

Additional help was given to the poor farmers in the form of loans at very low rates of interest or no interest at all. Usury was entirely abolished, but private lending, at rates fixed at a maximum of 10 per cent annually, was permitted. The ordinary government lending rate was 5 per cent. Several thousand agricultural implements made in the Red arsenals, and thousands of pounds of seed grain, were supplied to landless peasants breaking wasteland. A primitive agricultural school had been established, and I was told it was planned to open an animal husbandry school as soon as an expert in this field, expected from Shanghai, had arrived.

The cooperative movement was being vigorously pushed. These activities extended beyond production and distribution cooperatives, branching out to include cooperation in such (for China) novel forms as the collective use of farm animals and implements—especially in tilling public lands and Red Army lands—and in the organization of labor mutual-aid societies. By the latter device great areas could be quickly planted and harvested collectively, and periods of idleness by individual farmers eliminated. The Reds saw to it that a man earned his new land! In busy periods the system of "Saturday Brigades" was used, when not only all the children's organizations, but every soviet official, Red partisan, Red guard, women's organization, and any Red Army detachment that happened to be nearby, were mobilized to work at least one day a week at farming tasks. Even Mao Tse-tung took part in this work.

Here the Reds were introducing the germs of the drastically revolutionary idea of collective effort—and doing primary education work for some future period when collectivization might become practicable. At the same time, into the dark recesses of peasant mentality there was slowly penetrating the concept of a broader realm of social life. For the organizations created among the peasantry were what the Reds called three-in-one: economic, political, and cultural in their utility.

What cultural progress the Reds had made among these people was, by any advanced Western standards, negligible indeed. But certain outstanding evils common in most parts of China had definitely been eliminated in the score of long-sovietized counties in north Shensi, and a crusade of propaganda was being conducted among inhabitants of newer areas to spread the same elementary reforms there. As an outstanding achievement, opium had been completely eliminated in north Shensi, and in fact I did not see any sign of poppies after I entered the soviet districts. Official corruption was almost unheard-of. Beggary and unemployment did seem to have been, as the Reds claimed, "liquidated." I did not see a beggar during all my travels in the Red areas. Foot binding and infanticide were criminal offenses, child slavery and prostitution had disappeared, and polyandry and polygamy were prohibited.

The myths of "communized wives" or "nationalization of women" are too patently absurd to be denied, but changes in marriage, divorce, and inheritance were in themselves extremely radical against the background of semi-feudal law and practice elsewhere in China. Marriage regulations included interesting provisions against mother-in-law tyranny, the buying and selling of women as wives and concubines, and the custom of "arranged matches." Marriage was by mutual consent, the legal age had been moved up sharply to twenty for men and eighteen for women; dowries were prohibited, and any couple registering as man and wife before a county, municipal, or village soviet was given a marriage certificate without cost. Men and women actually cohabiting were considered legally married, whether registered or not—which seems to rule out "free love"—and their offspring were legitimate. No illegitimacy of children was recognized.

Divorce could also be secured from the registration bureau of the soviet, free of charge, on the "insistent demand" of either party to the marriage contract, but wives of Red Army men were required to have their husbands' consent before a divorce was granted. Property was divided equally between the divorcees, and both were legally obliged to care for their children, but responsibility for debts was shouldered by the man alone (!), who was also obliged to supply two thirds of the children's living expenses.

Education, in theory, was "free and universal," but parents had of course to supply their children with food and clothing. In practice, nothing like "free and universal" education had yet been achieved, although old Hsu Teh-lih, the commissioner of education, boasted to me that if they were given a few years of peace in the Northwest they would astound the rest of China with the educational progress they would make . . . it is interesting to know how the government was financing not only the educational program, such as it was, but this whole seemingly simple and yet in its way vastly complex organism which I have called soviet society.

4. THE KUOMINTANG CONFRONTS JAPAN

❧ Generalissimo Chiang Kai-shek and Wartime China

THE JAPANESE armies ate like acid around the edges of China for six years. Finally in 1937 they attacked the Marco Polo Bridge outside of Peking, and began a swift march southward to Nanking, the Chinese capital. For six years Chiang and the Kuomintang had procrastinated, hoping to destroy the last of the Communists before being forced to take up the gauntlet against Japan. The Communists had long since proclaimed war against Japan and were reaping significant propaganda victories by labeling the Kuomintang pro-Japanese and unpatriotic. "Why should we kill each other when we are being invaded from without?" they demanded.

Chiang was spared the agony of making this decision when he was kidnapped in 1936 at Sian, while ostensibly on an inspection trip of some of his anti-Communist pacification troops. The Sian Incident is still shrouded in mystery, and exactly what transpired is much contested. At any rate, Chiang agreed to form a second united front with the Communists in order to prosecute the war against Japan.

From 1937 until Japan's surrender in 1945, the Nationalist government was almost completely cut off from the outside world. Forced to retreat before the advancing Japanese armies, they moved their capital from Nanking to Hankow, and then finally hundreds of miles up the Yangtze River to Chungking, deep in Central China. The Chinese were thrown back on their own resources and bravery. Only one man seemed to be able to lead China out of this nightmare—Chiang Kai-shek, in whose hands lay China's destiny. He was the only hope for national salvation in China's darkest hour, and despite his shortcomings, the Chinese people rallied around him during this time of national crisis. No one was more aware of this than Chiang himself. In 1943, in *China's Destiny*, he wrote, "Without the Kuomintang there would be no China. In a word, China's destiny is entrusted to the Kuomintang. If the Kuomintang Revolution should fail, China as a nation would have nothing to rely upon." He might very well have added, without Chiang Kai-shek there would be no Kuomintang and no China. His words were telling but not very prophetic.

Because wartime China and Chiang Kai-shek were almost synonymous, it is fitting that we begin this chapter with a character sketch of the man who led China during the war.

The following selection, from White and Jacoby's *Thunder Out of China*, gives us a rare glimpse into Chiang's early life. They examine Chiang as the leader of the Chinese people, explaining that while he was frugal, incorruptible, and read his Bible every night, he was a frequently ruthless, shrewd, vain, short-tempered man of limited vision. Raised during the warlord period, he had learned "to revolve all his politics about the concept of force. . . . He had grown up in a time of treachery and violence," says the author. "There were few standards of human decency his warlord contemporaries did not violate. They obeyed no law but power, and Chiang outwitted them at their own game."

In the second passage they write about the war itself, during which White was a *Time* correspondent in China. He recalls the heroic but costly defense of Shanghai in 1937 and the confusion of the retreating government as it fell back inland to a series of temporary capitals. He describes the important role played by the Communist guerrillas north of the Yellow River in harassing Japanese supply lines and communications, and he concludes that the Japanese seriously underestimated Chinese defensive capabilities and tenacity. As one year became another, the war became hopelessly bogged down. Each side dug in along a static line of defense, waiting for a break in the military stalemate and the monotony. In the Chinese Army men died of starvation before they saw combat, and equipment rusted from disuse. There was not the slightest hope that the ragged, undernourished, ill-equipped Chinese Army could drive the Japanese from their soil, but they did prevent the Japanese from winning a conclusive victory in China.

THEODORE H. WHITE AND ANNALEE JACOBY *
Chiang Kai-shek

For all that any observer might see, the years of war dealt kindly with Chiang Kai-shek. His face changed by scarcely a line or a wrinkle. Always immaculate, always encased in an armor of self-discipline, he preserved his personality safe from the prying curiosity of the public. Countless mass meetings hung upon the short-clipped words he shrilled forth in his high-pitched Chekiang accent. None ever saw him kindled by the emotion that flickered from the adoring crowds; none ever saw him acknowledge the surging cheers with more than a slow, taut smile or the quick bobbing of his head.

Only the most convulsive moment of emotion can make him lift the hard casing of control in public and show the man beneath. In August 1945 Chiang sat quietly in a stuffy radio station in Chungking waiting to tell the Chinese people that the war was over. He was, as always, fixedly composed. His pate was shaven clean, and no telltale fuzz indicated graying hair. His spotless khaki tunic, barren of any decoration, was tightly buttoned at the throat and buckled with a Sam Browne belt; a fountain pen was clipped in his pocket. The studio was hot, and the twenty people in the room oozed sweat; only the Generalissimo seemed cool. He adjusted hornrimmed glasses, glanced at the scarlet flowers on the table before him, and slowly turned to the microphone to inform the people in his clear, high voice that victory had been won. As he spoke, a loudspeaker outside the building spread the news; and crowds, recognizing his conspicuous sedan, began to gather outside the stone building. He could hear the faint sound of cheers.

Chiang finished in ten minutes. Then suddenly his head

* White and Jacoby, *Thunder Out of China, op. cit.,* pp. 118–131, 40–67.

sagged; beneath his dark eyes the pouches of sleeplessness let go; the muscles of his slight body relaxed in profound exhaustion. For a fleeting moment the smooth exterior was punctured, the weariness and strain breaking through at the moment of victory to show the man. As quickly as the mood came it was gone, and he walked out of the studio, passed through the crowd with a smiling nod here and there, then sped back to his home. Watching him descend the stairs through the crowd to his sedan, no one could tell that here was a man who had just seen the defeat of his national enemy and who, only that night, was about to set in motion the wheels of machinery that was to engulf the country afresh in civil war.

Chiang's personal discipline is one of the first clues to his complex, involved character. It has been bred of a tempestuous, storm-tossed life and, like his lust for power, his calculating ruthlessness, his monumental stubbornness, has become more than an individual characteristic—it is a force in national politics. Chiang's character reflects and distorts fifty of the most turbulent years in Chinese history.

Chiang Kai-shek was born [in 1888] into the home of a small Chekiang farmer, a member of the governing group of the village, at a moment when China was entering a period of almost unprecedented chaos and disaster. His boyhood was sad. On his fiftieth birthday he wrote:

> My father died when I was nine years old. . . . The miserable condition of my family at that time is beyond description. My family, solitary and without influence, became at once the target of much insult and maltreatment. . . . It was entirely due to my mother and her kindness and perseverance that the family was saved from utter ruin. For a period of seventeen years—from the age of nine until I was twenty-five years old—my mother never spent a day free from domestic difficulties.

China, in Chiang's boyhood, was prey to every humiliation foreign arms could heap on her, and Chiang, moved by the national disaster, chose to become a soldier. He studied briefly in Japan, then returned to participate in the competitive examinations for admission to the first Chinese military academy, at

Paoting. He passed these examinations with distinction and within a year had marked himself as one of the academy's outstanding students. He was one of a handful chosen by the academy in 1907 to be trained in Japan, and there he was soon selected to serve with a Japanese field artillery regiment as a cadet. He did not like Japan and later spoke bitterly of his service there. But he did like military life. Once he told a group of Chinese students who had joined his army none too voluntarily:

> When I was a young man, I made up my mind to become a soldier. I have always believed that to be in the army is the highest experience of human existence as well as the highest form of revolutionary activity. All that I now possess in experience, knowledge, spirit, and personality I gained through military training and experience.

While he was in Japan, he was stirred, like other student thinkers, by Sun Yat-sen's vision of a new China, strong and great. In 1911 he returned to China to join the uprising that overthrew the Manchus and established the Chinese Republic. When the first republic proved a mockery, he went to Shanghai; what he did there is a matter of gossip and guess, for official biographies skip hastily over this period. It is known, though, that he was helped by a revolutionary named Ch'en Chi-mei, uncle of the CC brothers. In 1915 Chiang participated in another military coup aimed at seizing the Kiangnan arsenal near Shanghai. His comrades of that adventure, who are still among his intimate associates, fled the country, but Chiang disappeared somewhere into Shanghai's murky underworld. He lived a fast, hard life of personal danger, hunger, and abandon; then for a while he was an inconspicuous clerk on the Shanghai stock exchange. At that time, the underworld of Shanghai was dominated by the notorious Green Gang that controlled the city's rackets of opium, prostitution, and extortion. The Green Gang was an urban outgrowth of one of the many secret societies that have flourished in China for centuries. Such a gang has no counterpart in Western life; it sank its roots into all the filth and misery of the great lawless city, disposed of its gunmen as it saw fit, protected its clients by violence, was an organized force perhaps more powerful than the police. The border line between violent

insurrectionary and outright gangster was often blurred; men
passed between the two worlds with ease. No biographer can
trace Chiang's precise degree of association with the Green
Gang; but no informed Chinese denies the association, and no
account of China's Revolution fails to record that at every crisis
in Shanghai, the gang acted in his support.

Out from the mists of Shanghai, Chiang Kai-shek strode
forth into the full blaze of Chinese national politics at Canton
in the summer of 1924. Precisely how he arrived at this emi-
nence from his previous estate of penniless dependency on the
Shanghai publicans is obscure. He served briefly with a Fu-
kienese warlord after Shanghai; he had been brought to Sun
Yat-sen's attention by his Shanghai friends, and Sun sent him
to study Russian military techniques at Moscow in 1923. He
had returned to China and Canton with a huge distrust of the
Russians but a shrewd appreciation of the methods of the one-
party state. Canton in those days was bursting with fresh energy
and new ideas. Kuomintang leaders argued and competed; intrigue dissolved and remade political alliances. During the two
years of Chiang's stay in Canton he was never beaten in a
quarrel. He staged his first successful armed coup in the spring
of 1926 against the left wing of his own party; it was a master-
ful piece of timing, and after Sun Yat-sen's death he succeeded
to the post of party leader.

During the next twenty years both China and Chiang
changed, but his dominance in the Kuomintang was never once
seriously threatened. His one passion now became and remained
an overriding lust for power. All his politics revolved about the
concept of force. He had grown up in a time of treachery and
violence. There were few standards of human decency his early
warlord contemporaries did not violate; they obeyed no law but
power, and Chiang outwitted them at their own game. His false
starts in insurrection had taught him that he should show no
mercy to the vanquished and that the victor remains victor only
as long as his armies are intact. When he started north from
Canton in 1926 to seize the Yangtze Valley, he was an accomplished student in all the arts of buying men or killing them.

A full decade elapsed between the success of the Nationalist
Revolution in 1927 and the invasion by the Japanese in 1937,

a decade in which the frail, brooding figure of Chiang Kai-shek grew ever larger and more meaningful in the life of China. Chiang was shrewd—only a shrewd man could have built up his power from that of an insurrectionary to that of a leader willing and able to offer combat to the Japanese Empire. He knew how to draw on the Shanghai business world for support in money and goods; he was student enough to bring some of China's finest scholars into his administration. Power had come to Chiang Kai-shek as he rode the crest of a revolution to triumph over the warlords; the wave receded, but Chiang consolidated his victory on a new basis. He still spoke of a Nationalist Revolution—but the fact that the Revolution involved the will of the people escaped him. Chiang relied not on the emotion of the peasant masses but on an army and its guns.

The war against Japan made Chiang Kai-shek almost a demigod. For a brief moment at the war's outbreak he stood as the incarnate symbol of all China's will to resistance and freedom. Once again, as in the days of revolution, he was China —doing China's will, above reproach, above criticism, above all advice.

Chiang lived frugally by American standards. He breakfasted on fresh fruit, toast, and milk. On state occasions his cook prepared some of the most succulent delicacies of China, but at home with Madame Chiang the Generalissimo dipped his chopsticks into simple food. He took little exercise except for long walks in the country, with a covey of guards around him. He suffered from the back injury he had received during the Sian kidnapping, and his false teeth bothered him. The set he used during the war was made by a Canadian missionary in Western China; it was not quite comfortable, and he often went about at home without it. Once he had to cancel all public appearances while it was repaired. Except for these minor irritations his health was good. He always seemed composed and confident; during a conversation only his foot, tapping nervously, and the continual grunt of *"Hao, hao"* revealed the nervous tension that always seethed inside him.

As the leader of China at war Chiang was still harsh and ruthless, but he cloaked himself in the sanctity of a deacon; he became a devout and practicing Methodist. His utterances rang with the sincerity of a Puritan, but his ferocity was that of an Old Testament Joshua. He read the Bible every day and frowned on sin with the intensity of one who has sampled it and found it less rewarding than piety. He did not smoke; he rarely drank. It is true that American officers saw him at formal banquets when he would reach back into his past and toss down wine with the best, but among Chinese he was the ascetic. When the Communist leader Mao Tse-tung arrived in Chungking to talk about a truce in China's Civil War, Chiang lifted a toast to him, but only touched the cup to his lips.

Chiang was incorruptible. Chinese pointed out, however, that a man who had everything he could possibly want could afford to be honest. The government provided him with an un-limited budget, a fleet of limousines, and the best house wher-ever he went. The Americans gave him a private airplane. In Chungking he had a town house in his headquarters compound; across the Yangtze River, which he crossed by private launch, was a magnificent country home. Later in the war he built a group of villas as far outside Chungking in the other direction, named his own "Shantung," and used the others to entertain state guests. The houses, however modest by American stand-ards, were magnificent for Szechwan. They even had chrome-and-tile bathrooms, which so awed the workmen that at one guest cottage, later visited by Ambassador Hurley, they laid the entrance path straight to the bathroom door.

Now Chiang, reigning over China, was high above all or-dinary mortals. He was infuriated by gossip he would have shrugged off twenty years earlier. Once Chungking relayed the tale that during Madame's absence the Generalissimo had lived with a young nurse named Miss Ch'en, who cooked his native food for him. The story was idle gossip, but it galled Chiang so that he summoned Cabinet ministers, foreign missionaries, and two correspondents and proclaimed in the presence of Madame Chiang his Christianity, his true monogamous love, his com-plete denial of the gossip. Even during a month of disastrous military defeat this garden confessional got top billing in Chung-king conversation for days. Semiofficial transcripts of the Generalissimo's denial could be obtained from the government on request.

The New Life Movement was one of the more voluntary methods Chiang used for imposing the convictions and tastes of his maturity on his people. The movement frowned on luxury, smoking, drinking, dancing, permanent waves, gambling, spitting in the streets. Every now and then the police tried to make the rules stick; they stopped pedestrians from smoking in public and told people not to throw orange peels in the gutters. These outbursts of public piety passed away quickly; in the inner circle they were regarded as personal foibles of Chiang's. Though even Madame Chiang enjoyed cigarettes, the Generalissimo frowned especially on Western dissipations. No dance was held in Chungking till late in 1943, when the American Army garrison was so large that the prohibition could no longer be made to stick. Chinese were still forbidden to dance unless foreigners were present; once a private house was raided because of dancing and the guests arrested after the last American soldier had left.

No one knows how many positions Chiang Kai-shek held during the war years. At one time his secretary said there were at least eighty-two; he imagined a complete list could be found somewhere, but he had never compiled one. The Ministry of Information made up an incomplete list, which stated that among other things Chiang Kai-shek was: Chief Executive of the Kuomintang; President of the National Government; Chairman of the National Military Council; Commander-in-Chief of land, naval, and air forces; Supreme Commander, China Theater; President of the State Council; Chairman of the Supreme National Defense Council; Director-General of the Central Planning Board; Chairman of the Party and Political Work Evaluation Committee; Director of the New Life Movement Association; Chairman of the Commission for Inauguration of Constitutional Government; President of the Central Training Corps; President of the School for Descendants of Revolutionary Martyrs; President of the National Glider Association.

Chiang Kai-shek thought of himself first as a military leader. Though he may have been military director of his country's war effort, he was no strategist. General Wedemeyer was shocked when he arrived in China in 1944 to find that over half the Chinese soldiers were starving—not undernourished, but actually starving—and that Chiang had no effective over-all plan for either attack or defense. Chiang was not very successful in trying to outguess the Japanese or in moving defending forces to a position before a thrust came; he sent soldiers trudging to the front after battle had begun, though the Japanese had the advantage of mobility. American officers said, summing up his strategy, "He's a sucker for a feint."

Chiang thought of himself as a soldier, but his true genius lay in politics; he had no equal in the ancient art of hog trading. Ringmaster at a balancing act, he brought China together and kept it together. If his soldiers starved, that was the price of keeping the loyalty of dubious generals, who profited from their death. If he sent into battle soldiers who were doomed before they heard gunfire, that was one way of reducing the forces of a commander who might have challenged him.

As a politician Chiang dealt in force rather than ideas. Any concept of China that differed from his own was treated with as much hostility as an enemy division. In both Party and government, above honesty, experience, or ability, he insisted on the one qualification of complete, unconditional loyalty to himself. Since loyalty involved agreement, Chiang became a sage; Chinese tradition respects scholarship above all things, and the great ruler in Chinese eyes is the great teacher. Chiang's public speeches began to sound like an instructor chastening his pupils; he repeated over and over, "Be loyal; study hard; work hard; love your country." Every national decision was made by him, and he gradually came to believe that his knowledge and judgment were better than any subordinate's.

When inflation grew into one of the country's biggest problems, a high official of the government quipped, "The trouble with China is that the Generalissimo doesn't know anything about economics, and his Minister of Finance doesn't know anything, either." Nevertheless the Generalissimo wrote a book about economics. It was a windy, foggy book full of ignorant theories, and his own scholars recoiled from the shock of it; wiser men in the government bravely had the brochure withdrawn from circulation. Suppression made it a choice collector's item. During the fall of 1942 and early 1943, the Generalissimo spent long hours in his country home polishing his master work, *China's Destiny*. It was largely written by one of his personal secretaries, but the ideas and the final gloss were his own. Here was another omniscient textbook; it covered the anthropology of the Chinese people, the nation's history, its future recon-struction. His advisers took alarm at his interpretation of China's modern history, which was viciously, indiscriminately anti-for-eign. He heaped on foreigners the blame for warlordism, prosti-tution, gun running, opium smoking, gangsterism, and all the bloody chaos at the birth of the Chinese Republic; he bewailed the influence of foreign missionaries and their universities on Chinese culture. This book sold half a million copies before it was "withdrawn for revision," probably at the insistence of Madame Chiang. It too became a collector's item—but no for-eign correspondent was permitted by censorship to quote from it.

With government, army, and Party as his own private do-main Chiang's curiosity and whims reached down to the lowest levels. Sometimes he scolded, sometimes he punished, sometimes he taught; no decision was too trivial to interest him. When he saw the preview of the only big motion picture produced in Chungking during the war, a Chinese version of Amleto Vespa's thriller, *Secret Agent of Japan*, he sent it back to the studio with personal instructions to insert more footage on the work of the Kuomintang. The Minister of Information called on him once in a long gown; the Minister, Chiang said, was too young to wear an old-fashioned gown and should wear Western clothes. Chiang decided who should and who should not be allowed to go to America; he decided which students of the government Graduate School of Journalism should have scholar-ships to study abroad. Students of the National Central Univer-sity complained of their food, and the Generalissimo went out to have a meal at their mess himself; he decided the food was good enough.

When his troops were fighting north of Mandalay, he wired to General Stilwell: "I hear that watermelons are plentiful in the region of Mandalay. Chinese soldiers like watermelons. See to it that each company gets a watermelon each day." He deluged commanders at the front with orders about trivial details, without regard to the wretched state of China's communications. Each day he read the Chungking press, to mark little things that pleased or displeased him. When General Stilwell was relieved, the Generalissimo had foreign correspondents' dispatches translated into Chinese and censored them himself—totally. He sent out orders on tabs of paper; sometimes he was forgetful and the orders conflicted. "Make all provincial governments set the collection of grain before all things this year," he would write; later another tab would come down: "This year the gathering of new recruits is the primary task of all provincial governments."

To foreigners his outer reserve argued stability, a sweetly rational quality in a mad society. But sometimes Chiang erupted from his expressionless calm into a rage in which he threw teacups, pounded on tables, shrieked, and yelled like a top sergeant. When he dealt with a rare character who refused to scrape before him, like T. V. Soong, the results were dramatic. Their most violent argument over the Communist problem in 1935 resulted in Soong's disappearance from power for years. The British Ambassador Sir Archibald Clark-Kerr engineered another meeting in 1938; this, too, ended in a tempest. Early in 1944 Chiang met T.V. again, and the result was another prolonged exile of Soong from power. In the summer of 1944, Chiang was strolling along a country road when he saw an officer leading recruits roped together. Such sights were common in country places, but Chiang was infuriated and beat the officer until a bodyguard rescued the man. When the Generalissimo was reminded of the horror of Chinese conscription, he summoned the general in charge of conscription and beat him unmercifully; the general was executed the next spring.

High officials with Western training realized that the Generalissimo was a poor administrator. In guarded private conversations they admitted his faults but always set against them his one huge virtue—he meant to keep China in the war until Japan was defeated; other men might sicken and tire, but he was China, and he never faltered. No one else could keep all the balances in Chinese politics so nicely adjusted and still maintain resistance. He placed his armies so that they would fight together against the enemy but never against him; the warlords were placated by deft commitments; men who disliked him supported him because he was recognized by the world as the proper recipient of loans and supplies to China. He controlled all the massive misery of the countryside by the loyalty of the landlords and warded off pressure from America with promises of reform.

In the summer of 1940 morale had reached an all-time low. Everything was wrong. The Japanese were bombing day and night, and the clear sky that brought the bombers was also searing rice in the fields and bringing famine. The Japanese were in Indo-China; American policy were indecisive; the British announced that they were closing the Burma Road. Chiang burst out: *"Nimen ta suan pan!* (You people are counting beads on the counting board!) You count how many troops we have, how many rounds of ammunition, how many gallons of gasoline. But I don't care. When I started seventeen years ago, I had two thousand cadets in a military school. America, France, England, and Japan were against me. The Communists were stronger than they are today. And I had no money. But I marched north and beat the warlords. I united the country. Today I have three million men and half of China, and England and America are friends. Let them come—if they drive me back to Tibet, in five years I will be back and will conquer all China again." For Chiang it was his war, his enemy, his responsibility. He looked back not on three years of war against Japan but on seventeen years in his personal career. China was as much his own as the little academy in Canton had been.

Chiang felt just as personally about the only Chinese group he could not control, the Communists. Only the Communists could afford organized disobedience. They had their own territory and their own army, and they were beyond Chiang's reach. They defied him; therefore in his eyes they were disloyal to China, and he hated them. In 1941 he said: "You think it is important that I have kept the Japanese from expanding during these years. . . . I tell you it is more important that I have kept the Communists from spreading. The Japanese are a disease of the skin; the Communists are a disease of the heart. They say they wish to support me, but secretly all they want is to overthrow me." His was a personal war. He remembered the Communists as he had seen them last during the Long March. He had had the pilot of his plane follow the long, straggling line of Communist marchers fleeing over the hills for several hours so that he could look down and watch.

Just when it was that loyalty to Chiang's leadership began to crumble is difficult to say, but certainly disaffection set in about the same time among the warlords, in Chungking, and among the peasants. By the end of 1943 there was open discontent in the headquarters of various field commanders, many of whom had fought Chiang in past civil wars and followed his leadership now only because of the greater menace of the Japanese. In the Southwest, Cantonese and Kwangsi generals growled at Chiang with unconcealed anger from the security of their own camps; they had known him when he had been just another warrior; to them he was no god but a partner who ought to find money and supplies for them. Independent warlords far to the northwest and in Szechwan, Yunnan, and Sikang were kept in line by Chiang by the award of honorary titles; he let them pursue their private grafts, whether opium-running or simple double taxation, as long as they fulfilled his demands for new recruits for the army and new rice for the food tax. Chiang had contended with such enemies for years, and he knew how to handle them.

Criticism of Chiang had notably infected Chungking by 1944. Even those who felt that Chiang was the living embodiment of the Chinese state, the rock in the quicksands of defeat, felt that the "old man" was slipping—that he, like other leaders, was open to criticism. A more crucial sentiment against Chiang that grew with every month held that China was greater than Chiang and that Chiang himself was the point of paralysis. The group who felt this way believed that Chinese energies were being held back by the nature of Chiang's political balances and commitments, that he could not balance corruption, duplicity, and extortion and get a net effect of strength. Energy could come only from the people, and Chiang's alliances bound him to the oppressors of the people. Chiang emptied the vials of his wrath on this group of unorganized critics within and without his own party. He could deal with all, no matter how corrupt,

who held him in the same esteem he held himself; but any who
could not accept his formula that he was China were pariahs,
to be ferreted out and terrorized by his secret police. Some who
hated Chiang more than they loved China went over to the
Japanese; others sought a safe obscurity in a different province,
in private business, in the humdrum lower reaches of the bureaucracy. Except for a fortunate few the rest had to guard their
every word.

Among those who could talk were some of the most
honored names of the Nationalist Revolution. Gentle Madame
Sun Yat-sen, widow of the Kuomintang's founder, had a courage
of steel. She never attacked Chiang in public, but neither did
she hide her bitterness at the corruption and dissolution of the
nation. She preserved all the revolutionary ideals that had
brought the Kuomintang to power, and she gave quiet support
to harassed liberal and democratic groups. Dr. Sun Fo, for his
part, did not hesitate to speak his mind, either to Chiang or in
open meeting; Chiang could censor his accusations in both the
foreign and the domestic press, but he could not stop them. T. V.
Soong also was too fearless and too prominent to be intimidated;
he could be silenced only by admission once again to power.

The peasants too had had their fill of Chiang Kai-shek's
government by 1944. His picture hung in government offices in
every village, and his name was still a magic symbol, but the
men who did his will among the peasants were hated and ex-
coriated. As early as 1942 reports of peasant uprisings began to
seep into the capital. These reports—half gossip, half fact—
came from everywhere, from areas remote from Communist influence. Discontent was spreading through the hundreds of thousands of villages still under Kuomintang administration. There
were uprisings in Kweichow and Kansu, in Fukien and Hupeh.
In Szechwanese villages there were riots—angry, unorganized,
uncoordinated. Chiang lived in a state of increasing petulance;
bad news of this sort made him furious. His temper flared so
often that people sought to bring him only pleasant news and
flattery. The press was silenced, and signs hung in country tea-
houses: "It is forbidden to discuss national affairs."

Of all the grotesque elements of this personal government
perhaps the most incongruous was Chiang's assessment of his

own role. Chiang sincerely believed he was leading China to democracy; it enraged him to be called a dictator. Once Chou En-lai, chief Communist representative in Chungking, told him that the Communists would turn over control of their army only to a democratic government. Said Chiang, "Would you call *me* undemocratic?"

War

Out of the turbulence of thirty years the Chinese people had drawn a bitter but lasting education. The surging revolutionary tides that had swept the land had finally produced leaders who held themselves responsible for the nation in the eyes of history. Beyond all the hatred that the warring parties bore each other, they had come to share a conviction in China's unity and destiny. All Japan's plans were to be shattered on the rocks of this conviction. The first volleys of the war against Japan cut across all the discontent within China—across the slogans, the treachery and intrigue, the partisan zealotry. Even the imponderable working of the Revolution itself within the depths of Chinese society was suspended for a time while the nation turned to face the threat of the Japanese. There could be no China at all, neither Communist nor Nationalist, in submission to Japan; there could be no dignity whatever, either for rich or for poor.

The Japanese planned their 1937 operations on the main-land on two planes, the military and the political. For five years they had been biting into China above the Great Wall, section by section, while the Chinese stewed in their internal wars and protested to the League of Nations. This time the Japanese expected to wrench away the five provinces that lie below the Great Wall, within the bend of the Yellow River. Having seized the North, they hoped to persuade Chiang to yield them far-reaching concessions and special privileges in what remained of the land. Eventually the Japanese planned to tighten their economic-military-political grip till it clutched all China and the Chinese government had been reduced to the status of a subordinate colonial administration. If the Japanese had struck five years earlier, they might have succeeded, but in 1937 they were too late.

Their operations in the North proceeded according to plan almost to the split second. Their columns opened out from Peking and Tientsin, struck northwest through the famous Nankow Pass, breached the Great Wall from the south, then wheeled around to come down through it again from the north on the passes that guard the northern flank of the iron-rich, coal-producing province of Shansi. They struck south down the railway that leads from Tientsin to Nanking and within a few months stood on the banks of the Yellow River. The resistance that met the Japanese in Northern China was a combination of the very old and very new. The warlords, surprising everyone, chose to fight it out in alignment with the Central Government, rather than yield to Japanese threats or promises. Their armies, however, were ragamuffin hordes. They had no common body of military tactics and skills, no mutual confidence, no modern organization. They broke like a wall of dust before the impact of Japan's steel-tipped legion. It was summer, and the tank-led columns of the Japanese darted almost at will across the yellow plains of Northern China. Their air force ruled the skies; it strafed what little movement there was on Chinese highways. Japanese military intelligence in Northern China was superb. The first phases of the campaign ran like drillground maneuvers; the Japanese columns cut down the railways and highways to occupy successive objectives on schedule. By all calculations the occupation of the key rail and road junctions should have finished the job. These were the centers where political agitation had bothered the Japanese; these were the military keys to the land. And yet somehow, though no Japanese could quite tell why, the war went on. From the villages and mountains came rifle fire. The Japanese sacked and looted; they raped the women of the North till their lust was worn; they branded the centers they held with terror. And yet about them, picking at them, bleeding them, grew a conspiracy of resistance that seemed to nourish itself from the earth alone. This was the resistance of partisan China.

Partisan China was the domain of the Reds. By agreement with Chiang Kai-shek they were to leave positional warfare to him and wage guerrilla warfare behind the enemy lines. In the fall of 1937, starting from their small base in the barren sandlands of northern Shensi, the former Red troops, now restyled the Eighth Route Army of the Central Government, began in the fall of 1937 one of the most amazing adventures in arms of all times. It was to lift Communist military strength from eighty-five thousand men in 1937 to over a million by the end of the war, Communist political control from a million and a half to an estimated ninety million. In the early months of resistance Communist expansion raced over the hills. Their divisional and frontal units dissolved into regiments, the regiments into battalions and companies; and they trickled off through the Japanese lines into the countryside. Within four months after the outbreak of the war Communist troops were standing on the shores of the ocean, seven hundred miles from their starting point, and organizing a new war behind the enemy lines.

The wells of hatred and terror that the Japanese had opened by their ferocity were ready to be tapped, and the Communists tapped them. The soldiers of warlord armies who had fled the Japanese columns on the perilous highways had taken refuge in the hills; they were disorganized, lawless bands —but they had guns. Some were incorporated into Communist cadres of resistance. The weapons the others abandoned or sold were soon being used to arm a grass-roots peasant resistance. The students of the Northern universities had clamored for war against Japan; now that the war had arrived and was surpassing in barbarism anything they had conceived in their study halls, they too wanted to take part in it. They abandoned their classes, crossed the lines, and joined the resistance. Communist leadership was the rallying point for the entire movement north of the Yellow River, and every resource of human energy and intelligence, Communist, Kuomintang, and nonpartisan, was swiftly geared into a program of social reorganization that provided a stable base for continuing warfare. Relations between the Communists and the government were good. Some of the early campaigns were exemplars of co-ordination; the only major check the Japanese army received in the North came at the magnificent battle of Hsinkou. There in the mountain passes government troops held a frontal position long enough to let the Communists filter across the enemy communication lines and cut an entire division almost to pieces from the rear.

As the war in the North wore on, the Japanese columns closed down the channels of communication and supply till frontal warfare became futile and impossible. By early 1938 the Red Army abandoned all standard army framework; the divisions were now dissolved into a shifting net of marauding bands, depending on the people for support. The government of Chiang Kai-shek, realizing the strength the Communists had generated, grateful for the demands partisan resistance was making on enemy strength, recognized the new system and authorized the creation of an autonomous partisan base beyond the Yellow River, deep in the enemy's rear. At a town called Fuping in western Hupeh, a few days' march from Peking, the first guerrilla government was established in January 1938; it included Communists, Kuomintang members, and nonpartisan officials in a regime sanctified by the blessing of the Central Government.

Japanese calculations, which had been upset in Northern China by partisan resistance, were even more thoroughly upset by what happened in the lower Yangtze Valley. Long before the Communists rooted themselves in the North, the attention of the Japanese staff and the interest of the entire world had concentrated on the battle that was suffusing the entire Shanghai delta in flame and blood. This was Chiang Kai-shek's war.

Chiang watched the preliminary moves of the Japanese in Northern China with indecision. For a month he seesawed back and forth between the decision to fight and the knowledge of China's weakness. When he did decide to resist, he struck in a way that wrecked the smooth political-military structure of Japan's ambitions. The Japanese had hoped to fight in the North and to negotiate in the South. Chiang chose to precipitate a war of the entire people against the enemy by throwing down the gage of battle in his own bailiwick of the lower Yangtze, closest to his own internal bases, where his best troops were marshaled and ready. On August 13, 1937, he flung the best units of his German-trained army into action against the Japanese marine garrison in Shanghai. For a few days Chinese flesh and numbers compressed the Japanese into a narrow strip by the banks of the Whangpoo River. The Japanese realized that they were confronted not with an isolated incident in Northen China but with a war against the Chinese people. To win this war would require full mobilization of Japan's resources. The Japanese moved their fleet to offshore anchorages, marshaled their air force at Formosa, and proceeded to pump steel at the massed Chinese troops in overwhelming tonnages. Not even today is there any accurate estimate of the carnage at Shanghai; Chinese casualties mounted to the hundreds of thousands as the blood and courage of the soldiers absorbed the shock of Japan's barrages.

Chiang's decision to hold at Shanghai is now, as it was then, one of the most bitterly debated episodes of the entire war. It was symbolic, almost with the symbolism of caricature, of the personality of the man. There was no hope of success in matching Chinese flesh against Japanese metal; a withdrawal might have salvaged some of the good units of the Chinese army for later operations in the hinterland, where they could meet the Japanese on more nearly even terms. These, however, were factual considerations, and Chiang's stubbornness refused to submit to them. The soldiers standing in the wet trenches and fed endlessly into the slaughter were a projection of an inflexible will to resist. Since Chiang had accepted war with Japan, he meant to fight it out his own way—yielding no foot of ground that was not taken from him by force.

The resistance at Shanghai was futile in a military sense; in a political sense it was one of the great demonstrations of the war. It astounded the most world-weary of old China-hands, and it proved beyond further question in the record of history how much suffering and heroism the Chinese people could display in the face of hopeless odds. The demonstration at Shanghai was even more valuable internally. The tale of the battle, carried into the interior by word of mouth, kindled a spreading bonfire of patriotic fervor. The line at the Yangtze gave time to mobilize the nation. For two months the Japanese battered at Shanghai.

Then, by a clever outflanking movement to the south, they un-pinned the Chinese line and swept it away in utter confusion to Nanking.

Nanking, Chiang Kai-shek's capital, fell on December 12, 1937, and an historic orgy of several weeks of rape, lust, and wanton murder followed. The disaster all but unhinged Chinese resistance. The broken Chinese armies were so scattered and disorganized that some even advertised the whereabouts of their detachments in newspapers so that stragglers might rejoin their units. If the Japanese had struck inland immediately, they might have met no resistance more formidable than the hills and moun-tains; instead they waited. They felt that the loss of China's capital and great metropolis had eviscerated the nation's resist-ance and that Chiang would be willing to talk peace.

The winter of 1937–1938 worked a miracle in China. The seat of government was transferred to the upriver port of Hankow, eight hundred miles from the sea, and the most com-plete unity of spirit and motive that China had ever known existed there for a few months. The Hankow spirit could never be quite precisely defined by those who experienced it there and then. All China was on the move—drifting back from the coast into the interior and swirling in confusion about the tem-porary capital. Warlord armies from the South and Southwest were marching to join the battle. The Communists were speed-ing their partisans deeper into the tangled communications that supported Japan's front. In Hankow the government and the Communists sat in common council, made common plans for the prosecution of the war. The government authorized the creation of a second Communist army—the New Fourth—on the lower Yangtze behind the Japanese lines; the Communists participated in the meetings of the Military Council.

The elite of China's writers, engineers, and journalists con-verged on Hankow to sew together the frayed strands of resist-ance. By spring of 1938, when the Japanese resumed the campaign, with Hankow as their ultimate objective, the new armies and the new spirit had crystallized. In April 1938, for the first time in the history of Japan, her armies suffered a frontal defeat at the battle of Taierchwang. The setback was only tem-porary. Moving in two great arms, the Japanese forces closed

on Hankow from the north and the east to pinch it off in the
following fall. Almost simultaneously their landing parties seized
Canton, the great port city of the South, and the Japanese rested
on their arms a second time.

On paper the Japanese strategy was perfect. China falls
into a simple geographical pattern. Western China is a rocky,
mountainous land; Eastern China is flat and alluvial, with
scarcely a hill to break the paddies for miles on end. Both
Western and Eastern China are drained by three great rivers that
flow down from the mountains across the flatlands to the
Pacific Ocean. The Japanese Army now controlled the entire
coast and all the centers of industry. It also controlled the
outlets of the three great rivers. In the North it held the Peking-
Tientsin area and the outlet of the Yellow River. In Central
China it garrisoned both banks of the Yangtze, from Shanghai
through Nanking to Hankow. In Southern China it held Canton
and dominated the West River. With the cities, railways, and
rivers under control, the Japanese felt that they could wait until
a paralysis of all economic and transport functions brought
Chinese resistance to a halt, and they waited. They were still
waiting seven years later, when the Japanese Army surrendered
a ruined homeland to the Allies.

The Japanese blundered in China. Why they blundered was
best explained later by one of the shrewder statesmen of the
Chungking government, General Wu Te-chen, who said, "The
Japanese think they know China too much." Japanese political
and military intelligence in China was far and away the finest
in the world, but it had concentrated on schisms and rifts, on
personalities and feuds, on guns and factories. Its dossiers on
each province, each general, each army, contained so much of
the wickedness and corruption of China that the accumulated
knowledge was blinding. The one fact that was obscure to them
was that China was a nation. They had seen a revolution proceeding in China for thirteen years, but only its scum, its
abortions, its internal tensions; they had not measured its results. They were fighting more than a coalition of armies; they
were fighting an entire people. They had watched the infant
growth of Chinese industries on the coast, had marked the
new railways on the map. But the strength of the Chinese was

not in their cities; it was in the hearts of the people. China was primitive, so primitive that the destruction of her industries and cities, her railways and machinery, did not upset her as similar disaster disrupted Europe in later days. China was rooted in the soil. As long as the rain fell and the sun shone, the crops would grow; no blockade of the Japanese navy could interpose itself between the peasant and his land. China had just emerged from chaos, but she was still so close to it that the disruption of war could be fitted into the normal routine of her life; if, for example, it was necessary to move government, industry, people, and army into the interior, it could be done. There was an enormous elasticity in the system that Japan meant to wreck— when it was struck, it yielded, but it did not break. . . .

The early stages of the industrial hegira carried little glory. The removal from Shanghai started late; businessmen were reluctant to let their plants be moved; the government was slow in making its decisions. The first plant to go, the Shanghai Machine Works, one of the finest mechanical shops in the country, did not start up Soochow Creek till two weeks after the fighting began. Soochow Creek runs through the heart of Shanghai and skirted the battlefront. The machinery was loaded in rowboats, covered with leaves and branches for camouflage, and poled slowly upriver to the Yangtze; when air raids threatened, the rowboats sheltered in reeds by the side of the river. It was followed by other shops till the Japanese drive cut the city off from the Yangtze in early December. Because it was delayed too long, the Shanghai evacuation succeeded in moving only fourteen thousand tons of equipment before the enemy advance ended it.

Shanghai, however, had proved the thing could be done, and by the spring of 1938 dozens of movable plants in Northern and Central China were being taken down, repacked, and trans-shipped to the far interior. A major engineering operation was being performed while the national organism continued to function and resist. From the Yellow River one of the greatest textile mills in China, the Yufeng, set out on its trek to Szechwan, a province a thousand miles away and without a single railway. In February it packed its eight thousand tons of machinery and

bundled them off down the railway to Hankow. In May it
kissed the railhead good-bye and set off by steamer upriver to
the gorge mouth. In August it was repackaged again to fit on
some 380 native junks, which took it up the tumbling gorges to
Szechwan; 120 of the boats sank in the gorges, but the junkmen
raised all but 21 and carried on. The convoy arrived in Chungking in April 1939; a patch of hilly ground had been cleared for
its arrival, and by spring the company was busily training timid
Szechwanese peasant women to tend the rusting spindles.

An industrial wilderness stretched from Hankow on into the
West. Whatever went inland had to be moved by hand. Coolies
by hundreds and thousands hauled at blocks of steel weighing up
to twenty tons. By the last week of Hankow's resistance removals
had hit a stupendous pace. The Hankow power plant had been
operating up to the very last days, for it was essential to the
functions of life, but it was impossible to leave behind in Hankow
the enormous eighteen-ton turbine, which would be irreplaceable
after retreat to Szechwan. The dismantling process reached the
power plant early in October, but the turbine could not be inched
aboard a steamer until October 23, just two days before the
Japanese entered the city. The removal of such massive machinery presented problems that the tiny river steamers could
not handle; no steamer that could thread the gorges had a crane
capable of lifting more than sixteen tons. The Chinese settled the
problem by lashing heavy machinery to pontoons, floating the
pontoons, tying the pontoons to the steamers, and sending the
whole through the rapids in tow.

The new industries, resettled in Szechwan, were a Rube
Goldberg paradise. Steel factories were built with bamboo beams;
blast furnaces were supplied with coal carried in hand baskets.
Copper refineries consumed copper coins collected from the
peasantry, converted them into pure copper by the most modern
electrolytic methods, then shipped the metal to arsenals buried
deep in caves.

The migration of China's universities paralleled almost precisely the movement of her industries. Like industry China's
system of higher education had grown in thirty years of chaos;
it too had concentrated along the coast and in the great cities,
and it too was one of the elements of the new China that Japan

most feared. Every major turning point in modern Chinese history had been signalized by student uprisings and intellectual discontent. Students had generated the anti-Manchu uprisings. Their riots and demonstrations touched off the national uproar of 1919, when even corrupt warlords were forced to repudiate the Treaty of Versailles. Student-led riots struck some of the most important notes in the rising crescendo of revolution of the 1920s. Finally, the students and their professors were the most enthusiastic and vociferous demonstrators against Japan, outside of the Communist Party.

The four great universities of Northern China—Peking National, Tsinghua, Yenching, and Nankai—were particularly loathed by the Japanese. They singled out Tsinghua, which had been built with American money, for special treatment. They smashed its laboratories or removed its equipment to Japan and used the student gymnasium to stable Japanese horses. Nankai University was almost completely destroyed. In the basement of Peking University, the seat of China's intellectual renaissance, Japanese special police set up examination headquarters for their political and military inquisition.

When the Japanese attacked in the summer of 1937, most of the students were away on summer vacation. The Ministry of Education sent out a call for them to appear at two rendezvous. One was to be at Sian in the North, on the inner bank of the Yellow River, the other at Changsha, south of the Yangtze. From Sian the students of two colleges were told to move to southern Shensi. When they arrived at the end of the railway, they set out on the tail end of their journey for a 180-mile march over the rugged Tsingling mountain range. The deans of the university were the general staff of the march, and they divided their fifteen hundred-odd men and women into sections of five hundred each. Each unit was preceded by a police section, a foraging squad, and a communications squad; its rear was brought up by pack animals carrying rice and wheat cakes and by a few wheezing trucks crawling over unimproved roads. The foraging squads descended on villages, bought all the fresh vegetables they could find, and had enough greens on hand to start a meal when the rest of the students arrived with their cooking pots. The road they followed runs over some of the most primitive terrain in China. Local authorities quartered students in stables and farmhouses. Engineering students set up receiving stations to catch the evening broadcasts; next morning they hung up posters as news bulletins for the students farther back to read. For the villagers these bulletins were a first exposure to the phenomenon of current news.

As the Japanese drove farther inland, university after university packed up and moved away. Some evacuated their campuses within a few days of the Japanese entry; the students of Sun Yat-sen University were still poling boats bearing the college library out of the northern suburbs of Canton when the Japanese entered from the south. The agriculture department of National Central University decided that its prize herd of blooded cattle was too valuable to leave behind, and all through the summer of 1938 the cattle grazed their way inland just a few weeks ahead of the Japanese spearheads; not till the summer of 1939 did they finally reach the quiet interior, where the bulls settled down to bring joy to the scrawny, inbred cows of Szechwan. Of China's 108 institutions of higher learning, 94 were either forced to move inland or close down entirely. And yet the entire educational system had been re-established by the fall of 1939, and forty thousands students were enrolled in the refugee colleges, as against thirty-two thousand who had been registered in the last academic year before the war.

The transferred institutions of learning clustered mainly in three centers. One was near Chungking, another near Chengtu in Western China, the third at Kunming, capital of Yunnan. Each of these centers differed in texture and quality. The universities in the Chungking suburbs, under strict government control, were always infected by the capital's prevailing mood. The universities about Chengtu took refuge on the beautiful campus of the missionary West China Union University, where they were sheltered in relatively adequate quarters and, under the protection of Canadian and American missionaries, preserved their academic integrity almost inviolate; their scholastic standards remained consistently the highest throughout the war. The most important universities of Northern China, however, all trekked on to the far Southwest, where they combined at Kunming for the duration of the war as the National Southwest

University. The Northern universities had been noted before the war for their brilliant intellectual life, their advanced and sparkling political alertness; arriving in Kunming, they established themselves in squalor. The students were camped four, six, and eight to a room, some of them domiciled in a rat-ridden, cobwebbed abandoned theater; they ate rice and vegetables and not enough of these. The government, always suspicious of the advanced political views of the Northern universities, watched these refugee institutions like a hawk, tightening the net of surveillance closer about them with each passing year. In the beginning it did not matter—the universities were too happy at having escaped the Japanese to care. If the students lived hard, they knew that all China, too, was suffering. As the years wore on and teachers hungered, as budgets were made a mockery by inflation, the National Southwest University began to reassert itself politically and by the close of the war had become the principal seat of political discontent in Southern China.

The migrations of factories and universities were the most spectacular. How many more millions of peasants and city folk were set adrift by the Japanese invasion no one can guess—estimates run all the way from three to twenty-five million. The peasants fled from the Japanese; they fled from the great flood of the Yellow River, whose dikes had been opened to halt the Japanese armies; they fled out of fear of the unknown. The workers who accompanied the factories numbered perhaps no more than ten thousand; they came because without them the machines would be useless. The restaurant keepers, singsong girls, adventurers, the little merchants who packed their cartons of cigarettes or folded their bolts of cloth to come on the march, probably numbered hundreds of thousands. The little people who accompanied the great organized movements traveled by foot, sampan, junk, railway, and ricksha. Thousands crusted the junks moving through the gorges; hundreds of thousands strung out over the mountain roads like files of ants winding endlessly westward. There is no estimate of the number who died of disease, exposure, or hunger on the way; their bones are still whitening on the routes of march.

• • •

The war in China had settled into new molds by the summer of 1939. The trek was over; the wheels of what little industry had been salvaged were turning again in new homes; the universities were drawing up their fall curricula. The shattered armies were digging in on the hill lines. The front now ran in squiggly lines along the foothills of the West and along the rims of all the great river valleys. In the North the Communists began to dig deeper and deeper into the sleepy consciousness of the villagers; cut off from Chungking, they fashioned new tools of government and grew wiser and stronger each year. In Central and Southern China the loose federation of the Central Government and the warlords began to run in familiar ruts; only in Chungking, where the bombs fell from spring to autumn, the old spirit persisted for a few more years.

China did not realize for some time longer that it had arrived at a dead end. Meanwhile the Japanese hailed each of their new campaigns as a climactic thrust at Chungking, and the Chinese armies fought desperately to ward them off. These campaigns were small but bitter, part of a new pattern of war that the Japanese high command had settled on. The new pattern was to keep the fronts in a constant state of imbalance; new divisions and cadres were blooded in combat, then removed to reserve areas for use in future campaigns. The Japanese erected new industries along the coast in their rear and tied what remained of the Chinese economy into Japan's conveyor system.

The trouble with almost all the writing that war correspondents did in China was that it was built on press conferences and communiqués. We used phrases the world understood to describe a war that was incomprehensible to the West. Chinese communiqués, written by obscure men who had never smelled gunpowder or heard a shot fired in anger, spoke of thousands of men engaged, of bloody operations, of desperate attacks and counter-attacks. The Chinese put out such communiqués for years, in the beginning because they themselves believed that the Japanese were still intent on smashing through the mountains to the heartland beyond. Long after they had ceased to believe their own statements, Chinese wordsmiths were still glossing the grimy, squalid contests at the front with the polished rhetoric of earlier days. There were no real fronts, no barrages, no breakthroughs, anywhere on the China front, but men wrote of them—of supply trains, logistics, encirclements. The Chinese newspapers themselves did not believe the reported claims of thousands on thousands of Japanese being trapped or encircled, but they printed them just the same. The foreign press became cynical. Sometimes the exaggerations were too difficult to take straight. Once American Army intelligence found there were only 30,000 Japanese engaged in an action; the Chinese military spokesman reported 80,000 in action, but the communiqués recorded enemy casualties totaling 120,000.

The campaigns the Japanese fought between 1938 and 1944 were foraging expeditions rather than battles. They had no greater strategic objective than to keep the countryside in terror, to sack the fields and towns, to keep the Chinese troops at the front off balance, and to train their own green recruits under fire. Most of them were known as rice-bowl campaigns, because they occurred most frequently in Central China, the rice bowl of the land. The Japanese would concentrate several divisions, plunge deep into the front, ravage the countryside, and then turn back. The Chinese would counter by envelopment; their units would fall back before the thrusts, then close in on the flanks and rear to pinch off the garrison supply posts that the Japanese set up to feed their advance. The Chinese could never do more than pinch off the Japanese salients and force them back into their dug-in bases; to do more than that would have required a weight of metal and equipment that Wong Wen-hao's transplanted industry could not hope to provide. The result was the permanent exhausting stalemate known as the China War.

This China War was fought along a flexible belt of no-man's land, fifty to a hundred miles deep, all up and down the middle of China. In this belt of devastation the Chinese had destroyed every road, bridge, railway, or ferry that might aid the Japanese in one of their periodic thrusts; the only Chinese defense was to reduce the country to immobility. Japanese and Chinese troops chased each other across the belt for six years; the peasants died of starvation, the troops bled, the villages were burned to the ground, towns changed hands as many as six or seven times, and yet for six years the front remained stable with few significant changes.

One of the typical campaigns of this period was proceeding in southeastern Shansi in the summer of 1939. Shansi is an important province—it is laden with coal and has the most considerable iron ores in China south of the Great Wall. It nestles into the elbow of the Yellow River, and its rugged mountains dominate the plains of Northern China. By early 1939 the main Chinese positions in the province were cut into the slopes of the Chungtiao Mountains, which lie on the southern boundary, just north of the Yellow River. The guerrilla areas of the Communist Eighth Route Army were behind the Japanese strongpoints and around them; in front were Central Government troops.

I [i.e., Theodore H. White] went up to see this campaign in the fall of 1939—the first time I had visited the Chinese Army at the front. In the next six years I saw the same sights over and over again, each year more drab, each year less inspiring.

I started out with a column of Chinese troop reinforcements, marching north to the line from the railhead on the Lunghai line. The troops were strung out over the hills in long files, trudging along without discipline or fixed pace. The padding of their straw-sandaled feet made the dust lift knee-high about them, and for miles away eyes in the hills saw an army marching by serpentines of dust in the sky. The commander of each unit rode at its head on his bony horse. Behind him were the foot soldiers, and behind them came the baggage train— coolie soldiers carrying ammunition boxes slung from staves on their shoulders; men burdened with sacks of rice; the company kitchen, consisting of a single soot-blackened cauldron carried by two men, bringing up the rear. This column had several serviceable pack guns slung on mules. At that time the whole Chinese Army had about fourteen hundred pieces of artillery all told for a front of two thousand miles. A single pack howitzer loaded on muleback looked heavier, more powerful, more important, than an entire battery of Long Toms. Later in the war animal-drawn baggage trains became a rarity, but this was 1939, and the column I accompanied had one—it crawled along even more slowly than the slogging footsoldiers. It was loaded high with sacks of rice and with military gear. On the sacks of rice one or two soldiers would be stretched dozing in the sun; the driver cracked his whip smartly over the animals, and the wheels screamed for lack of greasing, but no matter how the cart pitched in the rutted road, the soldiers stayed sleeping on their sacks. There was no hurry, for the war had lasted a long time already and would last years more. On wet days the march was a column of agony, the soldiers soaked through and through, their feet encased in balls of clay and mud.

Traffic to the front was two-way. There was the insistent beat of the marching men plodding forward, and in the opposite direction came the derelicts of the battlefield. The sick and the wounded usually made their way back to the rear on foot, on their own. A serious head wound or a bad abdominal wound meant death at the front, for the medical service could never move these men to operating stations in time for help. Those who could walk but who obviously were no longer of military usefulness were given passes that permitted them to make their way back by themselves. These were pitiful men, limping along over the mountain passes, dragging themselves up by clutching rocks or trees, leaning on staves. You met them at the saddle of each pass as they sat resting from the long climb and looking out over the next valley and next hill with glazed eyes. More rarely you saw sick or wounded carried by stretcher to the rear. They smelled horribly of wounds and filth, and flies formed a cloud about them or even made a crust over their pus-filled eyes or dirty wounds.

We crossed the Yellow River in dirty flatboats and then moved up over thinner passes to the front. We followed hard on the heels of the Japanese army retreating through the Hsin River valley. It was fall, the season of the millet harvest, and the *kaoliang* too was ripe. Chinese valleys are beautiful to look at from the outside, before you know the burden of sorrow and superstition within each village wall. When the road was in the clear on the ridge, you could see clouds of chaff puffing into the air from threshing floors where the peasants were flailing the grain from the husks. The persimmons were ripe and red, glowing from the thin branches of trees from which the leaves had long been blown. The earth was being plowed for winter wheat, and it smelled good; in some of the fields the thin blades of the new crop colored the soil with green, while in the next patch the heavy pink-and-brown *kaoliang* ears hung down from tall stalks to brush our heads as we rode past.

The Japanese had just left, but they had blazed a black, scarred trail of devastation across the countryside. You might ride for a day through a series of burned villages that were simply huddles of ruins. In some places the roads were so torn that not even Chinese mountain ponies could carry you down the ditches cut across them. You had to pick your way down on foot and lead your horse after you or ride for hours on the crest of a barren ridge looking out into the hills beyond. Then there would be a single hut standing by itself in the vastness of the hills; with roof fallen in and timbers burned black, it would stand as a symbol of the desolation that ran from end to end of no man's land.

The stories the villagers told were such tales as I heard repeated later after every Japanese sortie. The peasants had fled before the Japanese advance. When they did not flee voluntarily, they were forced to leave by government edict, and they took with them everything from seed grain to furniture. They bundled their pigs and cattle off into the hills, hid their clothes and valuables in the ground, and retired to the mountains to build mat sheds and wait for the armies to force a decision. The Japanese entered a barren wasteland. They had been held up by floods, and when they reached their key objectives they had two weeks' growth of beard; caked with mud, they were exhausted and furious.

In some of the districts through which I passed, every woman caught by the Japanese had been raped without exception. The tales of rape were so sickeningly alike that they were monotonous unless they were relieved by some particular device of fiendishness. Japanese soldiers had been seen copulating with sows in some districts. In places where the villagers had not had time to hide themselves effectively, the Japanese rode cavalry through the high grain to trample the women into showing themselves. The Japanese officers brought their own concubines with them from the large garrison cities—women of Chinese, Russian, Korean, or Japanese nationality—but the men had to be serviced by the countryside. When the Japanese transport system broke down in the mud, peasants were stripped naked, lashed to carts, and driven forward by the Imperial Army as beasts of burden. Japanese horses and mules were beaten to death in the muck; on any road and all the hills you could see the carcasses of their animals rotting and the bones of their horses whitening in the sun. The Chinese peasants who were impressed to take their places were driven with the same pitiless fury till they too collapsed or were driven mad.

It took two weeks of riding and walking to get to the front. From a regimental command post I was led up the bank of a hill to the crest covered with stalks of tall wheat. With a soldier, I ran silently, crouching behind the wheat, and then dropped in convenient position. The man parted the wheat carefully and pointed down into the valley. There were whitewashed houses in the distance and the vague outline of a walled town. "Those are the Japanese," he whispered, pointing vaguely. I stared harder. Then I noticed something moving in the grain fields not far from us. "What's that?" I asked. The soldier did not even turn to follow my finger. "Those are the peasants," he said; "they have to harvest the grain, you know—it is the harvest season." Even the Japanese could understand that; they were peasants themselves. Except in the savagery of their raids they too could be neutral to the people who worked in the fields.

I traveled the front in Shansi for thirty or forty miles that week; in later years I traveled it for many more miles in many provinces. It was always anticlimax. I saw nothing anywhere but detached clusters of men in foxholes who were guarding rusting machine guns or cleaning old rifles. Chinese outposts were clusters of twenty or thirty men linked to their battalion headquarters by runner, from battalion headquarters to division command by telephone. The Japanese were usually disposed in villages with concentrations of two or three hundred men supported by light field artillery. You could look down on the Japanese from the hills for over a thousand miles; at any point there would be five times as many Chinese soldiers as Japanese. Yet always the Japanese had heavy machine guns and field artillery; before any armed Chinese could move across the open

268 REPUBLICAN CHINA

mile or two to get at the Japanese, he would be cut down by enemy fire, which no support in his army's possession could neutralize.

It was all quiet on the China front in 1939. It was to be all quiet in the same way, for the same reasons, for five more long years.

🏵 The United States:
A Critical Ally

THE JAPANESE attack on Pearl Harbor in December 1941 brought the United States into the war against Japan. Suddenly the United States found its future bound to China's as Western soldiers fought side by side with Asians for a common cause.

The problems of prosecuting the war in China against the Japanese were enormous. By 1942 the Chinese capital was almost as isolated from the outside world as Tibet, and China's coastline had been completely occupied by the Japanese. The last trickle of equipment to China had been pinched off when the Japanese took Burma and closed the Burma Road. In the spring of 1942 Washington sent General "Vinegar Joe" Stilwell to China as Commander-in-Chief of the China-Burma-India Theatre (CBI). Stilwell, said Theodore White, "was cut from no ordinary military cloth." A West Point graduate, veteran of World War I, and an old China-hand, in the previous twenty years he had made frequent trips to China. He knew China well, spoke Chinese, and had a deep respect and love for the Chinese people. But he could not abide the pompous, hypocritical, and corrupt bureaucracy which had grown up in wartime Chungking. First and always Stilwell was a military man bent on getting on with the war against the Japanese, and his impatience with inefficiency, procrastination, and lack of candor became his hallmark.

Stilwell's task was to keep the Chinese fighting on so that the Japanese would not be able to divert any troops from China to the Pacific battleground. To do this he had to train, feed, and equip the Chinese Army, which by 1942 had become a generally ineffective combat force. Nevertheless, Stilwell had unusual confidence in the average Chinese soldier's ability to fight if he was properly supplied. The difficulty was that Stil-well and his command were forced to work through the Kuomintang military clique. Personal politics, greed, and incompetence made Stilwell's fight a bitter one. He wanted to train a division of Chinese troops with American equipment and American trainers in India, and then send them and the British on a joint campaign into Burma to open up the Burma Road. China needed access to the coast desperately, for in 1943 her only source of supply was maintained by the Hump airlift over the Himalayas from North India, and the amount of equipment brought monthly into China was hardly enough to fill even rudimentary needs.

First the British, fighting for their lives in Europe, backed down on the Burma operation, then the Chinese began to balk. To many Americans this was very irritating, and, feeling used and abused, they claimed that since the American entry into the war, the Chinese had slackened their effort against the Japanese. While they fought on, the Chinese did almost nothing, assuming that the Japanese would eventually be defeated by American strength. Such critics, and Stilwell was among them, claimed that Chiang Kai-shek was reluctant to commit his troops to battle against the Japanese because he was saving them to use against the Communists. It was clear by 1942 that the Kuomintang-Communist United Front was faltering. The Nationalists had already clashed with the Communists in one major engagement—the Fourth Route Army Incident in 1941, a bloodbath which gravely crippled the Communist Fourth Route Army. By 1942 the Civil War had in fact resumed. Unfortunately the Japanese were far from being defeated.

This was the mess into which Stilwell plunged with a quick tongue and an obsession for getting things done. Stilwell soon concluded that further American aid to Chiang would be useless unless it was accompanied by some basic reforms in the Chinese government. He viewed the military crisis as a result of the breakdown of principle, policy, and administration in Chungking. Inflation, corruption, and starvation were endemic, and the political situation was further aggravated by the deadlock between the government and the Communists. Stilwell decided that the architect of the whole "manure pile," as he called it, was Chiang Kai-shek. Mutual antipathy rose until finally, at Chiang's request, President Roosevelt relieved Stilwell of his command in October 1944.

The following selection is taken from *The Stilwell Papers,* a collection of letters, notes, and a diary written by General Stilwell in China during the war. Some sections are extremely bitter and cynical. Stilwell is merciless in his criticism of Chiang Kai-shek. His criticisms were frequently accurate and perceptive, but less often constructive, yet below his cynical exterior one senses Stilwell's deep concern for China. His comments and criticisms were prompted not by contempt or superiority. Stilwell treated the Chinese with whom he dealt exactly as he treated his own countrymen, frequently enraging them with his complete candor. What incensed Stilwell was the tragedy that had befallen China and the incompetence of those trying to lead her out.

JOSEPH STILWELL*
From *The Stilwell Papers*

CHIANG KAI SHEK

I never heard Chiang K'ai-shek say a single thing that indicated gratitude to the President or to our country for the help we were extending to him. Invariably, when anything was promised, he would want more. Invariably, he would complain about the small amount of material that was being furnished. He would make comparisons between the huge amounts of Lend-Lease supplies going to Great Britain and Russia with the meager trickle going to China. He would complain that the Chinese had been fighting for six or seven years and yet we gave them practically nothing. It would of course have been undiplomatic to go into the nature of the military effort Chiang K'ai-shek had made since 1938. It was practically zero.

* Theodore H. White, Ed., *The Stilwell Papers* (New York: William Sloane Associates, 1948), pp. 315–322

Whether or not he was grateful was a small matter. The regrettable part of it was that there was no *quid pro quo*. We did what we could, furnished what was available, without being allowed to first ask what he would do, etc. The result was that we were continuously on the defensive and he could obstruct and delay any of our plans without being penalized.

[I have] faith in Chinese soldiers and Chinese people: fundamentally great, democratic, misgoverned. No bars of caste or religion. . . . Honest, frugal, industrious, cheerful, independent, tolerant, friendly, courteous.

I judge Kuomintang and Kungchantang [Communist Party] by what I saw:

[Kuomintang] Corruption, neglect, chaos, economy, taxes, words and deeds. Hoarding, black market, trading with enemy.

Communist program . . . reduce taxes, rents, interest. Raise production, and standard of living. Participate in government. Practice what they preach.

CHINESE ARMY

In 1944, on paper, the Chinese Army consisted of 324 divisions, 60-odd brigades and 89 so-called guerrilla units of about 2,000 men each. This looks formidable on paper, till you go into it closely. Then you find:

1. That the average strength per division instead of 10,000 is not more than 5,000.
2. That the troops are unpaid, unfed, shot with sickness and malnutrition.
3. That equipment is old, inadequate, and unserviceable.
4. That training is nonexistent.
5. That the officers are jobholders.
6. That there is no artillery, transport, medical service, etc., etc.
7. That conscription is so-and-so.
8. That business is the principal occupation. How else live?

How would you start to make such an army effective?

RADIOS I DID NOT WRITE

You don't have to join in singing "God Save the King," but you will at least stand up when the rest of them sing it.

I don't mind standing up. All I object to is (1) standing on my knees and (2) having my feet kicked out from under me when I do stand up.

Chiang Kai-shek is confronted with an idea, and that defeats him. He is bewildered by the spread of Communist influence. He can't see that the mass of Chinese people welcome the Reds as being the only visible hope of relief from crushing taxation, the abuses of the Army and [the terror of] Tai Li's Gestapo. Under Chiang Kai-shek they now begin to see what they may expect. Greed, corruption, favoritism, more taxes, a ruined currency, terrible waste of life, callous disregard of all the rights of men.

[An Undated Paper, on the dominant military doctrine of the Chinese Army.]

It wasn't just a question of recruiting, organizing, and training an army. The big job was to change the fundamentally defensive attitude of the Chinese to an offensive attitude. They were fixed and set by long years of custom—Chiang Kai-shek had made the defense his policy in the present war. He was going to trade "space for time," a very catchy way of saying he would never attack.

My own theory is that this predilection for the defensive wherever possible is based not only on the long succession of Chinese failures when in contact with modern methods and weapons, but also [on] the fact that most Chinese are Taoists at heart. Taoism teaches nonresistance to outside forces; it is foolish to struggle against a general trend. Float with the stream and avoid trouble. If you struggle, you will only bruise yourself on the rocks or be stilled along the shore and you will get nowhere. I have seen the subconscious effects of this feeling in action. The Chinese commander hesitates to challenge fate. If he makes a decision to take positive action and it results badly, it is his fault for having tried to influence events. If he lets nature take its course, everything may come out all right, but if it does not, he cannot be blamed for what has occurred, since he did nothing to bring it about. A scapegoat is always being sought for, under conditions where repeated failures must be explained and the inevitable tendency is to avoid any chance of being picked. This attitude is general in the Chinese Army. There is an added reason—a Chinese command is the property of the commanding general: if he risks it, he risks an investment. A division reduced to the strength of a regiment by an attack cannot expect to be filled up at once to its former strength. The division commander thus becomes in effect a regimental commander, and such reduction is to be avoided at all hazards.

The Chinese were dominated by the idea that the Japs were so superior in training, armament, and equipment that it was not practicable to attack them. Chiang Kai-shek has said on many occasions that a Chinese division did not have the firepower of a Jap regiment, and that three Chinese divisions were not a match for one Jap division. Naturally, his commanders eagerly accepted this statement as full excuse for running away. A new spirit had to be built up. It was vitally necessary that the fresh contacts should be successful. If they were, we could gradually build up confidence—if not, it would be almost impossible to keep them on the offensive.

The Chinese had no confidence in themselves. We started out to give them some.

PHILOSOPHY AS APPLIED TO SUPPLY

Conversation with the second in command of the Xth war zone:

> Q. General Wang, now that the Japs have taken the salt mines in south Shansi doesn't that seriously affect your supply?
> A. Oh, we've still got the salt in Yunnan to draw on.
> Q. Yes, but you have now lost the Tangku field, the Kiangsu field, and the Shansi field. Is there enough salt in Yunnan to supply the whole country?

A. Well, we won't have as much as we had before.
Q. Then there's the matter of gasoline. What are you going to do about that?
A. Oh, we'll get along all right.
Q. But you can't import any, and you don't produce any. As time goes on, you'll be in a bad fix. This matter of salt and gasoline supply is serious. Aren't you worried about it?
A. Oh, no, there's really nothing to worry about. Of course, without resupply, our stocks will get smaller and smaller, but you don't seem to understand that as the Japs occupy more and more of the country, the part left to us will get smaller and smaller, and we won't need so much salt and gasoline.

In time of war you have to take your allies as you find them. We were fighting Germany to tear down the Nazi system —one-party government, supported by the Gestapo and headed by an unbalanced man with little education. We had plenty to say against such a system. China, our ally, was being run by a one-party government (the Kuomintang), supported by a Gestapo (Tai Li's organization) and headed by an unbalanced man with little education. This government, however, had the prestige of the possession of power—it was opposing Japan, and its titular head had been built up by propaganda in America out of all proportion to his deserts and accomplishments. We had to back the existing regime in order to have any chance of getting China to pull her weight. To change the structure during the emergency would have been next to impossible. All through the Chinese machinery of government there are interlocking ties of interest . . . family, financial, political, etc. No man, no matter how efficient, can hope for a position of authority on account of being the man best qualified for the job; he simply must have other backing. To reform such a system, it must be torn to pieces. You build a framework to grow grapevines on: in the course of time, the vines grow all over it, twisting in and out and around and pretty soon the frame is so tightly held by the vines that if you start pulling them out, you will tear the frames to pieces. We could not risk it, we had to take the instrument as we found it and do the best we could. But because it was expedient to back this government to get action against Japan, it was not necessarily advisable to endorse its methods and policies. We could have required some return for our help.

Chiang Kai-shek made a great point of how badly the U.S.A. had neglected China, who had been fighting desperately for so long, while Lend-Lease materials had been poured into Great Britain and Russia by the billion. His case was that we owed him a great debt and that it was a crying shame that we didn't do more to discharge it. This attitude met with sympathy in the U.S. It was true that large quantities of Lend-Lease materials were going to Russia and Great Britain. It was also true that Russia and Great Britain, particularly Russia, were making good use of this material against Germany. It was also true that there was no possible way of delivering the goods to Chiang Kai-shek unless he made an effort on his part to help break the blockade. It seemed reasonable to expect Great Britain to use the huge Indian Army for the purpose. The U.S. was fighting Germany in Europe, and Japan in the Pacific. She was supplying enormous quantities of munitions and food to all the Allies. Under the circumstances it seemed reasonable for somebody else to display a little energy in Burma.

To keep the show going, I had to overlook some of these incongruities and pretend, like the other players. If not, the critics would say it was a bum show, and we are very much afraid of the critics in our show.

[*This paper was never finished.*]

SOLUTION IN CHINA [*Probably July 1944*]

The cure for China's trouble is the elimination of Chiang Kai-shek. The only thing that keeps the country split is his fear of losing control. He hates the Reds and will not take any chances on giving them a toehold in the government. The result is that each side watches the other and neither gives a damn about the war [against Japan]. If this condition persists, China will have civil war immediately after Japan is out. If Russia enters the war before a united front is formed in China, the Reds, being immediately accessible, will naturally gravitate to Russia's influence and control. The condition will directly affect the relations between Russia and China, and therefore indirectly those between Russia and U.S.

If we do not take action, our prestige in China will suffer seriously. China will contribute nothing to our effort against Japan, and the seeds will be planted for chaos in China after the war.

5. CIVIL WAR: THE TRIUMPH OF COMMUNISM

۞ The Strategy and Ideology of Communist Victory

THE YEARS 1945 to 1949 witnessed one of the greatest events of the twentieth century: the triumph of Communism in China. Communism not only altered the lives of six hundred million Chinese, but radically affected the world balance of power. The entire Eurasian heartland from Berlin to Pyongyang was under the red flag. The victory of Communism in China raised fears that a wave of Communist Revolution might begin to break out in the underdeveloped world and engulf the advanced West as Lenin and Mao Tse-tung predicted.

It was well known that Kuomintang China was corrupt, disorganized, and opposed by a large segment of its people. Yet as late as 1947 most people could not envisage the possibility of a Communist triumph. In this and the following set of selections, we offer material which we hope will shed some light on the reasons for the Communist victory.

Though the Civil War officially resumed in 1946, the conflict between the Nationalists and the Communists had a long history, as we have seen. There were repeated incidents following the Fourth Route Army clash of 1941. The war against Japan only delayed the inevitable mortal confrontation between the two foes, and almost as soon as Japan surrendered, Nationalists and Communists poured into the occupied areas, each trying to gain as much territory as possible. One of the main targets for both was Manchuria, which was to become the heartland of the Civil War struggle.

In February 1945 the United States, Britain, and the Soviet Union signed the controversial Yalta Pact in which Stalin was granted concessions in Manchuria in return for a pledge to enter the war against Japan shortly after the defeat of Germany. We will not debate the political wisdom of the Yalta Pact except to observe that it paved the way for Soviet occupation of Manchuria in the immediate postwar period.

Shortly after the Japanese surrender in August 1945 the Russians occupied Manchuria, where, by Allied agreement, they were to remain for only three months, until the arrival of Nationalist military units. (The Soviet Union was still technically allied to the Nationalist government by wartime treaty.) But by November 1945 it was obvious that the Nationalist takeover of Manchuria could not possibly be completed in the projected time, since Chiang was hampered by insufficient transport. As improbable as it may sound today, the Nationalists finally requested that the Russians remain in Manchuria longer than originally outlined, obviously fearing that the Chinese Red Army would take over if some foreign power did not fill the vacuum. In view of later statements accusing Stalin of conspiring with Mao, it is difficult to see how the Nationalists hoped to protect Manchuria from one Red Army with another Red Army.

What actually transpired between the Japanese surrender in August 1945 and the final Soviet withdrawal in March 1946 is still a source of much contention. There are, however, some known facts: the Soviets looted most of Manchuria's industrial plant equipment; Nationalist forces at this time totaled about three million, while the Communists had less than one million; it is also common knowledge that the United States supplied Chiang with large quantities of aid and the vital air transport required to move troops from Burma, India, and Central China to Manchuria. What has not been firmly established is the extent to which the Soviet Union collaborated with the Chinese Communists prior to the arrival of Chiang's troops in early 1946. What were Mao's relations with Stalin during this period? Did Soviet troops turn over the huge caches of Japanese equipment to the Chinese Communist Army in spite of their pledge to hold everything in abeyance until the Nationalists arrived? Was the ultimate Communist takeover of Manchuria a result of a Russo-Chinese Communist conspiracy? These are crucial questions and we shall return to them shortly in our discussion of the following selections.

The race to reoccupy China brought the subterranean Civil War out into the open. While the Americans were rushing Nationalist troops northward by air, the Communists were being marched by Lin Piao through North China into Southern Manchuria. As Lin's army moved, they expended great efforts to mobilize the countryside, thereby laying the foundations for future isolation of Manchuria from Central China. At the same time they constantly harassed the tenuous rail lines linking Manchuria to the main body of Chiang's forces.

Nationalist-Communist relations deteriorated rapidly. By the end of 1945 Chou En-lai had given up negotiating in the Nationalist capital and had flown back to Yenan. Clashes increased as troops from both sides poured into Manchuria. Tension had reached a high point by December 1945, when the Marshall Peace Mission arrived in China. Marshall made a heroic attempt to end the hostilities, and for a while it looked as though he might succeed. But in retrospect it is obvious that the shaky coalition he patched together was little more than a veneer of unity beneath which the desperate struggle continued. Intransigence on both sides moved the dispute from the conference table to the battlefield. Chiang refused anything short of complete Nationalist control over all of Manchuria. Unfortunately for him, the Communists were in far too strong a position in Manchuria to consider acquiescing so completely. Marshall's terms were finally unacceptable to both sides, for each wanted nothing less than total victory. By the spring of 1946 full-scale civil war was inevitable.

Actually Chiang appeared to be in a relatively strong position at this time. Having availed himself of the American airlift, he held over half of Manchuria's larger cities. He had received promises of considerable American aid, and his American-trained and -equipped army outnumbered anything that the Communists could put in the field. What is more, in early 1946 the Nationalists won a series of engagements with the Communists which gave them cause for optimism. In March 1947 Chiang's troops even took Yenan, the Communist capital. But these victories were deceptive. Still mustering their forces and avoiding a showdown, the Communists had not yet begun to go on the offensive. Before moving decisively, they deliberately allowed the Nationalists to overextend themselves, a mistake for which the Nationalists would pay dearly.

In the winter of 1947 Chiang's commanders, deluded by a false sense of confidence, ordered their men to dig in in the cities to wait out the cold Manchurian winter—a tactic referred to as "sitting the enemy to death."

In the spring of 1947 the People's Liberation Army (PLA), which had been formally constituted in March under Lin Piao's command, exploded in a series of quick offensives which left the citybound Nationalists dazed and confused. Lin swept town after town under his control until he had almost completely isolated the big Manchurian cities of Mukden, Kirin, and Changchun. This was the turning point in the Civil War, and except for the cities, Manchuria was lost. Initiative was clearly in the PLA's hands. Each Communist victory made Nationalist defeat more certain. Crippled from within by poor morale, corruption, poor strategy, and weak leadership, and battered from without by one of the world's finest fighting forces, the Nationalists disintegrated.

Chiang stubbornly chose to play his all-or-nothing game to its final conclusion, and as the situation grew more hopeless, his regime became more authoritarian and repressive in tactics, which resulted in mass disaffection among student and intellectual groups. Chiang's last crutch was American aid, but even Washington was becoming skeptical about pouring countless millions into China without any positive returns. They looked on critically as North China fell into Communist hands, leaving the Nationalist-held Manchurian cities isolated islands in a Red sea.

Mao had declared in December 1947 that "the Chinese people's revolutionary war has now reached a turning point." The PLA, whose ranks had been swelled with large numbers of defectors from the Nationalist armies, launched the final phase of its Mainland conquest in the beginning of 1948 with the siege of Mukden. By November the Nationalists had been cut to ribbons and Manchuria had fallen. The struggle then shifted to China proper as the Communists closed in for the kill. By April, P'eng Te-huai had retaken Yenan, reversing one of the few much-heralded Nationalist victories. In June, Chen Yi and

Liu Po-cheng took the old city of Kaifeng in Honan. Defeat followed defeat, severing the last threads of hope which held the shattered Nationalist cause together. In November 1948 the United States Embassy in Nanking reported that in the four battles of Tsinan, the Liaoning Corridor, Changchun, and Mukden alone, the Nationalists had lost 33 divisions and over 320,000 men, 85 per cent equipped by the United States. The situation was so bad that in November 1948 General David Barr reported the following to the Department of the Army:

I am convinced that the military situation has deteriorated to the point where only active participation of U.S. troops could effect a remedy. . . . Military matériel and economic aid in my opinion is less important to the salvation of China than other factors. No battle has been lost since my arrival due to the lack of ammunition or equipment. [The Nationalists'] debacles in my opinion can all be attributed to the world's worst leadership and many other morale-destroying factors that can lead to a complete loss of will to fight. The complete ineptness of high military leaders and the widespread corruption and dishonesty throughout the armed forces, could, in some measure, have been controlled and directed had the above authority and facilities been available. Chinese leaders lack the moral courage to issue and enforce an unpopular decision.

General Barr went on to recommend the withdrawal of the Joint United States Military Advisory Group from China.

Disaster followed disaster for the Nationalists, as the fighting moved into China's heartland. In November and December 1948 the Communists delivered the *coup de grâce* to the Nationalists at the epic battle of Huai-Hai. The battle lasted sixty-five days during which time a million troops maneuvered back and forth across the huge battlefield in a bloody slaughter. Once again the Communists, led by Ch'en Yi, used the strategy which had been so successful in Manchuria: the PLA concentrated on systematically cutting Nationalist communication lines until Chiang no longer had any means of resupplying or reinforcing his troops. The Nationalists' defeat at Huai-Hai was a crushing blow, from which they never even began to recover. Military chaos was accompanied by economic collapse and political disintegration. The Nationalists pleaded for American intervention, but there was little interest in Washington.

The Nationalists' final year on the Mainland was marked by a series of disorganized and humiliating retreats to the South, leading to their final flight to Taiwan. The Mandate of Heaven had clearly passed. By the fall of 1949 China was "lost."

The first selection is taken from *Red China's Fighting Hordes* written by Lieutenant Colonel Robert Rigg, who spent the Civil War years in Manchuria and North China as assistant military attaché to the American Embassy. He discusses the fall of Manchuria and the Nationalist forces' weaknesses as he saw them. In asking how the Communists won Manchuria he comments on Soviet Russia's role. While admitting that the Russians did not strain to keep Japanese supply depots from falling into the hands of Lin Piao's army, he admits that he saw no evidence of direct Soviet complicity with the Chinese Communists: "From 1946 on, the Chinese Nationalists were constantly pointing to Soviet help being given to the Communists, yet they were citing incidents and facts which they were unable to substantiate." He does not try to make a case for Soviet collaboration with the PLA during their period of occupation in Manchuria. He notes that when the PLA took Japanese supply dumps, they did so by attack and not agreement with Soviet troops. Rigg recounts a conversation with a Russian officer— "They [the Chinese Communists] attacked us," the Soviet Army officer said. "We shot at them, but our guards were few. They were overwhelmed and had to flee"—and then comments, "I found little variance to this pattern." Rigg concludes that the Nationalists were defeated as much by their own political inertia and corruption as by poor strategy and lack of equipment.

The second selection is taken from General Lionel Max Chassin's *The Communist Conquest of China*. Chassin, who commanded the French Air Forces in Indo-China from 1951 to 1953, discusses the Chinese Civil War from a French point of view. He sees Mao's victory in China as the triumph of an idea over military might, and says, "The profound lesson of the drama which was the Chinese Civil War is this: Even now, in this era of materialism and mechanization, spirit is always predominant, and it is morale that wins battles. Superiority in manpower and matériel means little if men make no use of their weapons."

Chassin goes on to discuss Communist ideology and Mao's role. He seeks to explain just what it was that made Communist soldiers dedicated and loyal, and made the people believe in their cause. He concludes that the Communist trumps were "agrarian reform, xenophobia, the steadiness and the discipline of the Red Army, the installation of honest officials and the careful avoidance of statism"—all of which, coupled with victory after victory, tended to vest the PLA with a legendary invincibility. Mao's generals built their military force out of zealous peasants, Nationalist defectors, and captured weapons. But they added to this a powerful ideology. The ideology was always foremost, the matériel was always secondary; but when the two were combined, they formed a force of immense power.

ROBERT B. RIGG *
Foundation of Victory

How did the PLA defeat the Nationalist Army? We can better see the PLA's future capabilities if we examine the circumstances and facts of its rise to dominance. I do not choose to record here a history of the China Civil War, but simply to name the more significant factors which built one army up to strength and whittled another down to defeat. The causes of Nationalist defeat in China are many, but too many of them have been oversimplified in journalistic clichés—and some have been overlooked. Here are the more significant causes.

* Robert B. Rigg, *Red China's Fighting Hordes* (Harrisburg, Pa.: The Military Service Publishing Co., 1951), pp. 243–259.

MANCHURIA UPSET THE BALANCE

If the wastelands of Mongolia extended to the Yalu River, Nanking, and not Taiwan, would still be the seat of the Nationalist government and UN soldiers would not have fought in Korea. One cannot argue with a land mass, however.

Manchuria's richness brought the Japanese to the mainland of Asia. Of all factors in the China Civil War, that invasion vaulted the Chinese Reds to their present military dominance of Asia. When the Communists of China were still hollowing out rocks to make mines for use against the Japanese, the United States dropped atomic bombs on Nagasaki and Hiroshima.

Ragged and poor, the Red military forces of China couldn't bring any semblance of formal military power to bear against the Japanese up to 1945; but with the collapse of the Japanese Kwantung Army and the Soviet dominance in Manchuria, the future of China's Red Army was made. The reservoir of manpower, factories, farms, and arms was there for the taking. With the generous assistance of the Soviet Army, the Chinese Reds immediately obtained the arms, gradually seized regions rich in manpower, and eventually occupied all of Manchuria, freeing Lin Piao's field army to swing the balance of military power in China proper.

From 1946 on, the Chinese Nationalists were constantly pointing to the Soviet help being given to the Communists, yet they were citing incidents and facts they were unable to substantiate. Captured Soviet weapons, reports of Russian officers with Communist battalions, were offered as evidence of Soviet assistance.

In April 1946 I had a long discussion, which was in the nature of an argument, with General Shiung Shih-huei, who maintained that a battalion of Soviet troops had participated in the April 1946 Battle of Changchun. Having just returned from the very midst of this battle, I remarked that I had seen not the slightest evidence of any Soviet armed participation, although I had observed Japanese manning light tanks and field artillery. General Shiung was insistent that his intelligence sources had actually seen Soviet troops in combat; but the weight of his argument was somewhat lessened when we compared notes as to the accuracy of his agents' reports. The same spies which reported the Soviet battalion had given Shiung a variety of inaccurate reports on my activities during and after the battle. They said that I had been arrested by the Soviets, and that later I had been taken away in a truck by the Chinese Reds and imprisoned. Although I was treated with open hostility by the few Soviets remaining in Changchun, I was not arrested. Lacking transportation, my pilot and I often flagged down Red Chinese trucks to "hitchhike" rides about the city. We were not made prisoners, as were the five American correspondents there.

On the subject of Soviet help to the Red Chinese, the Nationalists consistently missed the forest for the trees. In the first six months of Soviet occupation the Chinese Reds gained entry to the cities, obtained arms, and secured their biggest measure of Soviet assistance. So firmly entrenched were the Chinese Reds thereafter that there was no need for the Soviets to supply any advisors on the battalion, or even the division, level. Many observers have failed to grasp these facts.

LOOT AND PILLAGE

"It was like a scene from the French Revolution," a Soviet Russian in Mukden told me, "the mob lurched down the street in a 'drunken' frenzy, waving pots, pans, doorknobs, light fixtures, furniture, even doors—nothing was too small or too large for this looting mob to tear from the houses. Like locusts they swept through the residences and in a matter of minutes the homes were stripped bare of all furnishings."

This was mob looting—militarily insignificant but devastatingly destructive.

There were three phases to the looting of Manchuria: The organized industrial looting by the Soviets; the undisciplined pillaging by Chinese civilian mobs; and in between, and less publicized even to this date, the organized looting by Chinese Red military units. This looting by units was a quiet takeaway of cotton spindles, cloth, metals, and light machinery. While it was overshadowed in over-all significance compared to the Soviet effort and the spectacular sacking of homes by the Chinese mobs, it was nonetheless highly important to the economy of Lin Piao's growing field army. The Chinese Reds were careful never to inhibit their tactical mobility by carrying away heavy machinery; but they looted from Mukden, Changchun, and other cities that matériel which could directly serve their military interests or indirectly through the manufacture of shoes, clothing, and related quartermaster supplies.

There were other items the Chinese Reds also sought and gained. One day in early March 1946 a Japanese Army major knocked at my door in the former Yamato Hotel in Mukden. I received him somewhat skeptically and with a measure of hostility. I knew he wanted something. Minutes could tell, and they did; for after the rough treatment received from the Soviets the Japanese were still too frightened to spend much time running about in uniform.

"He is a medical officer," remarked the interpreter who stood near the Japanese major. Defeated and cowed by the Soviets, this man in uniform was still doctor and officer enough to care for his several hundred military patients. He was not afraid to appear publicly in uniform, although he was then coming into a new conqueror's realm—for the Nationalists had just assumed control of Mukden and were delighted to find any stray Japanese in military dress.

The case was simple enough; the major wanted me to see his looted military hospital—which I did a day later. Foul-smelling, sickeningly unsanitary, the hospital was a collection of wards wherein ex-Kwantung Army soldiers lay dying on the cold floors.

"The major only wants some UNRRA medical supplies and food," said the interpreter; and the major nodded, with a bow.

The drama of the story was in the looting—not the request. Dying men are not hard to recognize. There were many. The military hospital had been looted, not only of its surgical instruments and several hundred beds, but its Japanese technicians as well.

Who did the looting? The Soviets? No, it was principally the *Pa Lu*—the Chinese Reds. The Soviets had taken the beds, but the Chinese Communists took the technicians and the nurses. There was some doubt as to which party got the major share of the X-ray equipment and surgical instruments.

Sewage was backing up in Mukden, due to the Communist interruption of electric power. Plague was already taking its toll. The Japanese soldiers continued to die at the rate of a dozen a day. There were other hospitals—civilian ones—in which conditions were just as poor. Lin Piao's "People's Army" had supplied itself, in a brief few days, from the people who were a few years later to cheer the army as a liberator. This was how the present Fourth Field [sic] Army solved one of its initial logistical requirements. Its medical service was already well trained, even though foreign.

The technique was applied not only to hospitals, but also to stores of matériel.

"They attacked us," the Soviet Army officer said. "We shot at them, but our guards were too few. They were overwhelmed and had to flee!" The Soviet officer in Changchun gave me this explanation of how and why the Chinese Reds took over a military depot of Kwantung Army supplies in Changchun in 1945. I found little variance to this pattern. The Soviets placed a few guards over arms depots; but they were always "attacked." I confirmed this several times over. The attacks were usually at night. Whether the Chinese were invited to attack at a given time I cannot verify, but the results were always the same. The Reds of China got the arms. "We didn't want to kill Chinese; we didn't want to favor the Communists, but what could we do?" This was the conventional cliché used by the Soviet Army men in Manchuria. The Soviets even went so far as to photograph daylight "attacks" by the Chinese Reds, so as to document the Russian case. Thus Lin Piao's men in ochre obtained the arms with which a new field army was built. There was only the question of getting men to carry these arms and the Chinese had plans made to accomplish this, too.

THE FIGHT FOR MANCHURIA

Originally numbering some 100,000 Red soldiers from Shang-tung and North China, Lin Piao built up this cadre to about 230,000 by April 1946. By this time he had lost the railway line, from the Great Wall to points north of Mukden in Manchuria. Lin's forces were fighting the desperate Battle of Ssupingkai (1946) after having militarily reduced the isolated Nationalist stronghold of Changchun. The great coal center of Fushun, and Anshan (the Pittsburgh of Asia) were being lost to the Nationalists, but North Korea and the Soviet territory around Dairen and Port Arthur offered sanctuaries for Lin's troops if they were pushed too far to the east and south. Later these points of refuge were used to Chinese Communist advantage, but at this time (May 1946), the bitter Lin Piao was fighting delaying actions northward to hold as many of the rich regions of Manchuria as possible.

Lin's combat units had moved in key with the pattern of the Soviet withdrawal. Now he had reached a point where his military actions were to be more of a deterrent to the Nationalist advances than Soviet obstructionism had been, for the Soviets held only the big cities well behind him. Nationalist strength was growing. Two American trained armies (New First and New Sixth) now added their firepower and flexibility to General Tu Yu-ming's Northeast China Command. Lin's divisions had barely emerged from their old guerrilla past. Red units were padded with Manchurian manpower and studded with Japanese artillery and a few tanks, but they were neither consistent organizationally nor uniform in strength. The battles were growing larger; the weight of artillery fire had begun to have more telling effect on the outcome than maneuver. The Communists did not have a preponderance of heavier weapons and large-caliber ammunition supply was critically short. Depots were scattered and the Reds were generally lacking in motor transport. Furthermore, Lin Piao's officers were having to move divisions and not battalions; they were discovering that this was a new form of warfare with which they were not too familiar.

The 1946 Battle of Ssupingkai could have been decisive. It was a toe-to-toe slugfest, with the final outcome influenced by good generalship and a preponderance of artillery. It was the first real battle (by our standards) of the Civil War campaign in Manchuria. The Communists fought well and many died. But the Communists were outnumbered. Red infantry outfought the Nationalists, but the latter's artillery outgunned the Reds and slaughtered Communist infantry. Nationalist generalship forced Lin's hand when General Tu Yu-ming weakened his distant Southern Front (about 150 miles away) to bring the New Sixth Army up to outflank and outweigh the Reds. Lin Piao's good generalship was manifest in his decision to pull out of a fight that he was losing—and he withdrew with remarkable stealth and success. It was better not to fight the enemy on his own terms, Lin Piao reasoned—not until the Reds had more men. So he withdrew, abandoned hard-won Changchun, without a fight, and hesitated momentarily on the muddy shores of the Sungari River with his rugged but hastily composed army.

Then occurred one of those incidents which at the time appear to be quite simple and unimportant yet which later have in fact far-reaching and complicated effects on the war. A truce was imposed in Manchuria as of 6 June 1946. The combatants shot it out, to gain last-minute advantage, and were to maneuver and skirmish later; but, insofar as the general territorial occupations were concerned, each side settled down to consolidate and make ready for the showdown of 1947. This was the turning point not only of the Manchurian campaign but of the entire Civil War; for during the period of June 1946 through February 1947 Lin Piao consolidated his rear by establishing control over the greater portion of Manchuria, dividing up farmlands, recruiting and training Manchurians—who were to build up the Northeast Democratic United Army to about a half million men. Manchuria swung the balance of power in favor of the Chinese Communists, for it eventually gave them the weighty Fourth Field Army.

BLUE STRATEGY LOSES TO RED TACTICS

It became one of my tasks when flying low over Manchuria for the truce teams, to identify those towns which were held by the Nationalists and those controlled by the Communists. The battle lines were never continuously drawn and I remember days when I couldn't even locate a fighting front, for there was considerable maneuver in the spring and early summer of 1946. However, the problem of identifying the political color of a town was not usually too difficult. In the field troops of both sides looked almost alike from an altitude of four hundred feet; the Reds, however, would potshot at your plane, and they didn't possess much motor transport. In towns, however, you could never judge by the military activity which army was the occupying power. Over both Communist and Nationalist cities waved the red and blue Chinese National flags, but the key identity was whether or not the predominantly blue Kuomintang flag flew *with* the National flag. Gradually, as 1946 merged with the year to follow, another difference in the two territories became apparent from the air—moats and trenches. These came to signify government-held cities and railway bridges. The pattern began to appear all over China as these giant trenches slowly ringed the cities. Woven about the moats were systems of barbed wire, abatis, and pillboxs. How many new pillboxes were constructed, no one knows, but they numbered in the thousands. Then there was the inheritance of the thousands of Japanese pillboxes— solid structures of thick concrete and narrow embrasures. The Nationalists were not nearly as thorough as the Japanese in the construction of these installations of defense. The government forces made pillboxes out of brick, and even mud. One of the most ghastly masses of human flesh and splintered bones that I saw in China was outside the Shantung city of Yenchow, where one of these brick inclosures took a direct hit from a Red artillery piece at five hundred yards range.

Not only did all of these fixed defenses give a false sense of security to government troops, but they also bred an ill-fated "pillbox psychology" among Nationalist soldiers. The Communists never built them in any significant numbers. They ditched roads, tore up railroad tracks, and blew bridges in their territories; but they seldom sat down in one place to defend anything.

This was the influence of the truce—the Nationalists built defenses to protect their gains and insure city security; the Reds recruited and trained new troops, ranging their existing forces about to harass the enemy. Whereas military aggressiveness grew on the Red side, a defensive sluggishness took root on the Blue side. The side of numerical and technical superiority grew morally weaker; the "have-nots" strengthened their spirit and hopes. The Blues developed their buttocks; the Reds strengthened their legs and hardened their feet. By 1947 these facts were evident to any observers traveling in China.

It gradually became the high mark of success in the Nationalist Army for a general to hold onto a city. Generals, comfortable but stagnating militarily in their city headquarters, soon began to enjoy a false sense of security, just as their men in pillboxes and trenches gained confidence that their defense works would forever protect them. In the cold winter of 1946–1947, the monotonous duty of manning fixed defenses, after a long period of general inactivity, lowered morale of Chiang's troops, whose officers became more and more content to ward off the enemy at little cost in either casualties or effort. Government soldiers hugged fires and sought the indoors, whereas the poorly clothed Reds maintained their health by the exercise of marching. By harassing actions, the Communists confused their enemy as to their intentions.

The blue military side was being governed by a strategy which read—hold and secure the cities and the lines of communication; the countryside can wait. And the countryside was dangerous for the Blues, for when they ranged out into it the normal Red ambush and maneuver tactics were at their best.

In these actions the Reds sought to outnumber Nationalist units in a series of small engagements, and more often than not, the force of Red arms prevailed.

The Red hierarchy held to one main theme of strategy— leave the cities alone until they rot on the vines of communication. Theirs was the strategy of concentrating on tactics, pulling all their old tricks out of the bag and applying them with dash and vigor. Let the Red companies and battalions seek out their own targets and capitalize on local opportunities. Let them have the satisfaction of winning small battles, but don't over-commit them in masses to attacks we (Reds) may not win and which, if we don't will lower morale. Build morale, build fighting spirit, and manufacture hope by daily indocrination. This was the keynote of Yenan's instructions.

To the higher commanders, who were anxious to wield their growing armies in greater combat, Mao warned—be patient; time is on our side. Let inflation and other factors take full effect. Do with what you have; but above all, drain the enemy of supplies, arms, and men. Take them, even in driblets, but keep taking. Attrition isn't spectacular, but it helps win when applied against the other side.

Many Americans were reluctant to acknowledge at the time that the Nationalist strategical effort to try to take Manchuria was a *military* mistake. It was a gamble against great odds and distances, not to mention a struggle against foreign obstruction-ism. Later everyone could say, "Had the Generalissimo con-centrated on solidifying North China and subduing the Com-munists there, he might have later marched, with surety and success, to Mukden and Manchuli."

One very knowledgeable and highly intelligent observer, Mr. William C. Bullitt [see pp. 340–357], remarked on this strategic blunder to me in early 1947. Mr. Bullitt added that General Dwight D. Eisenhower also viewed the Nationalist ef-fort in the Northeast as a gross overextension of military forces. There is weight to that side of the question; but certainly the Chinese Communists, with even smaller forces (although Soviet help was to compensate greatly for this lack of numerical strength), *also* gambled strategically and overextended their troop units, which for a long time were even *isolated* in Man-churia. The difference, of course, lies in the fact that the Chinese Reds got to Manchuria first. They marched overland and poured in by sea from Shantung to the Kwantung Peninsula. They were received with hospitality; the Nationalists with hostility. But as to whether or not it was wise for the Generalissimo to embark on the military occupation of distant Manchuria, there is this big question: Could he have afforded delaying, for long, the order that history dictated to him at Yalta? Manchuria, with all of its cross currents and complications, had been again restored to China at the conference. Could any national leader of China have hesitated long in taking possession of the prize? Should he have let the Soviets hold it in trust for the year or two it might have taken him to consolidate North China? It would seem that the Generalissimo had to *make the effort* of takeover. He failed, but not because he did not try; failure came because of faults of technique in implementing his effort.

The Communists won Manchuria because of many factors. They must be given credit for their organizational ability which whipped the apathetic and leaderless Manchurian people together. Northeast China, as it emerged out of the chaos of Soviet occupation, was crying for leadership; and the region, so long under the tramp of foreign boots, had none to offer from its own population. The simple fact is, the Chinese Reds supplied the leadership, and the leaders, for all their brutality and other shortcomings, led or drove the people. The Nationalists, in spite of all of their efforts, could not or did not implement their strategy with any great leadership or political appeal. They even lacked an announced policy toward the significant Mongol and Korean minorities.

Elsewhere in China the pattern was much the same. Everywhere the Reds capitalized on Nationalist military mistakes. The Reds didn't need any real strategy; they just let the Blues apply their own. The Reds then nibbled, cut away, and isolated their enemy, not by the application of any real strategy, but by tactics, well conceived and well carried out. By multiplying many minor successes, the Reds began to gain a slight strategical edge. There were some big battles, some Communists defeats of note, but by and large when the Government marched out with its large bodies of troops in search of a showdown, the Communists would melt away. The Reds didn't want to fight large armies in 1946 or early 1947. . . .

LIONEL MAX CHASSIN *
The Roots of Mao's Victory

It is always easy to explain events after the fact—even for one who is always wrong in predicting the outcome of events while they are actually occurring. In reading this account one gains the impression that as early as 1946 the defeat of the Nationalists was inevitable. Yet, right up to the end of 1948, the best-informed and most impartial of observers—those who best understood what lay beneath the surface of superficial situation maps—hesitated to predict the complete victory of Mao Tse-tung. To Western observers Mao's solution to the problems of China, with all that it implied for the future of the world, posed the prospect of a disaster which none desired even to think about. They preferred to cling to the most improbable of possibilities. Even after the Communist victory at Suchow and the arrival of the Reds at the Yangtze, many still hoped for a partition of China, as had once occurred in the bygone days of the Sung Dynasty.

At the outset, as has been shown, Mao's chances of success were very slim. Clearly outclassed in numbers and matériel, he dominated only a small territory; he had no money, no resources, no allies. Worst of all, the masters of Russian communism had abandoned him; they had recognized Chiang Kai-shek, his mortal enemy, as the leader of China, and yielded Manchuria to Na-tionalist sovereignty. Opposing Mao was a man to whom prop-aganda had given the stature of a giant, a prospective member of President Roosevelt's world-governing Big Four, the master of more than three hundred fifty million people, of war-hardened armies, of enormous stocks of modern military matériel, an ally

* Lionel Max Chassin, *The Communist Conquest of China* (Cambridge, Mass.: Harvard University Press, 1965), pp. 247–259.

assured of the total support of the great American republic, which in 1945 was the world's most powerful state. Between these two champions, who could have hesitated in his choice?

Four years later Chiang Kai-shek, the Chinese hero, was to find himself a vanquished refugee on the small island of Formosa, while his adversary set himself up in Peking as the master of four hundred eighty million human beings. What happened? What were the causes of an event which means so much in the history of humanity?

The profound lesson of the drama that was the Chinese Civil War is this: Even now, in this era of materialism and mechanization, spirit is always predominant, and it is morale that wins battles. Superiority in manpower and matériel means little if men make no use of their weapons.

Here, in the Chinese Civil War, the adversaries were of the same race, of the same ancient civilization. How could the same man be a deplorably poor soldier under the Nationalists and then, after a few months of service with the Reds, become a veritable hero? How did hares so suddenly become lions? The answer is that the potential of man is enormous. He is as capable of heroism as of cowardice. But he will not become a hero unless he is inculcated with a faith, a belief, in a doctrine for which he will gladly give his life.

There is no such thing as a degenerate race or generation. The children of today possess the same innate qualities as did those of centuries past. The education of man—or, if one prefers, his "conditioning"—is everything. The cause of Mao's triumph lies in the fact that appealing as he did to ancient and deeply rooted reflexes, he gave a faith, a creed, to the peasants of China. Totalitarian doctrines are always based upon simple slogans, easy to exploit. Hitler chose, as the theme for Germany's external relations, abolition of the Treaty of Versailles; internally, the theme was the struggle against Jews and Communists. Mao had only to follow a beaten track. His external theme was the eternal theme of xenophobic nationalism, of the struggle against foreign imperialists, who themselves but barely emerged from barbarism, had "enslaved" the higher civilization that was China. As for internal themes, he cleverly appealed to the instincts of social justice and proprietorship which are so strong in the human heart. In proclaiming agrarian reform, in despoiling the landlords and lowering taxes, in giving landless farmhands plots to hold as their very own, Mao played the best of cards— to be cynically discarded once victory was won.

But beyond the achievement of these practical goals, it is undeniable that Mao knew how to make of his soldiers dedicated workers for "a powerful China, a respected China, where justice, truth, and peace would reign." He obtained this result by a sustained and patient effort of daily political education. In the everyday routine of the Red soldier, Marxist political indoctrination played a more important role than the manual of arms. Taken in hand by skillful political schoolmasters, the peasant-in-arms rapidly became a fanatic, an apostle of the new religion, ready to sacrifice his life for the better tomorrows. In this lies the essential reason for the victory of Mao Tse-tung. Victory, in a civil war, is almost always won by the side which knows how to gain the support of the people.

In order to win over the Chinese people, this Marxist leader chose the path of prudence. Although he had always been an orthodox Marxist, a believer who would do no rending violence to the classic doctrine, Mao did not hesitate to adopt a course of gradualism, so that the "first steps" would reveal to the peasants only the advantages of the new regime, and none of its fearsome flaws. This gradualistic policy was clearly reflected in the typical sequence of developments which followed upon the entry of the Red Army into a newly taken village. Even in those provinces where there were few landlords and the pattern of land tenure was already one of small holdings—as was often the case in Central China—there were always rich peasants, as well as pro-Japanese collaborators. And, always, there were miserably poor agricultural laborers among the villagers. First the villagers would be deeply impressed by the perfectly correct behavior of the Red troops, who far from giving themselves over to pillage, would ask only to be of help to the peasants. Then the Communist political leader would hold a meeting of all the villagers. He would promptly pillory, to the plaudits of all, the pro-Japanese bourgeois and the exploiting landowner. The lands of the condemned would then be distributed to the landless. The "politruk" (the Russian term for "political leader") would then announce that henceforth the people would be able to elect their own administrators and participate freely in public affairs. Since the officials of the Kuomintang regime were often incompetent and corrupt, the enthusiasm with which the population accepted the new representatives of the People's Republic can be easily imagined.

Moreover, Mao Tse-tung very cleverly resisted "leftism" in matters of agrarian reform, and so was always opposed to the despoliation of the so-called "middle peasants." His reasoning was based on the fact that the Communists had to have the support of the majority of the population; only a minority, then, need be despoiled. This was successfully done. Without, of course, renouncing collectivization, the final goal of Marxism-Leninism, it was declared that this ultimate stage of the Revolution would not be reached until the distant day of China's industrialization. For the moment the peasants were asked only to give their utmost support to the Red Army, which was liberating them from Kuomintang oppressors who were aided by American imperialists. It is easy to inflame a people against foreigners; in China this task was facilitated by the fact that the Nationalists used American aircraft, and that the bombs which fell on the civilian population were "Made in U.S.A."

The "Red Dragon" thus held important trumps: agrarian reform, xenophobia, the steadiness and discipline of the Red Army, the installation of honest officials, the careful avoidance of premature steps toward statism. But these trumps, without any doubt, would have been insufficient had Chiang Kai-shek been at the head of a strong political organization, and of a state which functioned in a normal manner. But such was not the case. Well before the end of the war against the Japanese, the Kuomintang was already completely rotten.

The drama in the Revolution of 1927 was that, unlike all the other revolutions in Chinese history, it failed to conclude with a general cleanup of corrupt officials and local lords. The customary pattern of Chinese revolutions is well known. Thanks to an uprising caused by the incompetence and corruption of a regime which oppresses and starves the people, a new dynasty mounts the throne. The new Emperor is a man of strong character, who in the unhesitating implementation of his plans for reform, cashiers corrupt officials and keeps careful watch over public order and the probity of his regime. But then he dies; and his son, already sinking into indolence, replaces him. After a few generations, the new aristocracy falls back into the old Chinese habits, and the tribulations of the people begin again. By nature long-suffering and patient, and brought up to respect their superiors, the people wait, sometimes for centuries, before rising once again. In this traditional cycle each revolution gave the people at least a temporary respite from oppression, if only of a decade or two. But Chiang Kai-shek, when he took power in 1927, was not strong enough to proceed with the necessary cleanup of corruption. On the contrary, Chiang, in order to secure acceptance of his authority, had to bargain with all the great warlords, the *tuchüns* who, like Chang Hsüeh-liang or Yen Hsi-shan, were the veritable proprietors of their provinces. Chinese administration, already corrupt and rotten under the Manchus, remained untouched by the Revolution of 1927, and a long-suffering people received no relief.

A second result of Chiang's incomplete victory was that he was never able to put his own ideas into practice, not even in the bosom of his own party. The Kuomintang rapidly fossilized, and soon became a totalitarian instrument for the oppression of the people, rather than a faithful agent of the reforms desired by the dictator. Moreover, the most intelligent doctrinaires of the Kuomintang, the brothers Ch'en Li-fu and Ch'en Kuo-fu, were convinced Confucianists who denied the need for any change in the ancient structure of Chinese civilization. Their opposition to agrarian reform, on grounds of its absolute uselessness, was particularly pronounced. Perhaps they were right, from a philosophical and even economic point of view, China being in general a country of extremely fragmented landholdings. And yet, for all that there was still much that could have been done; at the very least, farm rents and usurious interest on loans could have been diminished. At any rate, by refusing to undertake reforms the Kuomintang deprived itself of a powerful means of influencing the people, who thus were thrown into the camp of the Communist enemy.

Apart from these general reasons, the Chinese Nationalist Party owed its impotence to its immobilism, and to a deplorable conception of the economic and military requisites of the Civil War.

In the first place, despite the enormous sums donated by the Americans, and the wretchedly poor pay of Nationalist soldiers and officials, the Kuomintang was never able to put its financial house in order. Basically, this was because of corruption. Among those around Chiang—himself completely honest—and throughout all echelons of the Kuomintang, everyone stole, everyone made deals. Members of the Soong family prudently invested tens of millions of dollars in America. From Cabinet ministers right on down to the local Party representatives in the small villages, everyone took such private bites out of public revenue that nothing remained for the coffers of the state. Apart from American subsidies, the sole remedy was the classic recourse to the printing press, a solution which led only to inflation and misery. Under such pressures the people sometimes grumbled; thus the considerable growth of the Kuomintang police. Such growth was initially justified by the struggle against collaborators; but the police rapidly became a powerful instrument of oppression, manipulated solely by the right wing of the Party, the CC clique. In these conditions of growing misery, the people, who had manifested great qualities of patriotism and courage during the war against Japan, and had in general joyfully acclaimed the Kuomintang as well as the victory over Japan, became at first apathetic, and then resolutely hostile to the Kuomintang regime. In contrast, they soon favored the Reds, who appeared to the people as liberators; so did the Copts of Egypt, in their day, extend a cordial welcome to the Arabs.

The decline in the morale of the Chinese people, a direct consequence of the maladministration and corruption of the Kuomintang, had a direct impact upon the quality of the Nationalist Army. As pointed out at the beginning of this book, the Nationalist soldier, in the classic tradition of Chinese soldiery, was generally considered to be the scum of humanity. Except in several elite divisions, such a conception could not be changed, and morale remained low despite a multitude of promised reforms. No program of political education was launched, no valid mystique set forth: the soldier of Chiang Kai-shek knew not why he fought. Against the Japanese he could fight for his country

and his people; but in this civil war a peasant soldier from
Kwangtung had no idea why he should be fighting in Shansi and
Manchuria. Poorly fed, poorly paid, poorly clothed, poorly cared
for, poorly armed, often short of ammunition—even at decisive
moments—unsustained by any faith in a cause, the Nationalist
soldier was easy prey for the clever and impassioned propaganda
of the Communists.

In turning to military matters of strategy and tactics, one
can do no better than quote from the report of General Barr,
who as chief of the group of Chiang's American military advisers
from 1947 to the end of 1948, observed Nationalist troops and
leaders at first hand. Writing early in 1949, General Barr (see
pp. 282, 330) reported as follows:

> Many pages could be written covering the reasons for
> the failure of Nationalist strategy. I believe that the Gov-
> ernment committed its first politico-military blunder when
> it concentrated its efforts after V-J Day on the purely mili-
> tary reoccupation of the former Japanese areas, giving little
> consideration to long-established regional sentiments or to
> creation of efficient local administrations which could attract
> wide popular support in the liberated areas. Moreover, the
> Nationalist Army was burdened with an unsound strategy
> which was conceived by a politically influenced and mili-
> tarily inept high command. Instead of being content with
> consolidating North China, the Army was given the con-
> current mission of seizing control of Manchuria, a task
> beyond its logistic capabilities. The Government, attempting
> to do too much with too little, found its armies scattered
> along thousands of miles of railroads, the possession of
> which was vital in view of the fact that these armies were
> supplied from bases in central China. In order to hold the
> railroads, it was also necessary to hold the large cities
> through which they passed. As time went on, the troops
> degenerated from field armies, capable of offensive combat,
> to garrison and lines of communication troops with an in-
> evitable loss of offensive spirit. Communist military strength,
> popular support, and tactical skill were seriously under-
> estimated from the start. It became increasingly difficult to

maintain effective control over the large sections of predominantly Communist countryside through which the lines of communication passed. Lack of Nationalist forces qualified to take the field against the Communists enabled the latter to become increasingly strong. The Nationalists, with their limited resources, steadily lost ground against an opponent who not only shaped his strategy around available human and material resources, but also capitalized skillfully on the Government's strategic and tactical blunders and economic vulnerability.

Initially, the Communists were content to fight a type of guerrilla warfare, limiting their activities to raids on lines of communication and supply installations. The success of their operations, which were purely offensive, instilled in them the offensive attitude so necessary to success in war. On the other hand, the Nationalist strategy of defense of the areas they held, developed in them the "wall psychology" which has been so disastrous to their armies. As the Communists grew stronger and more confident, they were able, by concentrations of superior strength, to surround, attack, and destroy Nationalist units in the field and Nationalist-held cities. It is typical of the Nationalists, in the defense of an area or a city, to dig in or retire within the city walls, and there to fight to the end, hoping for relief which never comes because it cannot be spared from elsewhere. The Chinese have resisted advice that, in the defense of an area or a city from attack by modern methods of warfare, it is necessary to take up positions away from the walls where fire and maneuver is possible. Further, they have been unable to be convinced of the necessity for withdrawing from cities and prepared areas when faced with overpowering opposition and certain isolation and defeat, while the opportunity still existed for them to do so. In some cases their reasons for failure to withdraw and save their forces were political, but in most cases they were convinced that by defensive action alone, they could, through attrition if nothing else, defeat the enemy. Because of this mistaken concept and because of their inability to realize that discretion is usually the better part of valor, large numbers of Nationalist troops were lost to the Government.

It must be understood that all through the structure and machinery of the Nationalist Government there are interlocking ties of interest peculiar to the Chinese—family, financial, political. No man, no matter how efficient, can hope for a position of authority on account of being the man best qualified for the job; he simply must have other backing. In too many cases, this backing was the support and loyalty of the Generalissimo for his old army comrades which kept them in positions of high responsibility regardless of their qualifications. A direct result of this practice is the unsound strategy and faulty tactics so obviously displayed in the fight against the Communists.

Cooperation among and coordination of effort between the Armed Forces leaves much to be desired. The Ground Forces, being the old and dominant arm, is the source from which the large majority of top military positions are filled. These officers, mostly old and loyal contemporaries of the Generalissimo, have little or no knowledge of the newer arms: the Air Force and the Navy. The Chinese Air Force, consisting of 8⅓ groups, is far in excess of what a country bereft of gold credits can support. Although it has among its personnel over five thousand United States-trained pilots, it accomplished little, other than air-lifting troops and operating its transports for personal gains. There was an ever-present reluctance to take a chance on losing equipment or personnel, which was clearly reflected in their constant refusal to operate at other than high altitudes. There was an ingrained resentment in the Chinese Air Force against killing Chinese Communists who had no air support. All of these factors are important and unfortunate because the Chinese Air Force, unopposed, could have rendered invaluable support in ground operations had its capabilities been properly employed. From a military viewpoint, the case of the Navy is not so important since its employment, right or wrong, could have had little effect on the final outcome; all operations were land-based. From an economic viewpoint, the Navy could have been of inestimable value in suppressing smugglers in Hong Kong-Canton waters had it been willing to suppress and not participate. It was completely relieved of this mission in March 1948, and reputedly millions of dollars in customs revenue continue to be lost to the Government.

It might be expected that the Communists, being Chinese themselves, would also suffer from these faulty Nationalist traits and characteristics, and to a certain extent they do, but they have wisely subordinated them and made their ideology of Communism almost a fetish. By means of total mobilization in the areas they control, propaganda, and the use of political commissars within their armed forces, they maintain loyalty to the established order. Their leaders are men of proven ability who invariably out-general the Nationalist commanders. The morale and fighting spirit of the troops is very high because they are winning.

There is little to add to this analysis. At most, the additional observation must be made that the lessons of Western-type warfare, when learned by uncritical minds, have sometimes led to disastrous results. For example, even though the Reds had no air force, Nationalist units wasted endless time in confecting artful camouflage and digging innumerable shelters as protection against air attacks which obviously would never come. The emphasis which American instructors placed upon the importance of digging-in was further exaggerated by the defense-minded Nationalists, who were convinced that a three-to-one superiority was a minimal prerequisite to engaging the enemy. At each temporary halt, tired men were set to digging trenches. With training such as this, Nationalist troops were incapable of standing up to enemy fire: with the first volley they would hit the dirt and lie there, face down, without reacting. Lastly, the lavish American standards for estimating required expenditures of ammunition induced Nationalist commanders to discover that there was never enough ammunition for attacks.

Confronting the Nationalists was a Red Army with high morale and a remarkable zest for the offense. Frequent bayonet assaults, carefully coordinated with guerrilla activity which sowed a feeling of insecurity in the Nationalist rear, soon vested Red troops with a pervasive aura of invincibility. And by 1949 this army had performed a feat which is unique in the military history of the world: the entire conquest of an enormous country at a rapid pace averaging six miles per day, an advance which swept from the fall of Mukden on 8 November 1948 to the capture of Canton on 15 October 1949. Some of the battles it fought, particularly the battles of Liaoning and Suchow, stand as genuine models of strategy and tactics which merit careful study by the officers of Western countries.

One may well conclude that the Chinese Red Army constitutes a remarkably effective ground combat force. Yet it must be noted that the successes of this army were almost always obtained with ease: never in the Civil War were the Communists confronted by truly resolute, well-armed, and well-led adversaries. In fighting against the Nationalists, the Red Army habitually committed itself only to sure things, to certain victories, in which its own losses would be extremely low. Its strong point was guerrilla tactics, which are excellent in one's own country, but of little use in an alien land. Thus, before the outbreak of the war in Korea, one could rightfully ask how well this army would perform against a Western opponent. The response of the Chinese Red Army in Korea demonstrated that its defensive capabilities are as remarkable as its capabilities for offensive action. When the day arrives that this army is supported by a modern air force, it will prove itself to be a truly formidable foe for even the best of adversaries.

The same may be said for China itself. When this immense agricultural country achieves an industrialization backed by the natural resources of Manchuria and Sinkiang, it will assume a leading role not only in Asia, but in the world. And the average Chinese, who is intelligent, adroit, patient, enduring, and fully capable of manipulating machines, is ruled by a man of eminent qualities who well knows how to exact obedience. It is true that China, for the moment, is confronted by an immense task of reconstruction. But such was the case with Russia in 1918: this precedent proves that only twenty years suffice to industrialize a great agricultural nation—and the pace of history moves ever faster.

We must thus expect to see, a few years from now, the emergence of China as a very great power. For our descendants it will then be interesting to see whether racial instincts are stronger in man than the forces of ideology. In other words, will adherence to the same Communist faith suffice to silence, between a great USSR and an enormous China, the antagonisms arising from the color of skin or the shape of eyes? Here is the secret of the future; and there can be no doubt that upon the answer to this question depends, in large measure, the fate of Western civilization and even, perhaps, of the human race.

❧ Revolutionary Land Reform:
A Key Weapon in the Struggle

ONE OF the major acts of the American occupation forces in Japan after World War II was to initiate a land reform program. From there, American experts carried land reform projects to Taiwan, the Philippines, Vietnam, Nepal. Almost every new nation began to worry about its land problem. Underlying this concern was the fear that if the peasant was not given land, he would rise in wrathful revolt as he had in China.

The land reform movement in China began in the 1920s, when the Kuomintang and the Communists started organizing peasant associations. The Communists carried the movement into Kiangsi and Hunan, where it became the social basis of their revolutionary soviets. In Kuomintang China, scholars and officials talked constantly about land reform, but did little. During the Yenan Period the Communists introduced moderate programs of land reforms in the Red areas, and with the resumption of the Civil War, the Communists proclaimed a radical land reform which became a major factor in Communist victory.

In the following selection, Jack Belden, an experienced correspondent in China who witnessed the land reform of the Civil War period, describes the rise of a "new rural gentry" in wartime China: "the smaller bureaucrats and the militarists, unable to live on the paper money salaries given them by the Chiang government, also began amassing landholdings as a means of security in times of inflation." But the consequence was that "the number of peasants dispossessed from their land because of unpaid mortages and unpaid debts, both in Chiang's areas and in the Japanese-occupied areas, rose by untold thousands during the Japanese war." One of the gentry's strengths in the past had been its traditional double option of either seeking security in a stable government or, in times of trouble, finding it in landholding. As the old scholar-officials lost their positions in the new republican governments of Peking, they turned back to their local communities and the land. Tales of exorbitant tax collection are well known. But equally oppressive to the peasant were the staggeringly high rents demanded by this landlord gentry class.

Intolerable conditions on the Chinese land were exacerbated by war, chaos, and famine. The Communists, from their experience with earlier peasant rebellions, knew that deep conflicts divided the Chinese villages: poor peasants hated the rich, young struggled against old, debtors hated their usurers, and entire villages were bitter against landlords and officials. The Communists knew when the flag of revolt was raised, that thousands of peasants would rally to them as they had done for the Taipings and during the Kiangsi Period.

Over the years a new factor had entered the village picture: a changing peasant consciousness. The official, the landlord, and the Confucian schoolteacher no longer had their onetime allure of respectability. The peasants, despite their isolation, knew there was a modern world beyond their villages which had humiliated the collective body of their masters. China was a despised country. Young peasants returned to the villages with tales of a new life, and Communist cadres, many of them university students, propounded new ideas. In the past the peasant suffered but continued to respect his overlords. Now he tolerated his oppressors without respect, only because of the power they held over him.

The Communists realized that land reform could not just satisfy land hunger—it had to destroy the whole web of traditional socioeconomic relationships binding the peasant to ancient masters and to a perpetual existence as a slave of the soil. Hatred of the oppressor was as powerful a motivating force for the peasant as hunger for land. As Belden describes it in his introduction:

> It was passion and principally passion that overwhelmed Chiang Kai-shek. The radiant hopes and murderous hates

that the Chinese peasantry poured into the sphere of war and revolution released a flood of emotional energy that exploded with the force of an atomic bomb within Chinese society, nearly dissolving it.

Belden's story of "Stone Wall Village" is typical of the thousands of villages then undergoing land reform. The Communists did not bring the Revolution with "a flash of swift lightning": ". . . Five men brought the Revolution to Stone Wall Village." The Communists—a group of two intellectuals, two workers, and one peasant—entered quietly and began to talk with each peasant individually, asking every peasant to "speak his bitterness." Initially afraid, the peasants gradually came out of their shell of fear and began to denounce the landlord and his rich peasant assistants openly. The mood of collective fury built up until each peasant hurled his own accusations against the landlord. Before he was killed, however, the landlord bowed to the peasants, and so admitted his humiliation as a person and as a class.

From this great social ferment the Chinese Communists recruited peasants to fight in their armies. Some became regular soldiers, others guerrillas, and still others became support units for the Red armies. Revolution gradually swelled the size of the armies, but also brought in aroused, idealistic, and vindictive men. The morale and fighting ability of the new Red peasants contrasted starkly with the fearful conscripts who were the bulk of Chiang's armies. Inferior in numbers and weapons at first, the Communists, through their fighting strength, gradually overcame the Kuomintang's initial superiority.

After victory the Communists launched a systematic program of land redistribution, the first stage in a process of rural transformation which eventually led to the people's communes. Yet the revolutionary hatreds of the peasants against the old order, generated by centuries of oppression and unleashed by rebellion upon rebellion since the eighteenth century, did not disappear after 1949. As the Communists say repeatedly, the class war on the land has not ended.

JACK BELDEN *

The Land Problem

The Communists could not hope to overthrow Chiang Kai-shek without finding a mighty support in the hearts of the people. Such a support was guaranteed by the land problem. . . .

Dr. Sun Yat-sen, father of the Kuomintang, and the Communists both realized that China could not be freed unless the peasant were freed and they began preaching a program of land to the tiller—that is to say, they proposed to the peasant that he support them in their northward march against the warlords in exchange for their help in getting him land. This could obviously be achieved only at the expense of the landlords. The peasant did not react to the slogans of unifying the country or overthrowing imperialism presented him by the Kuomintang bourgeoisie. But he did react, and with impassioned violence, to Dr. Sun's slogan of "land to the tiller," because, choking in his narrow plot, he wanted to throw out the landlord. On this basis, the peasants rose up like a mighty flood, some pouring into Chiang Kai-shek's armies, some joining the peasant unions. On the broad backs of these farmers, Chiang Kai-shek swept to power.

The Chinese bourgeoisie, however, was so tied up with the landlord that it could not abide this ally and turned the peasant soldiers against their brothers in the village associations. Not all the peasants had risen, but those who had were suppressed. Thus the landlords were not settled with despite all the promises of soil to the tillers.

As soon as the mobsters of Tu Yüeh-shen's Green Gang had cut down the workers in Shanghai and given the signal for the counter-revolution, the higher army officers, most of whom

* Jack Belden, *China Shakes the World* (New York: Harper and Brothers, 1949), pp. 145–158, 174–185.

were large landowners, abandoned all thought of reducing land rents by 25 per cent in accordance with the adopted and passed program of the Kuomintang. Far from reducing rents, the landlords often demanded and received 65 per cent instead of 50 per cent of the tenant's rice or wheat crop. Should the tenant protest, the landlords would simply have their bailiffs throw him in their dungeons. The compensation the peasant received for putting Chiang Kai-shek in power was thus not land or even rent reductions, but threats, curses, blows and sometimes a coffin.

With the Party traitor to the program of their founding fathers, the learned economists in Chiang's government began to justify the betrayal by finding that the land problem was a myth and did not exist.

In adopting this attitude, they could conceivably find support if they wished in some very useful figures. On the morrow of Chiang Kai-shek's *coup d'état* in Shanghai all the arable land within China was estimated at one and one third billion *mow* (one *mow* equals approximately one sixth of an acre). The population of the country was around four hundred and fifty million, of which about three hundred and fifty million were farmers. In effect, and under the most ideal conditions, this meant that the peasant would have to extract taxes, food, fuel, clothing—in fact, everything he would ever use in his life from an iron hoe to a wooden coffin—out of no more than four *mow* (two thirds of an acre) of land. This fact by itself suggested that China would have to end feudalism or perish. But Chiang's agronomes now discovered in these figures proof of another sort. "What is the use of dividing the land?" they blandly asked. "There is not enough anyway." As for land concentration, it did not exist and hence there was no cause for revolution. No doubt the economists wished to rationalize their betrayal of the peasants. But their assumptions not only ignored the wishes of the farmer—as if this flesh-and-blood man were too insignificant to find a place in their figures—but also ignored the process of land concentration which was taking place before their eyes.

People who note the incredibly small plots of Chinese farms are apt to draw the conclusion that there are no larger landholdings in China. But small fields, far from showing no land concentration, illustrate the backward nature of an economy in which the landlords do not manage large farms for production, but parcel out their land to tenants in order to obtain rents. In Honan, south of the Yellow River, one might ride a donkey cart past scores of villages for a whole day and still be on the same family's land. In Shantung large areas of clan land were monopolized by the descendants of Confucius and in many places the writer came across associations of landlords known as the Hundred Ching Pai, or the Ten Thousand Mow Group. In northern Kiansu, there was a temple that owned two hundred thousand *mow* (thirty-three thousand acres) of land. The chief monks, engaged in rent collecting and the practice of usury, maintained big families, including concubines, and had dwellings far grander than even the magistrates. Utterly dependent on the monks for farm tools, the tenants were often conscripted for labor by the armed guards of these ecclesiastical landowners.

Although the National government had no nationwide statistics, there were nevertheless innumerable provincial statistics that formed a most impressive picture of the revolutionary situation engendered by the conditions of landownership. With every desire not to burden this text with figures, I cannot refrain from introducing the statistics of landownership in the home provinces of Chiang Kai-shek, T. V. Soong, H. H. Kung, and the brothers Ch'en Li-fu, and Ch'en Kuo-fu, Party bosses of the Kuomintang.

There is here before us a picture of a nation carrying in its womb a peasant war. In a backward and terribly overcrowded country such as China, where a plot of land often means the difference between life and death, these figures are of far greater significance than they would be in a land-rich country such as the United States. . . . [tables omitted]

. . . Chinese rulers, however, are traditionally contemptuous of the masses' ability to interfere in their own fate. Instead of seeking to alleviate these conditions by land reform, the Kuomintang bureaucrats adopted just the opposite policy. During the Japanese war, land became concentrated to an unheard-of degree in modern China. Despite the fact that an estimated fifty million *mow* of land were lying desolate in the provinces of Ho-

nan, Hupeh, and Hunan and despite the fact that an estimated
ten to fifteen million farmers died of starvation during and after
the war, Chiang Kai-shek's bureaucrats using their superior military force and their bureaucratic positions began a gigantic land
grab in the interior of China. At the end of the war, the land grab
by the Chiang government was even more callous and more open.
All the land that the Japanese had robbed from the Chinese
people, instead of being turned back to them was taken over by
the Kuomintang. Japanese land in Formosa was appropriated
by mainland carpetbaggers, while the North China Exploitation
Company seized several hundred thousand *mow* of land in
Hopei.

Taking a leaf from the book of their masters, the smaller
bureaucrats and the militarists, unable to live on the paper money
salaries given them by the Chiang government, also began amassing landholdings as a means of security in times of inflation.
Under the concerted drive for land by Chiang's interlopers from
the coast, even rich peasants and small landlords began to lose
their holdings. In Szechuan, it was estimated that during eight
years of war anywhere from 20 to 30 per cent of the total landlords were new landlords who occupied 90 per cent of the land
owned by the old landlords. This explosive bomb directed against
the native money-landlords brought forth a bitter reaction. "All
land under the sky belongs to the Emperor," used to be an old
Chinese saying. Now the dispossessed landlords complained:
"All land under the sky belongs to Chiang Kai-shek." Such a
way of speaking, of course, was mainly symbolic, but it had revolutionary significance.

This creation of a new rural gentry, however, had another
side. There was arising from the seized land not only a new
rural bourgeoisie but new paupers. The number of peasants dispossessed from their land because of unpaid mortgages and unpaid debts, both in Chiang's areas and in the Japanese-occupied
areas, rose by untold thousands during the Japanese war. In the
famine periods in North China, peasants who had to give land as
security for grain borrowed during the spring, within a space of
two or three years would lose everything. It was common for
three or four members of a family of seven to starve to death for

these reasons. Land concentration thus meant corpses to ferti-
lize the earth, but it also meant thousands of souls for agrarian
revolution. . . .

The failure of the Kuomintang not only to introduce reforms
in the villages, but rather to make conditions worse than they
ever had been, was not so much a personal failure of evil and
greedy men—though these there were in abundance—as it was
the failure of the Kuomintang to come to grips with the central
problem of Chinese rural civilization: feudalism. That Chiang
Kai-shek and his Party after twenty years still could not grapple
with this problem furnished abundant proof of the terrible contradictions with which their rulership was riven. It was quite
clear that the Kuomintang rulers, in addition to leaning on
foreign capital, and in spite of their urgent needs to modernize
the country, predicated their own rule on the rule of the landlords. In view of this fact, all the pious hopes of President Truman and the bitter blasts of General Marshall calling on the
Chiang regime to reform, were just so much wishful thinking.
The Chiang regime could not reform as long as it dared not attack the landlords. And it dared not attack the landlords because
in essence it represented feudalism itself.

What do we mean by feudalism? Technically speaking, the
name is incorrect. And certain learned philosophers, both Chinese and foreign, have taken great pains to point out that feudalism does not exist in China because there is no serfdom; that
is, men can sell their labor freely. It is true that China abolished
this formal type of feudalism many years ago, just as it is true
that the penetration of the West destroyed the self-sufficient
natural economy of the centralized feudal society and placed
much of Chinese life under the demands of a money economy,
though with few progressive results, as we have seen. But this
manner of looking at the problem of China is academic in the
extreme and takes no cognizance of the feudal remnants that
exercise such an important role in the lives, thoughts, customs,
habits, and emotions of the people. In abolishing serfdom, the
Chinese did not entirely do away with the power of the landlord
to conscript labor, to jail debtors, and to control the life and even
death of his tenants; it did not completely abolish child slavery,

the custom of buying and selling girls nor the system of con-
cubinage or forced marriage. All of these conditions are ir-
revocably bound up with the rule of the landlords and the gentry.

The power of the landlords in China was not everywhere
the same. In the provinces along the seacoast and in the Yangtze
Valley where foreign capital penetrated and where mercantile
and small industrial cities grew up, the power of the rural gentry
in many cases had to be shared with city merchants. In the
Western and Northern provinces, however, the landlords had
almost unlimited political power because of the thicker atmosphere of precapitalism. Even in northern Kiangsu, along the seacoast and not far from Shanghai, landlords lived like feudal
barons in mud castles, surrounded by armed guards and controlling tenants in fifteen or twenty villages. Such castles acted
as a trading center for tenants who were completely at the
mercy of the landlord or his bailiffs. Not only had the tenant
to bring 50 per cent of his crops to the manor, but also his
personal and family problems. In Shansi, I found that landlords
often governed all wedding ceremonies and funerals, so that no
one could get married or be buried without the approval of these
feudal lords. . . .

These excrescences on Chinese rural life would have been
enough to create thousands of impassioned soldiers for a peasant
war, but in themselves they were not decisive. That factor was
provided by the decline of Chinese agriculture as a whole.

The end of the Japanese war found the peasantry in this
condition. The army had carried away about twelve to fifteen
million fieldworkers, famine perhaps another ten million, and
there were untold millions of refugees. The landless farmers
went under first, the semitenants next. Those dispossessed from
the land increased by the hundreds of thousands. During the
third and fourth years of the war the middle peasants began to
go under. Then some of the rich peasants. By the end of the war
small and middle landlords and even large regional landlords
began to feel the pressure from Chiang's land-hungry bureaucrats and Japanese puppets. The desolate land ran into millions
of acres. Land hunger also spread like the plague. No longer
could the peasants live under the system of extortionate land

rents. The peasant's holdings had grown so small that he could
not afford to pay the traditional 50 per cent, to say nothing of
80, 90, and over 100 per cent, of his main crop. Rents not only
used up all his surplus labor, but encroached on the labor necessary to keep him alive. Everyone was asking, "When will these
Japanese dwarfs be driven out?" But when the Japanese war
ended and a new one started, the peasant found Chiang's new
rural bureaucrats even more hostile to him than the Japanese
or his old gentry had been. He began to grumble. From grum-
bling, he passed into banditry. Near the Eighth Route Army
areas he began to look for allies.

The ruling classes could not help but see that the peasant
was going to explode in a violent upheaval. But they kept putting
these black thoughts from their minds. Here is what Ch'en Li-fu,
graduate of the Pittsburgh School of Mines, Kuomintang boss,
and preacher of the Confucian way of life, revealed to one impressed foreign reporter: "To divide the land is not necessary
because when the head of a Chinese family dies, he divides the
land among his sons." Here is what T. V. Soong, after his appointment to the governorship of Kwangtung province, where
he is a large landholder, unveiled to another correspondent: "We
are not planning a land reform in Kwangtung because the system
we have had here for years is satisfactory." Finally, here is what
a liberal professor in a Christian university and at the same time
an official of the Shantung government had to say to this writer:
"China is not like Czarist Russia; we have no large landlords so
there is no need for land reform, but only a reform of the officials." (How one of these things was to be done without the
other, the Christian professor did not explain.) To introduce a
land reform into the countryside thus seemed in the eyes of
these Party bosses, governors, and Christians something alien
to the Chinese way of life. It is hardly necessary to remark that
such Oriental philosophizing was quite beyond the peasant. He
thought there was only one thing to do: throw out the landlord
and divide the land. That was the essence of the revolution to the
tenant, to the rural worker, to the coolie.

If the villages behind Chiang Kai-shek's lines remained
comparatively peaceful, that was only because the peasant was
awaiting leadership and an opportunity to rise. He had not for-

gotten about the land. Nor did the Kuomintang officials, despite their utterances, think he had forgotten either. All their remarks about there being no need for land reform were merely a camouflage for the deep-seated fears that Chinese rulers have always felt toward the peasantry. To the official the thought of this ignorant clod covered with the good Chinese earth rushing into his yamen was like some terrible dream out of the pages of the *Shui Hu Chuan*.

Well might the officials tremble!

For this simple man, born to tenant, feudal slavery, to an overworked and crowded plot of ground, stunned into obedience beneath the grasping landlord's hand, dispossessed from his land by crooked deals and savage violence, robbed of his wife's caresses and his children's laughter, suddenly rose with an impassioned thrill and, under the threat of death itself, began to demand land and revenge.

Stone Wall Village

The land in this region is rocky, bare of forest, and grudging in its fertility so that the hard-pressed farmers have been forced to build terraces and cultivate the hill slopes nearly to the top of every peak. For many centuries, the peasants have been struggling not only against the parsimonious nature of these mountains, but against the brutal exactions and dark superstitions of a civilization probably very much like that which Christ knew. These people, however, believed in no Supreme God, but rather knew many gods, including the God of Fate who made them poor, and ghosts, devils, and evil spirits whom they believed lurked in the rocks, trees, and the bodies of the animals which roamed their hills. As a consequence, they were easy prey for the intrigues of village witches who called down spirits to their incense tables and frightened peasants into doing the bidding of the landlords.

The common farmers, always hungry and always in debt, had a verse about their bitter lot which ran like this:

Harvest every year; but yearly—nothing.
Borrow money yearly; yearly still in debt.
Broken huts, small basins, crooked pots;
Half an acre of land; five graves.

About one hundred families lived in Stone Wall Village, many of them in caves hollowed out of the side of the mountain at the base of which the village was situated. South of the town ran a river, overhung with willows and cedars, on the banks of which was a mill where the people ground their wheat and Indian corn—the two crops raised yearly by Stone Wall Village. The barren aspect of the place was somewhat relieved by small orchards of peach, apricot, and pear trees.

Stone Wall Village had one peculiarity that set it apart from most Chinese villages: its women did not raise many children. The reasons for this were manifold. In the first place, many of the farmers were too poor to support a wife and did not marry. Secondly, girl babies were often strangled by their parents at birth because of poverty. Thirdly, the Japanese, who had occupied a strong point on the opposite bank of the river for six years, had raped many of the women, venereal disease had become widespread and many of the women had become sterile.

Politically, Stone Wall Village was in the hands of its village chief, a landlord named Wang Chang-ying. Although his personal characteristics are not germane to this story, it may be mentioned in passing that Landlord Wang was fifty years old, that he wore a small goatee and smoked a long-handled water pipe. In fair weather, it was said that he promenaded on the streets and beat any child who was unfortunate enough to bump into him. At sight of him, many of the village poor would immediately run indoors.

Wang's possessions included sixty-five acres (no one else owned more than three acres) of irrigated land, the riverside mill, a large store of grain, one wife, one son, one daughter, one daughter-in-law, and a vengeful nature. . . .

Such was the condition of Stone Wall Village when the Chinese Revolution suddenly descended on it. There had been

vague stories of this revolution in the village; there had been mur-
murings about the Eighth Route Army, about a thing called
democracy and about villages where there were no landlords
and everyone had an equal amount of land. But the people had
listened to these rumors with only half an ear; they were poor
and fated to be poor; they did not want to fight anybody, they
only wanted to be left alone.

Landlord Wang had also heard these rumors; he did not
take them seriously either. But as a precaution, he used to tell
the people: "Flesh cut from others won't stick to your own
body." The people, however, did not need this warning: they
had no intention of moving against Landlord Wang.

Nevertheless, the Revolution came to Stone Wall Village.

It did not come like a flash of swift lightning; for a revolution like everything else moves slowly in China. Nor did it announce itself like a clap of thunder, with the beat of drums, the
sound of rifle fire, or hot slogans shouted on the country air.

To be more exact, five men brought the Revolution to Stone
Wall Village. They were not soldiers nor were they Communist
Party members. One had been a schoolteacher, another a student,
a third a waiter, a fourth a shop assistant, and a fifth a farmer.
They were all members of the Hohsien County Salvation As-
sociation and their job was to "overturn" Stone Wall Village.

"Overturn" is a term of the Chinese Revolution that came
into being after the surrender of the Japanese. In Communist
terminology it means to turn over the social, political, and economic life of every village, to overturn feudalism and establish
democracy, to overturn superstition and establish reason. The
first step of the overturning movement is to "struggle" against the
landlords and divide the land.

To do this sounds easy. You have the guns and the power
and you just tell the landlord to give a share of his land to the
people. But it is never that easy. In Stone Wall Village, there was
no army, there was no militia. The Eighth Route Army was far
to the south. Even the guerrillas had gone elsewhere. Landlord
Wang was the power and the people were afraid of him.

The leader of the Hohsien Salvation team was a thirty-one-
year-old cadre, the son of a bankrupt rich farmer, named Chou
Yu-chuan. When Chou and his fellow workers arrived in Stone

Wall Village they posted proclamations of the Shansi-Hopei-Honan-Shantung Border Region government, announcing that every village had the right to elect their own officials and that land rents and rates of interest should be reduced. Then they called a meeting to explain these proclamations, but the people listened only halfheartedly, kept their mouths tightly shut, and went home without speaking further to the cadres.

For several days, the cadres went individually among the people asking them about local conditions and their own lives, but no one would talk. Whenever a cadre approached groups of people, they would break apart and move away. One or two men cornered alone admitted they were afraid of the landlord.

Under these conditions, the cadres could not carry on their work, so they decided to seek out one of the poorer men in the village and talk to him alone and in secret.

At this time, Chou and another cadre were living in a cave next door to one occupied by a tenant farmer, named Ma Chiu-tze. Ma had bought his cave before the Japanese war with six dollars earned by his wife in spinning thread. Now, his wife was sick and Ma often came to the cadre's cave and slept on the same *kang* with them. During the night, the three men always talked.

Ever since the Ch'ing Dynasty, Ma revealed, his family had been poor tenants, renting land and never having any of their own. Every year, he raised eight *piculs* of millet and every year he had to give four of these *piculs* to Landlord Wang. He could afford no medicine for his wife, whom he feared was dying. Two years before, his father had died and he had not been able to buy the old man a coffin, but had to wrap him in straw. Now he was thirty-five and he was still poor and it looked as if he would always be poor. "I guess I have a bad brain," he would say in summing up the reasons for this poverty.

Then the cadres would ask: "Are you poor because you have a bad brain or because your father left you no property?"

"I guess that's the reason: my father left me no property."

"Really is that the reason?" asked the cadres. "Let us make an account. You pay four *piculs* of grain every year to the landlord. Your family has rented land for sixty years. That's two hundred forty *piculs* of grain. If you had not given this to the landlord, you would be rich. The reason you are poor, then, is because you have been exploited by the landlord."

They would talk like this for hours and Ma would finally acknowledge that he was exploited by the landlord. Then he would say: "What can I do? Everyone looks down on me. When it's mealtime, the landlord eats inside the house, but I must eat outside, standing up. I am not good enough. Everyone looks down on me."

"And why is that?" said the cadres. "That is because you have no money and because you have no money you have no position. That is why we must overturn so that everyone can have an equal position and no man will look down on another."

Ma agreed that the landlords had to be overthrown before there could be any happiness for the poor, but he was only half convinced of his own statements. There was yet a long distance between words and action and the weight of two thousand years of tradition lay very heavily on Ma as on most Chinese peasants. . . .

[*Ma Chiu-tze became the Revolution in Stone Wall Village. But he needed help, so on the sixteenth day of the cadre's stay in the village, Ma brought three of his friends into the cave, including the old farmer Original Fortune Lee. However, it was feared that news of their talks had reached the ears of Landlord Wang; a few days later Original Fortune Lee was found murdered.*]

After the murder of Original Fortune Lee the people went about in terror and shut up again like clams. Even those who had attended the second meeting now said: "We haven't begun to struggle with the landlord, but one of us is gone already."

The cadres were very much surprised by the murder. They thought they had been too careless and had not placed enough belief in the peasants' fears. They also thought a hand grenade might be thrown at any time into their meeting cave. Their biggest fear, however, was that the peasants would give up the overturning movement altogether. Therefore they decided to hold a memorial meeting in honor of Original Fortune Lee, and by this meeting to mobilize the people.

On the stage opposite the Three Sects Temple, where semi-religious plays were held during festival times, the cadres placed pictures of Mao Tse-tung, Chairman of the Chinese Communist Party, and General Chu Teh, Commander-in-Chief of the Communist-led Eighteenth Group Army. Beside these pitcures they placed strips of paper saying: WE SHALL TAKE REVENGE FOR THIS PEASANT.

One hundred people of Stone Wall Village attended this meeting, but Landlord Wang did not come. The county magistrate came especially to make a speech and announced: "The government intends to clear up all murders. The people should continue to overturn and to establish a democratic government of their own."

The memorial meeting lasted four hours. After it was over, another meeting was called to decide how to continue "overturning." Only six farmers came to this meeting. No one said directly that he was afraid to attend, but weakly gave the excuse: "I have a little work to do."

These six men, however, decided that because of the murder they would have to "settle" with Landlord Wang immediately.

At the end of five days, thirty farmers mobilized by the other six gathered in the cave for another meeting. Until nearly midnight, they told stories of how they had suffered at the landlord's hands.

Suddenly, someone said: "Maybe Wang will run away."

"Let's get him tonight," said several farmers at once.

After some discussion, they all trooped out of the cave and started a march on Landlord Wang's home. Among the thirty men, there were one rifle and three hand grenades.

The marching farmers separated into two groups. One climbed on top of the cliffs and worked along the cave roofs until they were over the courtyard. The others marched directly to the gate, knocked loudly and commanded the landlord to open up.

Wang's wife answered the door and announced that her husband was not at home. Refusing to believe her, the peasants made a search and discovered a secret passage behind a cupboard. Descending through an underground tunnel, they found

Wang cowering in a subterranean cave. They took him away and locked him up overnight.

That night Wang's son fled to the county seat of Hohsien, ten miles away. Here landlords from other villages had organized bandits, former puppet troops, and some of the soldiers of Warlord Yen Hsi-shan into a "Revenge Corps." When the people learned of the flight of Wang's son, they grew anxious and said among themselves: "It is easy to catch a tiger, but it is dangerous to let him go back to the forest."

Nevertheless, they decided to go ahead with the struggle against Landlord Wang. That same day a mass meeting was called in a great square field south of the town, not far from the river. About eighty people came to complain against Wang, while the rest of the village watched—among them Wang's wife and daughter.

In the course of the morning and afternoon, the crowd accused the landlord of many crimes, including betrayal of Resistance members to the Japanese, robbing them of grain, forcing them into labor gangs. At last, he was asked if he admitted the accusations.

"All these things I have done," he said, "but really it was not myself who did it, but the Japanese."

He could not have chosen worse words. Over the fields now sounded an angry roar, as of the sea, and the crowd broke into a wild fury. Everybody shouted at once, proclaiming against the landlord's words. Even the nonparticipating bystanders warmed to something akin to anger.

Then above the tumult of the crowd came a voice louder than the rest, shouting: "Hang him up!"

The chairman of the meeting and the cadres were disregarded. For all that the crowd noticed they did not exist.

The crowd boiled around Wang and somewhere a rope went swishing over a tree. Willing hands slung one end of the rope around Wang's waist. Other eager hands gave the rope a jerk. Wang rose suddenly and came to a halt in mid-air about three feet above the earth. And there he hung, his head down, his stomach horizontal and his legs stretched out—a perfect illustration of what the Chinese call a "duck's swimming form."

About his floating body, the crowd foamed, anger wrinkling

their foreheads and curses filling their mouths. Some bent down and spit in the landlord's eyes and others howled into his ears.

As he rose from the ground, the landlord felt a terror which mounted higher as his position became more uncomfortable. Finally, he could bear it no longer and shouted: "Put me down. I know my wrongs. I admit everything."

The spite of the crowd, however, was not so easily assuaged and they only answered the landlord's pleas with shouts: "Pull him up! He's too low! Higher! Higher!"

After a while the anger of the people abated and cooler heads counseled. "If we let him die now, we won't be able to settle accounts with him." Then they allowed him to come down for a rest.

At this point, the wife of Original Fortune Lee came up close to Wang and said in a plaintive voice: "Somebody killed my husband. Was it you?"

Wang's face which had grown red from hanging in the air slowly was drained of all color. "No, I did not do it," he said.

"Tell the truth," said the crowd. "You can admit everything to us and nothing will happen. But if you don't tell us the truth, we will hang you up again."

"No, it was not me."

These words were hardly out of his mouth before someone jerked on the rope and the landlord flew into the air again. This time the crowd let him hang for a long while. Unable to bear the pain, Wang finally said: "Let me down. I'll speak."

Then, between sobs and sighs, he told how he and his son had seized Original Fortune Lee as he was walking home from the meeting, tied his hands together, held his head under water until he was dead and then had thrown him in the river, thinking he would float away.

A cry of rage went up as Wang finished speaking.

"You've already killed three of our men in the war," said Liu Kwang. "That could be excused. But now your own life can never repay us for the crimes you've done."

Again Wang was hung up and this time many shouted: "Let him hang until he is dead." But others said: "That is too quick; he must first have a taste of the suffering we've had."

At dusk, they let Wang down once more and put him in a cave under guard again.

As soon as the meeting was over, twenty or thirty men went to the landlord's house, drove the wife and daughter out of doors and sealed the house. The two women went to a nearby village to stay with relatives.

That evening the five cadres and those who had taken an active part in the struggle against the landlord walked around the village to listen to the gossip and sample public opinion. Such words were heard as: "Serves him right; he's so wicked. This is too light for him. Just count his sins."

Later that night another meeting of those of the village who wanted to struggle against the landlord was held in a courtyard. This time a hundred and twenty people attended.

When the cadres asked: "How do you feel? Have you done well?" the answer came back: "Oh fine! Fine!"

But exactly what to do with the landlord was a problem for which the people at first had no solution. Half of these in the meeting thought he should be beaten to death. A few said: "He is too old." Some had no ideas at all. Others thought that his clerk, the rich farmer Shih Tseng-hua, should be bound up with him at the same time in the struggle. This suggestion, however, was voted down when someone pointed out: "You should always collect the big melons in the field first. So we should cut off the big head first."

It was decided that Wang must die for his murders. But how? Should he be sent to the district government to be punished, should the people kill him or what?

"If he is tried before a court-martial for treason," said a farmer, "then there will be only one bullet, and that is too cheap for Wang. We ought to kill him first and report to the government afterward."

"Who dares kill him?" asked a farmer doubtfully.

At this everyone shouted at once: "We dare. We dare. He bayoneted our militiamen to death and we can also do that to him."

Three days after this meeting, the whole village breakfasted early, and shortly after sunrise, seven hundred men and women, including visitors from neighboring villages, many armed with pig knives, hoes, sickles, swords, and spears went out to the large field south of town where the landlord was to be killed. The cadres had written down Wang's crimes on large pieces of paper and these, hanging by ropes from the trees, now fluttered in the breeze.

"Traitor Wang Chang-ying killed three militiamen and one active farmer of the village," said one.

"Sinful Landlord Wang grafted money and grain during the War of Resistance," said another.

"Wang Chang-ying shifted the tax burden onto the people and looted the village," said a third.

A shout went up from the crowd as Landlord Wang was led onto the field. Three guards marched him, pale and shaking, to a willow tree where he was bound up. With his back against the tree, the landlord looked once at the crowd but quickly bent his head toward the ground again.

A slight shiver of apprehension went through the audience. They could not believe their enemy was helpless here before them. He was the lamb led to slaughter, but they could not quite believe they were going to kill him.

Ma Chiu-tze stepped before the crowd and called for attention. "Now the time has come for our revenge," he announced in a trembling voice. "In what way shall we take revenge on this sinful landlord? We shall kill him."

As he said this, he turned around and slapped Wang sharply across the face.

The crack of palm against cheek rang like a pistol shot on the morning air. A low animal moan broke from the crowd and it leaped into action.

The landlord looked up as he heard the crowd rushing on him. Those nearest saw his lips move and heard him say: "Two words, two words please."

The man closest shouted: "Don't let him speak!" and in the same breath swung his hoe, tearing the clothes from the bound man's chest and ripping open the lower portion of his body.

The landlord gave one chilling shriek and then bowed his head in resignation. The crowd was on him like beasts. Their faces had turned yellow and their eyes rolled. A big farmer swung his pig knife and plunged it directly into the landlord's heart. His body quivered—even the tree shook—then slumped, but still the farmer drew his knife in and out, again and again and yet once again.

Landlord Wang was quickly dead, but the rage of the crowd would not abate.

The field rang with the shouts of maddened people.

"It is not enough to kill him."

"We must put him in the open air."

"We must not allow him to be buried for three days."

But such convulsive passions do not last long. They burn themselves out. Slowly, the anger of the crowd cooled. The body of the landlord might rot in the open air and it were better that his wife and daughter be allowed to get him.

That evening, as the sun was going down behind the mountain, the landlord's wife and daughter brought a mule cart slowly across the field to where their husband and father lay. They wept no tears, but silently lifted the mutilated body into the cart and drove away.

Few saw them come and few saw them go. And no one said a word. For there was nothing left to say. The struggle against the landlord was ended.

Stone Wall Village had turned over.

❧ The Great Debate:
Could China Have Been "Saved"?

THE GREAT China debate in the United States began in 1947 and it has continued down to the present time, albeit in changed form. Influential American citizens, largely Republican, began to cry out: Why are we not helping the Nationalist government to prevent the triumph of Communism in China? As the Nationalist situation worsened, pressure on Washington increased to make a major effort to aid the Nationalists. When it was apparent that the Nationalist cause was doomed, accusatory voices were raised, seeking scapegoats for the debacle. The campaigns of Senator Joseph McCarthy rose out of this debate and brought about one of the most serious internal crises in American history.

Today voices can still be heard accusing the Truman Administration of having allowed China to go down the drain. In the light of America's inability to bring about reform and stability in South Vietnam and the indecisive results of the massive military involvement in that country, the argument that America could have prevented the Chinese Communist victory in the late 1940s seems doubtful. This argument appears to be even more questionable when considered in light of Chinese Communist accusations that the United States made every effort to bolster Chiang's military power, and that the Communists won the war essentially with captured American war equipment.

Republican criticism of China policy began in late 1946, but did not become widespread until the spring of the following year. Before that, even so adamant an enemy of Chinese Communism in later years as Representative Walter Judd gave his approval to Marshall's attempts to reach a settlement in China (in a speech on December 27, 1945). When the debate began, the Nationalist military position was still tenable. In March 1947 the Nationalists captured Yenan, and Chiang Kai-shek told Ambassador John Leighton Stuart that by autumn the Communists would be defeated. But early in May the Communists launched a powerful offensive in Manchuria that succeeded in isolating the main Nationalist-held cities: Kirin, Changchun, and Ssupingchieh. On May 30, 1947, the American Consul General in Mukden warned of a sudden debacle which would lay all of Manchuria open to the Communists.

The fortunes of war changed dramatically and rapidly in China, but it is important to note that when the debate began, the Nationalist situation by no means appeared to be hopeless. On March 12, 1947, President Truman proclaimed the Truman Doctrine for Greece and Turkey, implying a priority commitment to Europe rather than to Asia. The Republicans, always more Pacific-oriented than the Democrats, may have seen this as a sign of a decisive policy shift away from Asia. Whatever confidence American officials may have had that Chiang would finally win was increasingly dissipated during the summer of 1947.

In July, President Truman dispatched Lieutenant General Albert C. Wedemeyer to China on a fact-finding mission. Excerpts follow from his speech of August 22 before high members of the Nationalist government. Wedemeyer criticized the Nationalist government's corruption and inefficiency in no uncertain terms, noting, "today China is being invaded by an idea instead of strong military forces from the outside. The only way in my opinion to combat this idea successfully is to do so with another idea that will have stronger appeal and win the support of the people." He urged wholesale reforms of the entire Chinese government and Army, and steps to strengthen her economy. Despite this, after his return, Wedemeyer advocated long-term, large-scale military and economic assistance to China, though under strict American supervision.

By late 1947 the Nationalist situation although not yet desperate was becoming increasingly critical, particularly in Manchuria. Again the China debate broke out in Congress, with Republicans demanding a major effort to help the Nationalists hold Manchuria. The second selection presents excerpts from an article written in October 1947 by William C. Bullitt, former Ambassador to the Soviet Union. Bullitt stressed that America could not allow any outside nation to dominate China. At that time he saw the Soviet Union preparing to acquire control over the richest area of China, Manchuria; if Manchuria were taken, he predicted that all of China would fall. Bullitt, like Wedemeyer, noted the corruption and economic chaos, and proposed an eighteen-point reform program for China. On the military side he proposed that "the President should release immediately certain stocks of munitions and have them rushed to the government troops in Manchuria." He called for "the training and equipment in the American manner of ten new divisions" to drive the 350,000 Communists out of Manchuria. Like General Chassin, he claimed airpower would be of great use, but proposed mainly to turn over obsolete planes to the Nationalists. Nonetheless he was forced to admit that "all this aid will be ineffective unless the Chinese can revitalize their political life, arouse a new spirit in the country, and raise morale in the army." His final suggestion was to make General Douglas MacArthur the President's "Personal Representative" to Generalissimo Chiang Kai-shek.

In regard to Ambassador Bullitt's recommendations, one might only again note the comments made in November 1948 by General David Barr, head of the United States Military Advisory Group, that "no battle has been lost since my arrival due to lack of ammunition or equipment. [The Nationalists'] military debacles in my opinion can all be attributed to the world's worst leadership and many other morale-destroying factors that lead to a complete loss of will to fight."

Finally, we present excerpts from Dean Acheson's Letter of Transmittal of the State Department White Paper outlining the stages of the Nationalist collapse and American efforts to prevent it. The causes given for the collapse are largely those mentioned in other contemporary reports, including that of General Wedemeyer. Acheson concludes:

A realistic appraisal of conditions in China, past and present, leads to the conclusion that the only alternative open to the United States was full-scale intervention on behalf of a government which had lost the confidence of its own troops and its own people. Such intervention would have required the expenditure of even greater sums than have been fruitlessly spent thus far, the command of Nationalist armies by American officers, and the probable participation of American armed forces—land, sea, and air—in the resulting war.

Acheson maintained in substance that only if the United States had massively intervened and taken command of the war from the Nationalists was there a chance that the Communists could have been stopped.

The China debate continued well into the 1950s, but largely in the form of accusation and defense. The critics charged that China had been betrayed to the Communists by the secret Yalta agreements of February 1945, in which, in exchange for a Soviet promise to enter the war against Japan, the United States and Britain agreed to sacrifice China's vital rights in Manchuria to the Soviet Union. These critics noted that the Yalta betrayal led to the Soviet occupation of Manchuria. While hampering Nationalist efforts to re-establish control over Manchuria, the Soviets, as Ambassador Bullitt put it, planned "to use the time gained by the [Nationalist-Communist] armistice to transfer as many Communist troops as possible from North China to Manchuria and there to arm them with the abundant Japanese supplies and equipment which the Russian Red Army had seized when the Japanese Army in Manchuria surrendered." Dark hints of conspiracy were already voiced by Bullitt when he called for an investigation of China policy which "might at least fix responsibilities and reveal the names of men in our government and Foreign Service who are incompetent to preserve the vital interests of the people of the U.S." The conspiracy theme ultimately led to the purge of leading State Department diplomats allegedly responsible for the betrayal at Yalta and the loss of China.

Regardless of its sordid aspects, the China debate must be viewed as part of the changing history of American foreign policy. Tang Tsou, Professor of Government at the University of Chicago and brilliant student of United States policy toward China, found two contradictory themes in twentieth-century American policy toward China: espousal of the principles of the Open Door and refusal to go to war on China's behalf (*America's Failure in China,* p. 360). We suggest that the contradiction arose from the conflict over whether America's commitment to Europe or to Asia should have priority. Thus the Truman Doctrine proclaimed an American priority commitment to Europe and implied a relative de-emphasis of the Asian commitment. When, after years of Democratic rule, the Republicans sensed their star rising again, they began to press for a change in the priorities. The leading spokesman for this policy conception was General Douglas MacArthur.

There can be no doubt that the American commitment in Asia has grown steadily in the last two decades, and has reached a high point in the present Vietnam war. Tang Tsou's formulation of one aspect of traditional American Asian policy, namely its "refusal to go to war on behalf of China," must be broadened to mean a refusal to make major military commitments for the achievement of goals in the Far East. Tang Tsou maintains that "the acceptance of war with Japan" was "only a temporary resolution of the contradiction. . . ." From the present perspective, however, the contradiction appears to have vanished. Europe has been stabilized, and the threat of Soviet attack seems remote. Since 1950, America has twice committed herself to a major war in the Far East, not to mention an enormous buildup of permanent American military power in that part of the world.

As we shall see in Volume III, America today is in another China debate in addition to the Vietnam debate. Twenty years ago Democratic Party liberals argued for the priority of the European commitment. Today these same liberals, and younger men who have followed in their line, argue for *détente* with the Soviet Union but for firm containment, with the threat of using military force, of China.

As we reflect on the first great China debate, we might observe that it was strongly influenced by the actual course of events in China: the worse the situation became—that is, the more evident the collapse of the Chiang regime—the more

vociferous the conservative critique. Despite Administration
doubts about pouring more resources into China, Washington
decided to step up its aid program nevertheless. Thus, after initial discussion late in 1947 (when the Republican critique
reached a high point of intensity), Congress passed the China
Aid Act in April 1948, an effort which may have been insufficient
from the Nationalists' and the Republicans' point of view, but
which was made. The criticism had succeeded in pushing Washington toward a firmer commitment, and that criticism was tied
to the deteriorating situation in China.

The lingering echoes of the first China debate still suggest
that "if only America had done something," China could have
been "saved." The overwhelming bulk of testimony on this
period, pro and con, indicates that only full-scale mobilization of
American forces—sending of ground troops, dispatching of a
major part of the Air Force, and assumption of command over
Nationalist armies through American officers and advisers—provided a chance of averting the inevitable. Even assuming that
such mobilization could have been carried out at top speed, the
lessons of the Japanese invasion of China and the present American involvement in Vietnam indicate that at best only a holding
operation could have been mounted. The tide turned in the summer of 1947, though not yet decisively, and Communist victory
was certain by the end of 1948. Since large-scale foreign intervention was the only slight chance of changing events, one can
ask whether there ever was anything that America could have
"saved" in China.

ALBERT C. WEDEMEYER *
Summary of Remarks . . . Before Joint Meeting of
State Council and All Ministers of the
National Government August 22, 1947

TAXATION

Approximately 80 per cent of the people of China are hard-working peasants, their crops are visible and officials can easily appraise the amounts the peasants are able to give toward government. Corrupt officials in many instances take more than the peasants are able to give and this results finally in the peasants leaving the land and forming bandit groups.

In contrast to the taxation of peasants, Chinese businessmen and rich Chinese resort to devious and dishonest methods to avoid payment of proper taxes to their government. It is commonly known that Chinese business firms maintain two sets of books, one showing the true picture of business transactions and the other showing a distorted picture so that they do not pay as much tax as they should.

MILITARY

For the first year after the war, in my opinion, it was possible to stamp out or at least to minimize the effect of Chinese Communists. This capability was predicated upon the assumption that the Central Government disposed its military forces in such a manner as to insure control of all industrial areas, food-producing areas, important cities, and lines of communication. It was also assumed that the Central Government appointed highly efficient and scrupulously honest officials as provincial governors,

* United States Relations with China (With Special Reference to the Period 1944–1949) (Department of State Publication, 1949).

district magistrates, mayors, and throughout the political and economic structure. If these assumptions had been accomplished, political and economic stability would have resulted, and the people would not have been receptive, in fact, would have strongly opposed the infiltration or penetration of communistic ideas. It would not have been possible for the Chinese Communists to expand so rapidly and acquire almost undisputed control of such vast areas. I believe that the Chinese Communist movement cannot be defeated by the employment of force. Today China is being invaded by an idea instead of strong military forces from the outside. The only way in my opinion to combat this idea successfully is to do so with another idea that will have stronger appeal and win the support of the people. This means that politically and economically the Central Government will have to remove corruption and incompetence from its ranks in order to provide justice and equality and to protect the personal liberties of the Chinese people, particularly of the peasants. To recapitulate, the Central Government cannot defeat the Chinese Communists by the employment of force, but can only win the loyal, enthusiastic, and realistic support of the masses of the people by improving the political and economic situation immediately. The effectiveness and timeliness of these improvements will determine in my opinion whether or not the Central Government will stand or fall before the Communist onslaught.

During the war while serving as the Generalissimo's Chief-of-Staff, I tried to impress upon all Chinese military officials the importance of re-establishing excellent relationships between officers and enlisted men. I explained that officers must show sincere interest in the welfare of their men both in times of war and in peace. Wounded must be evacuated from the battlefield and cared for in hospitals or aid stations. Officers should visit their men in the hospital and find out if they can help them in any way. Officers should play games with their soldiers such as basketball and soccer. The junior officers should know all of their men in the unit by name. They should talk to them and encourage them to discuss their problems. Explain to them why they are fighting. Explain the objectives of their government and encourage open discussions. This will create a feeling of mutual respect and genuine affection. Discipline acquired through fear is not as effective as discipline acquired through affection and mutual respect. It would be so easy for the Chinese officers to win the respect and admiration of their men who are simple, kindly, and brave and who will gladly endure hardships and dangers if they are properly led and cared for.

CONSCRIPTION

I have received many reports that the conscription of men for military service is not being carried out honestly or efficiently. Again, as in taxation peasants are expected to bear the brunt of conscription, although in the cities there are thousands and thousands of able-bodied men, who should be under the conscription laws eligible for military service. Rich men's sons by the payment of money avoid conscription and the sons of rich men are being sent to school abroad instead of remaining here to help their country in a time of great crisis.

RELATIONSHIP BETWEEN MILITARY AND CIVILIANS

I cannot emphasize too strongly the importance of establishing and maintaining good relationship between military forces and the civilian population. Officers and men in the army and air corps should be very careful to be courteous, friendly, cooperative, and honest in all of their contacts with civilians. In Manchuria, I was told by many sources that the Central Government armies were welcomed enthusiastically by the people as deliverers from Japanese oppression. Today, after several months of experience with these Central Government armies, the people experience a feeling of hatred and distrust because the officers and enlisted men were arrogant and rude. Also they stole and looted freely; their general attitude was that of conquerors instead of that of deliverers. In Formosa the reports are exactly the same, alienating the Formosans from the Central Government. All of this is a matter of discipline. Of course if the officers themselves are dishonest or discourteous, one can hardly expect the enlisted men to be otherwise. Good relations between the military forces and the civilians are absolutely essential if the Central Government expects to bring about successful conclusion of operations against the Communists. At first the Communist armies were also crude and destructive and made the people hate them, but in the past few weeks, they have adopted an entirely new approach which requires their officers and men to be very careful in all their relations with civilian communities. You can understand therefore how important it is that your own military forces adopt steps immediately to improve the conditions I have mentioned.

Promotion in the military service should be by merit and merit alone. Older officers or incompetent ones should be retired and relieved. The retired officers should realize that they must make room for the younger ones and they must accept retirement patriotically and philosophically. There are entirely too many generals in the Chinese Army. Most of them are not well-educated and are not well versed in modern combat. Generals should never be used in civilian posts of responsibility, for example, as governors, mayors, and magistrates, except perhaps as Minister of Defense. Military men should not be permitted to belong to a particular political party. After the constitution goes into effect on December 25, they should be permitted to cast a vote, in other words, exercise the right of suffrage, but no military men should be permitted to hold government office or be active members of a political party.

CORRUPTION

One hears reports on all sides concerning corruption among government officials, high and low and also throughout the economic life of the country. With spiraling inflation, the pay of government officials both in civil service and in military service is wholly inadequate. I am sure that persons who are presently practicing dishonest methods would never consider doing so were it not for the fact that they receive insufficient remuneration to meet the bare necessities of life. Many of them are not trying to acquire vast fortunes, but are just trying to provide a standard of living commensurate with their position. On the other hand, certain rich families, some of whom have relatives in high positions of the government, have been greatly increasing their fortunes. Nepotism is rife and in my investigations I have found that sons, nephews, and brothers of government officials have been put in positions within the government, sponsored firms, or in private firms to enable them to make huge profits at the expense of their government and their people. It would be interesting and revealing if you would conduct an investigation into various large banking organizations and other newly created business organizations, to ascertain how much money has been made by such organizations and to what individuals or groups of individuals the money has been paid. To reduce corruption, it will be necessary to establish an index of the standard of living and as the exchange rises the pay of civil service and military service must be increased accordingly. I should emphasize that I am sure many patriotic and selfless Chinese are eking out a bare existence under difficult conditions. They are a great credit to China. However, it must be very discouraging to them to realize that many who already had amassed great fortunes have taken advantage of the present unfortunate situation in China to increase their wealth.

PUNISHMENT AND SECRET POLICE

I have had reported to me many instances of misdirection and abuse in meting out punishments to offenders political or otherwise. In Formosa there are many so-called political offenders who are still in prison without any charges or sentences. Some have been released but only after paying large sums of money and being required to sign a statement to the effect that they were guilty of an offense against the government. Actually in their hearts and minds they did not feel that they were guilty of such offense. Secret police operate widely, very much as they do in Russia and as they did in Germany. People disappear. Students are thrown into jail. No trials and no sentences. Actions of this nature do not win support for the government. Quite the contrary. Everyone lives with a feeling of fear and loses confidence in the government.

FINAL REMARKS

The government should not be worried about criticism. I think constructive criticism should be encouraged. It makes the people feel that they are participating in government; that they are members of the team. I have mentioned earlier the terrible economic conditions that exist in England. Criticism of the government is expressed freely in meetings on the streets, and in the press, and on the radio. This is in my opinion a healthy condition. The Government should point out that it is made up of human beings who are of course fallible and can make mistakes. The government should emphasize, however, that once the mistakes are pointed out, effective steps will be taken to remedy them. The government should publish information freely concerning expenditures, taxation. Let all the people know how much income tax each individual, particularly wealthy people and big business firms, are paying. Announce publicly when any official or any individual has been guilty of some crime or offense and also indicate the punishment meted out. By the same token, announce publicly the accomplishment or good work of individual government activities. All of these matters would contribute to confidence on the part of the people in the government. They want to know what is going on and they have a right to know. Open and public official announcements on the part of the government will also serve to stop malicious conjectures and adverse propaganda of opponents of the government.

I realize that many of the ideas that I have expressed are quite contrary to Chinese tradition. However, I have carefully studied the philosophy of Confucius and I am sure that all of these ideas are in consonance with the fine principles of conduct that he prescribed. I have confidence in the good sound judgment and in the decency of the bulk of the Chinese peoples. I hope sincerely that you will accept my remarks in the same spirit in which they were given, namely, in the interest of China. Anything that I can do to help China become a strong, happy, and prosperous nation, I would gladly do. Anything I could do to protect the sovereignty of China and to insure her a place of respect in the eyes of the world in the family of nations, I would gladly do.

WILLIAM C. BULLITT *
Report to the American People on China

To prevent the domination of China by any nation which might eventually mobilize the four hundred fifty million Chinese for war against us is a vital interest of the U.S.

Only two great powers have threatened to dominate China —Russia and Japan—and the U.S. has opposed whichever of those powers has been momentarily the more dangerous aggressor. Today Japan is no longer a great power. But Soviet imperialism, following in the footsteps of Czarist imperialism, and using the Chinese Communists as instruments of Soviet power politics, is striving to reduce China to the status of a satellite of the Soviet Union. Not merely the territorial integrity of China but her very independence is at stake. In our own self-defense, therefore, we must act to prevent Soviet domination of China and the eventual mobilization of Chinese manpower for war against us.

Can China be kept out of the hands of Stalin? Certainly— and at a cost to ourselves which will be small compared to the magnitude of our vital interest in the independence of China.

By what means? Before answering that question let us glance briefly at some events of the past twenty years and some aspects of the present situation which should influence our conclusions.

In the year 1928 Generalissimo Chiang Kai-shek completed his conquest of the Northern warlords and established the authority of the national government. The period from 1928 to 1937 was one of great progress, in spite of the seizure of Man-

* William C. Bullitt, "Report to the American People on China," *Life*, October 13, 1947.

churia by the Japanese in 1931. By 1937 the national revenues
had been trebled and the national budget brought close to balance. The New Life Movement [see pp. 150–154], started by
the Generalissimo, had infused a fresh, creative idealism into
many Chinese, especially the youth. The Communists, confined
to poverty-stricken Shensi, seemed powerless, and many believed
that, in spite of the loss of Manchuria, China could and would
win her way back quickly to economic health and national
strength.

The Generalissimo was wiser. In the private papers of
President Roosevelt will be found a report of a mission to Nanking on which I was sent by the President in the autumn of
1934. In the course of a series of long conversations the Generalissimo made predictions which for foresight and wisdom have
rarely been surpassed in the annals of statesmanship. He felt
certain that the Japanese would not permit China to recover
her strength but would strike again, because Chinese reconstruction was going too well and too quickly to suit them. He predicted that Japan would attack by 1937 at the latest. The attack
came in 1937. He predicted that the attack would be started by
a trumped-up incident in the area between Peiping and Tientsin.
It was started at the Marco Polo Bridge near Peiping. He said
that he would fight in North China and lose; that he would fight
at Shanghai, Nanking, and Hankow and lose them all; that he
would then place his capital at Chungking in the remote province
of Szechwan; that he had just invested $100 million (Chinese)
in the construction of small-arms factories in the Szechwan cities
of Chungking and Chengtu; that the Japanese would never get
into Szechwan; that he would never make peace with them so
long as he lived, and that in the end they would be defeated.
That is the exact history of the events from 1937 to 1945.

He then predicted that after the defeat of Japan, if he were
still alive, he would face his greatest difficulties. The country
would be ruined, the people exhausted. To lead the Chinese to
the peaceful establishment of democratic institutions and modernization of their ancient civilization was the ambition of his
life, but it would be a harder task than even the defeat of the
Japanese.

In that also he saw clearly. There is no truer saying than

the old French one: "To govern is to foresee." Chiang Kai-shek
foresees.

YALTA—DISGRACEFUL DOCUMENT

What Chiang Kai-shek did not foresee, however, was the possibility that China might be betrayed by her allies in the war.
In the latter part of November 1943 the Generalissimo met
President Roosevelt and Prime Minister Churchill in Cairo, and
at the close of their conference they issued the following joint
statement:

> Cairo Declaration, December 1, 1943. President
> Roosevelt, Generalissimo Chiang Kai-shek and Prime Min-
> ister Churchill.
> It is their purpose that Japan shall be stripped of all
> the islands in the Pacific which she has seized or occupied
> since the beginning of the first World War in 1914, and
> that all the territories Japan has stolen from the Chinese,
> such as Manchuria, Formosa and the Pescadores, shall be
> restored to the Republic of China.

But fourteen months later at Yalta, on February 11, 1945,
President Roosevelt signed with Marshal Stalin and Prime Minister Churchill, secretly, behind the back of China, an agreement
by which vital rights of China in her province of Manchuria
were sacrificed to Soviet imperialism. No more unnecessary, disgraceful, and potentially disastrous document has ever been
signed by a President of the U.S. Unnecessary, because at a time
when it was obvious that no power on earth could prevent Stalin
from declaring war on Japan at the last minute, we bought his
entry into the war at the expense of a major injury to our ally,
China. Disgraceful, because all the weasel words in the world
cannot convince any fair-minded man that we kept our Cairo
pledge to China. Potentially disastrous, because we handed to
Stalin a deadly instrument for the domination of China and
thereby paved the way for war in the Far East. . . .

CYNICAL INDECENCY

As all Americans now know, President Roosevelt after our entry into World War II based his foreign policy and his hopes of world peace on the gamble that he could convert Stalin from Soviet imperialism to democratic collaboration. Although on February 10, 1940, the President had stated, "The Soviet Union, as everybody who has the courage to face the fact knows, is run by a dictatorship as absolute as any other dictatorship in the world," he began to have the Soviet Union referred to in official communications as a "peace-loving democracy." Until President Truman's speech of March 12 this year the official doctrine of the U.S. government remained the farce that the Soviet Union was a peace-loving democracy and that the Chinese Communists were mere agrarian reformers who did not take orders from Moscow. This doctrine gave rise to spectacular actions in the Far East. Vice-President Wallace, then Ambassador Hurley, and finally General Marshall were sent to end the war between the Chinese government and the army of the Chinese Communists.

WE HELPED PROLONG CIVIL WAR

General Marshall reached Chungking, which was then the capital of China, on December 22, 1945, and so great was his prestige that he was able by January 10, 1946, to obtain signature of an armistice by the Chinese government and the Communists. Moreover just before leaving for Washington on March 11, 1946, he seemed to have paved the way for the enforcement of a truce in Manchuria. Thus it appeared that in less than three months General Marshall was well on his way toward stopping the fighting in China.

The surface appearance was deceptive. The Soviet government objectives were not those of General Marshall. On V-J Day there were no Chinese Communist troops in Manchuria. The Soviet plan was to use the time gained by the armistice to transfer as many Communist troops as possible from North China to Manchuria and there to arm them with the abundant Japanese supplies and equipment which the Russian Red Army had seized when the Japanese Army in Manchuria surrendered. To withdraw the Russian Army from Manchuria only when it could be replaced by a well-armed Chinese Red army and to use the Marshall armistice period for this purpose, was the Soviet plan. It worked perfectly.

On April 14, 1946, immediately after the evacuation of the capital of Manchuria, Changchun, by the Soviet Army, the Chinese Red Army attacked it. General Marshall returned to China on April 17 and the next day Changchun fell to the Communists.

General Marshall resumed his task with his customary determination and dignity. But, in truth, from the beginning he had no chance to succeed. The final verdict on General Marshall's actions in China must be that never was a distinguished soldier sent on a more hopeless and unwise political mission.

After the failure of General Marshall's mission American policy toward China fell into a tired apathy, marked by a weary and petulant inclination to "let China stew in her own juice." In order to bring pressure on the Chinese government to compel it to accept our erroneous thinking that the Soviet Union was a "peace-loving democracy" we cut off all aid to the Chinese government. The $500 million loan earmarked for China was withheld. The "Eight and One Third Air Group Program"— by which we agreed to equip and provide maintenance parts for eight and one third groups of the Chinese air force—was stopped by our unilateral action in September 1946.

Most serious of all, having equipped some Chinese divisions entirely with American artillery, machine guns, and rifles, and others partially, and promised to help maintain this armament, we had held up export licenses for munitions. In consequence Chinese divisions without ammunition and with worn-out American equipment were facing Communist troops newly equipped in Manchuria by the Soviet Union with abundant supplies of Japanese rifles, machine guns, and cannon. Our policy resulted in disarming our friends while the Soviet Union was arming our enemies. By the spring of this year it was evident that unless we changed our policy China would not "stew in her own juice" but in Soviet juice. Last July 11 General Albert C. Wedemeyer was sent to China to resurvey the situation. What is the situation?

Today the Chinese government holds firmly all China as far north as the Yangtze River. Small bands of bandits, some of whom call themselves Communists, hold remote areas south of the Yangtze; but the Shanghai fashion of calling the area south of the Yangtze "the zone of peace and reconstruction" is justified. The area from the Yangtze north to the borders of the Soviet Union is definitely a war zone.

The war there, however, in no way resembles warfare of the sort that our troops experienced in Europe in either World War. The Communists use guerrilla tactics, moving swiftly and attacking at night, hiding in villages and resting in the daytime. An observer in a plane may fly low over hundreds of miles of territory in North China and Manchuria through which these guerrillas are scattered and never see a single soldier or the slightest evidence of troop movement. At dusk the Communists assemble, march fast toward their objective, often covering as much as twenty miles, and strike in the night. They are attempting to bring down the government not by destroying its armed forces but by wrecking the economic life of the country. Hence they do not hesitate to burn towns and villages, destroy railroads, and blow up industrial installations, such as power plants, which they cannot carry away.

The government armies attempting to protect cities, towns, and villages are for the most part tied down to fixed points. They move more slowly than the Communists, and often when they attack they find that the Communists have quietly withdrawn in the night. A government drive to clear Shantung is now in progress, but already a large body of Communists has escaped into the adjoining province of Honan and is laying waste the rich country there. . . .

Whatever the issue of battle may be, the Chinese government cannot withdraw from Manchuria and must attempt to reinforce its troops in Manchuria at any cost. If Manchuria should be abandoned to the Communists or should fall into their hands by conquest, a course of events fatal to China would follow.

HOW STALIN COULD WIN

It is not difficult to foresee that the Communists would at once proclaim the "independence" of a "People's Republic of Manchuria," or that this "republic" would soon be recognized by the "Independent People's Republic of Outer Mongolia," which is entirely controlled by the Soviet government, and that the two "independent republics" would then enter into a mutual-assistance pact. And it is not difficult to imagine that the Chinese Ambassador in Moscow would then be summoned by Molotov and politely reminded that the Soviet Union has a mutual-assistance pact with the "People's Republic of Outer Mongolia." Therefore if the Chinese government should attempt by arms to regain its province of Manchuria and Outer Mongolia should go to the assistance of the "People's Republic of Manchuria," the Soviet Union under its pact with Outer Mongolia regretfully would be obliged to use force to prevent the Chinese government from inflicting injury on the forces of Outer Mongolia. Under penalty of Soviet intervention the Chinese government would be forbidden to attempt to recover its province of Manchuria— and Stalin's work at Yalta would be crowned with final success.

He would have all Manchuria firmly in his hands. And Manchuria is the finest piece of territory in Asia. As large as France and Germany combined, containing in its valleys agricultural land as rich as any in the world, where wheat, corn, soya beans, and all our Northern crops grow superbly; holding great deposits of coal and iron, and even gold; having immense wealth in forests and in waterpower both developed and undeveloped; containing before the war 70 per cent of Chinese industry but populated by only forty million people and offering immense possibilities for further settlement of overcrowded Chinese farmers, Manchuria is vital for the future development of China.

The urgent need of the government armies in Manchuria for ammunition and spare parts to use in their American arms and equipment is one which cannot be filled in a leisurely man-

ner. It requires immediate action. President Truman should act
at once as President Roosevelt acted after Dunkirk, when the
British and French were desperately short of munitions. President Roosevelt then had certain stocks of the U.S. Army declared no longer essential for use by the Army. They could
then legally be sold, and vast quantities were sold to Great
Britain at approximately ten cents on the dollar. We have hundreds of thousands of tons of such stocks today, rotting and
rusting throughout the world. Such of those stocks as can be
used in Manchuria should be released immediately and sold to
China and their transport rushed.

President Truman can legally take this action at once. He
does not need to wait for Congress to reconvene. He can act in
time to keep Manchuria out of the hands of the Soviet Union.
If he does not, one of the first acts of Congress when it re-
convenes should be an investigation of our policies with regard
to China. Such an investigation might at least fix responsibilities
and reveal the names of the men in our government and Foreign
Service who are incompetent to preserve the vital interests of
the people of the U.S.

INFLATION NOW CRIPPLES CHINA

By acting in time we can keep Manchuria out of the hands
of the USSR and thus insure China's territorial integrity. But,
essential as this is, it is not enough. China must not only be
preserved as a free national entity but made a healthy and strong
one—a power of such stature that in time she can serve as a
real counterweight to the Soviet empire in the Far East. To become strong she must have internal stability, and to achieve this
she must above all have financial stability.

China today is caught in the sort of vicious circle that has
become familiar to Europeans since World War I. She has been
at war since 1937. The Japanese occupied nearly all her great
cities, banking centers, and industrial regions. The sources of
such wealth as she had were in Japanese hands. Therefore she
could not finance her war against the invader by sales of bonds,

and she could cover only a small portion of the cost of the war by taxation. In consequence she covered her war costs by the only method open to her—the issuance of paper currency.

This means that China's war was in reality financed at the cost of the middle class and by reduction of the standard of living of such fixed-income groups as schoolteachers, college professors, government employees, both civil and military, and all who live on the income produced by securities bearing a fixed rate of interest. The cost of living today expressed in Chinese dollars is approximately thirty thousand times what it was in 1936, before Japan attacked China. The middle class is ruined.

In an effort to keep down expenditures for war purposes, the government has kept down the pay of its soldiers and officers. A private has been receiving in pay the Chinese equivalent of $1.50 a month. A major general receives the equivalent of $17 a month. For purposes of raising morale, as well as other reasons, pay in the army should be quadrupled. But there are more than four million officers and men on the rolls of the army, and a quadrupling of pay would add such a sum to government expenditures, which could be covered only by printing more paper money, that the present steady rise in the cost of living would be accelerated.

The salaries of all government employees from cabinet members to tax collectors are held down to fantastically low levels. In a time of great national peril it is proper to demand vast sacrifices of all who serve the government either as civilians or military men. But the underpayment of government employees in China has passed the limits of human endurance and is producing disastrous results. Soldiers who are grossly underpaid and hear from their families stories of increasing poverty have their morale deeply affected. Officers who cannot possibly support their wives and children on their salaries, if they are men of strong character and patriotism, sell all they possess to keep their families alive, and when they no longer have any possessions to sell, must either see their children starve or use their power as officers to graft or commit suicide. There have been many who have preferred suicide to dishonor, but many have turned to graft.

In the army, graft takes many forms. The simplest is the

padding of pay and ration rolls. The Chinese customs service, which before 1937 was one of the most efficient and honest in the world, is now riddled with graft. It still contains many honest men, but the majority expect "squeeze." Tax collectors of all sorts graft. An honest Chinese businessman who owes $10,000 to the government in taxes can declare and pay that sum only at his peril. The tax collector insists on his graft. He will settle for $5,000 for himself and $2,500 for the government. But if the businessman refuses him the graft he will report that the businessman is keeping fraudulent books and that in reality he owes $30,000. The Chinese judges have for the most part endured their sufferings and kept their honor clean. But there are grafting judges also. No item is too small to carry its tiny burden of graft. High-school and college diplomas in China must be registered. The registrars invent all sorts of excuses not to register them until they get their little "squeeze."

Most of these men graft to live, and there is no possible way to stop this sort of graft until all government employees, military and civilian, receive a living wage. But raising of government salaries will increase the inflation, inflation will raise the cost of living, the rising cost of living will quickly absorb the raises in salaries, graft will start again—nobody will be better off. How can China break this vicious circle?

There is only one ultimate answer to that question: finish the war. But how can victory be achieved if the vicious circle in which China is caught prevents the war from being fought effectively?

This is were the U.S. comes in. We can break the vicious circle at several points and at a cost to ourselves which will be small compared to the advantages to be gained for our own security.

The most astonishing facts to be found in China today are not in the realms of war or politics but in the field of finance. Chinese government expenditures, when translated into U.S. dollars at the prevailing rate of exchange, are on a Lilliputian scale. To govern the four hundred fifty million Chinese in a territory one third larger than the U.S. and to carry all the expenses of the war, the Chinese government now spends approximately the same sum annually as the municipal government of New York City.

It is a fact that the total government expenditures for the year 1947, at the present rate of exchange, will amount to approximately one billion dollars. It is a fact that all the trillions of Chinese government currency outstanding could theoretically be bought, at the present rate of exchange, for only $250 million.

These figures are of the first importance for only one reason —they prove that the problem of giving effective aid to China is within dimensions that we can handle. We can break the vicious circle of Chinese inflation without coming anywhere near breaking ourselves.

Before we go further into the question of aid to the Chinese government let us remember that wars are won not by arms alone but by fighting spirit, by patriotism, and great political leadership. What of political leadership in China today? Has it the qualities necessary to lift the tired, hungry nation to new heights of self-sacrifice?

The same men who led China during the period of great progress from 1928 to 1937 and through the heroic years of the war against Japan are still the leaders of China. Few question the honesty of the Cabinet members or their patriotism and good intentions or the first-rate ability of some of them—like the Minister of Communications, General Yu Ta-wei. But criticism of the government is universal. Why?

In no country in the world is disillusionment greater than in China. The Chinese people thought that when the Japanese invaders were driven out they would have peace. They had no idea that the defeat of Japan would be followed immediately by an attempt of the Soviet Union to use the Chinese Communists to destroy their independence and enslave them. At the time of the Japanese attack in 1937, the Chinese Communists had seemed a negligible band of brigands in a section of the poor province of Shensi. At that time, indeed, the Communist army consisted of only thirty thousand men.

But the Communists turned out to be the great profiteers of the war against Japan. While the government troops were fighting the Japanese they recruited their forces, and on August 15, 1945, when the Japanese surrendered, they had approximately 300,000 guerrillas under arms in North China. There was not a single armed Chinese Communist in Manchuria. But the Soviet government, which occupied Manchuria when the Japanese surrendered, began to rush Chinese Communists into Manchuria and to arm them with surrendered Japanese arms. In Manchuria they recruited not only local peasants but also Koreans, and their strength there is now close to 350,000. Scattered throughout North China they have now perhaps 400,000 men organized in small armies and guerrilla bands.

Today the tired Chinese people, who expected peace, have war, heavy taxes, rising costs of living and death. They want peace. And they blame the government because they do not have peace. It is the habit of all peoples after great wars to turn in disillusionment against their war leaders—the ejection of Winston Churchill and Charles de Gaulle are recent cases in point. And it is obvious that no Chinese government could be popular under present circumstances. Graft and inefficiency in the administrative services increase the government's unpopularity. But aside from the Communists and fellow travelers, even the Chinese who are most critical of the government do not speak ill of Generalissimo Chiang Kai-shek personally. They admit that his services to China have been greater than those of any man in modern times except Dr. Sun Yat-sen. They admit his complete personal honesty and devotion to his country's welfare. But they say that he is no longer well informed and does not know what is going on in the country, that he listens too much to old friends who helped him twenty years ago, that he has held supreme power so long that no one any longer dares to talk frankly to him, that he is too set in his ways to change either his policies or his intimate advisers, that he cannot, therefore, meet the terrible new problems which confront China today. But to the question, "By whom should he be replaced?" the answer invariably is, "There is no one to replace him."

A PROGRAM OF REFORM FOR CHINA

Those patriotic Chinese who feel the Generalissimo is not doing all he can to meet the present problems of China wish he would do the following things which compose a rational program of reform:

1. Retire half the generals and a third of the other officers of the army—this being the number they consider incompetent or corrupt or both.

2. Cut the rolls of the army to one half; first, by removing all nonexistent troops from the rolls; second, by disbanding units of the lowest quality.

3. Quadruple the pay of those officers and men who remain in the army and double their rations.

4. Punish severely all officers and men who, after having been given a living wage, graft.

5. Cut out all duplicate and useless government departments and agencies and dismiss all unnecessary government employes. It is estimated that this might reduce the government's civilian payroll by one third.

6. Raise to a living wage the pay of those who remain, then punish severely all who graft.

7. Stop putting the government into industry and business, government ownership being followed inevitably by nepotism, inefficiency, and graft. Sell to the highest bidder those industries now under government ownership and genuinely encourage private enterprise.

8. Welcome foreign capital, in acts as well as words.

9. Decentralize the government, reducing military forces and military authority in the whole area south of the Yangtze to the absolute minimum consistent with national safety, returning authority to the civilian provincial governors and permitting the provincial governments to receive directly at least 25 per cent of the land tax and to make decisions with regard to provincial projects.

10. Reform the land tax and all other taxes and demand absolute honesty from tax collectors, under the severest penalties.

11. Hire foreign specialists to direct the reform of taxation, the collection of taxes, the revamping of financial policy and the reconstruction of Chinese industry.

12. Compel all Chinese who have funds in foreign cur-

rencies or gold to deliver them to the government, and jail rich men who evade this measure or evade the full payment of their taxes.

13. Apply the draft law to the sons of the rich and influential as rigorously as to the peasants.

14. Eliminate the draft exemption of students, and draft immediately all those students who are working on the side of the enemy in the present war—the Communists and fellow travelers who comprise about 5 per cent of the student body—and put them through a course of re-education before sending them to the front. Permit patriotic students to make as many critical speeches and organize as many demonstrations as they wish.

15. Use Manchurians, as far as possible, in the administration of Manchuria.

16. Publish the exact facts about the Russian Red Army in Manchuria, its rapings and pillagings, publication of which, in fear of Russia, has been forbidden. Also publish the abundant evidence of the subservience of the Chinese Communists to Moscow.

17. Publish facts on smuggling from Hong Kong into China, which is greatly reducing customs revenues.

18. Go through with the nationwide October and December elections, and, when the democratic constitution is in full force, end in reality as well as name the period of "tutelage" by the Kuomintang inaugurated by Dr. Sun Yat-sen in 1924.

A program of this sort would unquestionably be popular throughout China, and with some American assistance it can be carried out.

THE COST OF SAVING CHINA

The new democratic constitution of the Republic of China, which was adopted by the National Assembly on December 25, 1946, will enter into force on Christmas Day this year. The Kuomintang, the government party, undoubtedly will win a majority of the votes, and Generalissimo Chiang Kai-shek will be re-elected President of the Republic of China. There will, therefore, be no break in the continuity of government and the U.S. government can begin today to concert with the Generalissimo plans to finish the war and to get China started again on the road to peaceful modernization of her ancient civilization. How shall we proceed? Neither Chinese internal reforms without American aid nor American aid without Chinese internal reforms can solve the problem of protecting the vital interests of the U.S.—and the very life of China. Simultaneously the U.S. and Chinese governments, hand in hand, must attack the problem.

It must be attacked at once on three fronts: 1) economic and financial, 2) military, 3) political. Since the essence of the problem is the ejection of every armed Communist from the soil of China, an intelligent project can be prepared only on the basis of an estimate of the time it will take to win the war. American military experts believe that this may take as long as three years. The Chinese are more optimistic. But let us accept the American estimate and try to sketch a Three Year Plan and estimate its cost.

During the next three years China will need to import large quantities of American cotton, tobacco, wheat, oil, gasoline, and many manufactured articles.

The sums she will need to spend for this purpose will far exceed the amount of foreign exchange she will acquire by exports and remittances from her emigrants throughout the world. She will therefore need credits for the purchase of food, raw materials, and manufactured articles. *The highest figure for such necessary credits given by American and Chinese economic experts is $250 million a year*—a tiny fraction of what is said to be Europe's requirements. Let us scale that down to $200 million and budget for our total Three Year Plan $600 million of credits for purchases in the U.S. from this autumn to the autumn of 1950.

The sale in China of the food, raw materials, and manufactured articles thus acquired would help to retard inflation. After cutting the numbers of the army and the civilian employees, it might be possible to quadruple the pay of all remaining government servants, civilian and military—which is essential for the elimination of graft—without producing a rise in the inflation. Since the task of preventing Stalin from taking over China must be a joint task of the U.S. and Chinese governments, there is no reason why the use of such credits should not be jointly controlled.

It is clear that unless the U.S. government acts rapidly the inflation will soon assume runaway proportions. To control the inflation China needs now a portion of the credits we have envisaged, perhaps $75 million. The remainder of the $200 million for the first year of our Three Year Plan can await action by the Congress: but either from the U.S. foreign relief program or the Export-Import Bank or some other source, this $75 million must be obtained in the next thirty days.

To combat inflation for the duration of our Three Year Plan, to curb speculators against the Chinese dollar, and to maintain China's international balance of payments, another fund will be required. All use of such a fund should require the countersignature of a representative of the U.S. government, and it should not be set up until certain corrupt practices are stopped. Let us assume that the Chinese government will act rapidly and effectively against the speculators and budget a $150 million exchange-stabilization fund for our total Three Year Plan.

Let us now turn to the military side of the problem, remembering that it is absolutely essential that the President should release immediately certain stocks of munitions and have them rushed to the government troops in Manchuria. This cannot be delayed, or by next spring we shall find Manchuria a Soviet satellite.

According to the estimates of the ablest American and Chinese military men, to drive out of Manchuria the 350,000 Communists will require the training and equipment in the American manner of ten new divisions. Furthermore, an efficient service of supply from the point of origin of the supplies to the front is essential. The great Manchurian port of Dairen cannot be used because by the Yalta Agreement it is now occupied by Soviet forces. Port improvements in Hulutao and Chinwangtao and the rehabilitation of at least one railroad will therefore be necessary. Until all graft shall have been eliminated from the Chinese Army,

it would be wasteful to turn over American supplies to a Chinese
service of supply. No American can take responsibility for commanding the Chinese Army, but American military men can
and should run the service of supply in Manchuria.

In North China, where the Communists hold no large cities
and are essentially raiders, the problem is one of cornering and
and capturing guerrillas. For this purpose light-armed, fast-mov-
ing troops are needed, equipped with jeeps, halftracks, light
trucks, small arms, machine guns, and 75s. The estimates of the
ablest American and Chinese officers who have studied this problem indicate that twenty divisions of such troops should be able
to clean up North China.

An air force, even of the smallest dimensions, would greatly
facilitate operations in both North China and Manchuria. We
have thousands of planes and millions of spare parts which are
obsolete in terms of our air force but first-rate material for the
Chinese air force. To release this material and turn it over to the
Chinese would cost us nothing but a bookkeeping entry.

It is obvious that the total cost to the U.S. of the military
element in the Three Year Plan we have sketched will depend
in large measure on the bookkeeping. If we choose to charge
the Chinese five or ten cents on the dollar for munitions and
estimate the total cost of aid in the military field on that basis,
the total costs will be low. But there will be real costs for transportation, oil, gasoline, food, and the services of Americans to
run the service of supply as well as to advise on training and
operations. Until a complete plan is drawn up, no estimate, even
approximate, can be made. But if we release the necessary munitions it seems unlikely that the costs could be more than $200
million a year—$600 million for the whole Three Year Plan.

If we add to that figure the $600 million envisaged for
credits and the $150 million for a monetary fund, we reach a
total for the Three Year Plan of $1,350 million—$450 million
a year for the next three years. As a price for preventing Stalin
from taking over China and organizing its resources and manpower for war against us, the figure is not high.

But all this aid will be ineffective unless the Chinese can
revitalize their political life, arouse a new spirit in the country,
and raise morale in the army. Can we help them to do that, or

will suggestions from us be considered impertinent? They will not be considered impertinent if they are made by the right man in the right way. Too many Americans, clothed with a little brief authority, when they go to China confuse the might, majesty, power and dominion of the U.S. with their own personalities and talk down to Chinese who, in truth as men, are their superiors. In the pages of history Generalissimo Chiang Kai-shek bulks larger than any living American. He and Winston Churchill will be remembered together as leaders who had the courage and will to rally their countries in their darkest hours. To protect a vital interest of the U.S. and to defend the very life of China, the closest cooperation between Americans and Chinese is essential. What American has the military knowledge, political skill, and personal magnitude to organize such cooperation?

We have in the Far East today a general of supreme stature who possesses all those qualities. If President Truman were to ask General MacArthur to add to his present duties and powers the title of Personal Representative of the President with the rank of Ambassador and to fly to China to organize with the Generalissimo a joint plan to prevent subjugation of China by the Soviet Union, the whole Far Eastern horizon would brighten with hope. The General would not have to abandon his work in Japan. He could divide his time between Tokyo and Nanking. His military, economic, and political proposals might well be those outlined in this report. He could establish rapidly with the Generalissimo the relations of two comrades in a front-line trench. They would work together as brothers for their common cause.

The cause is a common cause. If China falls into the hands of Stalin, all Asia, including Japan, sooner or later will fall into his hands. The manpower and resources of Asia will be mobilized against us. The independence of the U.S. will not live a generation longer than the independence of China.

DEAN ACHESON *

Letter of Transmittal Accompanying Report
on United States Relations with China

DEPARTMENT OF STATE
WASHINGTON, JULY 30, 1949

The interest of the people and the government of the United
States in China goes far back into our history. Despite the distance and broad differences in background which separate China
and the United States, our friendship for that country has always
been intensified by the religious, philanthropic, and cultural ties
which have united the two peoples, and has been attested by
many acts of good will over a period of many years, including
the use of the Boxer indemnity for the education of Chinese
students, the abolition of extraterritoriality during the Second
World War, and our extensive aid to China during and since
the close of the war. The record shows that the United States
has consistently maintained and still maintains those fundamental principles of our foreign policy toward China which include the doctrine of the Open Door, respect for the administrative and territorial integrity of China, and opposition to any
foreign domination of China. It is deplorable that respect for
the truth in the compilation of this record makes it necessary
to publish an account of facts which reveal the distressing situation in that country. I have not felt, however, that publication
could be withheld for that reason.

The record should be read in the light of conditions prevailing when the events occurred. It must not be forgotten, for
example, that throughout World War II we were allied with
Russia in the struggle to defeat Germany and Italy, and that a
prime object of our policy was to bring Russia into the struggle

* Dean Acheson, Letter of Transmittal Accompanying *United States Relations with China, op. cit.*, pp.III–XVII.

against Japan in time to be of real value in the prosecution of the war. In this period, military considerations were understandably predominant over all others. Our most urgent purpose in the Far East was to defeat the common enemy and save the lives of our own men and those of our comrades-in-arms, the Chinese included. We should have failed in our manifest duty had we pursued any other course.

In the years since V-J Day, as in the years before Pearl Harbor, military considerations have been secondary to an earnest desire on our part to assist the Chinese people to achieve peace, prosperity, and internal stability. The decisions and actions of our government to promote these aims necessarily were taken on the basis of information available at the time. Throughout this tragic period, it has been fully realized that the material aid, the military and technical assistance, and the good will of the United States, however abundant, could not of themselves put China on her feet. In the last analysis, that can be done only by China herself. . . .

After Pearl Harbor we expanded the program of military and economic aid which we had inaugurated earlier in 1941 under the Lend-Lease Act. That program, described in Chapter I of the attached record, was far from reaching the volume which we would have wished because of the tremendous demands on the United States from all theaters of a worldwide war and because of the difficulties of access to a China all of whose ports were held by the enemy. Nevertheless it was substantial.

Representatives of our government, military and civilian, who were sent to assist the Chinese in prosecuting the war soon discovered that, as indicated above, the long struggle had seriously weakened the Chinese government not only militarily and economically, but also politically and in morale. The reports of United States military and diplomatic officers reveal a growing conviction through 1943 and 1944 that the government and the Kuomintang had apparently lost the crusading spirit that won them the people's loyalty during the early years of the war. In the opinion of many observers they had sunk into corruption, into a scramble for place and power, and into reliance on the United States to win the war for them and to preserve their own domestic supremacy. The government of China, of course, had always been a one-party rather than a democratic government in the Western sense. The stresses and strains of war were now rapidly weakening such liberal elements as it did possess and strengthening the grip of the reactionaries who were indistinguishable from the warlords of the past. The mass of the Chinese people were coming more and more to lose confidence in the government.

It was evident to us that only a rejuvenated and progressive Chinese government which could recapture the enthusiastic loyalty of the people could and would wage an effective war against Japan. American officials repeatedly brought their concern with this situation to the attention of the Generalissimo and he repeatedly assured them that it would be corrected. He made, however, little or no effective effort to correct it and tended to shut himself off from Chinese officials who gave unpalatable advice. In addition to a concern over the effect which this atrophy of the central Chinese administration must have upon the conduct of the war, some American observers, whose reports are also quoted in the attached record, were concerned over the effect which this deterioration of the Kuomintang must have on its eventual struggle, whether political or military, with the Chinese Communists. These observers were already fearful in 1943 and 1944 that the National Government might be so isolating itself from the people that in the postwar competition for power it would prove itself impotent to maintain its authority. Nevertheless, we continued for obvious reasons to direct all our aid to the National Government.

This was of course the period during which joint prosecution of the war against Nazi Germany had produced a degree of cooperation between the United States and Russia. President Roosevelt was determined to do what he could to bring about a continuance in the postwar period of the partnership forged in the fire of battle. The peoples of the world, sickened and weary with the excesses, the horrors, and the degradation of the war, shared this desire. It has remained for the postwar years to demonstrate that one of the major partners in this world alliance seemingly no longer pursues this aim, if indeed it ever did.

When Major General Patrick J. Hurley was sent by President Roosevelt to Chungking in 1944 he found what he considered to be a willingness on the part of the National Government and the Chinese Communists to lay aside their differences and cooperate in a common effort. Already they had been making sporadic attempts to achieve this result.

Previously and subsequently, General Hurley had been assured by Marshal Stalin that Russia had no intention of recognizing any government in China except the National Government with Chiang Kai-shek as its leader. It may be noted that during the late war years and for a time afterwards Marshal Stalin reiterated these views to American officials. He and Molotov expressed the view that China should look to the United States as the principal possible source of aid. The sentiments expressed by Marshal Stalin were in large part incorporated in the Sino-Soviet Treaty of 1945.

From the wartime cooperation with the Soviet Union and from the costly campaigns against the Japanese came the Yalta Agreement. The American government and people awaited with intense anxiety the assault on the main islands of Japan which it was feared would cost up to a million American casualties before Japan was conquered. The atomic bomb was not then a reality and it seemed impossible that the war in the Far East could be ended without this assault. It thus became a primary concern of the American government to see to it that the Soviet Union enter the war against Japan at the earliest possible date in order that the Japanese Army in Manchuria might not be returned to the homeland at the critical moment. It was considered vital not only that the Soviet Union enter the war but that she do so before our invasion of Japan, which already had been set for the autumn of 1945.

At Yalta, Marshal Stalin not only agreed to attack Japan within two or three months after V–E Day but limited his "price" with reference to Manchuria substantially to the position which Russia had occupied there prior to 1904. We for our part, in order to obtain this commitment and thus to bring the war to a close with a consequent saving of American, Chinese, and other Allied lives, were prepared to and did pay the requisite price. Two facts must not, however, be lost sight of in this connection. First, the Soviet Union when she finally did enter the war against Japan, could in any case have seized all the territories in question and considerably more regardless of what our attitude might have been. Second, the Soviets on their side in the Sino-Soviet Treaty arising from the Yalta Agreement, agreed to give the National Government of China moral and material support and moreover formalized their assurances of non-interference in China's internal affairs. Although the unexpectedly early collapse of Japanese resistance later made some of the provisions of the Yalta Agreement seem unnecessary, in the light of the predicted course of the war at that time they were considered to be not only justified but clearly advantageous. Although dictated by military necessity, the Agreement and the subsequent Sino-Soviet Treaty in fact imposed limitations on the action which Russia would, in any case, have been in a position to take.

For reasons of military security, and for those only, it was considered too dangerous for the United States to consult with the National Government regarding the Yalta Agreement or to communicate its terms at once to Chungking. We were then in the midst of the Pacific War. It was felt that there was grave risk that secret information transmitted to the Nationalist capital at this time would become available to the Japanese almost immediately. Under no circumstances, therefore, would we have been justified in incurring the security risks involved. It was not until June 15, 1945, that General Hurley was authorized to inform Chiang Kai-shek of the Agreement.

In conformity with the Russian agreement at Yalta to sign a treaty of friendship and alliance with Nationalist China, negotiations between the two nations began in Moscow in July 1945. During their course, the United States felt obliged to remind both parties that the purpose of the Treaty was to implement the Yalta Agreement—no more, no less—and that some of the Soviet proposals exceeded its provisions. The Treaty, which was signed on August 14, 1945, was greeted with general satisfaction both in Nationalist China and in the United States. It was considered that Russia had accepted definite limitations on its activities in China and was committed to withhold all aid from the Chinese Communists. On September 10, however, our Embassy in Moscow cautioned against placing undue confidence in the Soviet observance of either the spirit or letter of the Treaty. The subsequent conduct of the Soviet government in Manchuria has amply justified this warning.

When peace came the United States was confronted with three possible alternatives in China: (1) it could have pulled out lock, stock, and barrel; (2) it could have intervened militarily on a major scale to assist the Nationalists to destroy the Communists; (3) it could, while assisting the Nationalists to assert their authority over as much of China as possible, endeavor to avoid a civil war by working for a compromise between the two sides.

The first alternative would, and I believe American public opinion at the time so felt, have represented an abandonment of our international responsibilities and of our traditional policy of friendship for China before we had made a determined effort to be of assistance. The second alternative policy, while it may look attractive theoretically and in retrospect, was wholly impracticable. The Nationalists had been unable to destroy the Communists during the ten years before the war. Now after the war the Nationalists were, as indicated above, weakened, demoralized, and unpopular. They had quickly dissipated their popular support and prestige in the areas liberated from the Japanese by the conduct of their civil and military officials. The Communists on the other hand were much stronger than they had ever been and were in control of most of North China. Because of the ineffectiveness of the Nationalist forces which was later to be tragically demonstrated, the Communists probably could have been dislodged only by American arms. It is obvious that the American people would not have sanctioned such a colossal commitment of our armies in 1945 or later. We therefore came to the third alternative policy whereunder we faced the facts of the situation and attempted to assist in working out a *modus vivendi* which would avert civil war but nevertheless preserve and even increase the influence of the National Government.

As the record shows, it was the Chinese National Government itself which, prior to General Hurley's mission, had taken steps to arrive at a working agreement with the Communists. As early as September 1943, in addressing the Kuomintang Central Executive Committee, the Generalissimo said, "we should clearly recognize that the Communist problem is a purely political problem and should be solved by political means." He repeated this view on several occasions. Comprehensive negotiations between representatives of the government and of the Communists, dealing with both military cooperation and civil administration, were opened in Sian in May 1944. These negotiations, in which Ambassador Hurley later assisted at the invitation of both parties between August 1944 and September 1945, continued intermittently during a year and a half without producing conclusive results and culminated in a comprehensive series of agreements on basic points on October 11, 1945, after Ambassador Hurley's departure from China and before General Marshall's arrival. Meanwhile, however, clashes between the armed forces of the two groups were increasing and were jeopardizing the fulfillment of the agreements. The danger of widespread civil war, unless the negotiations could promptly be brought to a successful conclusion, was critical. It was under these circumstances that General Marshall left on his mission to China at the end of 1945.

As the account of General Marshall's mission and the subsequent years . . . reveals, our policy at that time was inspired by the two objectives of bringing peace to China under conditions which would permit stable government and progress along democratic lines, and of assisting the National Government to establish its authority over as wide areas of China as possible. As the event proved, the first objective was unrealizable because neither side desired it to succeed: the Communists because they refused to accept conditions which would weaken their freedom to proceed with what remained consistently their aim, the communization of all China; the Nationalists because they cherished the illusion, in spite of repeated advice to the contrary from our military representatives, that they could destroy the Communists by force of arms.

The second objective of assisting the National Government, however, we pursued vigorously from 1945 to 1949. The National Government was the recognized government of a friendly power. Our friendship, and our right under international law alike, called for aid to the government instead of to the Com-

munists who were seeking to subvert and overthrow it. . . .
The National Government had in 1945, and maintained until
the early fall of 1948, a marked superiority in manpower and
armament over their rivals. Indeed during that period, thanks
very largely to our aid in transporting, arming, and supplying
their forces, they extended their control over a large part of North
China and Manchuria. By the time General Marshall left China
at the beginning of 1947, the Nationalists were apparently at
the very peak of their military successes and territorial expansion.
The following year and a half revealed, however, that their seem-
ing strength was illusory and that their victories were built on
sand.

The crisis had developed around Manchuria, traditional
focus of Russian and Japanese imperialism. On numerous occasions, Marshal Stalin had stated categorically that he expected
the National Government to take over the occupation of Manchuria. In the truce agreement of January 10, 1946, the Chinese
Communists agreed to the movement of government troops into
Manchuria for the purpose of restoring Chinese sovereignty
over this area. In conformity with this understanding the United
States transported sizable government armies to the ports of
entry into Manchuria. Earlier the Soviet Army had expressed a
desire to evacuate Manchuria in December 1945, but had remained an additional two or three months at the request of the
Chinese government. When the Russian troops did begin their
evacuation, the National government found itself with extended
lines of communications, limited rolling stock, and insufficient
forces to take over the areas being evacuated in time to prevent
the entry of Chinese Communist forces, who were already in
occupation of the countryside. As the Communists entered, they
obtained the large stocks of matériel from the Japanese Kwantung Army which the Russians had conveniently "abandoned."
To meet this situation the National Government embarked on a
series of military campaigns which expanded the line of its
holdings to the Sungari River. Toward the end of these campaigns it also commenced hostilities within North China and
succeeded in constricting the areas held by the Communists.

In the spring of 1946 General Marshall attempted to restore peace. This effort lasted for months and during its course

a seemingly endless series of proposals and counterproposals
were made which had little effect upon the course of military activities and produced no political settlement. During these negotiations General Marshall displayed limitless patience and
tact and a willingness to try and then try again in order to reach
agreement. Increasingly he became convinced, however, that
twenty years of intermittent civil war between the two factions,
during which the leading figures had remained the same, had
created such deep personal bitterness and such irreconcilable
differences that no agreement was possible. The suspicions and
the lack of confidence were beyond remedy. He became convinced that both parties were merely sparring for time, jockeying
for military position, and catering temporarily to what they believed to be American desires. General Marshall concluded that
there was no hope of accomplishing the objectives of his mission.

Even though for all practical purposes General Marshall,
by the fall of 1946, had withdrawn from his efforts to assist in
a peaceful settlement of the Civil War, he remained in China
until January 1947. One of the critical points of dispute between
the government and the Communists had been the convocation
of the National Assembly to write a new constitution for China
and to bring an end to the period of political tutelage and of
one-party government. The Communists had refused to participate in the National Assembly unless there were a prior military settlement. The Generalissimo was determined that the
Assembly should be held and the program carried out. It was the
hope of General Marshall during the late months of 1946 that
his presence in China would encourage the liberal elements in
non-Communist China to assert themselves more forcefully than
they had in the past and to exercise a leavening influence upon
the absolutist control wielded by the reactionaries and the militarists. General Marshall remained in China until the Assembly
had completed its work. Even though the proposed new framework of government appeared satisfactory, the evidence suggested that there had been little shift in the balance of power.

In his farewell statement, General Marshall announced the
termination of his efforts to assist the Chinese in restoring internal peace. He described the deep-seated mutual suspicion
between the Kuomintang and the Chinese Communist Party as

the greatest obstacle to a settlement. He made it clear that the salvation of China lay in the hands of the Chinese themselves and that, while the newly adopted constitution provided the framework for a democratic China, practical measures of implementation by both sides would be the decisive test. He appealed for the assumption of leadership by liberals in and out of the government as the road to unity and peace. With these final words he returned to Washington to assume, in January 1947, his new post as Secretary of State.

As the signs of impending disaster multiplied, the President in July 1947, acting on the recommendation of the Secretary of State, instructed Lieutenant General Albert C. Wedemeyer [See pp. 334–340] to survey the Chinese scene and make recommendations. In his report, submitted on September 19, 1947, the General recommended that the United States continue and expand its policy of giving aid to Nationalist China, subject to these stipulations:

1. That China inform the United Nations of her request for aid.

2. That China request the United Nations to bring about a truce in Manchuria and request that Manchuria be placed under a five-power guardianship or a trusteeship.

3. That China utilize her own resources, reform her finances, her government, and her armies, and accept American advisers in the military and economic fields.

General Wedemeyer's report, which fully recognized the danger of Communist domination of all China and was sympathetic to the problems of the National Government, nevertheless listed a large number of reforms which he considered essential if that government were to rehabilitate itself.

It was decided that the publication at that time of a suggestion for the alienation of a part of China from the control of the National Government, and for placing that part under an international administration to include Soviet Russia, would not be helpful. . . .

The reason for the failures of the Chinese National Government appear in some detail in the attached record. They do not stem from any inadequacy of American aid. Our military observers on the spot have reported that the Nationalist armies did not lose a single battle during the crucial year of 1948 through lack of arms or ammunition. The fact was that the decay which our observers had detected in Chungking early in the war had fatally sapped the powers of resistance of the Kuomintang. Its leaders had proved incapable of meeting the crisis confronting them, its troops had lost the will to fight, and its government had lost popular support. The Communists, on the other hand, through a ruthless discipline and fanatical zeal, attempted to sell themselves as guardians and liberators of the people. The Nationalist armies did not have to be defeated; they disintegrated. History has proved again and again that a regime without faith in itself and an army without morale cannot survive the test of battle.

The record obviously cannot set forth in equal detail the inner history and development of the Chinese Communist Party during these years. The principal reason is that while we had regular diplomatic relations with the National Government and had the benefit of voluminous reports from our representatives in their territories, our direct contact with the Communists was limited in the main to the mediation efforts of General Hurley and General Marshall.

Fully recognizing that the heads of the Chinese Communist Party were ideologically affiliated with Moscow, our government nevertheless took the view, in the light of the existing balance of forces in China, that peace could be established only if certain conditions were met. The Kuomintang would have to set its house in order and both sides would have to make concessions so that the government of China might become, in fact as well as in name, the government of all China and so that all parties might function within the constitutional system of the government. Both internal peace and constitutional development required that the progress should be rapid from one-party government with a large opposition party in armed rebellion, to the participation of all parties, including the moderate non-Communist elements, in a truly national system of government.

None of these conditions has been realized. The distrust of the leaders of both the Nationalist and Communist Parties for each other proved too deep-seated to permit final agreement, notwithstanding temporary truces and apparently promising negotiations. The Nationalists, furthermore, embarked in 1946 on an overambitious military campaign in the face of warnings by General Marshall that it not only would fail but would plunge China into economic chaos and eventually destroy the National Government. General Marshall pointed out that though Nationalist armies could, for a period, capture Communist-held cities, they could not destroy the Communist armies. Thus every Nationalist advance would expose their communications to attack by Communist guerrillas and compel them to retreat or to surrender their armies together with the munitions which the United States has furnished them. No estimate of a military situation has ever been more completely confirmed by the resulting facts.

The historic policy of the United States of friendship and aid toward the people of China was, however, maintained in both peace and war. Since V-J Day, the United States government has authorized aid to Nationalist China in the form of grants and credits totaling approximately two billion dollars, an amount equivalent in value to more than 50 per cent of the monetary expenditures of the Chinese government and of proportionately greater magnitude in relation to the budget of that government than the United States has provided to any nation of Western Europe since the end of the war. In addition to these grants and credits, the United States government has sold the Chinese government large quantities of military and civilian war surplus property with a total procurement cost of over one billion dollars, for which the agreed realization to the United States was $232 million. A large proportion of the military supplies furnished the Chinese armies by the United States since V-J Day has, however, fallen into the hands of the Chinese Communists through the military ineptitude of the Nationalist leaders, their defections and surrenders, and the absence among their forces of the will to fight.

It has been urged that relatively small amounts of additional aid—military and economic—to the National Government would have enabled it to destroy Communism in China. The most trustworthy military, economic, and political information available to our government does not bear out this view.

A realistic appraisal of conditions in China, past and present, leads to the conclusion that the only alternative open to the United States was full-scale intervention in behalf of a government which had lost the confidence of its own troops and its own people. Such intervention would have required the expenditure of even greater sums than have been fruitlessly spent thus far, the command of Nationalist armies by American officers, and the probable participation of American armed forces—land, sea, and air—in the resulting war. Intervention of such a scope and magnitude would have been resented by the mass of the Chinese people, would have diametrically reversed our historic policy, and would have been condemned by the American people.

It must be admitted frankly that the American policy of assisting the Chinese people in resisting domination by any foreign power or powers is now confronted with the gravest difficulties. The heart of China is in Communist hands. The Communist leaders have foresworn their Chinese heritage and have publicly announced their subservience to a foreign power, Russia, which during the last fifty years, under Czars and Communists alike, has been most assiduous in its efforts to extend its control in the Far East. In the recent past, attempts at foreign domination have appeared quite clearly to the Chinese people as external aggression and as such have been bitterly and in the long run successfully resisted. Our aid and encouragement have helped them to resist. In this case, however, the foreign domination has been masked behind the façade of a vast crusading movement which apparently has seemed to many Chinese to be wholly indigenous and national. Under these circumstances, our aid has been unavailing.

The unfortunate but inescapable fact is that the ominous result of the Civil War in China was beyond the control of the government of the United States. Nothing that this country did or could have done within the reasonable limits of its capabilities could have changed that result; nothing that was left undone by this country has contributed to it. It was the product of internal Chinese forces, forces which this country tried to influence but could not. A decision was arrived at within China, if only a decision by default.

And now it is abundantly clear that we must face the situation as it exists in fact. We will not help the Chinese or ourselves by basing our policy on wishful thinking. We continue to believe that, however tragic may be the immediate future of China and however ruthlessly a major portion of this great people may be exploited by a party in the interest of a foreign imperialism, ultimately the profound civilization and the democratic individualism of China will reassert themselves and she will throw off the foreign yoke. I consider that we should encourage all developments in China which now and in the future work toward this end.

In the immediate future, however, the implementation of our historic policy of friendship for China must be profoundly affected by current developments. It will necessarily be influenced by the degree to which the Chinese people come to recognize that the Communist regime serves not their interests but those of Soviet Russia and the manner in which, having become aware of the facts, they react to this foreign domination. One point, however, is clear. Should the Communist regime lend itself to the aims of Soviet Russian imperialism and attempt to engage in aggression against China's neighbors, we and the other members of the United Nations would be confronted by a situation violative of the principles of the United Nations Charter and threatening international peace and security.

Meanwhile our policy will continue to be based upon our own respect for the Charter, our friendship for China, and our traditional support for the Open Door and for China's independence and administrative and territorial integrity.

Chronology

ℰ Chronology

1911: Manchu Dynasty overthrown; Republic founded; Sun Yat-sen loses power to General Yüan Shih-k'ai

1913: Yüan Shih-k'ai becomes President of China and is recognized by foreign powers; Sun Yat-sen flees to Japan

1915: Japan presents Twenty-one Demands to China; anti-Japanese demonstrations; Yüan Shih-k'ai proclaims himself Emperor

1916: Yüan Shih-k'ai dies; military and civil governors become supreme commanders in provinces and declare provincial autonomy (period of warlordism begins); "Chinese Renaissance" begins

1917: Canton government declares war on Germany in World War I; China declares war on Germany; Russian Revolution begins

1919: Violent anti-Japanese demonstrations; May Fourth Movement in Peking; China's first general strike takes place in Shanghai

1920: General Strike of Manchurian Railway workers; Ch'en Tu-hsiu, father of Chinese Communism, becomes Chinese delegate to Comintern and founds Chinese Socialist Youth League

1921: Kuomintang revived; Sun Yat-sen becomes President of Kwangtung government; Chinese Communist Party founded; first contacts between Sun Yat-sen and Comintern; publication of Lu Hsün's great novel *The Biography of AH Q*

1922: Hong Kong seamen strike, other workers follow suit; Sun Yat-sen flees to Shanghai from Canton

1923: Kuomintang-Comintern collaboration begins; Sun Yat-sen returns to power in Canton; Soviet military advisors attached to Kuomintang; Chiang Kai-shek goes to Russia for military training

1924: First Kuomintang Congress; "Northern March" to unify China begins; Sun Yat-sen goes to Peking

1925: Sun Yat-sen dies; May 30 general strike in Shanghai spreads to other cities; Chiang's power grows with help of Soviet advisor Borodin

1926: Peasant association movement spreads, notably in Kwangtung and Hunan; Canton Coup, first break between Chiang Kai-shek and Communists; Chiang launches final stages of "Northern March"

1927: Chiang unleashes "White Terror" against Communists; left Kuomintang-Wuhan government overthrown; Mao Tse-tung leads peasant insurrection in Hunan; Canton commune crushed; Soviet government proclaimed in Hailufeng districts of Kwangtung

1928: Mao Tse-tung and Chu Teh establish guerrilla base in Kiangsi; revolutionary land reform carried out by Communists; Nanking government proclaimed and recognized by foreign powers; "Northern March" completed

1930: Chiang Kai-shek begins "bandit extermination" campaign against Communists

1931: Japanese occupy Manchuria; Nanking government prohibits anti-Japanese demonstrations; Chinese Soviet Republic formed in Kiangsi

1932: Communists declare war on Japan; Kuomintang concludes armistice with Japan

1934: Chiang Kai-shek launches last and greatest "bandit extermination" campaign; New Life Movement begins; Red Army's "Long March" begins

1935: Mao wins undisputed control of CCP; Communists reach Northern Shensi; anti-Japanese united front proclaimed

1936: Anti-Japanese student demonstrations erupt throughout China; Sian Incident, Chiang Kai-shek kidnaped

1937: Kuomintang and Communists agree to cooperate; Sino-Japanese War begins, Japanese attack Marco Polo Bridge

1938: Japan occupies large areas of China; clashes between Kuomintang and Communists resume; Chinese capital moved to Chungking

1939: Wang Ching-wei sets up puppet government in Japanese-occupied Nanking

1941: Communist "New Fourth Route Army" attacked by Kuomintang; U.S. enters war in the Pacific after Japanese bomb Pearl Harbor

1942: Party "rectification" movement begins in Communist areas; Burma Road closed

1943: Village cooperativization movement launched in Communist areas; Cairo Declaration restores Taiwan to China

1944: Constitutional convention in Chungking attended by Communists; Stilwell is relieved of command

1945: Yalta Conference: Seventh Congress of Chinese Communist Party; Russia enters the Pacific war and occupies Manchuria; Japan surrenders; treaty of friendship and alliance signed by Soviet Union and Nationalist China; civil war between Communists and Kuomintang resumes; Marshall mission dispatched to China

1946: Marshall wins short-lived armistice; Soviets evacuate Manchuria, U.S. airlift helps Nationalists take the cities; American Military Advisory Group formed; Communist armies enter Manchuria in large numbers; Communists resume revolutionary land reform; full-scale civil war erupts

1947: Uprising in Taiwan against Chiang's occupying armies; Nationalists occupy Yenan; Nationalists reach peak of military success in civil war; Wedemeyer Report recommends support of Nationalists but sharply criticizes the regime; Communists consolidate control over Manchurian hinterland; U.S. refuses increased assistance to Chiang

1948: Communists go on the offensive in Manchuria, North, Northwest, and Central China; Party rectification movement; anti-American student demonstrations in the cities; China's first National Assembly convenes in Nanking, Chiang Kai-shek elected President, Li Tsung-jen Vice-President; cities fall; Nationalists abandon Manchuria; China Aid Act restores limited U.S. assistance to China

1949: Tientsin and Peking fall; Mao Tse-tung proposes eight-point peace plan to Nationalists; Nationalist government moves to Canton; Chiang abdicates, Li Tsung-jen succeeds him; peace moves fail; Shanghai falls and most of Mainland China occupied by the Communists; U.S. State Department issues White Paper; preparations made for setting up the People's Republic of China with the capital at Peking

Bibliography

❦ Bibliography*

Brandt, Conrad, *Stalin's Failure in China* (Cambridge, 1958).
Brandt, Conrad, Schwartz, Benjamin, and Fairbank, John K., *A Documentary History of Chinese Communism* (Cambridge, 1952).
Ch'en, Jerome, *Mao Tse-tung and the Chinese Revolution* (London, 1965).
Chiang Kai-shek, *China's Destiny* (New York, 1947).
Ch'ien Tuan-sheng, *The Government and Politics of China* (Cambridge, 1950).
Clubb, O. Edmund, *Twentieth Century China* (New York, 1964).
Feis, Herbert, *China Tangle: The American Effort in China from Pearl Harbor to the Marshall Mission* (Princeton, 1953).
Hsia, C. T., *A History of Modern Chinese Fiction, 1917–1957* (New Haven, 1961)
Johnson, Chalmers, *Peasant Nationalism and Communist Power* (Stanford, 1962).
North, Robert C., *Moscow and Chinese Communists* (Stanford, 1963); *Chinese Communism* (New York, 1966).
Schram, Stuart R., *The Political Thought of Mao Tse-tung* (New York, 1963); *Mao Tse-tung* (London, 1966).
Schwartz, Benjamin, *Chinese Communism and the Rise of Mao* (Cambridge, 1951).
T'ang Liang-li, *The Inner History of the Chinese Revolution* (London, 1930).
Tang Tsou, *America's Failure in China, 1941–1950* (Chicago, 1963).
Tawney, R. H., *Land and Labour in China* (London, 1932).
Wei, Henry, *China and Soviet Russia* (Princeton, 1956).

* This bibliography does not include works cited in the text.

Index

🕉 Index

FRANZ SCHURMANN is Director of the Center for Chinese Studies at the University of California at Berkeley. Born in New York City, he received his Bachelor's degree from Trinity College and his Doctorate from Harvard University; he served in the United States Army during World War II. He is the author of *The Ideology and Organization of Communist China*, and co-author of *The Politics of Escalation in Vietnam*. Professor Schurmann writes frequently on Chinese History and Southeast Asian current affairs for both scholarly and popular periodicals. He makes his home in Oakland, California.

ORVILLE SCHELL was also born in New York City. He has been educated at Harvard, Stanford, and Taiwan National Universities. He is presently a graduate assistant in Chinese Studies at the University of California at Berkeley. Mr. Schell has worked for the Ford Foundation Overseas Development Office in Indonesia and has been a newspaper correspondent in Southeast Asia.